DATA MINING TECHNIQUES AND APPLICATIONS

AN INTRODUCTION

DATA MINING TECHNIQUES AND APPLICATIONS
AN INTRODUCTION

Hongbo Du

COURSE TECHNOLOGY
CENGAGE Learning™

Australia • Brazil • Japan • Korea • Mexico • Singapore • Spain • United Kingdom • United States

**Data Mining Techniques
and Applications: An Introduction
Hongbo Du**

Publishing Director: Linden Harris

Publisher: Brendan George

Development Editor: Rebecca Hussey

Content Project Editor: Adam Paddon

Senior Production Controller: Paul Herbert

Marketing Manager: Vicky Fielding

Typesetter: MPS Limited, A Macmillan Company

Cover design: Adam Renvoize

While the publisher has taken all reasonable care in the preparation of this book, the publisher makes no representation, express or implied, with regard to the accuracy of the information contained in this book and cannot accept any legal responsibility or liability for any errors or omissions from the book or the consequences thereof.

Products and services that are referred to in this book may be either trademarks and/or registered trademarks of their respective owners. The publishers and author/s make no claim to these trademarks.

For product information and technology assistance, contact **emea.info@cengage.com.**

For permission to use material from this text or product, and for permissions queries, email **clsuk.permissions@cengage.com.**

The Author has asserted the right under the Copyright, Designs and Patents Act 1988 to be identified as Author of this Work.

British Library Cataloguing-in-Publication Data
A catalogue record for this book is available from the British Library.

ISBN: 978-1-84480-891-5

Cengage Learning EMEA
Cheriton House, North Way, Andover, Hampshire, SP10 5BE, United Kingdom

Cengage Learning products are represented in Canada by Nelson Education, Ltd.

For your lifelong learning solutions, visit **www.cengage.co.uk**

Purchase your next print book, e-book or e-chapter at **www.CengageBrain.com**

Printed by C&C Offset, China
1 2 3 4 5 6 7 8 9 10 – 12 11 10

BRIEF CONTENTS

CONTENTS

PREFACE

Data mining has become a popular and interesting subject of computing in recent years. Since its conception in the early 1990s, the subject has received a huge amount of attention from the research community, the IT industry and beyond. Knowledge matured over the past two decades has started to flow from research and practice into postgraduate and undergraduate degree programmes.

The author was among the first group of university teachers who introduced a course module in the subject area in the mid-1990s. At the time, there were very few texts on the subject of data mining. Indeed, we had to rely on research papers and articles in magazines to prepare teaching materials. Early texts started to appear in the late 1990s (Berry and Linoff 1997; Fayyad et al. 1996), but they were either too superficial or too theoretical for an undergraduate computing audience. The situation has started to improve since 2000, particularly after (Han and Kamber 2001; Hand et al. 2001) appeared. These early texts were followed by (Witten and Frank 2005; Tan et al. 2006). Some well-established database texts, such as (Connolly and Begg 2005; Elmasri and Navathe 2007), merely included extra chapters on the subject.

Is there a need for yet another text on data mining? Certainly. Compared with the abundance of texts on databases, texts about data mining are relatively few, particularly for undergraduate computing students. Options for lecturers and tutors to choose suitable texts for their data mining courses are still rather limited.

This book aims to introduce the basic concepts, principles and, most importantly, methods and techniques for data mining. It is meant to enable sound understanding of data mining technology and effective use of the technology in practice. The book starts with the fundamental concepts and principles of data mining and the data mining process. It then describes characteristics of real-life data and data sets, and possible ways of exploring and understanding features of data sets. The book mainly concentrates on three core types of data mining task: cluster detection, classification and association rule discovery. It describes commonly used data mining solutions for these tasks. Besides technical details of the solutions, the book also attempts to address practical issues in relation to effective use of the solutions. Throughout the book, the Weka data mining software toolkit is used to demonstrate the practical use of data mining solutions. At the end, the book puts data mining into the perspective of a decision-support system environment and highlights data mining applications and real-life case studies. The text tries to combine the best parts of (Tan et al. 2006) with the extended practical flavour of (Witten and Frank 2005).

The book is primarily aimed at final year undergraduate students in computing disciplines and information systems. Taught masters students can also use the book for an entry-level course to the subject. Researchers and practitioners who are developing an interest in data mining can use the book as a starting point. Because of the intended audience, the book restricts its coverage of data mining techniques. It is not intended to serve as a complete survey of all existing data mining solutions and systems, or to catch up with the latest development of the technology. The amount of theoretical content is limited. Most necessary theories, such as proximity measures and information gain, are discussed within the context of data mining solutions, rather than being addressed on a general and theoretical footing.

The book assumes that you have a basic knowledge of data structures and algorithms, programming and databases. Such knowledge is normally obtained from the first two years of undergraduate programmes of study in the related disciplines, and hence an expected prerequisite for the book. Some understanding of the time complexity of algorithms is needed to appreciate performance issues in data mining solutions. Although no extensive programming experience in a specific language is required, readers must feel comfortable with control structures used in the pseudo-code descriptions of mining algorithms and be able to appreciate issues regarding algorithm implementations.

APPROACHES TO THE SUBJECT

The book selects a mixture of data mining techniques originating from statistics, machine learning and databases, and presents them in an algorithmic approach. As well as introductory chapters on data mining concepts and principles, the book contains a number of key chapters about data mining techniques. These chapters are organized according to the type of data mining task rather than the origins of the data mining techniques. Each of the key chapters starts with a description of the problems faced by the task and a description of input data sets. The chapter then presents in pseudo-code data mining algorithms that are later illustrated with comprehensive but small examples. After presenting the algorithms, the chapters discuss how to evaluate patterns mined from input data sets. In order to give a practical flavour, the chapters use the Weka software to demonstrate the mining process. This enables students to observe the mining procedure and practise the type of data mining by using the relevant algorithms provided by Weka. One advantage of Weka is the wide range of solutions available in the software environment. Most algorithms and solutions described in this book are available in Weka. To further strengthen the practical side of understanding, some exercises using Weka are provided at the end of each chapter. Some chapters also contain a discussion section on the practical use of data mining solutions. The underlying theme is thorough coverage of a specific type of data mining in a self-contained presentation.

Examples are used extensively in the book. These examples can be categorized into two types: demonstrative examples and case studies. The demonstrative examples illustrate data mining concepts and algorithms, whereas the practical case studies demonstrate how data mining solutions provided by software tools are used in practical problem solving. Exercises using examples are also provided at the end of each chapter for revision purposes. These exercises make use of data sets that come with the software toolkit, so there is no need for students to look for data sets from other sources for the purpose of the exercises.

PEDAGOGY

The book presents a *white-box* rather than a *black-box* view of the techniques of data mining, explaining in detail how data mining algorithms work. This approach has academic merit and a practical intention. First, understanding of algorithms and their implementation is well within the realm of computing disciplines. The understanding is essential for critical evaluation of performance of the algorithms, appreciation of the strengths and limitations of the algorithms, and development of new solutions. Second, the understanding also enables appropriate choice of solutions, necessary data pre-processing, proper settings of solution parameters, and interpretation of the results produced. In other words, it enables effective use of data mining solutions in practice. It is my opinion that a black-box approach cannot achieve all the objectives mentioned above. That approach might be more suitable for an information systems type of degree programme.

The book attempts to strike a balance between depth and breadth: basic data mining methods are described in detail whereas advanced methods are outlined in principle. This approach enables readers to grasp basic methods, understand their strengths and weaknesses and hence appreciate the need for advanced solutions. At the same time, undergraduate students only need to be aware of the principal ideas of advanced methods. Therefore, a clear outline description should be sufficient. For those who want to go further, the book serves as a reference point and provides bibliographical notes at the end of each chapter.

Figures and diagrams are extensively used so that the examples are easy to follow. Many existing textbooks on data mining techniques do not provide complete examples; they use examples to illustrate a certain aspect of a data mining technique. This textbook provides examples that walk through a mining algorithm from beginning to the end. These examples enable readers to have a complete view of the algorithm concerned.

The book contains 10 chapters. Each chapter begins with a list of objectives that inform readers what to expect from the chapter. It also serves as a checklist for readers to determine whether they have met the intended goals after studying the chapter. Each chapter ends with a summary of key issues addressed in the chapter. The summary is useful for revision. Each chapter provides a set of exercises at the end. For the first two chapters, most exercises are related to the concepts and principles of data mining. For each key chapter on data mining techniques, the exercises include revision exercises, demonstration exercises, practical exercises using Weka, and discussion exercises. In Chapter 10, data mining projects are suggested as exercises.

The book is written primarily for final year undergraduate students undertaking a course in advanced database technology and systems, data warehousing and data mining, and applied data mining techniques. Typical courses are assumed to be 12 weeks in length, and each week coincides with one chapter. For a comprehensive understanding of the subject, every chapter is needed and they should be studied in the same order in which they are presented. The material in Chapters 4, 6 and 8 can be taught in any order, but Chapter 5 must follow Chapter 4, Chapter 7 must follow Chapter 6 and Chapter 9 must follow Chapter 8. A shorter and more intensive introductory course on data mining techniques can be created by selecting Chapters 1, 2, 3, 4, 6 and 8. You may also want to include Chapter 10.

OTHER MATERIALS FOR INSTRUCTORS

All teaching materials for the book, including a comprehensive collection of lecture slides, tutorial sheets, coursework assignments and outline answers to the questions in the exercises are available from the book's website, www.cengage.co.uk/du. A list of other useful reference materials and websites are also listed for people who want to explore the field of data mining.

ACKNOWLEDGEMENTS

Many people deserve my full gratitude. First, I wish to thank my students (undergraduate, postgraduate and research) in the University of Buckingham from 1996 to the present day, the students in the Computing Department of the City University London between 1998 and 2004, and the students in Sarajevo School of Science and Technology (SSST) from 2007 onwards. Those students have experienced my courses in data mining from the very early days. Their enthusiasm in the subject and their support to me have made the whole experience of teaching the subject very enjoyable. Through the courses, I still maintain contact with some of the students as friends even to this day. Many thanks. I want to single out, Mr Amer Hadžikadić of SSST, for working with me to create an exciting new course in data mining at SSST in 2007.

I especially want to thank Gary Saarenvirta of Makeplain Corporation for allowing me to use one of his highly successful data mining projects, the customer segmentation, as a case study for this book. I have referred to this project many times in teaching in over several years and it is my opinion that the project is still one of the best-conducted data mining projects reported in the literature. At a time when data mining can be perceived as a closely guarded secret weapon in a shroud of mystery, Gary's permission for me to use his work is indeed a gesture of generosity. I am also grateful to my colleagues Professor Sabah Jassim, Dr Harin Sellahewa and Dr Naseer Al-Jawad for allowing me to use their highly successful SecurePhone project as examples in the book. I have collaborated with them in applying data mining solutions in image processing on a number of occasions. Their support to the book and valuable discussions are fully appreciated.

I wish to thank many people within the Department of Applied Computing in Buckingham and outside for interesting discussions on the subject of data mining. If their names were to be mentioned individually, the list would certainly go over several pages.

I must, of course, also thank my close family members for their continuing support, patience and comfort. My wife Linda has done everything to ensure that I have time to work on the book at weekends and evenings without much complaint. Her support is essential for the completion of this book. I also wish to thank my young daughters, Vivienne and Iris, for not complaining too much about their dad's absence from their side during the development of this book. I thank my parents, Mr Chunrong and Mrs Lishan Du, for their limitless love and constant encouragement. In particular, the book is dedicated in loving memory to my late father, Chunrong.

I specifically thank the anonymous reviewers for their valuable comments and constructive criticisms that have helped in shaping up the chapters and sections throughout the book. Their encouraging comments regarding the weaknesses, the style and the good points of the book strengthen the author's confidence in the book itself.

Last, but not least, I owe a debt of gratitude to *every* member of the publication team at Cengage Learning. In particular, it was Gaynor Redvers-Mutton who initially encouraged me to write this book. Although Gaynor has left Cengage by the time this book is published, I owe her a heartfelt thank you. The same gratitude should also go to Patrick Bond and Matthew Lane for their continuing support and patience. Matthew helped to finalize the design of the book cover, but then moved on to other projects. I also thank Rebecca (Bex) Hussey who must have exhausted her entire stock of carrots and sticks in moving this book forward to completion. I sincerely hope that her lifespan is not shortened in any way by her hard work on this book. Tons of thanks, Bex.

Hongbo Du, 2010

WALK THROUGH TOUR

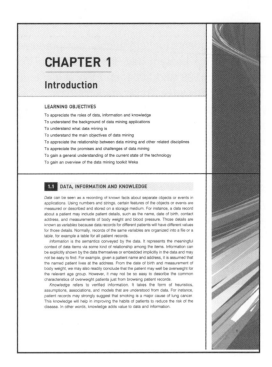

Learning Objectives   Featured at the beginning of each chapter, you can check at a glance what you are about to learn.

Figures and Screenshots   Graphs, charts and diagrams help to illustrate the examples being discussed in the text. Screenshots help to familiarise you with the screens you will see when mining data using Weka.

Summary and Exercises   A summary at the end of each chapter helps to clarify and consolidate key concepts. This is followed by Exercises which offer a chance to test and reinforce your knowledge of the chapter's main issues.

that fit all the requirements of the criteria, but sometimes there may be no solution to suit the criteria completely. Existing solutions may need to be tailored or new solutions may have to be developed. Whenever possible, data analysis often use more than one clustering solution over the same data set in order to consolidate the resulting clusters.

5.10 SUMMARY

This chapter has presented a number of more advanced clustering algorithms of different categories. Based on the evaluation of limitations of the basic K-means and agglomeration methods, density-based, graph-based and model-based clustering approaches were broadly described. For each approach, a specific algorithm was studied: the DBSCAN algorithm for density-based methods, the CHAMELEON algorithm for graph-based methods, and the EM algorithm for model-based methods. In addition, the CLIQUE algorithm designed for subspace clustering was also explained against the backdrop that clusters may not exist in high-dimensional spaces. For each algorithm, the chapter broadly described and illustrated its process, discussed its performance and outlined its strengths and weaknesses. Some of the algorithms described in the chapter are also available in Weka and we demonstrated the use of these methods.

Due to their complex nature, the descriptions of some of the algorithms, such as CHAMELEON, are kept brief and only small examples were used for illustrative purposes. The theories behind some algorithms such as the EM/GMM method are also kept to the minimum to appeal to most readers. To achieve more thorough understanding of the algorithms, readers are recommended to read the reference materials given in the Bibliographical Notes.

Proximity between data objects is a broad concept and can be interpreted differently in different circumstances and for different types of data. Taking a meaningful measure of proximity during a clustering process determines the success or failure of the process. Because of the importance of the issue, this chapter further explored how to measure similarity between data objects according to the principles of commonly shared nearest neighbours and the time-warping measure for sequential data records.

Clustering projects have their own unique procedures and issues for consideration. The chapter therefore outlined general principles for conducting clustering tasks. Applying the right solution to the right data is also essential for clustering and the chapter explained how to select a clustering solution.

EXERCISES

1. Use the random number generation facility of either Weka or Microsoft Excel to create an artificial set of 200 uniformly distributed data records. Then use the simple K-means method in Weka to appreciate the limitations of the method in the following aspects:
   (a) Artificial clustering results even though there is no tendency towards clusters in the data set.
   (b) Different clustering results when the random seed for the initial centroid selection is changed. Observe this by saving cluster memberships for different calls of the method and comparing any changes in memberships.
   (c) Convex clusters. Observe this by using the visualization facility in Weka.
2. Discuss, with suitable examples, the major limitations of the agglomeration method.

10. In medium- and large-scale network systems, accesses to switches, computers and printers are recorded by system log records. Log records are generated very fast and in large volumes. The system administrators are keen to track the log records and monitor the network traffic. Discuss the dynamic nature of the scenario, the scale of data changes, and the need for an incremental data mining solution.

11. In Section 9.7, three categories of parallel solution are described. It has been reported that the count and data distributions can be combined into a hybrid solution. Conduct an investigation in the literature into such a hybrid solution. Outline the working principles of the hybrid solution.

BIBLIOGRAPHICAL NOTES

Due to extensive interest in association rule mining, much research work has been conducted in this field, resulting in a large collection of literature on the subject. A number of survey papers have been published, for example, Ullman (2000), Hipp et al. (2000), Zhao and Bhowmick (2003), and Kotsiantis and Kanellopoulos (2006b). All the papers give a thorough review of the concepts of association rules of different kinds, techniques for mining those rules and the performance of the techniques. The work by Bayardo and Agrawal (1999) provides a theoretical underpinning to various measures for optimal (best and most interesting) rules that can be useful for some researchers. Besides the survey articles, this text has also used Tan et al. (2006) and Han and Kamber (2006) for general reference.

Three types of association (generalized, quantitative and sequential) were first introduced by the QUEST project team at IBM's Almaden research centre. The original articles by the researchers from the QUEST team (Agrawal and Srikant 1995; Srikant and Agrawal 1995, 1996) are mainly referred to for details of the adapted algorithms. Discussions over rule redundancy are also based on the papers by Srikant and Agrawal. For sequential pattern discovery, this chapter refers to a survey article by Zhao and Bhowmick (2003) and an article by Joshi et al. (1999). Two more references have been used for sequential pattern mining: the GSP algorithm was first reported in (Srikant and Agrawal 1996) and the MFS algorithm was first reported by (Zhang et al. 2001).

The literature about incremental mining of association rules is extensive and research is continuing. Early works include Cheung et al. (1996) and Cheng et al. (1997) on the FUP algorithm and its improvement (the FUP2 algorithm), and an algorithm known as CARMA, by Hidber (1998). The Borders algorithm is reported in Aumann et al. (1999). A similar algorithm using the concept of negative borders, known as ICAP, is reported in Ayad et al. (2001). The SWF algorithm is reported in Lee et al. (2001).

Unlike the extensive coverage of incremental mining of association rules, the literature's coverage of parallel solutions for association rule mining appears limited. This chapter mainly draws references from two sources: the first paper to parallelize the sequential Apriori algorithm (Agrawal and Shafer 1996) and an excellent broad survey by Zaki (1999).

Bibliographical Notes   At the end of each chapter the Bibliographic Notes direct you to further print and online material on the chapter's topics.

CHAPTER 1

Introduction

LEARNING OBJECTIVES

To appreciate the roles of data, information and knowledge

To understand the background of data mining applications

To understand what data mining is

To understand the main objectives of data mining

To appreciate the relationship between data mining and other related disciplines

To appreciate the promises and challenges of data mining

To gain a general understanding of the current state of the technology

To gain an overview of the data mining toolkit Weka

1.1 DATA, INFORMATION AND KNOWLEDGE

Data can be seen as a recording of known facts about separate objects or events in applications. Using numbers and strings, certain features of the objects or events are measured or described and stored on a storage medium. For instance, a data record about a patient may include patient details, such as the name, date of birth, contact address, and measurements of body weight and blood pressure. Those details are known as *variables* because data records for different patients will have different values for those details. Normally, records of the same variables are organized into a file or a table, for example a table for all patient records.

Information is the semantics conveyed by the data. It represents the meaningful context of data items via some kind of relationship among the items. Information can be explicitly shown by the data themselves or embedded implicitly in the data and may not be easy to find. For example, given a patient name and address, it is assumed that the named patient lives at the address. From the date of birth and measurement of body weight, we may also readily conclude that the patient may well be overweight for the relevant age group. However, it may not be so easy to describe the common characteristics of overweight patients just from browsing patient records.

Knowledge refers to verified information. It takes the form of heuristics, assumptions, associations, and models that are understood from data. For instance, patient records may strongly suggest that smoking is a major cause of lung cancer. This knowledge will help in improving the habits of patients to reduce the risk of the disease. In other words, knowledge adds value to data and information.

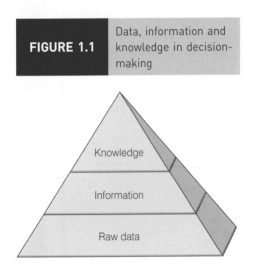

FIGURE 1.1   Data, information and knowledge in decision-making

Data enable an organization to keep records about events that occur. Information enables the organization to react and respond to the events. Knowledge enables the organization to anticipate events and act appropriately when the events occur. Figure 1.1 presents a structure of data, information and knowledge; it illustrates that knowledge is drawn from information which, in turn, is drawn from quality raw data. It can be seen that the quantity of raw data is greater than that of information which, in turn, is greater than the quantity of knowledge. Information-based decision-making makes use of data, information and knowledge. Data may come from sources external to the organization. Heuristics may be accumulated from experience. Information-based decision-making is becoming increasingly important and challenging in the modern dynamic and uncertain world.

1.2   BACKGROUND OF DATA MINING

Computerization of operational activities in commercial, governmental and scientific organizations has generated large volumes of data. Storing such data in a database is an operational necessity for the daily running of a business or office. Banks need to store customer transaction details in order to produce monthly bank statements. Telephone companies must record itemized phone calls in order to send quarterly bills to their customers. Hospitals must keep patient records so that a trail of medical treatments received by the patient can be recorded and monitored.

Recent years have seen rapid advances in computer hardware technology. The cost of storage media with massive capacity is constantly reducing. Various data-gathering devices, such as barcode readers, scanners and CCTV cameras, can acquire a large amount of digital data very rapidly. Many organizations, large and small, can now afford to maintain a large database. Millions of databases are currently in use. Supermarkets and department stores accumulate customer transaction details every day. Software agents constantly collect data from the web to update databases that support search engines. High-powered microscope cameras capture images of organs and cells in microscopic detail. Data collected from these areas of application are measured in gigabytes or terabytes. Fast data access and transfer over the Internet have fuelled the growth of the amount of data even further. There are mountains of data. Can any nuggets of valuable information be discovered from the vast mountains of data? Can databases be treated as potential gold mines?

Having access to data does not necessarily mean having access to valuable information. Possessing more data does not necessarily mean possessing more information. Large department stores still appear to know little about their customers' habits. Promotion companies spend hundreds of thousands of pounds to produce marketing leaflets that are dumped directly into recycle bins. Some flagship companies have made wrong decisions that have caused the loss of millions in share values. Law enforcement agencies still find it hard to catch criminals. Scientists find it increasingly difficult to investigate natural phenomena with traditional experimental approaches. We are living in an age that can be called 'data rich but information poor'. The situation is reflected vividly in a comment made by Lord Leverhulme, once the president of Unilever. He is quoted as saying, 'I know half the money I spend on advertising is wasted, but I can never find out which half!' This situation may be worsening because the speed of data comprehension does not seem to match the speed of data acquisition. In other words, the data mountains are growing. Better tools to keep up with the growth are desperately needed.

Computers are good for their speed and accuracy in handling repetitive tasks. Can computers be used to assist in the understanding of data?

Database management systems (DBMS) have matured over the past four decades. Existing DBMSs are equipped with powerful database design and query tools and effective data maintenance tools. However, most DBMSs are not equipped with adequate data analysis tools because they are online transaction processing (OLTP) systems for an application, rather than for data analysis. Although the situation has improved in recent years, data analysis tools have yet to become a standard on every desktop DBMS.

Statistics is a discipline about data analysis. Its methods and principles have been used extensively in the past. So can traditional statistical software such as Minitab help in meeting the challenge? The answer is, unfortunately, 'not quite'. Most statistical applications deal with 'clean' data, where the data are normally of good quality. Most statistical software tools can only deal with data sets of a reasonably small size. However, real-life databases are often large. It is worth mentioning that there have been encouraging developments in recent years. The most recent edition of SPSS, for instance, can now handle data sets measured in gigabytes. Statistical software tools also have limitations. Most of them perform better on numerical and continuous data than on discrete and nominal data. Real-life databases tend to be a mixture of different types of data value.

There is, therefore, an urgent need for a new approach to data analysis and data comprehension.

1.3 DATA MINING AND KNOWLEDGE DISCOVERY IN DATABASES

Knowledge discovery in databases (KDD) refers to the efficient process of searching through large volumes of raw data in databases to find useful information patterns that are implicitly embedded in the raw data. Strictly speaking, the term KDD tends to refer to the complete cycle of discovery from unprocessed raw data to knowledge. The term *data mining* normally refers to the integral step of the KDD process that discovers and outputs hidden information patterns from prepared raw data. In practice, however, the two terms are often used interchangeably, causing some degree of confusion. Some key phrases in that description need further explanation.

1.3.1 Useful Information

The output of data mining is *information patterns*. Unfortunately, there is no standard definition of the term *pattern*. However, a broad description does exist. Given a set of data, a pattern is a statement that describes some kind of relationship among a subset of the data with a degree of certainty. The statement should normally be more general than what the data directly represent and simpler than the complete enumeration of the data themselves.

Information patterns discovered from a database can take different forms such as rules, models and statements (see Chapter 2). For instance, a supermarket may find, from its customer transactions, a rule suggesting that customers who purchase beers are 98% likely to buy nappies. A life insurance company may discover, from claim records, a model that estimates the amount of insurance premium for a new customer. From application records, a credit card company may derive a statement that customers who have an income of between £20,000 and £40,000 and own a house are safe.

Useful information patterns normally lead to a course of action that brings positive effects for the intended application domain. For instance, if a supermarket discovers the rule about beer and nappies, the store can put beer and nappies in nearby locations to increase the customer throughput in the store, and even promote the sale of either nappies or beer. It must be said that not all patterns discovered are useful. It may well be the case that, after a long and costly process, the patterns discovered merely state commonsense understandings or that no clear action can be taken as a result.

1.3.2 **Non-trivial Information**

Information discovered from the database must be non-trivial in the sense that it is implicitly embedded *inside* the data rather than explicitly stored as a fact or easily summarized via simple computations.

In order to assist the understanding, all forms of information retrieval and discovery can be put into a spectrum. At one end of the spectrum is the most trivial form of retrieval, the retrieval of explicitly stored data through a query. For instance, a query operation 'find names of students who are 23 years old' will search the database and return the names of those students whose age is equal to 23. Data retrieval also includes simple data aggregations such as sum, count, maximum, etc. For example, a query may find the average age of all students in the computer science department. Although the average age is not explicitly stored in the database, it is trivial to derive it. Both queries can be described simply in a language such as SQL.

At the other end of the spectrum is data mining. Information retrieval at this end is the most non-trivial. It aims to discover hidden patterns within the data by exploiting sophisticated algorithms. For instance, finding the rule that states 'customers who purchase a T-shirt are 98% likely to purchase jeans' may require the use of a new algorithm which may search the entire database many times to establish a strong association between the two data items. Quite often, these kinds of algorithms can only be implemented in a programming language rather than as simple statements of an SQL-like query language or script language.

In the middle of the spectrum are various forms of data reporting and summarization, including online analytic processing (OLAP). This form of information retrieval is more sophisticated than direct retrieval of raw data. It performs complex queries, data drilling and data summarization based on segmentation of the data. These reporting actions are non-trivial compared to data retrieval but trivial compared to data mining. The outputs from OLAP are data or summary information. The discovery process is interactive but manual, assisted by OLAP tools. An example of an OLAP query is 'find the monthly sales totals for each category of products for the last three years'. This reporting brings together a number of relevant items of data but the action itself does not explain the trend behind the sales figures. It is the user who interprets the outcome.

1.3.3 **Real-life Databases**

Data mining deals with real-life data, which are different from laboratory-controlled data collections for scientific experiments. The characteristics of real-life data can be summarized as follows:

■ The database size can be very large. Databases measured in megabytes are now common. Databases measured in gigabytes or even terabytes are not rare. These databases are stored on secondary storage devices. It is unrealistic to assume that the entire data set can always be fitted into main memory. This is different from artificial intelligence applications where the database component of a reasoning mechanism is normally assumed to be stored in the main memory.

■ Different databases may be built for different application purposes for the same organization. The access barriers between the different database systems mean that data integration can be a difficult issue to resolve when data in their entirety are needed for analysis.

■ A data set can have very high dimensionality. It is quite common for real-life databases to have hundreds of variables. Some applications, such as image processing, may push the number of dimensions to thousands or even hundreds of thousands, depending on the resolutions of the images.

■ Attributes can be of heterogeneous types. Mixtures of numbers, strings and other types are a norm. It is common for a business database to contain customer name, date of birth and bank account balance in a single record. Transforming non-numeric values to numbers may not be always meaningful or convenient.

■ Data objects may not be traditional record structures. The widespread use of the web and multimedia materials results in data sets of different complexities. Unstructured text, semi-structured web pages, time-series audio files, spatial images and video clips can all be stored in databases. Data objects in such data sets have various relationships.

■ Database contents may be dynamic and evolving. OLTP databases contain current data records that may change rapidly. Archival databases accumulate data records from the start. For both kinds of database, the content evolves over time.

■ Data quality can be poor in terms of consistency, correctness, preciseness, completeness and timeliness. Data in most real-life databases are entered by hand. A data-entry system without rigorous data-verification procedures means that the data entered can be wrong or recorded imprecisely. Data records may also have null values for certain fields, indicating that the values for those fields are missing or not available. Poor quality data may result in the discovery of poor quality information patterns. Extremely polluted data sets are of little use.

■ Data values can be sparse. Data values for an attribute can be extremely skewed to one end of a spectrum or in a series of ranges rather than uniformly or normally distributed. For instance, the ages of university students are skewed to the range between 18 and 22.

In a typical data mining context, the data set given is what we have. Often, we have little or no control over the collection of the data from the original data source. To discover good-quality information patterns from poor-quality data is a challenge.

1.3.4 Efficient Discovery Methods

The problem of discovering non-trivial information patterns from a large set of data can be computationally hard. Many discovery problems such as association rules are combinatorial in nature. Certain patterns can only be found after many different combinations of data values are attempted. The number of possible combinations (i.e. the search space) may be extremely large. Simple solutions are unlikely to scale up well to cope with large data sets and may take too long to find the patterns. A discovery method has little practical use if it takes excessively long to return any patterns.

Any discovery method must therefore be efficient. A method is generally considered efficient if its execution time and space complexities are comparable to those of sorting algorithms. The problem is that efficient algorithms are hard to find. Useful improvements of efficiency include using powerful hardware platforms, adopting efficient implementation techniques, exploiting domain knowledge or human intervention, and adopting approximate algorithms that return some results in time, but not all.

1.4 OBJECTIVES OF DATA MINING

The main objectives of data mining can be broadly categorized into *classification*, *estimation*, *prediction* and *data description*. Objects are classified into one of a set of pre-defined classes. In order to do this, a classification model is built from a set of data examples. The accuracy of the classification by the model is then evaluated to give some degree of confidence to the result. Once a reliable classification model has been developed, it is then used to classify data records whose class outcomes are unknown. For instance, a classification model for determining whether a credit card application should be granted can

1

be built by using historical credit card application records. The model can then be used to determine whether to accept or reject an application.

Estimation is similar to classification. Instead of classifying an object into a discrete class, this task involves building a model, again based on a set of data examples, to estimate the value of a continuous outcome variable. For example, an estimation model can be built on records about house sales. The model produces an estimated value of a house according to features such as the number of bedrooms, the facilities (e.g. en-suite, and garage) and the total area of floor space. An estimation model can also be used for classification purposes. In a two-class scenario, an estimated value close to one end of the output value range can be taken as the prediction of one class and an estimated value close to the other end of the range can be taken as the prediction of the other class.

Prediction overlaps significantly with the classification and estimation. Prediction is more concerned with a future outcome of the output variable. For instance, historical data recordings on weather conditions are used to predict tomorrow's weather. Solutions for classification and estimation are widely used for prediction.

Data description is about describing general or specific features of the selected data set. It includes summary statistics, clustering and characteristic rule mining. One powerful data description method is data visualization – using visual vocabulary to describe features and trends in a data set.

1.5   DATA MINING AND OTHER DISCIPLINES

Data mining is a field of study that emerges from statistics, machine learning and database systems. As a discipline for data analysis, statistics contributes significantly towards data mining in terms of fundamental theories and methods for data analysis, measures for evaluating significance and relevance of patterns, and so on.

Machine learning, particularly inductive learning from data as a branch of artificial intelligence, has a long history dating from the 1950s. Over the decades, a large number of machine-learning methods and algorithms have been developed. The application of these methods to data mining problems is a major issue of interest. Most of the time, these methods and algorithms need to be modified in terms of performance efficiency in order to scale up and solve problems with real-life databases.

Over the past four decades, the technology of database management systems has matured. Fast storage and searching structures on secondary storage devices have been developed. Generations of query languages have also been developed and standardized. Most DBMSs are equipped with query optimization mechanisms to ensure fast evaluation of query operations. The technology advances in databases can offer data mining with fast access to secondary storage, making discovery tasks efficient and practical. Database query languages may be used in steps of data mining algorithms. It is interesting to see how to integrate data mining algorithms with the fast storage and search structures of databases.

1.6   PROMISES AND CHALLENGES

Data mining technology has a wide range of applications. The following list outlines some major areas:

- finance and insurance, including discovery of financial and insurance frauds, investment risk analysis, and credit history analysis;

- marketing and sales, including customer profiling, computer-aided marketing and promotion, and sales analysis;

- medicine, including diagnosis of diseases, analysis of functions of genes, and analysis of the effects of new drugs;

- agriculture, including diagnosis of plant diseases and the planning of agricultural produce within a region;

- social development and economics, including city resource planning, national and local government policy making, and local and global economy monitoring;

- engineering and manufacturing, including evaluation of computer-aided design and manufacturing and fault detection in production lines;

- natural sciences, including study of observed or experimental data, generation of new hypotheses, induction of new theories, and relationships between important variables;

- military and intelligence, an area that is highly classified;

- law enforcement, including criminal profiling, identification of criminals and terrorists, and detection of money-laundering activities.

There are many other areas where data mining can be useful that have not been included in the list. It can be said that the technology can find its use in any area as long as there is a need for sophisticated data analysis and data comprehension.

Besides the promises, there are also serious challenges due to the characteristics of real-life databases, as discussed in Section 1.3.3. The extremely large size of real-life databases mean that many mining solutions may not scale up. Therefore, efficient mining algorithms and new implementations are constantly required. The fact that real-life databases are kept on secondary storage media further enhances such need. For large-scale data analysis, machines with high processing power may also be needed. Some data mining projects, such as clustering large data sets and mining association rules, have been conducted on computers with parallel processing capabilities.

High dimensionality of data casts a vast multidimensional search space where it is not only difficult to detect patterns but also time-consuming to find them. When data are scattered, no patterns converge in the high-dimensional space. This phenomenon is known as the *curse of dimensions*. Data mining solutions should consider how to find patterns in sub-spaces of fewer dimensions. In other words, the most relevant and significant dimensions should be considered and the least relevant and least influential dimensions should be ignored.

Traditional data analysis methods, such as statistical methods and some machine-learning methods, work well for homogeneous variables, either numeric or categorical, within a table of records. However, when different data types are present, even finding a sensible and effective way of measuring similarity among data objects becomes less than straightforward. When data of complex structures, such as multimedia data sets, are involved in data mining, various relationships among data objects, such as spatial relationships, time series and containment properties, must also be considered.

When the data quality is of concern, actions such as error correction, data imputation and data summarization should be taken to improve the data quality, if possible before data mining starts. Improving data quality is not always an easy task. There is a limit on how much the quality can be improved. 'Garbage in and garbage out' is still a statement that largely makes sense. Data sets with skewed value distributions can cause distortion of the discovered information patterns if the user is not careful. It is also possible that certain patterns do not easily converge when data values are extremely skewed. Effort should also made to ensure the mining solutions are more robust to the effects of poor-quality data.

The evolving content of a database means that the information patterns discovered from the database should also evolve in order to reflect the truth of the database content. Many data mining methods are designed to work with static data, and cannot easily be applied to dynamically changing databases. More effort is needed to develop data mining methods of incremental nature that are adaptive to change.

It is important to correctly understand the meaning of the discovered information patterns. Comprehensibility of the patterns is as important as validity. Visualization has been used extensively to assist in comprehension of patterns. Correct visualization can certainly improve comprehensibility. It can even enable the discovery of new patterns by human eyes. However, inappropriate visualization with inappropriate visual vocabulary can be misleading and may cause serious misinterpretations. It should also be recognized that some patterns may be hard to interpret.

1.7   CURRENT STATE OF DATA MINING

Data mining is a new and active area of technological development. Statisticians once used the term to refer to an undisciplined approach of *torturing* data to suit any conclusions. Until the mid 1980s, analysis of data in databases was studied as a branch of database systems under the name of 'statistical databases'. Data mining started to emerge in the late 1980s. It was established as a new discipline of study in the early 1990s and has quickly gained popularity among academic researchers and industrial practitioners. From the mid 1990s to the early 2000s, the technology flourished. Machine-learning solutions and statistical methods were adopted. Many new data mining solutions and algorithms for classification, cluster detection, association, and anomaly detection were developed. Commercial data mining software tools, such as IBM Intelligent Miner for Data and Clementine, started to appear on the market, and a number of tools, such as Weka, are now widely used. Existing software tools, such as SPSS, Matlab and Microsoft SQL Server, have been extended to include some data mining facilities. Recent efforts largely focus on developing the technology further for specific problems in various application areas, such as medicine, biology, life sciences, finance, and so on.

Although data mining has delivered benefits to a wide range of applications, there is also a certain degree of hyperbole about it. 'Turn your machine loose on your data, and it will find what you want' is a misleading statement, no more than a myth. Such trivialization also underestimates the degree of difficulties involved in applying the technology successfully. Successful cases of data mining are reported but a large number of data mining projects are not so successful – some do not even get off the ground. Occasionally a long and costly process may end with nothing.

After nearly 20 years of research and development, *first-order discovery* (from data to information patterns) has been addressed to a certain extent. New data mining methods are needed for discovery of more sophisticated patterns from primitive patterns. This *second-order discovery* requires integration of different data mining methods. For instance, association among values of attributes may be used for discovering possible associations concerning attributes themselves.

1.8   WEKA MACHINE-LEARNING TOOL

The Waikato Environment for Knowledge Analysis (Weka) is a machine learning toolkit developed at the University of Waikato in Hamilton, New Zealand. The software provides many machine-learning, statistics and other data mining solutions for various types of data mining task, such as classification, cluster detection, association rule discovery and attribute selection. The software is also equipped with data pre-processing and post-processing tools and visualization tools so that complete data mining projects can be conducted via a number of different styles of user interface. The toolkit is written in Java and can, therefore, run on various platforms, such as Linux, Windows and Macintosh. It is distributed under the terms and conditions of the GNU General Public License. Figure 1.2 shows the root interface window of

FIGURE 1.2 Weka machine-learning toolkit for data mining

the Weka Version 3.6.1. The software offers four application *routes* for accessing its tool set. Selecting one of the options from the Applications group opens a task window in the main window area.

The *Explorer* route provides an interactive way of performing a data mining investigation. Through a simple yet effective graphical user interface, the end user can open an input data set and observe and understand its features via controls on the *Pre-processing* and *Visualize* tab pages. The user can also select a data pre-processing operation to prepare the data before mining. Through the Explorer, the user performs a mining task by selecting a mining solution and setting the relevant parameters. The discovered patterns and the evaluation results are displayed, and some patterns can be visualized. For most parts of this text, only the Explorer route is needed. The Explorer has limits. By default, it can only deal with an input data set of several thousands of data records, because the entire data set is loaded into the main memory. Although it is possible to change the default setting of memory sizes, the amount of available memory may not be able to accommodate the entire data set.

The *Experimenter* interface is particularly designed for evaluation and selection of classification techniques. It allows the user to automate the process by setting different learning algorithms with parameters upon a number of chosen data sets, collecting performance statistics, and testing the significance of the accuracy of the classification models produced by different classification solutions. This useful facility is used in Chapters 6 and 7.

The *KnowledgeFlow* interface allows the user to set up a more serious batch-processing mining task for larger data sets. Via the controls on the graphical user interface, the user can specify a sequence of pre-processing and mining tasks in the form of a task flow chart. Functions in the Knowledge Flow mode of the system have incremental algorithms behind them to overcome the memory space limits. We shall use an example to illustrate this route in Chapter 10.

The *Simple CLI* route offers an interface that allows the end user to call a Java function by issuing commands with command-line parameters to start mining or data pre-processing functions.

Weka is a robust data mining software tool that is ideal for teaching and learning. The Explorer interface enables interactive test running of many different data mining solutions upon a reasonable-sized data set. The Explorer interface and the KnowledgeFlow interface allow students to perform small data mining projects. The tool set is freely available for download under the GNU license. These are the main reasons why Weka is selected to support this text. An example of performing a data mining task in Weka is shown in Chapter 2.

The Weka installation process is quite straightforward. There are two versions of the software that can be downloaded: one with a Java Virtual Machine and one without. Choose one of them according to the local environment setting. Under Microsoft Windows, the installation wizard goes through a sequence of standard installation steps. The wizard extracts all files automatically into appropriate folders on the local disk drive.

1

1.9 SUMMARY

This chapter has briefly introduced the concept of data mining. It started by describing data, information and knowledge and the respective roles they serve. It then introduced the background of data mining and highlighted the urgent need for data mining. The chapter thoroughly explained what data mining is in detail, from non-trivial useful information to real-life databases and efficient mining solutions. The chapter mentioned classification, estimation, prediction and description as the main objectives of data mining and explained the origins of data mining.

The potential applications of data mining technology were mentioned. The main challenges and difficulties were also highlighted. The chapter briefly described the current state of the technology and introduced the Weka software toolkit that supports the text.

EXERCISES

1 In a typical university's academic department, the essential aims are to effectively deliver courses and teach students knowledge in subjects of a discipline area. Describe example raw data, valuable information and knowledge and discuss their roles in monitoring and ensuring the effectiveness of teaching.

2 In a fictional database about customers purchasing tour packages to various places at different prices, data operations of different kinds are performed. Try to categorize the following operations into data retrieval, online analytic processing, or data mining:

   (a) Find names of customers who have purchased tours that cost less than £300.

   (b) List the names of the customers, the number of tour packages that the customers have purchased, and the total cost for the tours.

   (c) Calculate the differences in quarterly sales of tours between this year and the previous two years.

   (d) Find a rule such as 'If customers purchase a tour package to France, then it is 85% likely that the same customers also purchase a tour package to Spain'.

   (e) From the customer purchase history, build a model for predicting the kinds of customer who are likely to purchase tours to a certain country.

3 Discuss the most distinct feature of each of the following real-life databases:

   (a) The UK government has been conducting Family Expenditure Surveys over the past four decades. As a result, a deposit of survey records has been accumulated and stored at the National Data Archive Centre. Each survey may contain around 70 variables. There are about 2000 survey records every year. From year to year, some variables do change. For instance, the cost of petrol in a month may be a variable for one year's survey but it was not a variable in surveys during the early 1970s.

   (b) A supermarket chain issues loyalty cards to their customers. The card enables the supermarket chain to monitor purchases made by each individual customer. Each customer transaction consists of a number of purchased items that are scanned into the database via barcode readers. Each day, a typical store processes thousands of customer transactions. The stores of the supermarket chain are open for most days during a year. There are hundreds of stores throughout the country.

(c) A consortium of insurance companies closely monitor claims for car accidents. When a car accident happens, the parties involved are asked to fill in an accident report form by their insurance company which is a member of the consortium. Besides personal details and insurance policy details, the form requires information about the location of the accident, a description of the accident and a diagram indicating the positions of the vehicles involved. Sometimes but not always, a report from the police may also be added.

4 Categorize each of the following data mining activities as classification, estimation or description. State clearly the reasons behind your decision. Can any patterns discovered be used for prediction purposes?

(a) An estate agency has accumulated a large number of property sale records. The properties can be studio flats, semi-detached houses, detached houses or mansion houses. The agency wants to investigate from the data set what kinds of customer are likely to purchase which types of property.

(b) It is interesting for the same estate agency to make significant links between different descriptors of the properties sold and the characteristics of their customers. For instance, customers who are married with young children may be more likely to purchase a three-bedroom, detached house with a single garage.

(c) In recent years, we have seen increasing amounts of toxic waste dumped into our environment. Waste water from manufacturing processes, farming land run-off and sewage water from treatment plants have broken the chemical balance of the water in our rivers. The organic matter in the water has resulted in excessive growth of algae, which in turn leads to a reduction of the oxygen level in the water, causing the deaths of fish and other wild life. Therefore, environment agencies want to monitor closely the growth of algae in the rivers and lakes. One agency has collected water samples from a number of different sites and analyzed them for various chemical substances. They have also collected algae samples at the same locations to determine the population distributions of different types of algae. The agency wants to use the sample data to build a model that can approximate the distribution of algae population based on amounts of the chemical substances.

5 Data mining is a powerful technology that can bring about positive benefits but it has also caused a certain degree of suspicion and concerns over ethical issues. Find suitable examples to highlight that such concerns are valid and reasonable.

BIBLIOGRAPHICAL NOTES

The area of data mining has matured over the last two decades. Many papers, journals and, more recently, an increasing number of textbooks have been published. Early introductory texts to the concept of data mining include (Fayyad *et al.* 1996; Berry and Linoff 1997). Popular magazines such as *Communications of the ACM* also ran special editions to introduce data mining, data warehousing and their applications (CACM 1996). Hand *et al.* (2001) and more recently Luan and Zhao (2006) describe the major differences between statistics and data mining. Witten and Frank (2005) underline close relationships between machine learning and statistics. Chen *et al.* (1996) present a survey of data mining from a database perspective. A broad description of information patterns is given by Frawley *et al.* (1991). The famous quote from Lord Leverhulme of Unilever appeared in an editorial article about data mining in *The Economist* magazine (1995).

Textbooks on data mining include Han and Kamber (2001), who give the subject a database perspective, addressing issues in relation to data mining techniques and data mining systems.

Hand *et al.* (2001) builds the subject on the solid ground of statistical theory and modelling. Witten and Frank (2005) offer coverage of the subject with a strong emphasis on machine-learning techniques and tools. Tan *et al.* (2006) emphasize data mining techniques and algorithms with a strong note on evaluation of mining results. Other more general texts include a shorter text by Larose (2005) and a business-oriented text from Berry and Linoff (1997; 2004).

A good reference website for KDD and data mining is maintained by Piatetsky-Shapiro (2007). This website provides many useful links to a variety of references on the subject. Weka can be downloaded as a self-extracting executable file under a GNU license from the site at Weka (2008).

CHAPTER 2

Principles of data mining

LEARNING OBJECTIVES

To understand the process of data mining

To understand different approaches to data mining

To appreciate the main categories of data mining problem

To recognize output patterns of information

To achieve a general understanding of data mining solutions

To appreciate the importance of evaluation

To undertake a data mining task in Weka

To review basic concepts in statistics and probability

Chapter 1 explains *what* data mining is. This chapter addresses issues about *how* data mining is conducted. Instead of the specifics of a particular data mining method, this chapter concentrates on the general principles of data mining.

It first outlines steps of the data mining process and explains approaches to undertaking data mining tasks. The roles of participants in a data mining project are also discussed. The chapter then introduces the main categories of problem that data mining is set to solve and the types of information pattern that are produced. The chapter also surveys a range of existing data mining methods and solutions, particularly those to be covered by the rest of this text. Information patterns deduced from data are fundamentally probabilistic and uncertain. This fact highlights the importance of evaluating any discovered patterns.

In order to enhance your understanding of the data mining process, the chapter uses an example to demonstrate how to perform a data mining task using Weka.

Since probability and statistical methods and measures are extensively used in data mining, it is necessary to provide a brief review of some basic concepts in probability and statistics. The coverage is maintained at an elementary level in order not to overburden readers with theoretical rigour in statistics.

2.1 DATA MINING PROCESS

Generally, the data mining process consists of three key steps: preparation of input data, mining of data, and post-processing of output patterns (see Figure 2.1).

2

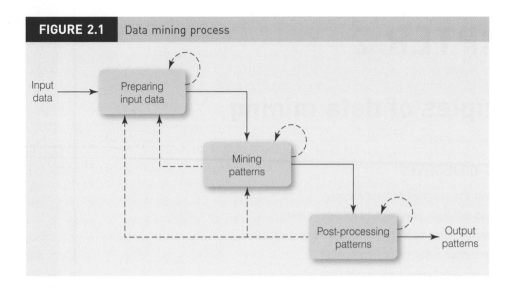

FIGURE 2.1   Data mining process

2.1.1 Data Preparation

The data preparation step is a complex process that may involve data collection and selection, pre-processing and formatting. Data collection involves the identification of data sources and the gathering of relevant data details from the sources. Data may be collected from different parts of the same database, different databases within the same organization, or even from external data sources. For instance, for the purpose of analyzing the possibility of bad debts, a credit card company may collect credit card application data from the sales department and credit card usage data from the accounts department. The company may also collect credit history data from external credit bureaus. It is rare, unless the database is very small, that data mining starts with the whole database. Normally, a target data set is selected from the database by performing a query or sampling. For instance, the credit card company may select records from a specific period of time.

What makes data mining different from conventional experimental studies is that data are not generated and collected under controlled conditions, but are simply given. The data collection and selection stage is more about focusing on relevant variables and selecting a relevant subset of data from available data sources than on generating data.

The selected target data set normally needs to be pre-processed before data mining can begin. The objectives of pre-processing include cleaning data, dealing with unknown data values, reducing data dimensionality, transforming data values from one domain to another, and so on. Data pre-processing is discussed in Chapter 3. Besides pre-processing, the data set may need to be re-formatted in order to suit the chosen data mining solution. For instance, Weka requires data sets to be in ARFF or CSV format before they can be mined.

2.1.2 Data Mining

The second step of data mining is the actual mining from the input data to patterns. At this stage, a sensible data mining task must be properly designed to comply with the objectives of the investigation. For example, if preventing bad debts is the business objective, a credit card company may want to develop a classification model to forecast the likelihood of an account going bad. In order to develop the classification model, the available data set may be divided into two separate subsets, one for constructing the model and the other for testing its accuracy. Indeed, the specification of the mining task may also provide useful feedback on how the data should be organized and prepared.

At the mining stage, an applicable data mining solution is selected. The selected solution should be able to cope with the types of data in the input and should be suitable for the mining task. A data mining solution normally needs a number of external parameters. The settings of the parameter values affect the patterns found. For instance, mining association rules require setting a minimum support threshold and a minimum confidence threshold. Increasing the thresholds reduces the number of association rules found. Using the right parameters is crucial for discovering good patterns. Unfortunately, there is always an element of trial and error before the right setting can be found.

2.1.3 Post-processing of Patterns

The post-processing stage refers to any further processing of the discovered patterns after mining. The post-processing includes pattern evaluation, pattern selection and pattern interpretation. First, the credibility and significance of the patterns are vital for the purpose of data mining, and hence must be evaluated objectively using appropriate methods. Often, not all patterns are of interest, and therefore a further selection may be needed. A ranking criterion for *interestingness* may be deployed in the selection process. It is then important that the credible, significant and interesting patterns are understood and interpreted correctly. Appropriate visualization of the patterns can assist the interpretation. This is because human eyes are a powerful tool to identify visual patterns and trends.

As indicated in Figure 2.1, the whole data mining process is iterative: each step may be repeated and it may be necessary to go back to earlier steps. The data preparation step, particularly the data pre-processing, normally takes most of the time allocated to a data mining project.

2.1.4 Standard Process

In recent years, major data mining software vendors and practitioners, particularly SPSS, have proposed an industrial standard process for data mining. Known as the cross-industry standard process for data mining (CRISP-DM), it proposes a thorough and rigorous methodology for undertaking data mining projects. CRISP-DM version 1.0 outlines activities of data mining in six phases consisting of a number of generic tasks. Each generic task consists of a sequence of specialized tasks that in turn can be undertaken via process instance activities. Chapter 10 explains the methodology in more detail.

2.1.5 Roles in Data Mining

There have been extensive debates about human involvement in the data mining process. Early definitions of data mining use the word 'automatic' or 'semi-automatic' to describe the process, indicating a large degree of autonomy from human intervention. The main reason against heavy human intervention is a valid one: to prevent biased discovery of anticipated patterns and ignoring important but previously unknown patterns. However, this cannot mean that data mining is a self-initiated and fully automatic process from gathering of data to the delivery of valid patterns. To conduct a data mining project using software tools must, at least for the foreseeable future, involve humans in the process due to the cognitive nature of the tasks.

The primary human operators are *business data analysts,* or *data miners*. Business data analysts are involved in every stage of the mining process, ranging from selection of data to evaluation of resulting patterns. The debate about human intervention must not and should not target the data miners.

It should focus on the role of another type of human operator, known as the *domain expert*, who has extensive knowledge about the areas of the business application. In fact, the involvement of domain experts at the post-processing stage is very desirable: the experts can advise on which patterns are interesting and useful and what actions to take in correspondence with the patterns. There is also a role for domain experts to play in selecting and pre-processing data and in advising on the types of mining task to perform. However, the degree of involvement of the domain experts in those activities must be carefully considered. One must appreciate the advantage of saving time and finding patterns of real interest and, at the same time, realize the risk of introducing bias into the investigation. The best compromise lies with the effective exploitation of the strengths of both machines and humans: machines are good at searching quickly through a large volume of data; humans are good at spotting general trends and patterns that emerge from the discovery. The ideal team for data mining therefore should include both data analysts and domain experts.

2.2   DATA MINING APPROACHES

There are basically two approaches to conducting data mining: hypothesis testing and discovery. Hypothesis testing is a traditional approach used by statisticians and experimental scientists. In this approach, a preconceived statement (a hypothesis) is formed, a set of data requirements is developed and relevant data details are collected. Experiments may be needed to generate the data required. The data are then prepared and analyzed. The resulting patterns with their evaluation results should then either substantiate or disprove the original hypothesis. Normally, the evidence supporting the hypothesis is compared with that for a default belief, the *null* hypothesis. The proposed hypothesis is only accepted when support is *significantly* higher than support for the null hypothesis.

For instance, the human form of 'mad cow disease' (BSE) might be related to people's eating habits. An initial hypothesis may state that excessive consumption of burgers leads to a high risk of having the disease. Data about burger consumption by people who have the disease and people who do not, such as frequencies and amounts of regular burger consumption and other diets are collected. After the data are prepared, association rules that express a link between burger consumption and the disease may be discovered. The lift factors of the rules are measured. The result of the measurement may indicate that the lift of any of the association rules is so low that it is not significantly different from the lift factor of the null hypothesis: that the presence of the disease is not correlated with the consumption of burgers – it happens by chance. Therefore, the original hypothesis has not been substantiated. This is not to conclude that there is no link but merely to state that the link is not strong.

Unlike the hypothesis testing approach, the discovery approach starts with data and induces possible patterns without a specific hypothesis in mind. This approach is investigative in nature. To a certain extent, this is the main factor that differentiates data mining and machine learning from more traditional statistical analysis. Learning from data can be directed or undirected. A directed discovery, also known as *supervised learning* in machine-learning terms, means that the discovery is driven by the outcomes of an output variable. The discovery is to find patterns relating to the outcomes. A typical piece of data mining in this approach is classification, where we select the target variable and direct the computer to tell us how other variables are related to the outcome of the target variable. In undirected discovery, also known as unsupervised learning, there is no specification of a target variable. The computer investigates relationships of some kind between variables or between data objects and measures their degrees of significance. A typical example of this approach is association rule discovery.

The procedures and activities of directed and undirected discovery are similar. Both start without a specific hypothesis in mind, collect and prepare data, mine possible patterns from the data and evaluate the strength of the resulting patterns. However, directed discovery has more specific issues to consider. In the data preparation stage, the target variable must be specified. Data pre-processing in relation to the outcome of the target variable may be needed. For instance, values of a descriptive attribute may be discretized by considering the outcome of the target variable. Specific mining solutions that build a computer model for the target variable are selected. The evaluation of the model again considers the performance of the model in relation to the outcomes of the target variable.

Take the previous example about the human form of BSE. A directed discovery can be described as follows. The process starts without forming an initial hypothesis, but with an objective of learning patterns in relation to the presence of the disease. Data regarding burger consumption and other factors, such as diet, body weight, age, home region, long-term illness, may be included in the investigation. The target variable is therefore a Boolean variable that describes the presence (positive) or absence (negative) of the disease. Possible factors of the investigation become input descriptive features. The intention is to establish what factors contribute to the presence of the disease. A classification method is then used to build a classification model for the target variable. The accuracy of the classification in predicting the presence and absence of the disease, based on the input features, is then measured to provide some confidence in the model. According to the classification method used, for example a decision tree induction method, the important and most influential factors for the disease are indicated.

2.3 CATEGORIES OF DATA MINING PROBLEM AND OUTPUT PATTERNS

In Chapter 1, the main objectives of data mining were outlined as classification, estimation, prediction and description. In this section, the main categories of data mining problem and possible output patterns corresponding to the data mining objectives are presented in more detail.

2.3.1 Classification

Classification is about determining the class of a given data record by applying a classification model (Figure 2.2). Such a model is developed from a set of data records known as *examples*.

As shown in Figure 2.2(a), each example consists of a list of *descriptive features* and a class label that is already known. For instance, an example (overcast, hot, high, FALSE, P) represents a weather condition of 'overcast outlook, high temperature, high humidity, and not windy' and is assigned a class label P, which indicates that a game of golf can be played in those weather conditions. Through the chosen model-building method, a classification model can be induced from the examples. Figure 2.2(b) shows the use of the classification model to classify a data record whose class is unknown. Such a record is known as an *unseen data record*. Since the record outlook is sunny and humidity is high, the model, according to what it has learnt from the examples, has made the decision that the class for this weather condition is N, indicating that a game of golf cannot be played. A more practical example of classification is to build a model to predict whether an application for a credit card should be accepted or rejected.

Output patterns for classification refer to the forms that a classification model takes. There are a variety of forms that have been used to represent classification models.

Instance space An *instance space* is a multidimensional space defined by descriptive feature variables. Training examples are considered as points in the space like stars in a galaxy. Each training example may have a weight attached to it, like the force of gravity, indicating its sphere of influence.

Normally, the entire instance space is held in the computer memory when the model is used to classify an unseen data record. To classify an object, the distance between the object and each example is measured, and the *nearest* or *k nearest neighbours* of the object are located. The weight attached to an example influences the distance measurements. The class of the object is then decided by the class of its nearest neighbour or k nearest neighbours.

2

FIGURE 2.2 An illustration of classification process

Example data set

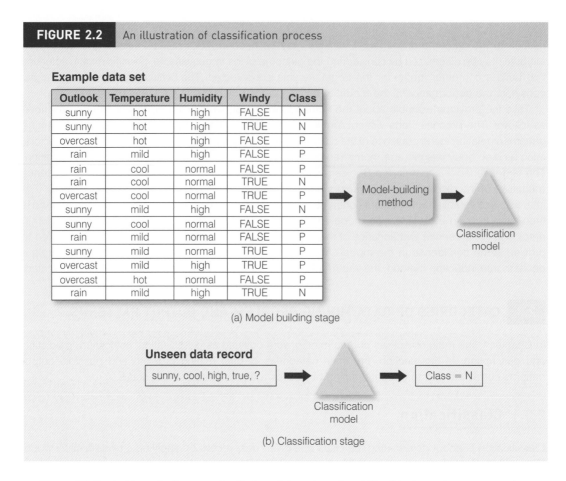

Outlook	Temperature	Humidity	Windy	Class
sunny	hot	high	FALSE	N
sunny	hot	high	TRUE	N
overcast	hot	high	FALSE	P
rain	mild	high	FALSE	P
rain	cool	normal	FALSE	P
rain	cool	normal	TRUE	N
overcast	cool	normal	TRUE	P
sunny	mild	high	FALSE	N
sunny	cool	normal	FALSE	P
rain	mild	normal	FALSE	P
sunny	mild	normal	TRUE	P
overcast	mild	high	TRUE	P
overcast	hot	normal	FALSE	P
rain	mild	high	TRUE	N

Model-building method

Classification model

(a) Model building stage

Unseen data record

sunny, cool, high, true, ?

Classification model

Class = N

(b) Classification stage

Figure 2.3 illustrates an instance space that contains several real-life objects such as an aeroplane, a bicycle, a clock, etc. If an unseen data object of a specific shape needs to be classified, we measure the *distance* between each example and the unseen object. The nearest neighbour, i.e. an aeroplane, is then located. The output from the model is the class label of the nearest neighbour, i.e. *aeroplane*, which is used to label the unseen record.

Classification rules A rule is an IF..THEN assertion that states a fact about the data set. A classification rule has a conjunctive description of features in the IF part and a class outcome in the THEN part of the rule. Most of the time, a conjunctive description of features in the IF part of a rule involves the feature variables and specific values that the variables take. Such rules are known as *propositional* rules. For instance, the following classification rule may be discovered from a credit card application data set:

```
IF (20,000 < Income < 40,000) AND (OwnHouse = 'yes')
THEN Class = 'safe customer'
```

Rules may also involve several values of variables. Such rules are known as *rules involving relations* or simply *relations*. For instance, the following rules may be discovered and used to distinguish whether an object is lying or standing:

```
IF width > height THEN lying
IF height > width THEN standing
```

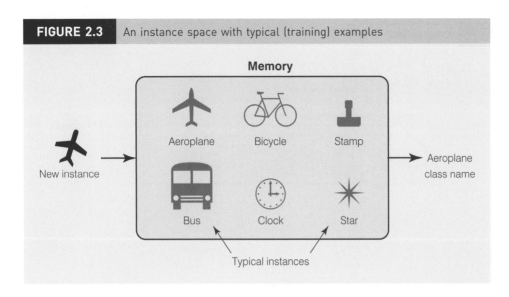

FIGURE 2.3   An instance space with typical (training) examples

Decision trees A decision tree is a tree structure consisting of internal nodes, leaf nodes, and links connecting internal nodes to leaf nodes. In a typical decision tree (see Figure 2.4), a leaf node represents a class label, an internal node represents a variable, and a link from a parent node to a child node represents a value of the variable denoted by the parent node.

If a decision tree involves a numeric variable, a link represents a range of values for the variable. As shown in Figure 2.4(b), the internal node for drive mileage has two links, one labeled '< 10000' and the other '≥ 10000'.

A specific form of decision tree is a binary tree where the leaf nodes still represent class labels, but an internal node specifies a Boolean test. In this case, a link is associated with true or false, representing the outcome of a Boolean test that involves a variable and its value. Figure 2.4(c) shows the binary tree version of the example in Figure 2.4(b).

With a decision tree, classification decisions can be made by traversing the tree from the root towards the leaf nodes. While traversing a path, a sequence of tests is conducted. When a leaf node is reached, a decision is made. For the decision tree in Figure 2.4(a), if a customer is middle-aged and the drive mileage is short, then the customer is classified as *safe*. Classification rules can be derived from a decision tree.

2.3.2 Estimation

Estimation is very similar to classification except that the output of a continuous target variable is of interest. The process of estimation is similar to that for classification, which also involves building an estimation model and then using the model to estimate the value of the outcome variable. The output patterns, i.e. an estimation model, may take the form of a function, a theorem or a network.

Functions A function represents a mapping pattern from arguments to value. For estimation, a function can be a precise pattern such as the speed function:

$$f(n) = n^2 + 2n - 10$$

where n represents the force pressed on the accelerator pedal. This function is obtained by exhaustively testing the mappings between different speed values with corresponding n values.

FIGURE 2.4   Decision trees

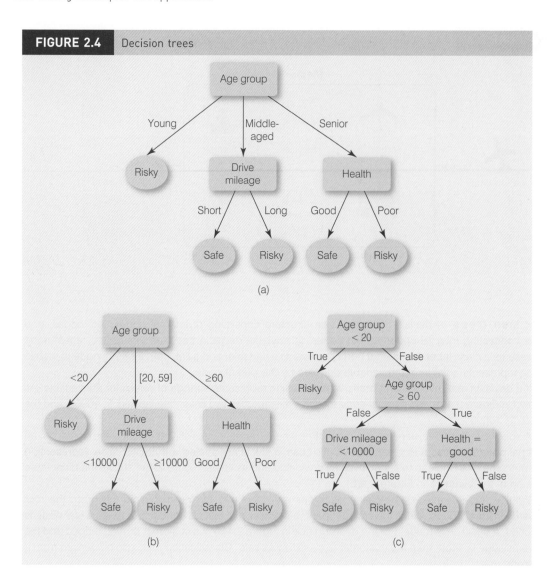

Most of the time, functions are approximate – no precise mapping can be found from arguments to values. Finding a best-fit line among the data points is known as *regression analysis*. If it is to find a straight line, the task is called linear regression analysis. If it is to find a curve, the task is called non-linear regression. Figure 2.5 shows examples of regression graphs.

Theorems   Related to functions are theorems, e.g. the Bayesian theorem. Based on statistical theories, the parameters in the theorem can be tuned to best fit the examples in a training set. The theorem is then used to predict the outcome of an output variable (see Section 7.3.3 for an example).

Artificial neural networks   Emulating the human brain, an artificial neural network (Figure 2.6) consists of nodes and links located on different layers. Each node, also known as a neuron, consists of functions that summarize the input data and transform the result into an output value, which can feed into another neuron as input. Weights are attached to the links, influencing the results of computation. Further details of neural networks are described in Chapter 7.

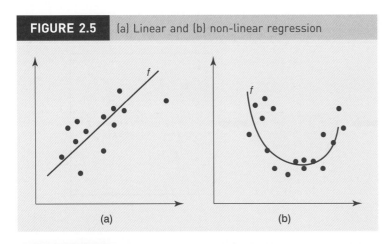

FIGURE 2.5   (a) Linear and (b) non-linear regression

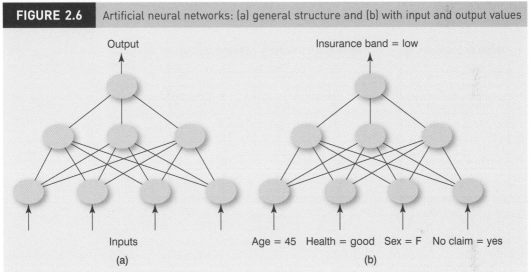

FIGURE 2.6   Artificial neural networks: (a) general structure and (b) with input and output values

2.3.3 Cluster Detection

A *cluster* is a group of data objects among which there exist some degree of similarity. Cluster detection, also known as clustering, is a process that divides a given data population into an appropriate number of clusters. Data objects within a cluster are known as *members* of the cluster. It is expected that similarity among members of a cluster should be high and similarity among objects of different clusters should be low. The objectives of clustering include knowing which data object belongs to which cluster and understanding common characteristics of the members of a specific cluster.

Figure 2.7 illustrates a clustering process in which points of close geographic locations are grouped together into a cluster. There are four clusters in the data population.

There is some similarity between clustering and classification. Both classification and clustering are about assigning appropriate class or cluster labels to data records. However, clustering differs from classification in two aspects. First, in clustering, there are no pre-defined classes. This means that the number of classes or clusters and the class or cluster label of each data record are not known before the operation. Second, clustering is about grouping data rather than developing a classification model. Therefore, there is no distinction between data records and examples. The entire data population is used as input to the clustering process.

2

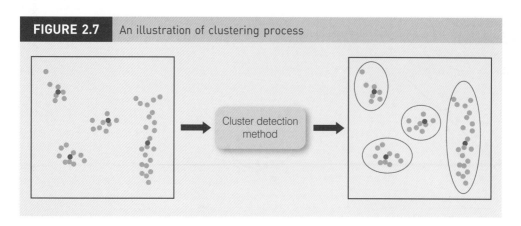

FIGURE 2.7   An illustration of clustering process

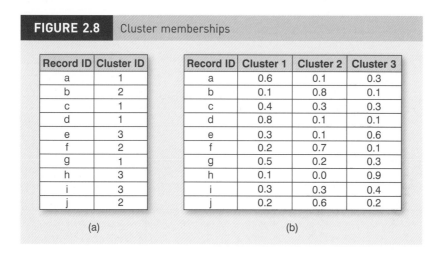

FIGURE 2.8   Cluster memberships

Record ID	Cluster ID
a	1
b	2
c	1
d	1
e	3
f	2
g	1
h	3
i	3
j	2

(a)

Record ID	Cluster 1	Cluster 2	Cluster 3
a	0.6	0.1	0.3
b	0.1	0.8	0.1
c	0.4	0.3	0.3
d	0.8	0.1	0.1
e	0.3	0.1	0.6
f	0.2	0.7	0.1
g	0.5	0.2	0.3
h	0.1	0.0	0.9
i	0.3	0.3	0.4
j	0.2	0.6	0.2

(b)

An example application of cluster detection is to identify customer groups according to their expenditure habits so that cross-sale opportunities across some groups may be found (see the customer segmentation case study in Section 10.2).

Although there are various ways of describing clusters, the primary output pattern for clustering is the assignment of cluster membership to each data object. Moreover, a general summary of the characteristics of each cluster, such as cluster size, cluster centre and within-cluster variations, is expected.

Figure 2.8 shows two ways to represent cluster membership. In Figure 2.8(a), each object has a single and exclusive membership. Figure 2.8(b) shows a table that indicates the likelihood of the cluster to which a data object belongs.

2.3.4 Association Mining

Association mining identifies co-occurrences of groups of data items in a data set. Such associations may exist between values of the same variable. If values of the variable can be categorized, association may exist between different categories. Associations may also be found between values of different variables. Associations may occur in temporal order and become sequential patterns.

An example of association mining is to identify significant associations between products on sale in a transaction database, as shown in Figure 2.9. The association mining method can find *association rules*

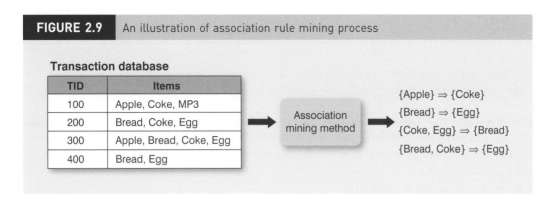

FIGURE 2.9   An illustration of association rule mining process

in an IF..THEN ($\Rightarrow$) clause format. For instance, the method has found that a customer who buys bread also buys eggs. One area of practical application for association mining is the retail industry, such as supermarkets, shops, supply chains, etc. However, association patterns have a much wider range of applications in general.

As indicated, the output patterns for association mining are either affinity groups or association rules. In an affinity group, data objects are grouped not because they are similar but because they occur more often together in data recordings than other object combinations. In other words, the existence of such a group is justified by the frequency of co-occurrence of data objects within the group. For instance, the group {Coke, Crisps} may occur in many shopping transactions. Unlike clusters, such groups do not need a group identifier to assign the membership of each object in the group nor are the general characteristics of the group under study.

A *sequential pattern* is an ordered sequence of co-occurrence groups. For instance, the sequential pattern ({Coke, Crisps}, {Ice cream, Mint}) may exist, indicating that purchases for Coke and Crisps are followed by those for Ice cream and Mint. For sequential patterns, only the order of groups is of interest. That makes sequential patterns different from time series patterns.

Another form of output pattern for association mining is an association rule with an IF..THEN clause. A special form of association rule may have a value or a combination of values in the IF part and another value or a combination of values in the THEN part, for the same attribute. This type of association is known as a Boolean association rule. For instance, there may be a Boolean association rule in the context of a retail shop:

```
IF T-shirt AND jeans THEN trainers, ice cream
```

The rule states that people who purchase both a T-shirt and jeans are likely to purchase trainers and ice cream. In the same retailing context, data objects may belong to a certain category. Association rules may exist between categories. For instance, if 'cake' and 'apples' from the food category and 'Newsweek' and 'Hello!' from the magazine category are present in shopping transactions, the following rule may exist:

```
IF food THEN magazine
```

Rules can have exceptions, indicating special circumstances where the rule does not apply. For instance, the following rule may exist:

```
IF (Income > 20,000) AND (OwnCar = 'yes')
THEN Class = 'safe customer'
Except IF Age = teen THEN Class = 'risky customer'
```

Associations may exist among values of different attributes. For instance, the rule below states that married couples with one child are likely to live in a detached house and own a car:

```
IF (Married = 'yes') AND (NoOfChildren = 1)
THEN (HouseType = 'detached') AND (OwnCar = 'yes')
```

Besides the three main categories of data mining problems, there are many other problems from various applications where data mining can also be applied. Examples include anomaly detection, time-series analysis, and taxonomy mining, which are beyond the scope of this text.

2.3.5 Data Mining Example

Table 2.1 shows data about students who have just graduated from university. The table records some personal details about the students, the major subjects that the students studied and the results that they obtained at graduation. We use this example to illustrate the major data mining problems that have been described in this section.

With this table, we can build a classification model that predicts the degree classification of a student. The model may predict that students with a computing major from the UK tend to have a first-class degree. Clustering among records in the table may be conducted when similarity is measured upon gender, major subject, age and degree class. A cluster may be formed containing young UK males majoring in computing with first-class degrees. Association rules between attributes within the table may also be discovered. For instance, there seems to exist a strong association between a history major and an upper second-class degree.

TABLE 2.1	An example data set about students					
StudentID	**Gender**	**Country**	**Major Subject**	**Age**	**TotalUnits**	**Degree Class**
1	M	UK	Computing	22	360	1st Class
2	F	UK	Computing	21	360	2nd Lower
3	M	FRANCE	Psychology	24	345	2nd Lower
4	M	SPAIN	Accounting	23	360	1st Class
5	F	UK	Psychology	22	300	Pass
6	F	USA	History	30	345	2nd Upper
7	M	UK	Computing	35	360	1st Class
8	F	FRANCE	Psychology	25	360	3rd Class
9	F	GERMANY	History	23	360	2nd Upper
10	M	UK	Accounting	22	360	1st Class
11	M	SPAIN	History	20	345	2nd Upper
12	F	UK	Law	45	300	Pass

2.4   OVERVIEW OF DATA MINING SOLUTIONS

Many data mining solutions have been developed. The solutions can be categorized according to the data mining tasks. This section provides a brief overview of those solutions for clustering, classification and association rule discovery.

A large number of clustering solutions have been developed. There are different ways of categorizing those solutions, such as by clustering result or by similarity functions used. Clustering solutions can be roughly divided into two categories by clustering result: partition-based methods and hierarchical methods. Partition-based methods divide the whole data population into a number of disjoint groups. A typical method of this category is the k-means method. Hierarchical methods, on the other hand, produce a hierarchy of possible levels of groupings of data, from individual data objects as clusters up to a single large cluster containing all data objects. According to user requirements, one or more levels of the hierarchy may be of interest and therefore taken as the result of the clustering. A typical method of this category is the agglomeration method.

Other categorizations of clustering solutions also exist. For instance, DBScan is a method that is based on density measure whereas Chameleon is a method that measures similarity by relative closeness and connectivity. Clique is a method that searches for clusters in subspaces of a given high-dimensional data set.

Solutions for classification are largely categorized according to the model produced. Section 2.3 outlines five types of classification model: instance space, decision tree, classification rule, artificial neural network, and classification theorem. The classification methods that produce an instance space as the model are known as 'nearest neighbour methods'. These methods find, from the instance space, one or k nearest neighbours of the unknown record to determine its class. A typical method of this category is the k-nearest neighbour (kNN) algorithm.

Classification methods that construct a decision tree are known as 'decision tree induction methods'. These methods use training examples of data to construct a decision tree. At classification time, the tree is traversed from the root to a leaf according to the attribute values of the data record. The leaf node determines the class of the record. A typical decision tree induction method is the ID3 algorithm.

Neural network solutions construct an artificial neural network as the classification model; during the training period, the topology of the network is decided and the weights attached to the links are tuned according to the output produced by the training examples. At the classification stage, descriptive attribute values are entered via the input layer of the network and the classification result is collected from the nodes on the output layer.

Rule-based classification methods induce a set (or a sequence) of classification rules. Again, during the training period, rules are learnt from training examples. In the classification period, rules that match the data records are applied or *fired* to determine the class of the record. A typical method is the covering method.

Classification methods that use theorems as a classification model are normally categorized as 'statistical methods' because of the statistical nature of the theorems. During the training time, examples are used to best estimate the parameters or coefficients of the theorem. During classification, the theorem with its trained parameters is applied to the unknown data records to determine their class. A number of methods fall under this category such as Naïve Bayes, regression analysis, Gaussian Mixture Model, etc.

Data mining solutions for association rules tend to focus on the discovery of various types of association such as Boolean, generalized and quantitative rules as well as sequential patterns. The most used algorithm is the early-developed Apriori algorithm, which is based on the *round-robin* principle of testing combinations of data items.

Most of the algorithms and methods are explained and discussed in detail in the following chapters. Clustering methods are the subject of Chapter 4 and 5. Chapters 6 and 7 are devoted to classification methods. Chapters 8 and 9 cover association rule solutions. However, it is impossible to describe all the data mining solutions that have been developed. We emphasize the basic methods and the most popular and widely-used advanced methods.

2.5   EVALUATION OF MINING RESULTS

Once information patterns are mined from the input data, they should be evaluated. Without proper evaluation, patterns may reveal relationships that happen by chance and may not lead to any useful actions. Then the patterns are hardly of any practical use.

How to evaluate patterns has been an active area for on-going research since the inception of data mining. Various measures have been suggested. Broadly known as *measures of interestingness*, these measures evaluate conciseness, coverage, reliability, peculiarity, diversity, novelty, surprisingness, usefulness and applicability of patterns.

- *Conciseness* is concerned with the number of resulting patterns and complexity in pattern description. A small number of concise patterns are easier to understand and hence add more value in understanding of the data. An example measure is the *minimum description length* of a rule.

- *Coverage* of a pattern refers to the portion of the data set whose data support the pattern. Coverage is related to generality. The greater the portion the pattern covers, the more general the pattern is. Support of frequent itemsets in association rule discovery is such a measure.

- *Reliability* of a pattern means that the pattern occurs in a high percentage of applicable cases. Reliability is reflected by the accuracy of classification models and confidence of association rules.

- *Peculiarity* of a pattern is its difference from the norm. A peculiar pattern is normally induced from data that are very different from the norm. Peculiar patterns normally mark the unknown features about the data, such as anomalies.

- *Diversity* of a pattern refers to its difference from other patterns and the differences among elements within the pattern itself. Diverse patterns are different from the uniformity of data and hence may underline something special about the data. In clustering, for example, diversity among clusters is desirable whereas diversity among cluster members is not.

- A pattern is said to be *novel* if it is not known before and is not trivial enough to be inferred from the already known patterns. After all, mining unknown, non-trivial patterns is the primary objective of data mining. On the other hand, it is difficult to objectively measure novelty unless an intelligent management system that manages all known patterns is in place. In practice, measures of novelty involve the domain expert in the evaluation process.

- A pattern is said to be *surprising* if it contradicts existing knowledge or user's expectations. Surprising patterns are interesting because they reflect the limitations of existing knowledge.

- A pattern is *useful* if it helps to achieve any objectives laid out at the beginning of data mining. A measure of usefulness is highly related to the intended application and hence the *application-specific utility function* must be used in the evaluation.

- A pattern is said to be *actionable* or *applicable* if it leads to certain actions being taken that in turn lead to a positive return of some kind for the client. For instance, the applicability of the association rule nappies⇒beer may be measured by additional sales for either of the items after taking the action of putting the two items together in stores.

The measures evaluating conciseness, coverage, reliability, peculiarity and diversity are based directly on the data and patterns. No additional knowledge of the intended user or application is required. They are therefore called *objective* measures. Most objective measures are based on statistical theory and probability. The use of some of these measures is seen in later chapters. The measures evaluating novelty, surprisingness, usefulness and applicability are not directly based on the data, but depend on the user and domain knowledge of the intended applications. Therefore they are known as *subjective* measures. Subjective measures are harder to use than objective measures.

The interestingness measures mentioned in this section are not entirely independent. In fact, a lot of them are correlated in certain ways. Conciseness is related to coverage in the sense that the more concise a pattern is, the more general it becomes and the bigger fraction of the data set it covers. For instance, the association rule {nappies}⇒{beer} is more concise than {nappies, towels}⇒{beer, biscuits}. The first rule is more general and has greater support than the second rule. The more general a pattern is, the less sensitive it is to noise data and hence the more reliable it becomes. For instance, a pruned smaller decision tree is normally expected to have better accuracy.

This list of interestingness measures is not exhaustive. More may be added as better understanding of the issue is obtained. In practice, different measures may be used for different types of data mining task. For instance, measures of reliability and conciseness are more relevant to classification and association whereas measures of coverage and diversity are more relevant to association and clustering.

2.6 DATA MINING IN WEKA

In this section, we use an example to demonstrate how to perform a data mining task in Weka. The data set to be used is the Iris data set that comes from the UCI Machine Learning Repository and is provided with the Weka package. There are 150 instances in the data set, describing characteristics of three types of iris flower: setosa, versicolor and virginica. The characteristics of each type of flower are described by four variables: sepal length, sepal width, petal length and petal width, all measured in centimetres. The reason for choosing this particular data set is that the data set is small, clean and with no missing values. The three types of flower are uniformly distributed: there are 50 instances of each type. Our intention is to demonstrate how to build a classification model from the data set.

The session starts by launching the Weka application and selecting the Explorer route from the Applications menu. In the Explorer, data mining operations are provided on a sequence of tab pages in the main window. By default, the first enabled tab page is for pre-processing. It is here that an input data set is located, loaded and pre-processed. At the top of the Preprocess tab are buttons for opening an input data set from different sources, editing a data set and saving an opened and processed data set. Under the buttons is an area for selecting pre-processing operations called filters (see Chapter 3).

Press the Open File... button. In the dialogue box, locate the file `iris.arff` in the `data` folder and press the Open button. Descriptive information about the data set is then displayed in the pane areas as shown in Figure 2.10.

Summary information about the data set name, size and number of attributes are listed in Current relation pane. In the Attributes pane, every attribute of the data set is listed with a unique numeric attribute index and a checkbox. The buttons allow attribute selection. Once an attribute is selected, summary information about that specific attribute is displayed in the Selected attribute pane. For instance, the summary information for the sepal length attribute includes the minimum (4.3), maximum (7.9), average (5.843), standard deviation (0.828), number of unique values (35) and percentage of missing values (0%). The bottom right pane displays the distribution of the three types of flower for different ranges of sepal lengths; each type of flower is marked by a specific colour

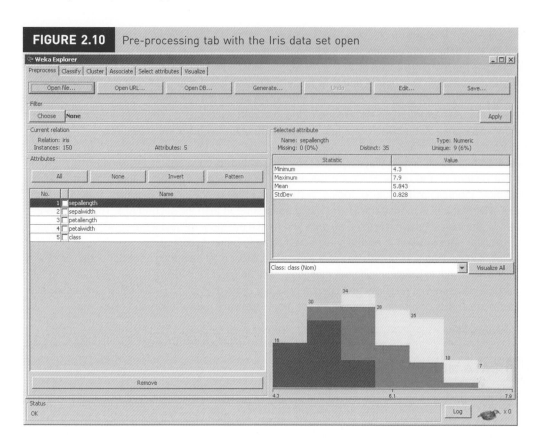

FIGURE 2.10   Pre-processing tab with the Iris data set open

code. Weka takes the attribute with the name 'class', the final attribute in the list, as the target class variable.

By pressing the Edit. . . button at the top of the tab, you can browse the data set as a table in a pop-up window as in Figure 2.11(a). You can also visualize the distributions of attribute values and their associated classes by pressing the Visualize all. . . button, as shown in Figure 2.11(b). The visualizations provide an opportunity for the user to gain an understanding of the data set. For instance, a certain petal length and petal width determines the flower type to be setosa, the leftmost bar in the charts.

From the descriptive information about the data set and the visualization of class distributions, it is understood that different types of flower are concentrated in certain ranges of the four descriptive attribute domains. This means little pre-processing is needed if a data mining solution that can deal with numeric attributes is chosen. To conduct a classification task, select the Classify tab. At the top, the Choose button allows you to select a classifier (classification method) from a tree view window. Select the classifier J48 from the 'trees' category. The classifier name and default parameter settings are listed, in command format, in the textbox next to the Choose button. If you click the command, a pop-up dialogue box enables you to edit the command-line parameters. In the Test options pane, you can select an option to test the accuracy of the model; by default, it is set to Cross-validation with 10 folds. Details of classifiers and test options are discussed in later chapters.

Press the Start button above the Result list to commence the task. A log record is created for the task and listed in the Result list, so that you can select and perform this specific task again. The output of the data mining task is displayed in the Classifier output pane (see Figure 2.12).

FIGURE 2.11   Viewing and visualizing data

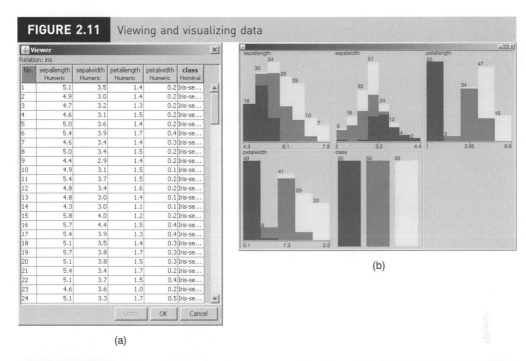

(a)

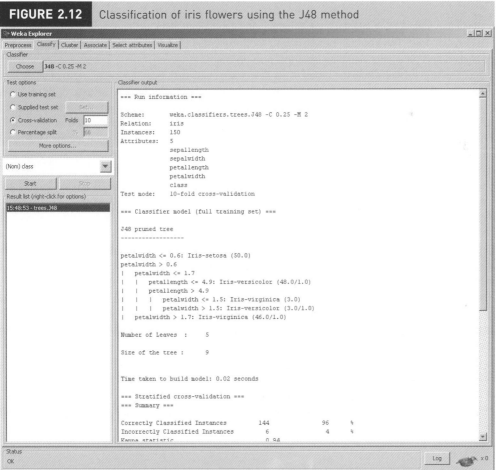

(b)

FIGURE 2.12   Classification of iris flowers using the J48 method

2

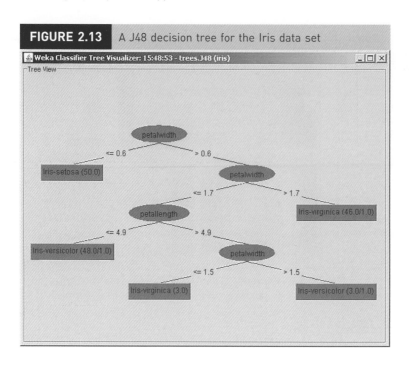

FIGURE 2.13 A J48 decision tree for the Iris data set

The Classifier output pane displays information about the input data set and then the model in the form of a decision tree. The tree can be visualized more naturally (see Figure 2.13) by right-clicking the task log record and selecting Visualize from the pop-up menu.

The decision tree explains how the types of iris flower are classified. First, the petal width of the flower is tested. If the width is less than or equal to 0.6 centimetres, the flower type is setosa. If the width is greater than 1.7 centimetres, the flower type is virginica. If the width is in between, the petal length of the flower is tested. If the length is less than or equal to 4.9 centimetres, the flower type is versicolor. If the length is greater than 4.9 centimetres, the flower type depends again on the petal width. If the petal width is less than or equal to 1.5 centimetres, in fact in the range (0.6, 1.5], the flower type is virginica; otherwise, if the petal width is in the range (1.5, 1.7], the flower type is versicolor.

The rest of the Classifier output pane displays results of the model evaluation, as shown in Figure 2.14. We do not explain every detail here but highlight the overall accuracy measurements.

In Figure 2.14, overall accuracy rate is indicated by the figures in the top box. Of the 150 examples of the training set, 144 are correctly classified by the tree and 6 are misclassified, representing an overall accuracy rate of 96% and overall error rate of 4%. The confusion matrix in the bottom box gives a more detailed performance picture. The rows represent the actual classes in the training set, and the columns represent the predicted classes by the decision tree. The matrix shows that out of 50 examples of each type of flower, 49 setosa, 47 versicolor and 48 virginica are classified correctly. One setosa is misclassified as versicolor, three versicolor instances are misclassified as virginica, and two virginica instances are misclassified as versicolor. Therefore, the tree performs best for the setosa class and worst for the versicolor class.

After the classification task has been performed, the output model can be saved in a file for future reference by right-clicking the task log record and selecting Save from the pop-up menu.

This completes the simple classification mining task. We have not looked into any pre-processing, nor have we tried different classification techniques or selected a good result. Those things are revealed progressively in later chapters.

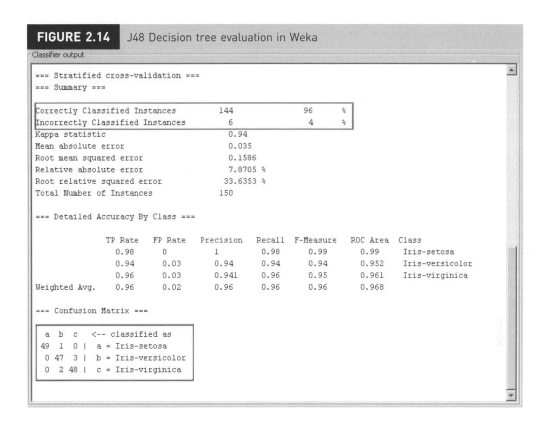

FIGURE 2.14   J48 Decision tree evaluation in Weka

```
Classifier output

=== Stratified cross-validation ===
=== Summary ===

Correctly Classified Instances        144               96      %
Incorrectly Classified Instances        6                4      %
Kappa statistic                         0.94
Mean absolute error                     0.035
Root mean squared error                 0.1586
Relative absolute error                 7.8705 %
Root relative squared error            33.6353 %
Total Number of Instances             150

=== Detailed Accuracy By Class ===

               TP Rate  FP Rate  Precision  Recall  F-Measure  ROC Area  Class
                 0.98      0         1        0.98      0.99      0.99     Iris-setosa
                 0.94      0.03      0.94     0.94      0.94      0.952    Iris-versicolor
                 0.96      0.03      0.941    0.96      0.95      0.961    Iris-virginica
Weighted Avg.    0.96      0.02      0.96     0.96      0.96      0.968

=== Confusion Matrix ===

  a  b  c   <-- classified as
 49  1  0 |  a = Iris-setosa
  0 47  3 |  b = Iris-versicolor
  0  2 48 |  c = Iris-virginica
```

2.7   REVIEW OF BASIC CONCEPTS OF PROBABILITY AND STATISTICS

This section reviews some fundamental concepts, assumptions and theories in probability and statistics that are essential for the understanding of data mining solutions and the evaluation of patterns. Due to space constraints, the review is brief and concise without rigorous examination of the statistical and mathematical background. The bibliographical notes list further texts for those who want to gain a more thorough understanding of the subjects.

2.7.1   Events, Probability and Conditional Probability

A *random experiment* is an act of observation that leads to an independent outcome that cannot be predicted with certainty. The set of all possible outcomes (also known as observations) of a random experiment is called the *sample space*. An *event* corresponds to a subset of the sample space with some commonality among the members of the subset. A data set collected from a practical application can be considered as a sample space where each data record is an observation and an attribute taking a specific value is an event. Strictly speaking, the data set itself is only a sample or subset of the real sample space which is the multi-dimensional space defined by the domains of the attributes. In reality, a data set that covers the entire sample space is either impossible or very rare.

The probability P of an event E, denoted as $P(E)$, is roughly defined as the fraction of the number of outcomes that convey the event in the experiment against the total number of possible outcomes, i.e.

$$P(E) = \frac{\text{the number of outcomes conveying } E}{\text{total number of possible outcomes}}$$

$P(E)$ takes a value between 0 and 1, indicating the *likelihood* of event E occurring. If $P(E) = 0$, it means that E never occurs whereas if $P(E) = 1$, it means that E always occurs. The probability that E *does not* occur is represented as $P(\text{not } E) = 1 - P(E)$.

Given two events E and F, the probability that E or F occurs is represented as $P(E \text{ or } F)$. The probability that the two events occur together is denoted as $P(E \text{ and } F)$. The following law exists:

$$P(E \text{ or } F) = P(E) + P(F) - P(E \text{ and } F)$$

E and F are said to be *mutually exclusive* if and only if $P(E \text{ and } F) = 0$ and, therefore, $P(E \text{ or } F) = P(E) + P(F)$. For a given sample space S and k mutually exclusive events $E_1, E_2, \ldots, E_k$ in S, $P(E_1 \text{ or } E_2, \ldots, \text{ or } E_k) = P(E_1) + P(E_2) + \ldots + P(E_k) = 1$. This means that the events are exhaustive and that one of the events will definitely occur but it is not known which one.

Events E and F are said to be *statistically independent* if and only if $P(E \text{ and } F) = P(E) \times P(F)$. Statistical independence means that the co-occurrence of the two events is random by chance.

The *conditional* probability of event E occurring given that event F has already occurred, denoted as $P(E|F)$, is defined as:

$$P(E|F) = \frac{P(E \text{ and } F)}{P(F)}$$

The conditional probability $P(E|F)$ indicates the influence of the occurrence of event F on the occurrence of event E in terms of degree of certainty. If $P(E|F) = 1$, it means that when F occurs, E also occurs. If $P(E|F) = P(E)$, it means the occurrence of F has no effect on the occurrence of E because E and F are statistically independent.

Taking the student data in Table 2.1 (page 24) as an example, the data set can be considered as a sample space. 'Country = Spain' can be considered as an event.

$$P(Country= Spain) = 2/12 = 1/6$$
$$P(Country \neq Spain) = 1 - 1/6 = 5/6$$
$$P(Country= China) = 0$$

Also, 'Gender = F' and 'Gender = M' are two mutually exclusive events. Let E_1 represent 'Gender = M' and E_2 represent 'Major = Computing'. Then,

$$P(E_1) = \frac{6}{12} = \frac{1}{2}$$

$$P(E_2) = \frac{3}{12} = \frac{1}{4}$$

$$P(E_1 \text{ and } E_2) = \frac{2}{12} \neq P(E_1) \times P(E_2)$$

It is concluded that the two events are not statistically independent. In other words, the two events have some influence on each other. Also,

$$P(E_1|E_2) = \frac{P(E_1 \text{ and } E_2)}{P(E_2)} = \frac{2}{3} = 0.67$$

The conditional probability of 67% is more than $P(Gender = M) = 50\%$. Therefore, knowing that the major is 'Computing' gives a bit more confidence in the gender being 'M'.

2.7.2 Random Variables and Probability Distribution

In a random experiment, a quantity of interest may be recorded as a *random variable*. Random variables take a value with an associated probability and can be discrete or continuous. For a discrete random variable, the probability of the variable taking a specific value corresponds to an event in the random

TABLE 2.2	Rolling two dice: values and their probabilities									
X	2	3	4	5	6	7	8	9	10	11	12
P(X)	1/36	2/36	3/36	4/26	5/36	6/36	5/36	4/36	3/36	2/36	1/36

experiment. For instance, let X be a discrete random variable that adds the total number of points appearing on the faces of two dice. There are $6 \times 6 = 36$ possible outcomes and 11 possible values for the variable. Table 2.2 lists the values and their associated probabilities. Figure 2.15 shows how the probabilities are distributed. This kind of distribution is known as binomial distribution.

A data set such as in Table 2.1 (page 24) can be seen as recordings of observations of a random experiment. An attribute of the data set can be taken as a random variable. Each value has an associated probability of occurring estimated from the given data set. If a value is not observed in the data set, its probability is considered to be 0.

For a continuous random variable X, the probability that X takes a value within a range (a, b), denoted as $P(a<X<b)$, is defined as the integration of a probability density function $f(x)$ from a to b. One well-known probability density function is the Gaussian function. The probabilities follow a normal distribution, as shown in Figure 2.16. The probability $P(a<X<b)$ refers to an area under the curve line between values a and b.

Besides binomial distribution for discrete random variables and normal distribution for continuous random variables, there are other forms of probability distribution (such as Poisson distribution for a discrete random variable).

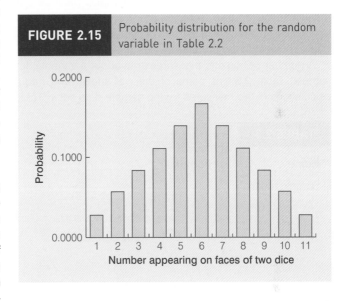

| FIGURE 2.15 | Probability distribution for the random variable in Table 2.2 |

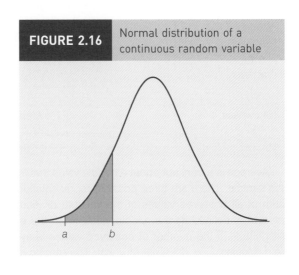

| FIGURE 2.16 | Normal distribution of a continuous random variable |

2.7.3 Basic Statistical Concepts

Statistics is a discipline about analyzing a limited sample of data in order to draw conclusions about a data population and even data at large. This process is known as *statistical inference*.

A *data population* refers to the whole set of data under an investigation about which some conclusions are to be drawn. A *sample* is a selected subset of the population. *Sampling methods* are used to select a sample of data from the population. Known sampling methods include random sampling, systematic sampling, stratified random sampling, etc. Sampling methods are discussed in more detail in Section 3.4.2.

There are different reasons why samples have to be drawn from a data population. The main reason is to save resources in studying the population. Conclusions about a population can be made from a sample if it is properly selected. In data mining, particularly classification, data may play different roles in the development of a model. Different samples must be obtained to serve different purposes. In the manufacturing domain, samples are drawn from the population for quality assessment. It is either impractical (in the case of millions of cars) or undesirable (in the case of fireworks) to assess the quality of every object in the population.

A number of numeric measurements about a variable, known as *statistics*, can be derived from a sample. Table 2.3 lists some of the well-known and frequently used statistical measures with the calculations of the measures for the sample data set in Table 2.1.

TABLE 2.3   Statistical measures and examples

Name	Formula	Example
Sample mean	$$\bar{x} = \frac{\sum x_i}{n}$$	$\overline{age} = 26$
Sample median	$\left(\frac{1}{2}n + 1\right)^{th}$ value if n is odd $\frac{1}{2}\left(\left(\frac{n}{2}\right)^{th} \text{ value} + \left(\frac{1}{2}n + 1\right)^{th} \text{ value}\right)$ if n is even	$Median_{age} = 23$
Sample mode	The most frequently occurring value of the variable	$Mode_{age} = 22$
Standard deviation	$$s_x = \sqrt{\frac{\sum(x_i - \bar{x})^2}{n - 1}}$$	$s_{age} = 7.324$
Variance	$$s_x^2 = \frac{\sum(x_i - \bar{x})^2}{n - 1}$$	$s_{age}^2 = 53.636$
Skewness	$$\frac{3(\bar{x} - Median_x)}{s_x}$$	$Skewness_{age} = 1.229$

Average is a concept about a *middle* value that is meant to represent all the values of the variable in the sample. There are three possible representations of average. The *sample mean* is defined as the sum of all observed values of the variable divided by the number of observed values. The *sample median* is defined as the middle value when the observed values are ranked in ascending order of magnitude. If the number of observed values is even, the median is the mean of two middle values (e.g. $Median_{age} = (23 + 23)/2 = 23$). The *sample mode* is defined as the observed value that occurs most frequently. The sample mode may not be unique.

The sample mean is mostly used when the variable is a continuous variable. It is also preferred over the others when the frequency distribution of the variable is symmetric. The sample median is normally used for numeric discrete variables or ordinal variables when the sample mean makes little or no sense. It is preferred when the frequency distribution of the variable is skewed, because the sample mean can be distorted by a few extreme values. For nominal variables, the sample mode is the only sensible measure of average. Measuring an average without measuring variations does not provide a true picture of the sample. For example, a sample's mean temperature of 20 °C may be derived from {10, 10, 40} or {19, 20, 21}. However, the *middle value* represents the second sample better than the first because individual temperatures in the second sample are much closer to the middle value.

Variance is defined as the sum of the squares of the differences between individual values of variable x and the sample mean divided by $n - 1$, where n represents the number of observed values of the variable. The *standard deviation* is the square root of the variance. Other indicators of variation include the measure of *skewness*. The skewness measure in Table 2.3 has a result near to 0, less than 0, or greater than 0 depending on whether the distribution is symmetric, negatively skewed or positively skewed. For the data set in Table 2.1, $skewness_{age} = 1.229$ indicates that the distribution is positively skewed, i.e. the mean is greater than the median.

A measure of the average together with a measure of the variation provides a reasonably clear understanding of a data set. The distribution of the variable also enhances understanding; it may be specifically useful for samples when the distribution of values is not that 'standard'. Graphical options, such as histograms, are often used to visualize the distribution to enhance the understanding. In a normal distribution, most values of the variable concentrate towards the middle with comparatively few extreme values at the ends of the distribution. The distribution has a symmetric bell shape with the peak at the centre (Figure 2.17). The peak corresponds to the mean value of the variable (μ). Standard normal distribution has a mean value $\mu = 0$ and standard deviation $\sigma = 1$, denoted by N(0, 1). In Figure 2.17, approximately 68% of the area under curve lies within one standard deviation from the mean (the darker shaded area), i.e. $P(\mu - \sigma < X < \mu + \sigma) \approx 0.68$. Approximately 95% of the area lies within two standard deviations from the mean (the light and dark shaded areas), i.e. $P(\mu - 2\sigma < X < \mu + 2\sigma) \approx 0.95$.

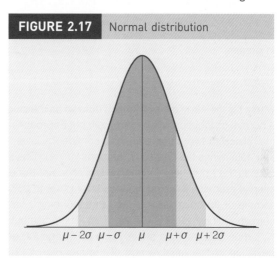

FIGURE 2.17   Normal distribution

$$\mu - 2\sigma \quad \mu - \sigma \quad \mu \quad \mu + \sigma \quad \mu + 2\sigma$$

2.7.4 Confidence Interval Estimation

When a sample is drawn from a population with a mean μ_X and standard deviation σ_X for variable X, the sample mean, $\overline{X}$, is a point estimate of μ_X. This single value estimate is unlikely to be precise, particularly when the sample size is small. A range of estimates may be considered by adding a margin of error to the sample mean. This is known as an interval estimate. We expect a high probability, i.e. confidence, that the mean of the population is within the range. In general, this can be expressed as

$$P(\overline{x} - e < \mu < \overline{x} + e) = c$$

where e represents the margin of error and c is the confidence level. The expression states that on $c \times 100\%$ occasions when such intervals are calculated, the population mean falls within the calculated interval but on the other $(1-c) \times 100\%$ occasions, it falls outside the calculated interval. The range is known as $c \times 100\%$ *confidence interval*. The process of finding out the appropriate interval is called confidence interval estimation.

One important theory in statistics is known as the *central limit theorem*, which states the following fact. Suppose that we draw many samples of size n from the population. When n is large, the distribution of the sample means is a normal distribution with the following properties:

- the mean of the distribution of the sample means is μ_X;

- the variance of the distribution is σ_X^2/n;

- the standard deviation of the distribution is $\sigma/n^{(1/2)}$.

These properties are independent of the kind of distribution of the original data population. The distribution of the sample means can be transformed into a standard normal distribution by the following expression and by approximating σ_X by s_X when n is large:

$$z = \frac{\bar{x} - \mu_X}{\sigma_X/\sqrt{n}} \approx \frac{\bar{x} - \mu_X}{s_X/\sqrt{n}}$$

Then, properties of normal distribution apply. For instance for a large sample,

$$P(-s_X/\sqrt{n} < \bar{x} - \mu < s_X/\sqrt{n}) = P(\bar{x} - s_X/\sqrt{n} < \mu < \bar{x} + s_X/\sqrt{n}) \approx 0.68$$
$$P(-2s_X/\sqrt{n} < \bar{x} - \mu < 2s_X/\sqrt{n}) = P(\bar{x} - 2s_X/\sqrt{n} < \mu < \bar{x} + 2s_X/\sqrt{n}) \approx 0.95$$

In general,

$$P(\bar{x} - ts_X/\sqrt{n} < \mu < \bar{x} + ts_X/\sqrt{n}) = 1 - a$$

where t is the value of t-distribution (known as the student test distribution). The t-distribution is not exactly a normal distribution when n is small, but approaches a normal distribution when n is large. The value of t is related to two parameters: the confidence level that determines the value of a and the sample size that determines the degree of freedom $(n - 1)$. The value of a refers to the area of the normal distribution outside the t number of standard deviations at the ends of the distribution. For a two-sided confidence interval estimate, if the confidence level is set to 95%, then $1 - 2a = 0.95$, and hence $a = 0.025$. For a sample of 30 observations, the corresponding t value is 2.042; for a sample of 200 observations the corresponding t value is roughly 1.96. The t-distribution table is available in every statistics text.

Let us take the data set in Table 2.1 (page 24) as an example. The sample mean and the standard deviation of the variable age of the sample of 12 observations are respectively 26 and 7.324. At a confidence level of 95%, $a = 0.025$, $v = n - 1 = 11$, and hence $t = 2.201$. The interval estimation of the population mean is therefore [21.347, 30.653]. This rather wide interval is largely due to the fact that the sample size is too small. If a larger sample were to be drawn, the interval would be narrower and the sample mean would be closer to the population mean.

2.7.5 Hypothesis Testing

Hypothesis testing as a data mining approach was explained at the beginning of this chapter. This section describes it within the context of a statistical inference. In statistics, hypothesis testing is conducted through the following steps:

1 Decide on and create a null hypothesis and an alternative hypothesis. The null hypothesis is a statement expressing the idea of 'no difference', whereas the alternative hypothesis is a statement

that expresses the idea of 'some difference'. The alternative hypothesis can be one-sided, e.g. the average height is greater than a given value, or two-sided, e.g. the average height does not equal a given value (it may be greater or less than the value).

2   Decide on a level of significance p, as a percentage. This is the risk factor that we take in rejecting a given null hypothesis in favour of its alternative when the null hypothesis is in fact true. Normally, p = 5% or p = 0.05 is a common level of significance adopted by many statistical studies.

3   Decide on and calculate a suitable test statistic and compare the result with the appropriately tabulated test statistics. The comparison determines whether the null hypothesis should or should not be rejected in favour of the alternative. We assume that the test statistics are distributed normally. If the calculated test statistic falls within the area under p, the null hypothesis should be rejected in favour of the alternative; if the calculated test statistic falls within the area under $1 - p$, the null hypothesis is not rejected (see Figure 2.18).

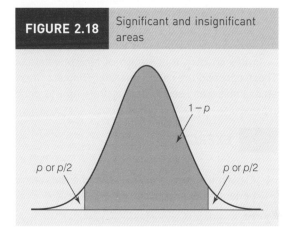

FIGURE 2.18   Significant and insignificant areas

Again, take the data set in Table 2.1 (page 24) as an example. Suppose that the average age of the student population is $\mu = 25$. We would like to use the sample mean of the data set to estimate the population average. By hypothesis testing, two hypotheses are formed: the null hypothesis states that $\overline{X} = \mu$ and the alternative hypothesis states that $\overline{X} \neq \mu$. Although it is clear that $\overline{X} \neq \mu$, is the difference significant? Suppose that the level of significance p is set to 5%. From the sample data set, we obtain $\overline{X} = 26$, $s_{age} = 7.324$ and $n = 12$. The following test statistic is calculated:

$$t = \frac{\overline{x} - \mu}{s_{age}/\sqrt{n}} = \frac{26 - 25}{7.324/\sqrt{12}} = 0.473$$

Since the alternative hypothesis is two-sided, $a = 0.05/2 = 0.025$. The tabulated t statistic for the degree of freedom of $v = n - 1 = 11$ is 2.201. The calculated t value from the sample is less than the tabulated value and hence the null hypothesis cannot be rejected in favour of the alternative. In other words, the apparent difference between the sample mean and the population mean is insignificant.

2.8   SUMMARY

This chapter described three key stages of a general data mining process. The importance of each stage and the iterative nature of the process were highlighted. Two alternative approaches to data mining, i.e. the hypothesis testing approach and the discovery approach, were presented. In real-life applications, both approaches are exploited. It is quite common for people to have a certain 'expectation' before data mining starts. The data mining results not only confirm or reject the expectation, but may also provide new leads in understanding the data. The chapter also highlighted the roles of humans in the discovery process. It is the author's experience (and the experience of many other data miners) that a data mining project cannot be successful without the participation of a domain expert. In this chapter, the issue about how to conduct a data mining project from the participant's point of view has not been fully addressed. This task is left for Chapter 10.

This chapter briefly surveyed different types of data mining problems, possible output information patterns and data mining solutions. Simple examples were used to illustrate different types of data mining task. The aim was to gain a general and basic awareness of different types of data mining before each type and its various solutions are studied in much more detail in later chapters.

The chapter also highlighted the importance of pattern evaluation in the data mining process. Various possible understandings of the interestingness of patterns were broadly explained. It concluded that objective measures of interestingness are relevant to specific types of data mining task and subjective measures of interestingness are relevant to the intended applications. Specific measures of interestingness are discussed in the individual chapters for data mining techniques. The subject of measuring interestingness is far from settled.

In this chapter, a collection of fundamental concepts of probability and statistics were reviewed. These concepts are used in the later chapters when data mining techniques are studied. In this chapter, an example was used to demonstrate how to perform a data mining task in Weka.

EXERCISES

1 Explain the three primary steps of a data mining process. Describe the tasks that need to be performed at each step of the process.

2 Discuss the main differences between the hypothesis testing and discovery approaches to data mining.

3 A successful estate agency is considering expanding its business into a new city. The company wishes to conduct market research about the housing market in that city. It is interested in what types of houses sell quickly and what types of houses sell slowly. The main source of data is a local free newspaper that contains weekly advertisements of house sales by existing local estate agencies.

　(a) Describe any work that should be undertaken in order to prepare the input data for a sensible data analysis.

　(b) If the company is interested in determining which types of houses sell quickly (within two weeks of the advertisement first appearing), what data mining tasks do we need to perform on the input data prepared in (a)? What types of pattern can be useful for the purpose?

　(c) How do we measure the interestingness of the patterns discovered in (b)?

4 Use appropriate examples to illustrate the following scenarios: (a) data mining with human intervention that saves resources but is prone to bias and (b) data mining without human intervention that avoids bias but consumes resources.

5 Use the data set in Table 2.1 (page 24) as an example to illustrate output patterns for classification, clustering and association besides those mentioned already. For each output pattern, explain how to evaluate its interestingness.

6 Explain the differences between the following data mining methods and solutions:

　(a) K-nearest neighbour methods and decision tree induction methods for classification;

　(b) Partition-based methods and hierarchical methods for clustering.

7 Explain and discuss what is meant by *objective* and *subjective* interestingness measures. Use suitable examples to illustrate the measurement of different aspects of interestingness such as conciseness, coverage, reliability, peculiarity, diversity, novelty, surprisingness, usefulness and applicability.

8 Calculate probabilities for the following events.

   (a) For a deck of playing cards, calculate the probability that the card drawn is a diamond. Also calculate the probability that the card is a king given that we already know the card is a diamond.

   (b) The National Lottery Draw is performed every week in the United Kingdom. Fair balls with numbers between 1 and 48 are put into a lottery machine and then six balls are drawn randomly from the machine. The numbers on the six balls (in combination not permutations of the numbers) form the Jackpot number. Calculate the probability of selecting six unique numbers between 1 and 48 that match the Jackpot number.

   (c) A not-so-perfect device is used to detect a rare disease in a population of mice. The device may give a positive reading for a healthy mouse and may fail to detect the disease in a mouse even it is present. Let P(Disease) represent the probability that the disease is present and P(Positive|Disease) represent the probability that the reading is positive given that the disease is present. Suppose that P(Disease) = 0.0005, and P(Positive|Disease) = 0.98. Calculate P(Disease|Positive).

9 The sample in Table 2.4 is drawn from a data population. Calculate the sample mean, sample standard deviation, sample median and sample mode for the variables Body Height and Body Weight. Are the probability distributions for the two variables symmetric, positively skewed or negatively skewed?

10 For the data set in Table 2.4, perform a 95% confidence interval estimation of population mean for variable Body Weight.

11 For the data set in Table 2.4, conduct a hypothesis test with 5% level of significance that the sample mean for variable Body Height is greater than the population mean of 170 cm.

TABLE 2.4	Sample data for Exercises 9 to 11	
SubjectID	**Body Height (cm)**	**Body Weight (kg)**
s1	125	61
s2	178	90
s3	178	92
s4	180	83
s5	167	85
s6	170	89
s7	173	98
s8	135	40
s9	120	35
s10	145	70
s11	125	50

BIBLIOGRAPHICAL NOTES

The process of data mining has been described differently in a number of texts and papers. Fayyad *et al.* (1996) describe a process for knowledge discovery in databases (KDD) with five stages: data selection, data pre-processing, data transformation, data mining, and pattern interpretation and evaluation. Similar to the process described in this chapter, Tan *et al.* (2006) describe a data mining process in three stages but do not highlight the iterative nature of each stage and across the stages. The description of two main approaches to data mining follows the lines presented by Berry and Linoff (1997), but is much less specific. Specification of the CRISP-DM 1.0 methodology can be found in CRISP-DM (2000).

The roles of human participants in the mining process are a controversial issue, mentioned in a number of texts (Berry and Linoff 1997; Hand *et al.* 2001; Larose 2005). Ma and Drury (2003) is the first piece of work that studies the human factors in data mining thoroughly; it refers broadly to everyone involved without much emphasis on the role of domain experts. Although there is no general consensus yet on the issue, we argue strongly the importance of the involvement of domain experts in data mining projects.

There is no clear agreement in the literature regarding what are counted as essential types of data mining problem. Witten and Frank (2005) tend to concentrate on classification problems from a machine-learning perspective, whereas Hand *et al.* (2001) concentrate more on solutions with strong statistical origins. In general, however, classification, cluster detection and association rule discovery have been mentioned in most published texts. We therefore consider those three to be the most essential types of data mining problem with the most mature knowledge.

The literature on cluster detection methods is extensive. Recent surveys of the subject include Fasulo (1999), Jain *et al.* (1999) and Berkhin (2002). Classification is also an area that has been extensively and intensively studied over many years. Many articles of a review nature have been published. Due to the scope of the field, there is no single survey that covers all of the classification approaches. Witten and Frank (2005) can be considered a systematic review of classification techniques. Murthy (1998) provides a recent survey of decision tree induction techniques. Association rule discovery is relatively new compared to clustering and classification. Recent surveys include Hipp *et al.* (2000) and Zhao and Bhowmick (2003).

The importance of pattern evaluation has been realized by the data mining community. A number of articles have tried to address the issue. Our description of different ways of evaluating interestingness is mainly based on a recent article by Geng and Hamilton (2006). Witten and Frank (2005) devote an entire chapter to evaluation and to evaluation techniques primarily for classification models. How to measure interestingness is still an on-going research topic in data mining.

Some existing texts either assume some knowledge of statistics or put relevant materials into an appendix. This text does not assume you have basic knowledge of statistics and putting the statistics into an appendix is inappropriate because of the importance of understanding to the evaluation of data mining results. Due to space limitations, however, our coverage of statistics has to be brief. Many textbooks are available for a thorough coverage of probability and statistics. We have based our section mainly on the short text by Rees (2001), which provides readers with a quick review of basic concepts in probability and statistics. The text itself is very easy to follow.

CHAPTER 3

Data, pre-processing and exploration

LEARNING OBJECTIVES

To understand different types of data from the point of view of data analysis

To understand and appreciate the applicability of operations to data of different types

To understand the origins of data sets and problems associated with data sources

To appreciate issues regarding data quality

To learn techniques for pre-processing data

To observe ways of exploring, visualizing and understanding data before data mining

To learn to pre-process, explore and visualize data in Weka

As explained in Chapter 2, data preparation and pre-processing before data mining is an important step of the data mining process. It is therefore necessary to understand and appreciate issues concerning input data such as the implications of different data types and data quality.

Effective data mining also requires a good understanding of data. Understanding data helps in preparing data more sensibly, selecting data that are more relevant to the investigation, formulating the data mining tasks more accurately, and evaluating the importance of the patterns more objectively and realistically. Data exploration and visualization are major ways of achieving this understanding.

The Weka data mining tool is equipped with a variety of data pre-processing and exploration tools. It is useful to demonstrate how the pre-processing and exploration is conducted with practical examples.

3.1 INPUT DATA AND DATA TYPES

3.1.1 Data Objects, Attributes and Measurements

A data object is an individual, and normally independent, recording of some real-life object or event. A data object is represented by its values for a pre-defined set of features, *attributes* or *variables* that collectively describe certain aspects of the real-life object or event. For example, a data object ('John Smith', 23, 'Oxford', 'Computer

Science', 1) may represent a student named John Smith who is 23, from Oxford and in his first year studying Computer Science.

A value for an attribute of a data object is measured and recorded according to a measurement scale. It is very important to use the appropriate scale in order to accurately record the measurement result and correctly reflect the meaning of the attribute. During the measuring process, measurement errors may be introduced and affect the quality of the data recorded.

The main measurement errors are bias, imprecision and inaccuracy. When a biased measuring instrument is used, a systematic variation from the true value may be introduced. Such bias can be quantified only when the true value is known. For instance, a person's height is measured in metres five times by a tape ruler with the results {1.742, 1.741, 1.743, 1.740, 1.741}. The sample mean of the measurements is calculated as 1.7414. If the true height is known as 1.740 metres, the amount of bias is measured as the difference between the true value and the sample mean, which is 0.0014. Imprecision of measurement can also be introduced randomly when the measurement is taken. Imprecision is normally caused by not using a sufficient number of significant digits. For instance, using two significant digits to measure a person's height is less precise than using three. However, the level of precision is relevant to the attribute and can vary from application to application. In order to be precise, an attribute may be measured repeatedly. The amount of precision can be indicated by the closeness of the repeated measurements. In the example of measuring someone's height five times, the standard deviation (known also as the *standard error*) among the measurements, i.e. 0.00114, can be used as an indication of precision. Accuracy refers to the closeness to the true value and is related to bias and precision. Inaccuracy can be caused by high bias and low precision. Only measurements with low bias and high precision lead to accurate results. Figure 3.1 illustrates the relationship among accuracy, bias and precision. Image that the innermost circle represents the true value. Only measurements in the low bias and high precision situation are considered accurate.

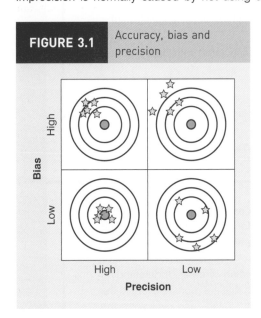

FIGURE 3.1 Accuracy, bias and precision

Besides possible data measurement errors, there are also potential data collection errors. Incorrect data entry is one type of data collection error. *Incorrectness* refers to randomly introduced incorrect measurement results, caused by human error or instrument error. For instance, the name John Smith may be recorded incorrectly as John Smyth. When recording a piece of music, additional incorrect signals, e.g. background noise, may be recorded together with the correct sound signals. Other types of data collection error include unnecessary data duplicates and inconsistent data entries. These incorrect data are also known as *noise*.

It is important to minimize measurement and collection errors when data are first recorded. However, for data mining, data miners have little or no control over errors of these kinds because the data are already recorded and are simply presented to the data miners. Nevertheless, understanding the existence of the errors is still useful. If the causes of errors become known, it may be possible to correct the errors. For instance, if the amount of bias measurement for an attribute becomes known, the recorded data can be updated to correct the amount of bias. Some errors, such as inconsistent data, may be corrected or dealt with at the data pre-processing stage.

3.1.2 Attribute Domain Types and Operations

The domain of an attribute is a set of permitted values for the attribute. In the context of data analysis, the domain of an attribute is categorized as nominal, ordinal, interval or ratio. Values of a *nominal* domain are distinct names. Among the names, no concept of order or difference of any kind exists. The only sensible operations that can be applied are $=$ and $\neq$ for comparing two nominal names from the same domain. For instance, a nominal attribute 'country' may have 'Britain', 'France' and 'China' as its values. Both 'Britain $=$ Britain' and 'Britain $\neq$ China' make sense but 'China $>$ Britain' and '(France $-$ Britain)/China' do not. Sometimes a less rigid operation such as *match* or *agree* can replace the $=$ operator. In food appreciation, 'good' and 'nice' may be considered as 'agree' in meaning although the two words are literally different. However, this operator may differ from application to application. In word processing, for instance, even Smith and SMITH may not be considered as equal.

Values in an *ordinal* domain are also names. There exists a certain order among the names, but any difference between the names is not defined. In general, all comparison operators, such as $>$, $<$, $\leq$, $\geq$, $=$ and $\neq$, are applicable in an ordinal domain. For instance, a day may be described as 'cold', 'warm' or 'hot' and there is a general belief that 'cold' is colder than 'warm' and 'warm' is colder than 'hot', but how much colder that 'cold' is than 'warm' is not known, and the result of 'warm $-$ cold' cannot be defined.

Interval domains contain numeric values. Interval quantities are measured in fixed and equal units. Both concepts of order and difference exist among the values. Therefore, how much bigger one value is than another can be defined. All operations applicable to ordinal domains are also applicable to interval domains. Some arithmetic operations such as addition and subtraction can also be applied. However, an interval type has no definition of an absolute zero and arithmetic operators such as multiplication and division cannot be applied. For instance, the calendar year of birth is an interval attribute. If John is born in 1978 and Susan in 1980, we can calculate that John's year of birth is two years earlier than Susan's.

Ratio quantities are similar to intervals but they have an absolute zero point. For ratio domains, all arithmetic operators and comparison operators are applicable. For instance, the distance between two places on a map is of ratio type. The distance from a place to itself is considered to be zero. The distance from London to Birmingham is longer than the distance from Oxford to Cambridge. The distance between London and Glasgow is more than twice the distance between London and Birmingham. The zero point is inherent in the sense that it is related to knowledge and culture. The Fahrenheit temperature measure does not have an absolute zero point clearly defined and hence it is an interval measure rather than a ratio measure. The Kelvin measure has an absolute zero point and hence it is a ratio measure. Therefore, we can say that $100\,^{\circ}K$ is twice as hot as $50\,^{\circ}K$ whereas $100\,^{\circ}F$ ($\approx 38\,^{\circ}C$) is not twice as hot as $50\,^{\circ}F$ ($10\,^{\circ}C$).

Understanding different types of attribute domain is very important. The domain type determines whether a data processing operation makes sense. With a given data set, one should not just 'take the data as they are presented'. For instance, it is common practice in a database to define the data type for a userID attribute as a long integer. However, these integers are labels used for convenience, not for arithmetic operations such as addition and multiplication. Even comparing whether one user identifier is smaller than another makes little sense.

Often, nominal and ordinal types are called *qualitative* types and interval and ratio types are called *quantitative* types. Nominal and ordinal types are also known as *categorical* types whereas interval and ratio types are known as *numeric* types. A domain with enumerable values is *discrete* and a domain with real numbers is known as *continuous*.

3.2   **INPUT DATA SETS**

An input data set consists of individual data objects, also known as data records, instances or examples. All data sets have the following common properties:

- *Type*. The data objects in a data set are organized in a particular structure, where components of the structure correspond to attributes. Different types of data file may be used to represent data sets from different data sources. The type is normally indicated by the file extension. For instance, Weka takes data sets of table type represented in ARFF format; See5 requires two separate files: the name file describing the attributes and the data file of table type presenting the data values. Data sets of different types are discussed in more detail shortly.

- *Size*. The size of a data set can be measured in terms of the number of data objects or the total number of bytes. These days, it is common for a data set to contain tens or hundreds of thousands of data objects. Data files are often measured in megabytes, gigabytes or terabytes. The size of a data set can directly affect the speed of data mining and the memory resources requirement. Some data mining solutions cannot cope with data sets of a large size.

- *Dimensionality*. Dimensionality refers to the number of attributes in a data set when data objects are considered as points in a multi-dimensional space. Real-life data files vary significantly in dimensionality. A survey often has tens of dimensions for recording answers to the survey questions. A shopping transaction may have well over 100 dimensions, if each dimension corresponds to a purchased item. A digital image of 120×200 pixels can be considered as a record of 24,000 dimensions if the colour value of each pixel needs to be recorded. The dimensionality for a short digital video of tens or hundreds of frames is even higher. Data sets with very high dimensionality can make meaningful and effective data mining extremely difficult. Known as the *curse of dimensionality*, data can be very diverse and therefore any patterns can be easily lost in a high-dimension space. Computation for data analysis in high-dimensional space can also be very costly in terms of computation speed and memory resources required.

- *Sparsity*. Data values collected in a real-life environment can be different from those collected in a controlled environment. The values may not be distributed normally or uniformly. Often, data values are skewed to a small number of diverse subranges. Sparsity can be a challenge as well as an opportunity for data mining. On the one hand, it is difficult to see patterns in extremely skewed data and some form of data transformation is often required to 'spread' the data out before patterns can be identified. On the other hand, the sparsity of data may speed up the discovery process if efforts are concentrated only on the subranges.

- *Abstraction*. Data can often be presented at different levels of abstraction. At the least abstract level, data are presented as they are recorded, known as the *raw* data. Summarization and approximation on the raw data can produce a level of more abstract representation. For instance, in an analysis of student intake numbers over the years, individual student record details are not of interest but the total number of students each year is of interest. The latter value is summarized by query operations over the original data records. Approximation of original data is another way of achieving data abstraction. For instance, a person's height may be measured in centimetres and then summarized as *tall*, *medium* or *short*. It is worth noting that, at different abstraction levels, data properties may be different. In the previous example, a person's height is measured in a ratio scale but summarized on an ordinal scale. The different data properties may have an effect on the patterns to be mined. The level of data abstraction to be used is about the types of pattern to be mined, which in turn is determined by the intended purpose of discovery.

TABLE 3.1	Relational table			
Outlook	**Temperature**	**Humidity**	**Windy**	**Class**
Sunny	85	High	FALSE	Negative
Sunny	80	High	TRUE	Negative
Overcast	83	High	FALSE	Positive
Rain	70	High	FALSE	Positive
Rain	68	Normal	FALSE	Positive
Rain	64	Normal	TRUE	Negative
Overcast	64	Normal	TRUE	Positive
Sunny	72	High	FALSE	Negative
Sunny	69	Normal	FALSE	Positive
Rain	75	Normal	FALSE	Positive
Sunny	75	Normal	TRUE	Positive
Overcast	72	High	TRUE	Positive
Overcast	81	Normal	FALSE	Positive
Rain	71	High	TRUE	Negative

A data set can be viewed as a flat table of rows and columns. The most common form of table is that in which a column corresponds to an attribute and a row represents a specific data object (see Table 3.1). The value of an attribute for a data object is a measurement of the attribute for the object. This two-dimensional table structure is widely accepted by most data mining solutions. Such a table can be exported from a relational database, can be a plain text file with comma or tab separators, or can be a spreadsheet.

A *transaction database* is a special type of table with two columns: the transaction identifier and a set of items contained in the transaction as shown in Table 3.2. Similar to a transaction database, a *sequential* transaction database contains the record identifier and a list of sets of items as shown in Table 3.3. Each set of items has a timestamp t_i associated with it. The list therefore signifies a temporal

TABLE 3.2	Transaction database
TID	**Items**
100	Apple, lamb, rice
200	Apple, sugar, rice
300	Apple, beef, rice
400	Apple, pear, sugar
500	Apple, pear
600	Beef, rice

TABLE 3.3	Sequential transaction database
Record ID	**Items**
100	t1:{apple, beer}, t4: {newspapers}
200	t1:{apple, beef}, t3:{beer, newspapers}
300	T2:{beef, potato}
400	t4:{beef, rice}

order between the sets of items. Because the Items columns in Tables 3.2 and 3.3 contain a set of values, they are not first normal form relational tables such as the one in Table 3.1.

When a table contains only numeric data values, it is normally known as a *data matrix*. Data matrices include tables created by a cross-tabulation query, in which the columns are values of an attribute and the table contents represent summary data for every row and attribute value. A table of numbers that is transformed from another table is also a data matrix.

Besides the commonly used flat tables, there are other forms of data set where there is some structure among data objects. A *graph-based* data set describes not only individual data objects within the set but also some form of reference relationship among the data objects. For instance, a page of a website can be considered as a data object. The reference structure among the web pages of the website is a directed graph among individual data objects. Representing the connectivity among the data objects is as important as the data objects themselves. A *sequence* data set describes a sequence among individual objects. For instance, a sequence may represent the results of medical tests over a time period for monitoring development of a disease in a patient. A sequence that represents measurement results recorded over a period of time is also known as a *time series*. A typical example of a time series is a sequence of audio signals. *Spatial data* that represents positions, areas, etc. of data objects are also sequence data sets. A typical example of spatial data is a digital image. A value in the sequence represents, for example, the colour value of a pixel at a specific x and y co-ordinate position. Details of sequential data are further discussed in Chapter 9.

Data objects may have a unique identifier. Data mining that relates output patterns to data object identifiers is known as *discovery with signatures*; otherwise, it is known as *discovery without signatures*. Whether to have signatures in the discovery depends on the business need and the law.

3.3 DATA SOURCES

Data may come from internal sources, such as operational database systems within the organization, and external sources, such as third-party data sources. As mentioned before, most data mining techniques consider a data set as a single flat table of rows and columns. Such a table may be directly taken from a database or may be the result table of a join query that connects a number of relevant tables together.

Taking data from an operational database may require breaking data barriers set by the database application software and may run the risk of disrupting the normal service of such systems. Because of possible on-going changes taking place in the operational database, the table should be uploaded to a separate and more stable place before mining. A recent development is the use of *data warehouses*.

A data warehouse is an organization-wide database that is designed to support both tactical and strategic decision-making. A data warehouse possesses a central data repository, separate from operational database systems within the organization. Besides routine data maintenance operations, one type of important operation performed in a data warehouse is data analysis. A data warehouse therefore contains not only detailed raw data but also various pre-computed data summarizations. It is equipped with a wide range of query and data analysis tools. Data warehouses enforce the consistency and quality of organization-wide data in order to minimize the effects of poor quality data and ensure the validity of data analysis. Table 3.4 highlights the differences between an operational database and a data warehouse. Issues regarding data warehouse architectures and management operations are further described in Section 10.4.

A data warehouse possesses a central data repository. For data analysis purposes, the central repository contains data details, pre-computed data summaries and descriptive data, known as

TABLE 3.4	Major differences between databases and data warehouses
Operational Database	**Data Warehouse**
Current data	Historical data
Detailed original data	Detailed and summarized data
Dynamic data	Largely static data
Repetitive processing	Ad hoc reporting
Small size, high-frequency transactions	Medium or large size, low-frequency transactions
Fixed pattern of usage	Flexible pattern of usage
Transaction driven	Analysis driven
Supports day-to-day decisions	Supports strategic decisions
Serves operational users	Serves decision makers

metadata. Most, if not all, current data warehouses use a relational data model to represent data in tables. A typical relational database schema consists of a set of relations in normal form that are logically connected via foreign key attributes. Databases for different application purposes tend to have different schema structures. A *star schema* is considered to be particularly suitable for data warehouse purposes (Figure 3.2).

A star schema consists of two types of table: a *central fact table* and *dimension* tables. The central fact table stores most facts that make up data objects and

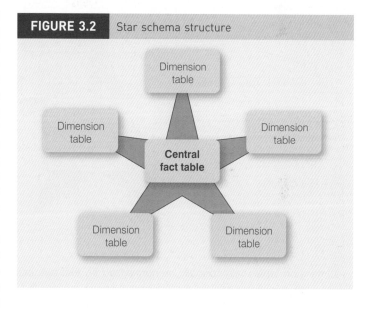

FIGURE 3.2	Star schema structure

are frequently used for data analysis purposes (see Figure 3.3(a)). Pre-computed data summaries can also be stored in the central fact table for convenience. The fact table may have very few details on specific entities: those details are stored in the dimension tables. The central fact table interacts with the dimension tables via foreign keys. Dimension tables surround the central fact table like satellites (see Figure 3.3(b)). One join operation is sufficient to recover details of specific entities with the facts in the central table.

The central fact table is normally large and changes proportionally little over time. The fact table must constrain its number of columns so that retrieval can be performed fast. Join is an expensive operation in a relational database and can significantly slow down the discovery process when it is repeatedly used within the iterative process of discovery. Therefore, foreign keys should be carefully selected so that the need for natural join operations is minimized.

3

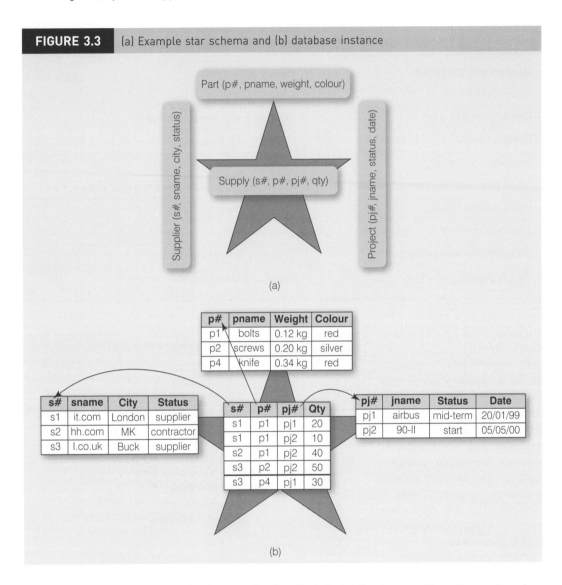

FIGURE 3.3   (a) Example star schema and (b) database instance

Dimension tables are normally *de-normalized* so that all details of a specific entity are kept in a single table, avoiding the need for join operations to recover the details from several tables in higher normal form. For better performance, join operations between the central fact table and dimension tables via pre-computation at the data pre-processing stage should be considered as performed. However, doing so is at the expense of having redundant data in the central fact table as well as the dimension tables.

3.4 DATA QUALITY

The issue of data quality has a direct relevance on the quality of data mining results. 'Garbage in, garbage out' has a certain degree of truth. Although almost everyone accepts the importance of data quality, in reality, it is not always rigorously controlled. There is a significant difference in attitudes towards product quality and data quality. For the former, rigorous procedures and mechanisms are in place in many manufacturing companies. For the latter, however, poor quality data are common in many databases. Decision-makers often make their decisions on the basis of *soft data*, i.e. incorrect and biased data reports, speculations and personal opinions. The plea for total data quality control, similar to total product quality control, has largely fallen on deaf ears.

In general, data quality can be judged by accuracy, correctness, completeness, consistency and redundancy.

- *Accuracy* is concerned with whether data are recorded with measurements that are sufficiently precise without bias. For instance, using three significant digits to measure a currency exchange rate is normally imprecise (Section 3.1.1 explains about precision and bias in relation to accuracy).

- *Correctness* is about whether data are recorded without spurious objects and errors. For instance, a currency exchange rate between sterling and the US dollar may be measured accurately but may be incorrectly recorded in the database as the exchange rate between the euro and the US dollar. Normally, incorrectness is caused by human error or measurement instrument limitations. For instance, when temporal and spatial data are recorded, almost inevitably background noise is added into the data set. There are de-noising tools available to reduce or eliminate noise of this kind. Incorrect data entry may also lead to the creation of *outlier* data objects that are out of the norm. The existence of outlier objects distort statistical figures from the truth.

- *Completeness* is concerned with whether any attribute value of a data object is missing and why. For instance, the attribute Age may have a null value for a certain data object. This may be because the person concerned does not want to record a value, because the person's age is not known, or because the person's age cannot be determined at the time of recording. A lack of understanding of why the value is missing affects correct understanding of the data. How to deal with missing values is discussed in Section 3.5.7.

- *Consistency* indicates whether the data recorded violate any established constraints that should be respected. Inconsistent data affect the truth of the discovered patterns. Data integrity of different kinds may be violated. For instance, a domain integrity constraint may specify that university students cannot be less than 15 years old. If the database contains records of students who are younger than 15, the constraint is violated. Inconsistency may also exist across attributes and across tables. For instance, a record about a book being borrowed may be recorded with a return date earlier than the date borrowed. A customer identifier may be referred to in a shopping transaction but there may be no such customer.

- *Redundancy* is concerned with whether a data set contains unnecessary duplicates. Data redundancy is not only just about wasting memory, but also about data consistency and validity. For data mining, data redundancy may affect how data values are distributed and hence influence the significance of the discovered patterns. For instance, repeated entry of the same customer shopping transaction may be taken to be multiple transactions from different customers purchasing the same items and hence support for the purchased items is invalid.

Data quality can be quantified by calculating the quality ratio on every aspect mentioned above. For instance, the ratio of the number of data records with null values to the total number of data records can be used as a measurement of completeness. However, not every data quality dimension is easy to quantify. For instance, it is extremely difficult to identify erroneous data entry.

Most of the quality indicators mentioned above are related to data measurement and collection. For data mining, it is often difficult or even impossible to address data quality issues at source when the data are generated. The only options available are to conduct some kind of 'data cleaning' before data mining starts. An integrity constraint on data objects may be enforced by removing objects that violate the constraint; a data imputation method may be used to fill in missing data fields; outliers may be identified and isolated or removed before data mining starts. Alternatively, quality-tolerant mining algorithms can be developed and used. For instance, some classification algorithms have a certain degree of tolerance towards missing data.

Data quality is related to the intended purpose of data analysis. A collection of seemingly poor quality data may not be acceptable for certain analysis but may well be acceptable for others. For instance, an investigation into customer shopping behaviours can tolerate errors in the spelling of customer names but cannot tolerate errors in the items that customers purchase. Errors in items purchased can be tolerated if only the quantity of items purchased is of interest. On the other hand, even a high-quality data set, if not used properly, can turn into a poor-quality data set as far as the intended application is concerned. For instance, a high-quality data set of two classes may be used to build a classification model. If the training examples are selected inappropriately and the training set contains mostly of examples of one of the classes, the classification model is not accurate. Similarly, if some important attributes are not included in the training set, the classification model may also be inaccurate. When a profile of online shopping behaviours of customers is to be built, it is not very helpful if the shopping behaviour data are more than three years old, because of the dynamic nature of online shopping.

3.5   DATA PRE-PROCESSING

As explained in Chapter 2, data pre-processing is an important part of data preparation. The purpose of data pre-processing is to ensure speedy and cost-effective data mining that delivers high-quality output patterns. Data pre-processing involves many tasks of various kinds. This section emphasizes data aggregation, feature selection and creation, data discretization, data transformation and handling of missing values. Due to space limitations, we explain only the general principles of the pre-processing methods. Examples of how to use the methods in Weka are shown in Section 3.7.

3.5.1 Data Aggregation

Data aggregation, also known as data summarization, is a task of deriving the right level of data detail for data mining. There are a number of reasons why it is important to have the right level of detail. First, a data set with every detail as recorded may be too big to handle within the time constraint. Second, the finest details result in only a few examples of a similar nature. This makes any patterns insignificant. Third, not all details may be of interest to the investigation. For instance, an investigation for annual sales patterns for the last decade may only include the detail of monthly sales figures, rather than every sale for each working day. In an investigation into the associations between items that customers purchase, the investigator may be interested only in associations between categories of items rather than between items themselves.

Data aggregation involves combining a number of existing data objects into a single object in a new and more abstract data set. A variety of methods can be used for this purpose. Aggregate functions such as sum, average, mode, standard deviation, etc. are normally available in database query languages such as SQL. The functions can be applied to attribute values for all data objects or groups of data objects. Figure 3.4 shows an example of the use of the 'count' and 'sum' aggregate functions in SQL.

Using aggregate functions is not the only way to perform data aggregation. You can also replace data values with a more abstract concept. One early data mining solution known as the *attribute-oriented induction* is such an example. Taking a relational table and a set of data abstraction hierarchies as inputs, the method repeatedly substitutes the data values of every attribute in the table by their abstract concepts immediately above them in the hierarchy. At any time, if duplicate objects occur in the table as result of the replacements, they are removed. For attributes that do not have a data abstraction

FIGURE 3.4 A data aggregation example in SQL

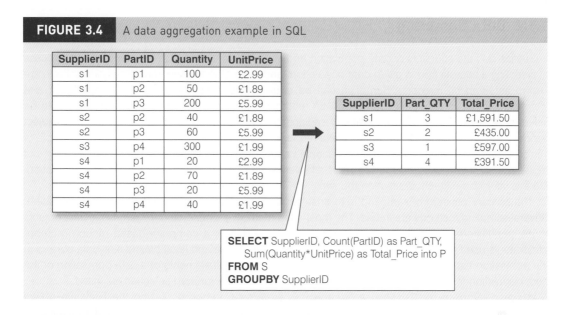

SupplierID	PartID	Quantity	UnitPrice
s1	p1	100	£2.99
s1	p2	50	£1.89
s1	p3	200	£5.99
s2	p2	40	£1.89
s2	p3	60	£5.99
s3	p4	300	£1.99
s4	p1	20	£2.99
s4	p2	70	£1.89
s4	p3	20	£5.99
s4	p4	40	£1.99

SupplierID	Part_QTY	Total_Price
s1	3	£1,591.50
s2	2	£435.00
s3	1	£597.00
s4	4	£391.50

SELECT SupplierID, Count(PartID) as Part_QTY,
Sum(Quantity*UnitPrice) as Total_Price into P
FROM S
GROUPBY SupplierID

FIGURE 3.5 Attribute-oriented induction for data aggregation: (a) input hierarchies, (b) input table and (c) output table

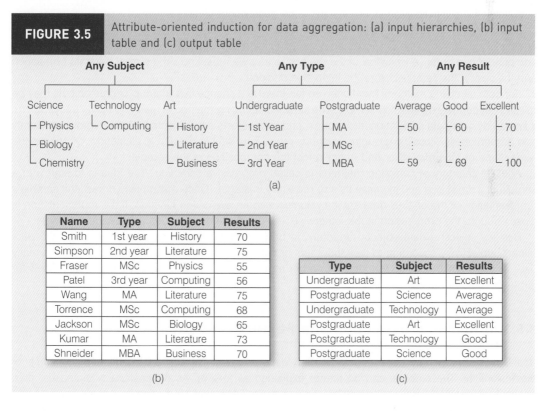

Name	Type	Subject	Results
Smith	1st year	History	70
Simpson	2nd year	Literature	75
Fraser	MSc	Physics	55
Patel	3rd year	Computing	56
Wang	MA	Literature	75
Torrence	MSc	Computing	68
Jackson	MSc	Biology	65
Kumar	MA	Literature	73
Shneider	MBA	Business	70

(b)

Type	Subject	Results
Undergraduate	Art	Excellent
Postgraduate	Science	Average
Undergraduate	Technology	Average
Postgraduate	Art	Excellent
Postgraduate	Technology	Good
Postgraduate	Science	Good

(c)

hierarchy, it is considered that the attribute values cannot be further generalized and hence they are dropped from the table. When the process terminates, a much smaller table containing abstract concepts about data is obtained. Figure 3.5(c) shows a data aggregation result table created from the input table Figure 3.5(b) by referring to the input abstract concept hierarchies Figure 3.5(a).

3.5.2 Data Sampling

In Section 2.7, the concepts of data population and samples were defined. Data sampling is a process of selecting a sample from a given data population, and the methods used in obtaining the sample are known as *sampling methods*. Sampling can be done in two ways: *sampling with replacement* and *sampling without replacement.* Sampling with replacement means that the same data object can be selected again whereas sampling without replacement means that, once selected, the data object cannot be again selected. A computer-based random number generator can be seen as an example of sampling with replacement whereas the National Lottery draw is a typical example of sampling without replacement. When the size of the sample is relatively small compared to the size of the data population, there is very little difference between the two.

The primary concern of sampling is to ensure that the sample is representative of the population. Several sampling methods are in use. The most-used method is *simple random sampling*: Data objects in the population are listed and then selected randomly. Often, a computer-based random number generator is used for the random selection. This method is simple and least biased if all data objects in the population can be listed. Sometimes, it is impossible to list all elements of a data population or the data population is too large to be enumerated and therefore the random selection is limited.

Another sampling method in use is known as *systematic sampling*. Taking the first data object randomly from the data population, the method then selects each subsequent data object from the data population list at a fixed interval. For instance, the quality control mechanism of a production line may select every 20th product as a sample product. Again, this sampling method is very simple to implement and performs as well as the simple random sampling if the data population list is not sorted according to any pre-defined order. A limitation of the method is that we must know the size of the data population and the size of the sample before the interval is decided.

For both sampling methods mentioned so far, there is a chance that a group of data objects may be missed out completely from the sample. The *stratified sampling* method is meant to tackle this problem. It first divides the data population into groups, and then selects data objects from each group randomly and proportionally. Possible grouping methods range from simple division to clustering. Of course, the sizes of the groups may differ and hence affect the composition of the sample.

Another category of sampling methods is called *progressive sampling*. The idea is to start with a sample of a small size and increase its size gradually in stages. Once a sample is drawn, the sample's representation of the original data set is evaluated with an evaluation function. If the representation is close enough, the progression stops; otherwise, the progression continues with a bigger sample.

Besides selecting data objects randomly, in practice, data objects may be selected by the data miners subjectively according to their judgment or convenience. Such sampling methods are normally used in initial small-scale investigations in order to locate areas of interest but are not often used for large-scale quantitative studies.

3.5.3 Dimension Reduction and Feature Selection

Real-life databases may contain data of high dimensionality. Section 3.2 mentioned the curse of dimensionality. The problem can be further explained as follows. As dimensionality increases, data become increasingly diverse, spread-out and uniform. Data analysis becomes harder because the mined patterns are more specific and less significant. Measures of distance between data objects such as the Euclidean distance (see Chapters 4 and 5) become less and less effective. It gets harder for any pattern to emerge. As dimensionality increases, the size of the search space increases exponentially. The time for data analysis therefore increases dramatically, making timely discovery of patterns increasingly difficult. The problem can be lessened by reducing the number of dimensions because not all attributes are equally significant in describing patterns. There may exist a certain degree of redundancy among the dimensions.

Various methods have been used for *dimension reduction*. One type of method measures the significance of attributes. Principal component analysis (PCA) uses linear algebra techniques to transform values of existing attributes of a data set to values of a new set of attributes, known as *eigenvectors*. Each original attribute becomes a linear combination of the eigenvectors. Each new attribute has an associated *eigenvalue* indicating some degree of significance of the new attribute. New attributes with low eigenvalues are insignificant and hence may be ignored, reducing the number of dimensions without too much loss of information. Similarly, independent component analysis (ICA) transforms existing attributes into a set of fewer, independent attributes, removing information redundancy in the data set. A rudimentary example of using PCA to pre-process data in Weka is attempted as an exercise, but more details on PCA and ICA are beyond the scope of this book. Interested readers can refer to the bibliography for further references.

Closely related to dimension reduction is *feature selection*, which is primarily about removing redundant and irrelevant attributes from a data set. Dimension reduction techniques are applicable. Other methods of feature selection include manual selection based on domain knowledge, embedding feature selection into the data mining solutions and automatic or semi-automatic filtering and wrapping. Manual selection based on domain knowledge is a decision made by domain experts and data analysts. For instance, domain experts may decide on the basis of their experience that the address of customers has little to do with the level of customer loyalty and hence it is removed from the data set. However, this manual selection approach runs a risk of omitting important features.

Embedded selection means that feature selection is determined by the data mining method. For instance, the decision tree induction method ID3 may build a decision tree without using the temperature attribute of Table 3.1 (page 45) because temperature has little influence on the outcome of the class. This type of selection avoids bias but works only when the number of features and the number of data objects are relatively small.

Recently, a number of new feature selection algorithms have been proposed. These algorithms can be categorized into *filtering* algorithms and *wrapper* algorithms. Filtering algorithms use an independent search and evaluation method to determine the relevance of feature variables to the data mining task, whereas wrapper algorithms use a search method coupled with a targeted data mining solution as the evaluation mechanism. For instance, a filtering algorithm may measure the pair-wise correlation between a feature variable and the class variable to determine if the feature variable should be selected. A wrapper algorithm may select a subset of features and use a decision tree induction method to develop a tree and measure its accuracy, which is then compared with the accuracy of a tree developed with another subset of features. The main challenge to the algorithms is that the complete enumeration of all subsets of features is exponential to the number of the features; the search space is therefore too large for trivial solutions and specific solutions are needed. The bibliographical notes provide a number of references for filtering and wrapper algorithms.

3.5.4 Feature Creation

Feature creation refers to the creation of new features based on existing ones such that, in the new feature space, more meaningful patterns can be mined. *Feature extraction* uses an extraction method to draw descriptions of data. For instance, from original image pixel values, the image colour, texture and shape can be extracted. *Feature mapping* is the same as variable transformation (Section 3.5.6), which maps feature values from one domain to another. For instance, images can be transformed from a spatial domain to a frequency domain using wavelet transformation filters and methods. *Feature construction* refers to defining new attributes based on existing ones. For instance, we can create a new 'customer tenure' feature variable that counts the number of months that the customer has been with the company from customer transaction records. This new feature variable can be used to indicate a degree of loyalty of the customer to the company.

Some dimensionality reduction methods, such as PCA, also create new variables based on the existing variables, but the new features exist in the transformed space.

3.5.5 Data Discretization

Discretization refers to the process of converting continuous numeric values to discrete categorical labels. Some data mining solutions only work for categorical attributes, in which case discretization is absolutely necessary. Some mining solutions assume that numeric data are normally distributed. These solutions do not work well if the data are distributed differently. Discretization may be able to improve the quality of the results of such mining tasks. Although some solutions, such as decision trees, can handle numeric attributes, these solutions take too much time because numeric data may need to be sorted repeatedly. Many existing data mining tools, such as IBM Intelligent Miner for Data and Weka, are equipped with data discretization facilities.

In general, a discretization process involves two tasks. First, the number of categories (intervals) and the locations of split points for the categories are determined. Secondly, all values of the continuous attribute are sorted, all split points are specified, and all values within an interval between two split points are replaced by the category label. The second task is quite straightforward and so the first task is normally the focus of attention.

Supervised discretization means that the discretization is guided by the knowledge of a target class variable, ensuring a homogeneous outcome of class. *Unsupervised discretization* quantizes each numeric attribute regardless of a class variable. It is the only possibility when dealing with clustering and association rule discovery problems, where the classes are unknown or nonexistent. Simple unsupervised discretization methods include equal-interval binning, equal-frequency binning and clustering methods.

The principal idea of the equal-interval binning method is to divide the domain of a continuous attribute into a number of equal-length intervals. For instance, if we have an attribute representing a person's age, we can divide the domain [0, 99] into intervals [0, 9], [10, 19], ..., [90, 99]. The obvious problem with this method is that, given a data set, there may be many data objects within some intervals and very few or no objects in other intervals. For instance, if we have an attribute representing the ages of university students, there would be hardly any objects in [0, 9], and very few objects in the intervals beyond age 50, but many objects in [10, 19] and [20, 29]. Then the discretized attribute would have a distribution that is skewed towards the two intervals.

As an alternative, equal-frequency binning divides the range of the attribute into a predetermined number of intervals of variable lengths, ensuring that each interval contains the similar numbers of data objects. For instance, instead of equal interval discretization of university student ages, we can have variable-length intervals such as [15, 17], [18, 19], [20, 22], [23, 30] and [31, 99]. This method, also known as the 'equal-depth method', overcomes the problem of sparseness of value distribution.

Clustering methods for discretization mean that a clustering algorithm with a similarity function over numeric attributes is used to divide data into clusters. The intervals are determined by the projection of the clusters to the attribute dimension: an interval is formed by the range of attribute values of the members of the cluster.

For classification, certain attributes may have strong association with the class variable. The class may determine the subrange of attribute values and the attribute values may determine the outcome of the class. Therefore, attribute values should be better discretized in the light of the knowledge about classes. There are several supervised discretization methods, mainly categorized into entropy-based and error-based methods. Entropy-based methods use average information to determine the best possible split points. Similar to building a decision tree, information gains over all possible split points (the middle point between two adjacent values) over the whole domain are calculated first. The split point with the highest information gain is then identified and the whole range is split into two. Then, for each half, the same process is repeated, looking for the next split point. The process continues until each subrange has examples of only one class or an evaluation criterion is satisfied.

The principle of error-based methods is to treat every numeric value initially as an interval in itself and to repeatedly consider merging the adjacent intervals into a wider interval. The process is controlled by a confidence threshold, a reflection of errors made on classes. When the threshold is exceeded, the merging process stops.

A special type of discretization, known as binarization, converts a discrete attribute into a number of binary attributes. There are two alternative approaches for binarization. One approach is to convert each value of the discrete attribute to a binary representation of n bits where $n = \log_2 m$. Then a combination of n binary values corresponds to a discrete value of the attribute. Another approach is to use m asymmetric binary variables to represent each of the m values. The mth binary variable takes the value 1 while all other binary variables take the value 0. Binarization works fine when the discrete attribute does not have too many values. It leads to dimension explosion if it is used for numeric attributes of many values.

3.5.6 Variable Transformation

Variable transformation is a process that transforms all values of an attribute from one domain to another by applying a transformation function to the original domain. We emphasize an artificial difference between 'variable transformation' and 'dimensionality reduction via transformation'. The latter methods normally combine a number of attributes into a single new attribute but we exclude them from this discussion for convenience.

One reason for variable transformation is for convenience of data use and management. It is therefore appropriate to transform from one domain to another without altering the data properties, for instance, to transform one nominal domain to another nominal domain, as long as a 1:1 mapping scheme is followed. All data of one ordinal domain can be transformed to those of another ordinal domain as long as the same order among the data is preserved. One interval or ratio domain is transformed to another interval or ratio domain via linear transformation such as converting a temperature from Fahrenheit to Centigrade. However, cross-type variable transformation, e.g. from nominal to ordinal, must be controlled with caution because the transformation changes the domain type.

Another reason for variable transformation is to make the data values across different attributes more comparable. For instance, the number of houses sold by an estate agency may be measured in hundreds whereas the house sale values may be measured in millions of dollars, causing a huge difference between measurement scales for the two attributes. This topic is further discussed in Chapter 4.

Another important reason for variable transformation is to minimize or remove the effects of outlier objects. The existence of outliers can cause distortion in scales of measurement and can change the distribution of data values. For instance, if most customers have an income between £10,000 and £20,000 and the data contains one or two people earning millions of pounds, the measurement scale can be distorted as most of the income data are concentrated in a relatively small range, causing difficulties in understanding the data. In such cases, transformation can be carried out by applying a function, such as log(x). As the result of transformation, data properties and distribution may be changed. For instance, using logarithmic transformation can spread the data across the measurement scale, changing a skewed data distribution to a near normal distribution.

Other reasons for transformation also exist. For instance, in order to study human facial features, some researchers transform pixel values of face images from a spatial domain to a frequency domain through wavelet transformation. Facial features are then extracted from wavelet coefficients in the frequency domain.

3.5.7 Dealing with Missing Values

Data objects with attribute values missing are seen as incomplete. Section 3.4 provided a number of reasons for missing values. The different reasons mean that null values should be interpreted differently, leading to different ways of dealing with them. For instance, if the missing value is deliberate, imputing a replacement value is not correct, because the very fact that the value is not entered reveals something important about the data object. The best approach, therefore, is to know why values are missing. The difficulty faced in data mining is that information regarding why data are missing is often scarce.

There are normally three approaches to handling missing values: removal, imputation, and special coding. When plenty of data are available and the overwhelming majority of them have no missing values, removing a few records with missing values from the data set may be considered a plausible option. Such a removal may not affect mining of significant patterns. In fact, some data analysis methods simply ignore variables with missing values implicitly. However, this simple removal makes some data no longer available. Those data may well be the source of an important pattern. The removal method cannot be used in situations where many data records have missing values like the data records in the Family Expenditure Survey in exercise 3(a) in Chapter 1.

Imputation is a way of handling missing values by replacing them with meaningful replacement values. Available options for replacement include the default, a measure of average (sample mean, sample median or sample mode), and a randomly generated value according to the known value distribution. If the default option is used, it must be sensible for the variable. For instance, if we do not know how many other credit cards a customer has, it may be sensible to suggest that it should default to 0. However, it does not make sense to use 0 to replace a missing value for age. Instead, the average age of all customers would be a more sensible alternative. For ordinal non-numeric attributes, the sample median and mode can be considered instead of the sample mean. For categorical attributes, only the mode can be used. For instance, the median 'C' may be used to replace a missing student examination grade, and the mode 'sunny' may be used to replace an unknown weather outlook. Using a random value generated according to the value frequency distribution of the attribute is also an alternative. For instance, instead of using the average, a random salary value can be generated according to the frequency distribution of known salaries.

These simple methods of replacement can distort the frequency distribution of the attribute values, particularly when a large number of missing values are replaced by the same value. Although the method that bases the replacement on the value distribution has a lesser effect, it amplifies the variation of the data. The simple methods can be improved on by segmenting the data records according to values of another attribute. The average, median, mode or randomly generated value is then calculated according to the local value distribution within the segment to replace missing values in each segment. The results can be very good if the variable used for segmentation is correlated to the variable being treated. Segmentation can also be created by using a number of different attributes.

Besides the simple methods, more sophisticated solutions have been developed, such as methods based on information content and statistical methods. Information-content-based methods construct a classifier to impute the missing values. Statistical methods use techniques such as regression analysis to induce a regression model from known data values and fill in the missing values according to the predicted values of the regression model.

Although there are different ways of dealing with missing values, there is no ideal solution to the problem. What method to use depends very much on the specific situation. The best way of handling missing data, as a researcher claimed, is not to have any (if we can manage it, of course).

Missing values can be introduced by the process of *data integration,* even if the data are complete before integration. For instance, the sales, marketing and customer support departments of a company may have their own data sets about customers. For some data analysis purpose, the different data sets need to be integrated into a single table of rows representing customers and columns representing useful variables from the different departments. If the original data sets contain the same customers, no missing values are introduced by integration. However, if there are differences among the customer data sets, the integrated table has missing values for variables from some departments for customers of other departments. How to solve this problem of introducing missing values depends on the purpose of the data analysis. For instance, we may concentrate on the common customers across the departments.

3.6   UNDERSTANDING DATA BY EXPLORATION

Knowing your data is essential for the success of data mining. Data exploration is a preliminary investigation of data in order to better understand the characteristics of the given data set. In particular, data exploration helps to identify the necessary data pre-processing tasks and select appropriate data analysis techniques. Through data exploration, certain patterns normally discovered by data mining solutions may even be revealed. This section briefly overviews three categories of exploration method: statistical summary, data visualization and online analytic processing.

3.6.1 Summary Statistics

Summary statistics helps with the understanding of a particular variable and the understanding of relationships between variables. In Section 2.7, some basic measures were introduced. The sample mean, sample median and sample mode are three different ways of measuring average. Standard deviation and variance reflect the variations of values from the mean. Skewness serves as an indication of the shape of value frequency distribution for the variable, indicating whether the sample mean is less than, equal to or greater than the sample median.

Besides those measures, a number of other measures also assist with understanding a single variable of the sample data set. The *trimmed* sample mean and median of $p\%$ refer to the mean and median of the values after the top and bottom $(p/2)\%$ of the values of the variable are excluded. The trimmed measures provide a more accurate estimate of the *average* with less effect from extreme outlier values. The *percentile* x_i for a variable x is a value of x such that $i\%$ of observed values of x are less than x_i. Percentile provides an understanding about percentage coverage of values for an ordered, i.e. ordinal or continuous, variable.

In the data set of Table 3.1 (page 45), the trimmed mean for the variable temperature with $p \approx 40\%$ is 73, which is marginally different from 73.5, the sample mean. The trimmed median with $p \approx 40\%$ is 72, the same as the sample median. The 57% *percentile* for the same attribute is 75.

For a data set with multiple variables, vectors of summary measures can be used to gain an understanding of the data set. For instance, the sample means of the variables can be organized into a mean vector, represented as:

$$\bar{x} = (\bar{x}_1, \bar{x}_2, ..., \bar{x}_n)$$

In the case where there is a mixture of different data types across the variables, we might still use a 'pseudo mean vector' that includes other suitable means of measuring averages. For instance, in the vector ('sunny', 73.5, 'high', FALSE, 'positive'), sample mean is used for temperature and sample mode is used for outlook, humidity, windy and class.

Covariance is a measure of data variation between two numeric variables x and y. It combines the effect of each of the two variables varying from its own mean. It is calculated as follows:

$$\text{covariance}(x, y) = \frac{1}{m-1} \sum_{i=1}^{m} (x_i - \bar{x})(y_i - \bar{y})$$

In a data set where n attributes are present, a matrix is normally constructed to record covariance between any pair of variables. The ijth entry of the matrix is the covariance between the ith variable and the jth variable. The covariance between the ith variable and itself is the variance of the variable. In other words, the diagonal line of the matrix lists the variances of all the variables.

Correlation is a measure indicating how much two variables x and y are 'related'. It is calculated as follows:

$$\text{correlation}(x, y) = \frac{\text{covariance}(x, y)}{\sigma_x \sigma_y}$$

where σ_x and σ_y are respectively the standard deviations of the two variables x and y. The correlation(x, y) ≈ 1 when x and y are *positively* related, i.e. values of y increase or decrease in accordance to the increase or decrease of values of x. The correlation$(x, y) \approx -1$ when x and y are *negatively* related. That means that values of y increase and decrease as the values of x decrease and increase. The correlation $(x, y) \approx 0$ when x and y are not related, that is, the increase or decrease of the values of x have nothing to do with the increase or decrease of the values of y.

Table 3.5 presents a data set about student homework and examination results. The covariance matrix is shown in Figure 3.6(a) and the correlation matrix is shown in Figure 3.6(b), (both these figures can be found on page 60). The correlation matrix shows that there is quite a strong positive correlation between the results of the first homework and the exam, whereas the result of the third homework and the exam are hardly related.

3.6.2 Data Visualization

Visualization has been recognized as an effective way of revealing the information patterns embedded in a data set. This is because people are good at spotting patterns, trends and regularities in visual images. Data visualization is about mapping data (attributes, records, relationships) to visual forms in terms of points, lines, shapes and colours. In general, the primary forms for data visualization are *tabular*, *graphical* and *point-and-link*. The most commonly used visual form is tabular, which presents a set of data in a simple table format, providing an overview of the entire collection of data. Graphical forms use pictures and drawings to offer a possible view on how a data object is composed. Point-and-link forms typically use points for individual data objects and links for some relationships between data objects. Many commonly used visual forms are available in standard office software, such as Microsoft Excel. Figure 3.7 illustrates some common forms:

■ A *pie chart* presents data values as segments of a circle. Because there is no apparent order among the segments, a pie chart is suitable for visualizing nominal attributes. Figure 3.7(a) shows a pie chart for a distribution of examination grades.

■ *Histograms* and *bar charts* are used to show the frequency distribution of data values. They are normally used for ordinal and continuous attributes. Histograms and bar charts also exist for nominal attributes but any artificial concept of order among categories should be ignored. Figure 3.7(b), presents a bar chart showing the frequency distribution of phone calls of different costs.

TABLE 3.5	An example table for student results

Student ID	Home-work 1	Home-work 2	Home-work 3	Exam	Student ID (*Cont.*)	Home-work 1	Home-work 2	Home-work 3	Exam
1		94	34	42	28	45	90	21	63
2	35	94	85	45	29	62	95	38	63
3	31	46	22	48	30	38	94	40	64
4	46	90	60	50	31	50	90		64
5	52	94	49	50	32	32	90	38	64
6	58	94	30	51	33	44	90	43	65
7	47	90		52	34	57	94	52	68
8	37	94	25	52	35	50	94	39	70
9	35	94	45	54	36	55	90	62	71
10	57	94	100	54	37	43	94	54	72
11	51	94	5	54	38	50	90	30	74
12	45	94	33	55	39	54	90	82	77
13	44	0	35	55	40	64	95	5	78
14	52	95	56	56	41	85	95		79
15	35	94		57	42	63	90	62	82
16	57	97	57	57	43	75	90	35	83
17	45	90	71	57	44	86	97	39	84
18	39	94	54	57	45	77	95	79	84
19	31	94	63	57	46	79	94	35	86
20	45	94		59	47	86	98	57	87
21	35	90	84	59	48	71	90	9	89
22	37	90	40	61	49	45	94	72	90
23	83	97	26	61	50	90	94	68	92
24	68	97	55	62	51	89	94	53	93
25	50	95	56	62	52	90	98	79	98
26	77	93		63	53	57	92	40	
27	84	48	18	63	54	36	94	54	22

■ *Stem and leaf plots* are used to obtain an understanding on data value distribution for a single integer or a continuous attribute (see Figure 3.7(c)). Data values are divided into groups and, in each group, the common digits of the values are used as stems that are listed vertically and the remaining digits of the values are plotted as leaves, one after another, horizontally.

■ *Scatter plots, contour plots* and *surface plots* allow the plotting of points, belts and surfaces in a 2D or 3D space. Figure 3.7(d) shows an example of a 2D scatter plot of points.

■ *Parallel* and *star dimensions* are a way of visualizing data of high dimensionality. A data point in a high-dimensional space is treated as a sequence of line segments. Each point in the sequence represents the value of one attribute of the data object, and the line segments connect different attribute values for the same data object. The difference between a parallel dimension, Figure 3.7(e), and a star dimension, Figure 3.7(f), is that all dimensions in a star dimension start from a common origin. The sequence of line segments in the star dimension looks more like a closed web.

FIGURE 3.6   (a) Covariance and (b) correlation between variables

	Homework 1	Homework 2	Homework 3	Exam
Homework 1	329.3537037			
Homework 2	59.2787037	264.071405		
Homework 3	−21.73573676	64.755571853	447.9999479	
Exam	205.5303355	72.4061214	12.21695964	257.1074

(a)

	Homework 1	Homework 2	Homework 3	Exam
Homework 1	1			
Homework 2	0.199341524	1		
Homework 3	−0.056272414	0.17839233	1	
Exam	0.706192401	0.275427052	0.034233438	1

(b)

Data visualization is not a trivial exercise of turning data into any arbitrarily chosen, subjectively pleasing visual shape. The meaning of the visualization must be clear and easy to interpret. Appropriate visual representation must be suitable to the data types of the attributes involved. For instance, continuous attributes can be visualized by dimensions with position-related values whereas nominal attributes cannot. The visualization must try to represent not only individual data items, but also the implicit relationships behind the items. The ultimate objective of visualizing data is to tell the truth about the data. For instance, the bar chart in Figure 3.7(b) may give people the illusory expectation that the percentage of calls costing more than 80 pence is even smaller. The correct interpretation should be that the chart shows the frequency distribution of known costs. It does not tell us anything beyond the percentages of existing costs of calls.

Using visualization to interpret the meaning of data is a large subject that cannot be explained in detail within a section of a chapter. The exercises encourage you to explore data visualization using Microsoft Excel and Weka. The bibliographical notes include references to the subject.

3.6.3 Online Analytic Processing

As described briefly in Chapter 1, online analytic processing (OLAP) is a reporting and presentation process that enables manual discovery of timely information based on the up-to-date content of a database or data warehouse in order to support fast decision-making. OLAP tools are highly interactive. Data analysis is conducted through constant dialogues between the user and the system: the user specifies an OLAP request and the system feeds back the results, based on which the user specifies a further request. OLAP tools perceive the data store as a multidimensional hypercube. Data within the cube can be summarized in different ways. OLAP requires fast execution of an analysis operation and fast delivery of the results. OLAP tools tend to support real-time, tactical decision-making rather than strategic decision-making. OLAP is not strictly data mining. It relies on human users to identify patterns behind different summarizations of data. The following examples of OLAP requests are illustrated in Figure 3.8:

■ Find the total number of customers registering at each branch of the bank in April 2000 compared with the same month over the past two years (Figure 3.8(a)).

FIGURE 3.7 Some common forms of data visualization: (a) pie chart, (b) histogram, (c) stem and leaf plot, (d) scatter plot, (e) parallel dimension and (f) star dimension

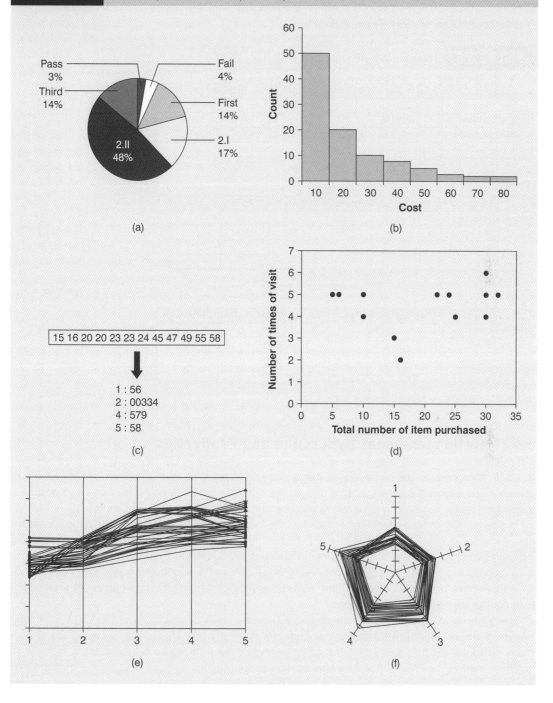

- Find the total number of dwellings viewed by prospective buyers according to type for each month of 2005 (Figure 3.8(b)).

- For each product, find its market share in its category this month minus its market share in its category in October 1994 (Figure 3.8(c)).

FIGURE 3.8	Results of OLAP requests

Branch Name	Total in April 2000	Total in April 1999	Total in April 1998
Buckingham	23,345	20,234	15,333
Milton Keynes	22,234	13,000	12,800
Northampton	2,000	3,000	10,000
....	....	....	....

(a)

Property Type	January	February	March	April	....
Detached house	383	400	380	402	....
Semi-detached	1,000	3,000	4,000	3,800	....
Apartment	10	300	20	40	....
....	....	....	....	....	....

(b)

Products	Market Share Today	Market Share in 1994	Difference
Dell 17"	17%	10%	7%
HP 15"	83%	90%	–7%
Intel MotherB	56%	93%	–37%
....	....	....	....

(c)

3.6.4 Multidimensional Hypercube and Properties

In OLAP, data objects are perceived as points within a hypercube that is defined by dimensions of various kinds. Figure 3.9 shows a table of customers at different bank branches can be viewed as a three-dimensional cube along dimensions representing branch name, year and month.

In general, a multidimensional hypercube has the following properties. First, a large cube contains a set of smaller cubes. The number of sub-cubes is determined by the domains of the dimensions, independent of the number of data records in the data set. Each sub-cube may contain a number of data records represented as points. Data summarization can be conducted over these points. Sub-cubes can have different densities. Some sub-cubes may contain many data points whereas others may contain very few or no data points.

The 3D cube in Figure 3.9 consists of 180 sub-cubes, each of which is identified by a particular branch, year and month (we assume that there are five bank branches). This is regardless of how many customer records the data table contains. A sub-cube in Figure 3.9 contains a number of customer names together with a data aggregation about the total number of customer points within the sub-cube. The number of data points in each sub-cube is determined by the actual data objects in the data set.

There are three categories of dimension: *attribute*, *measure* and *aggregation*. Attribute dimensions correspond to the variables of the data set. Measure dimensions refer to dependent variables. For

FIGURE 3.9   A three-dimensional hypercube

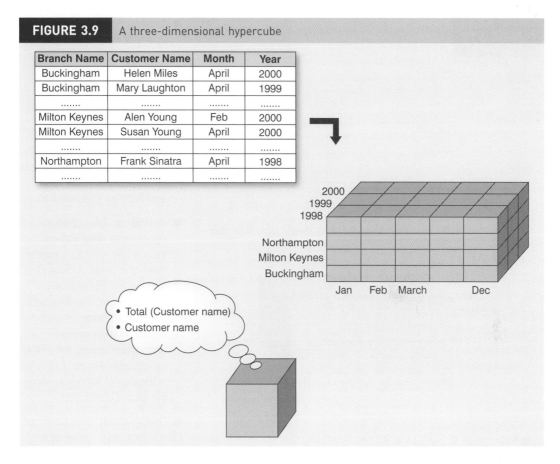

Branch Name	Customer Name	Month	Year
Buckingham	Helen Miles	April	2000
Buckingham	Mary Laughton	April	1999
....	....	....	....
Milton Keynes	Alen Young	Feb	2000
Milton Keynes	Susan Young	April	2000
....	....	....	....
Northampton	Frank Sinatra	April	1998
....	....	....	....

• Total (Customer name)
• Customer name

instance, based on unit price and quantity, a measure of the total amount is derived. Aggregate dimensions refer to data aggregations and summarizations produced by some aggregate function. For example, an aggregate dimension may describe the total number of customers from a particular region with a certain postcode.

Hierarchies of various kinds can be defined along a dimension, resulting in different gradients of measurements upon that dimension. A hierarchy can be an is-a hierarchy of classes, a data aggregation hierarchy, an is-a-part-of hierarchy, and so on – any form of data abstraction is acceptable. For instance, given a hierarchy over the Month dimension, the 3D cube in Figure 3.9 can be portrayed as the one in Figure 3.10.

3.6.5 OLAP Operations

OLAP provides operators that operate on cubes for grouping and summarizing purposes. The most basic operators include:

■ *Pivoting*: This operator selects the dimensions of the multidimensional space upon which the cube is projected and viewed. Visually, the operator rotates the cube to bring the selected dimensions into view. Functionally, the operator allows the end-user to define the dimensions upon which data are to be summarized. For instance in Figure 3.9, the user can view the cube from Month, Branch Name and Year dimensions and count the number of customers in every combination of values of the three dimensions.

3

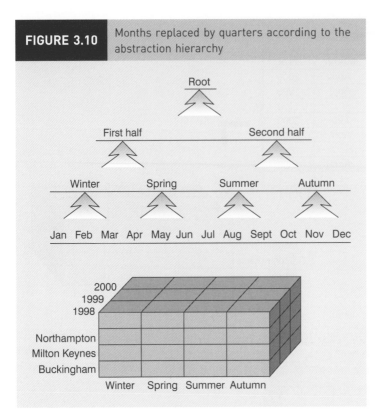

| FIGURE 3.10 | Months replaced by quarters according to the abstraction hierarchy |

- *Slicing and dicing*: This operator selects a particular sub-cube or a particular collection of sub-cubes whose values of certain dimensions satisfy a condition. It is the same as the SELECT operator in SQL. For instance in Figure 3.9, the sub-cubes between June and September for years 1999 and 2000 can be selected.

- *Rolling up*: This operator aggregates data values from a low level to a higher level of a chosen hierarchy, making the measurement coarser along the selected dimension. Data summarization can be undertaken during the rolling-up process. Figure 3.10 is an illustration of rolling up along the Month dimension.

- *Drilling down*: This operator is the inverse of rolling up. It drills down along a chosen hierarchy from a high level down to a lower level, making the measures along the dimension finer and hence revealing more details behind a certain data summary.

3.6.6 Using an OLAP Model

In this section, we consider a multidimensional hypercube OLAP model from an IBM research and development project, called the 'AGS model' here (after the main investigators' initials). Although not yet fully adopted by any commercial system, this model has some good features. It defines a small set of algebraic operators over cubes and OLAP requests are specified as a combination of algebraic operations. Each algebraic operator can be translated into an SQL statement and used as a function in an application program.

The example data set shown in Table 3.6 is about quantities of products of different categories supplied by suppliers on various dates. A multidimensional hypercube for the data set is shown in Figure 3.11. Inside the hypercube are integer numbers representing supply quantities. Along the Product dimension is a hierarchy describing categories that the products belong to, as shown in Table 3.6. Along the Date dimension, there is also a hierarchy describing the months to which the dates belong.

We want to issue the following OLAP request:

For each product, find its share in its category in March 2007 minus its share in its category in October 2006.

TABLE 3.6	Data details for the hypercube in Figure 3.11			
Supplier#	**Product#**	**Product Category**	**Date**	**Quantity**
s1	p1	Appliance	03/10/2006	20
s1	p2	Appliance	15/10/2006	10
s1	p1	Appliance	04/03/2005	20
s1	p4	Tools	15/10/2006	5
s2	p2	Appliance	03/10/2006	10
s3	p1	Appliance	20/03/2007	25
s3	p2	Appliance	04/10/2006	5
s3	p3	Tools	10/02/2004	20
s3	p4	Tools	12/03/2007	10

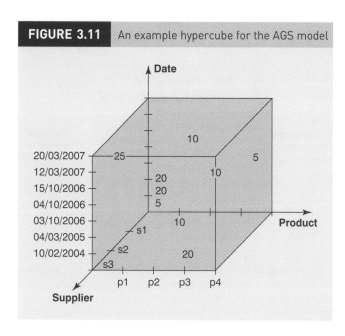

FIGURE 3.11	An example hypercube for the AGS model

The purpose of this request is to understand whether the share has increased (positive), remained the same (zero) or decreased (negative) over the period. The main steps of the OLAP operation, illustrated in Figure 3.12, are as follows:

1 The *restrict* operator (similar to slice-and-dice) is applied to the initial cube in Figure 3.11 with a selection condition: *Date* = '*/10/ 2006' or Date = '*/03/2007,'* where * serves as a wild card. The operation creates a new hypercube C_0 as shown in Figure 3.12(a) that contains layers of the original cube with the relevant dates.

2 A *merge* operation rolls up values along the Supplier dimension to a single root point. During the rolling-up, the SUM function is applied to add the quantities of the same product supplied on the same date by different suppliers into a single subtotal. A similar merge operation is conducted to roll up to Month along the Date dimension, applying the SUM function to the quantities on different dates of the same month for each product. The resulting cube C_1 has only two dimensions, Month and Product, as shown in Figure 3.12(b).

3 Another merge operation is performed on cube C_1. This time, data are rolled up Product Category along the Product dimension of the cube and the SUM function calculates the total quantity of products in each category for each of the two months. The resulting cube C_2 is shown in Figure 3.12(c).

3

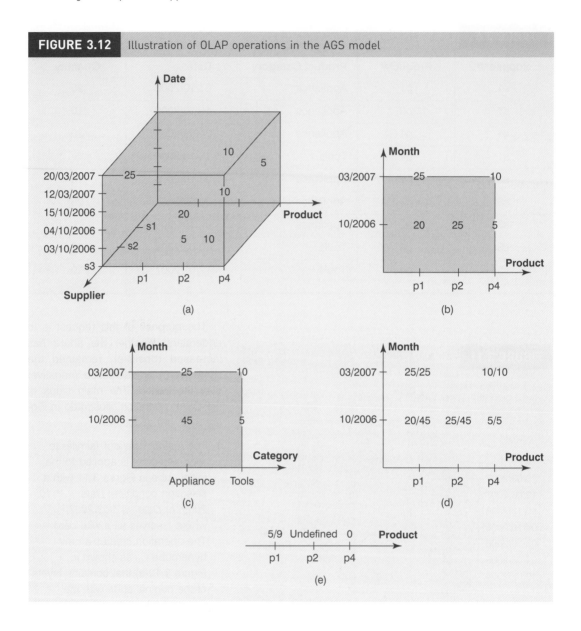

FIGURE 3.12   Illustration of OLAP operations in the AGS model

4   The *associate* operation is applied to the input cubes C_1 and C_2, aiming to calculate the market
    share of each product in its category in the two months. It applies the division operation to each
    pair of Product quantity and Category quantity, to obtain the ratio of each product's share in its
    category. The resulting cube C_3 is shown in Figure 3.12(d).

5   A final merge operation is performed on cube C_3 to reduce the Month (Date) dimension to a
    single root point, creating an opportunity to summarize along that dimension. A function subtracts
    the product share ratio for October 2006 from the product share ratio for March 2007. The
    resulting one-dimensional cube along the Product dimension contains data values representing
    the differences of the share ratios for each product between the two months (see Figure 3.12(e)).
    The result shows that, over the period, product p1 experienced an increase in its category share

by a factor of 5/9 and product p4 experienced no change in its category share. There is no result for product p2 because we do not have data for March 2007.

3.7 DATA PRE-PROCESSING AND VISUALIZATION IN WEKA

Weka, like many other data mining tools, is equipped with various utilities for data pre-processing, data exploration and data visualization, most of which are provided on the Preprocess tab in the Explorer (see Figure 3.13 and Section 2.6). In the Filter block, you can choose and apply a data pre-processing operation, known as a filter.

In Figure 3.13, no filter has been applied to the data set loaded from the file named `weather.arff`. You can see that the data set has five attributes and 14 instances. The highlighted temperature attribute is a numeric attribute with 12 distinct values and no missing values. The minimum, maximum, mean and standard deviation of the attribute are listed. The histogram shows that eight instances have values between 64 and 74.5 and six instances have values between 74.5 and 85. In both intervals, there is a mixture of yes and no classes for the attribute play, taken by default to be the class attribute.

FIGURE 3.13   The Preprocess tab in Weka

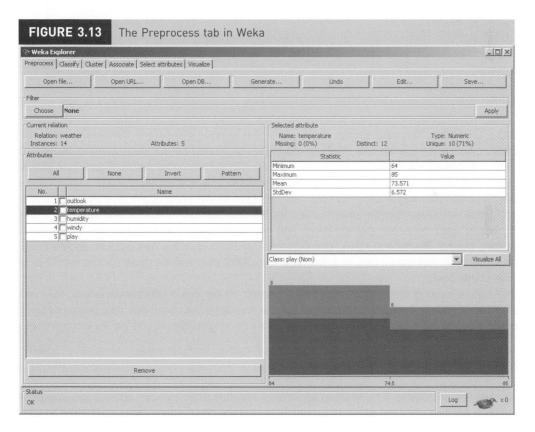

3.7.1 Weka Data File Format

Native Weka files are plain text files with data in the ARFF format, as shown in Figure 3.14(a). Lines starting % are comments. The line starting @relation names the data set. Attribute names and their data types are described by lines starting @attribute. Four data types can be specified: numeric, string,

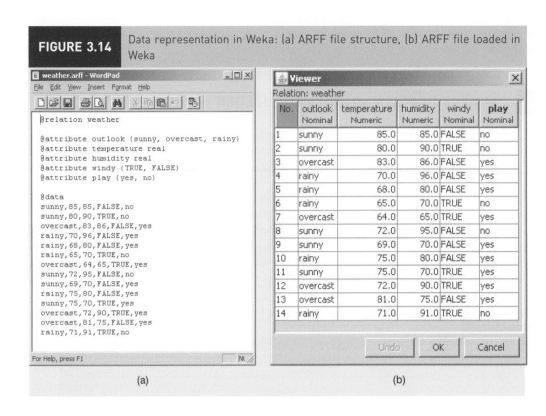

FIGURE 3.14 Data representation in Weka: (a) ARFF file structure, (b) ARFF file loaded in Weka

(a)

(b)

date and enumeration. The data section starts with a line labelled @data and contains the data for each data object on a separate line. Attribute values are separated by commas. Missing values are marked by a single question mark, ?. Strings are enclosed in double quote marks. Figure 3.14 shows the content of an ARFF file in both a text editor and the Weka Viewer window.

Weka can also open files in other formats, such as comma-delimited (CSV) files. For example, a Microsoft Excel worksheet can be saved as a CSV file and opened by Weka. The first row of the spreadsheet is used to name the attributes and the data types for the attributes are derived automatically but not always accurately. Once opened, you can save the data set into an ARFF file. Weka can also open files from a URL or a database with JDBC connectivity; these options are beyond the scope of this book.

In the Explorer mode of Weka, when a data file is opened, all the data details are loaded into the main memory. That is why the Explorer mode cannot handle very large data sets. Any data pre-processing operates on the data set in memory. The data file contains the original details until the file is overwritten.

3.7.2 Data Pre-processing in Weka

In Weka, data pre-processing is done using attribute or instance *filters* that can operate supervised or unsupervised. *Attribute* filters are applied to attributes (columns) and *instance* filters are applied to data objects (rows). *Supervised* filters perform with consideration of a class attribute whereas *unsupervised* filters do not.

A filter is applied through the following standard procedure. In the Filter block on the Preprocess tab, the user presses the Choose button and browses the tree structure to locate the required filter. Once selected, the filter name and its property parameters with default values are listed in the display box next to the Choose button. The user can modify the default values of the filter parameters in the editor that appears when the user clicks on the display box. The filter is applied to the loaded data set when the Apply button is pressed. In the rest of this section, the functions and effects of the filters are described, with an emphasis on unsupervised attribute and instance filters.

Remove attribute filter   The user selects this filter and lists the indices of the attributes to remove from the loaded data set. Attributes can also be removed by selecting them and then pressing the Remove button in the Attributes block. Similar filters include *RemoveType,* which deletes the attributes of a given data type, and *RemoveUseless,* which deletes attributes with constant values (e.g. all students from the same department) and nominal attributes that have too many distinct labels (e.g. student names). Automatic feature reduction is also possible (see Exercise 9).

Add attribute filter   The user selects this filter and specifies the location, name and the labels (values) of the new nominal attribute. Once created, the value of the new attribute can be entered manually in the viewer window for data objects. New numeric features can be added with the *AddExpression* filter, which applies a mathematical expression based on the values of other attributes. Figure 3.15 shows a creation of a new attribute named HomeworkAverage that takes an average of the homework marks for the data set in Table 3.5 (page 59). In the expression for calculating the average, a2, a3 and a4 refer to the indices of the three homework attributes. The *AddExpression* filter can be used for data transformation in general. Once the new attribute is created, the original attribute can be removed at the user's discretion.

Numeric transformation attribute filters   *MathExpression* allows transformation with a valid mathematical expression that uses arithmetic operators and built-in functions, such as absolute (abs),

FIGURE 3.15	Feature creation in Weka: (a) filter parameters and (b) the new attribute in the Viewer

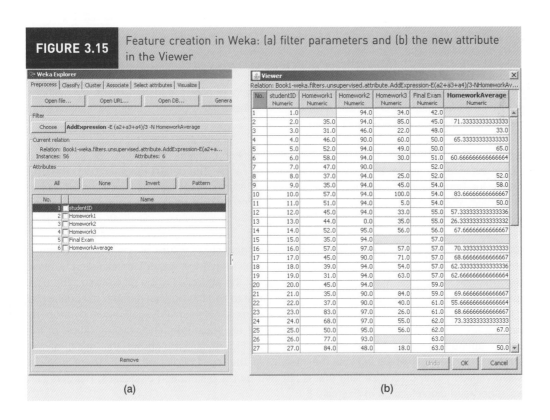

(a)   (b)

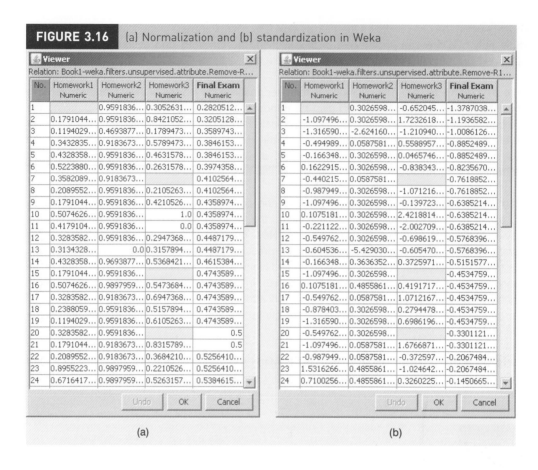

FIGURE 3.16 (a) Normalization and (b) standardization in Weka

logarithm (log), square root (sqrt), etc. *NumericTransform* only allows transformations by methods supported by the Java math library. Unlike *AddExpression*, these filters do not create new attributes but replace the current values with the transformed values.

Transformation attribute filters The *Normalize* filter converts the values of all numeric attributes in the loaded data set to those within a common range. The default range is [0,1]. The user can change the normal range if needed. The *Standardize* filter standardizes all numeric attributes to have zero mean and unit variance. Figure 3.16 shows the results of normalization and standardization for the student marks data set in Table 3.5 (page 59).

Discretize **filter** The unsupervised version of the filter discretizes values of one or more numeric attributes into nominal intervals of equal width or equal frequency without considering a class attribute. The user selects the filter and lists the indices of the attributes to be discretized. The user then specifies the number of equal-width bins or asks Weka to find the optimal number of equal-width bins. If equal-frequency discretization is required, the user must set the userEqualFrequency property to True. Figure 3.17(a) shows the parameter settings of an equal-frequency discretization of the sepallength attribute for a data set `iris.arff` and Figure 3.17(b) shows the result of the discretization. The nominal labels indicate the intervals as the result of discretization. There is also a supervised version of the Discretize filter that is affected by the distribution of classes. Readers can practise supervised discretization in Exercise 5.

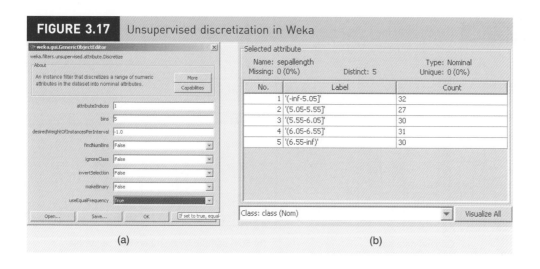

FIGURE 3.17   Unsupervised discretization in Weka

ReplaceMissingValues filter   This rudimentary filter fills in missing values; numeric values are replaced with the sample mean and nominal values are replaced with the sample mode. The user can also fill in missing values manually in the viewer window. For numeric attributes, the user may enter any value. For nominal attributes, the user can only select one of the nominal labels that already exists in the attribute domain. If the label does not exist (for instance, it is a special code indicating unknown), the label can be added into the attribute domain by using the *AddValues* filter.

Resample instance filter   This filter selects a random sample of a certain percentage (SampleSizePercent parameter) of the loaded data set, with or without replacement (to sample without replacement, set the noReplacement parameter to True). The unsupervised Resample filter draws the sample from the entire data set reflecting the real distribution of attribute values including class values; the supervised Resample filter draws samples according to either the real distribution of classes (set the biasToUniformClass parameter to 0) or a uniform distribution of classes (set the biasToUniformClass parameter to 1). Figure 3.18 illustrates the application of the Resample filter to `soybean.arff`, which contains 683 instances.

Many unsupervised filters have a supervised counterpart. Supervised filters must be used with care for classification tasks; test examples must be pre-processed in the same way as the training examples. This issue is reviewed again in Chapters 6 and 7.

The many other filters for data pre-processing have not been described due to limitations of space. Filters in Weka are continuously developed and new filters are constantly added in new versions.

3.7.3 Data Visualization in Weka

Weka provides a number of utilities for data exploration and understanding. Summary information about the loaded data set and the selected attribute and the histogram of the selected attribute are readily displayed on the Preprocess tab. The Viewer window enables browsing of the data set and filling in or changing data values. Weka also provides an *InterQuartileRange* filter that identifies extreme values and outlier data objects.

Weka is equipped with limited visualization utilities for both data and patterns. Histograms and scatter plots are two forms of data visualization. The user can display the histograms for all attributes by pressing the Visualize All button. Figure 3.19 shows the histograms for all attributes of the weather

3

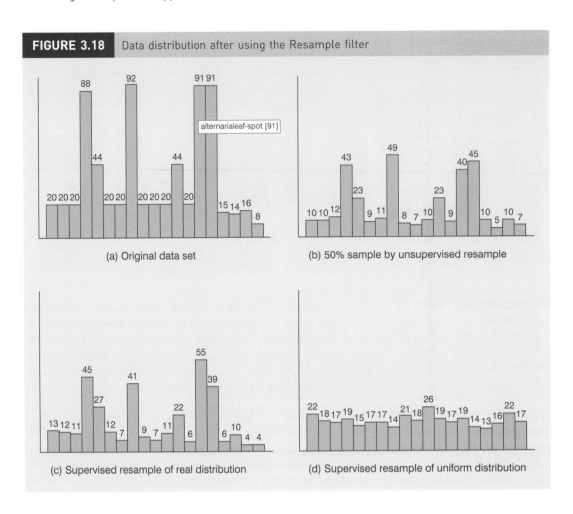

FIGURE 3.18   Data distribution after using the Resample filter

(a) Original data set

(b) 50% sample by unsupervised resample

(c) Supervised resample of real distribution

(d) Supervised resample of uniform distribution

data set. By browsing the histograms, one may conclude that the outlook attribute serves best in distinguishing the given classes.

Weka's Visualize tab, Figure 3.20(a), shows a matrix of scatter plots for every pair of attributes. Data objects are shown as points in the scatter plots. By default, the points are coloured according to their classes (sharp discrete colours for nominal class attributes and a spectrum of colours for numeric class attributes). For a clearer view of nearby data points, an amount of *jitter*, a random displacement of the co-ordinates of each point, is introduced to separate the data points. The amount of jitter and the plot and point sizes can be changed by the user using the sliders below the plots. The Select Attributes button enables the user to select attributes. All modifications take effect when the user presses the Update button. Figure 3.20(a) shows the visualization of the student marks data set in Table 3.5 (page 59).

The user can select a specific scatter plot by clicking on the plot area within the plot matrix. The selected plot appears in a pop-up window. The user can 'browse' through the plots in the matrix by changing the X and Y dimensions at the top of the pop-up window. The user can also further select an area of the displayed plot by drawing a rectangle or polygon and then pressing the Submit button (see Figure 3.20(b)).

FIGURE 3.19   Histograms for all attributes of the weather data set in Weka

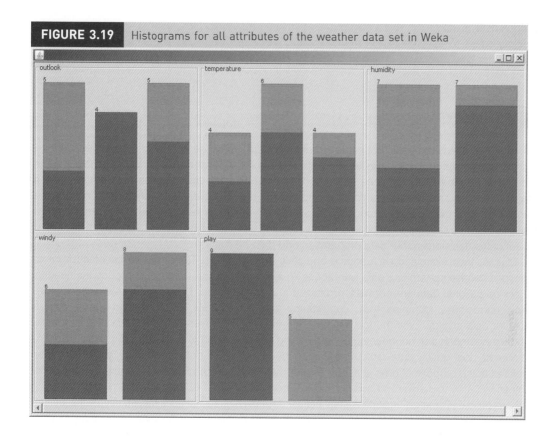

FIGURE 3.20   Visualizing a data set in Weka

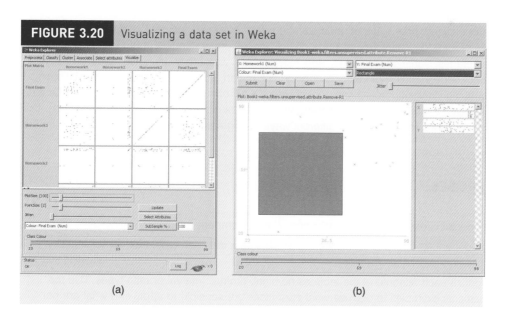

(a)   (b)

Besides data visualization, Weka also provides limited visualization for patterns. For instance, Weka uses colour codes to visualize cluster memberships. Weka also visualizes some classification models such as a decision tree and a neural network. These visualization methods are described and demonstrated in later chapters.

3.8 SUMMARY

This chapter first described basic concepts about input data. Precision and bias in data measurement were discussed in relation to data quality when input data are first created. The concepts of data objects, their attributes and their domain types were also explained. Correct understanding of domain types is essential for deciding what data manipulation operations are sensible. Data transformation from one domain to another is permissible as long as features of the original domain type are preserved. Common features of input data sets were highlighted. Understanding both the common and the distinct features of a data set helps decisions about data preparation and data mining.

The chapter then examined data source and data quality issues. Data may be collected from an operational database system or a data warehouse. In a data warehouse, in order to reduce the need for costly join operations, data are normally organized in a star schema. Data can be evaluated for their accuracy, correctness, completeness, consistency and redundancy. Having good-quality data is desirable for data mining. Even though we have no or little control over the generation of good-quality data, it does not mean that no meaningful data mining can be performed. Good data mining solutions should tolerate poor-quality data without degrading the quality of the output patterns. Data quality is an issue related to the purpose of data analysis. Quality may be a serious concern for one analysis but not for another.

Data pre-processing is an important step before data mining that affects the quality of the mining results. A large part of this chapter was therefore devoted to this topic. A range of techniques were outlined for data aggregation; data sampling (or case selection); attribute selection, reduction and creation; data discretization, data transformation, and treatment missing data. The principles of the techniques were explained and some of them were demonstrated using Weka filters.

This chapter outlined three ways of understanding data: summary statistics, data visualization and online analytic processing. Summary statistics offer a general understanding about values of attributes in terms of averages, variations in value, and relationships with other attributes. Data visualization enables a direct understanding of value frequency distribution, summary statistics, and relationships with other attributes via visual projections and images. OLAP offers different ways of viewing the data and performing data aggregation along different view angles at different levels of data abstraction. The different angles of views on the data and different ways of aggregating data offer more insight into the data.

EXERCISES

1 Table 3.7 contains data about the employees of an IT company.
   (a) Sum up the following characteristics of the table as a data set: type, size, dimensionality, sparsity and level of abstraction.
   (b) Categorize each attribute of the table as nominal, ordinal, interval or ratio types. Use the attributes as examples to discuss what operations are sensible to apply and what are not.

2 A team of researchers conducts research into face recognition. The team has created a database of short colour video clips of frontal face images for 50 human subjects of different

TABLE 3.7	Sample data for Exercises 1, 5 and 10				
Emp ID	**Name**	**Year of Birth**	**Gender**	**Status**	**Salary**
100	Smith	1954	M	Director	£100,000
125	Jones	1967	F	Technician	£18,000
167	Highley	1975	F	Senior Technician	£35,000
200	Millns	1987	M	Technician	£16,000
205	Dujevic	1985	M	Technician	£17,000
216	Isovic	1985	F	Technician	£17,000
220	Sun	1986	F	Senior Technician	£33,000
301	Bean	1955	M	Deputy Director	£80,000

genders and ethnic groups. Each video clip consists of 100–120 frames (still images) of 120 × 80 pixels and is stored in a separate file. Describe how to compose a table from the video clips for classification purposes. In your description, you must state clearly what the rows and columns of the table represent. Which type of data set does the table belong to?

3 Give examples, different from those used in the chapter, for the following types of data set: transaction database, graph and sequence.

4 A medium-sized company is keen to design its own data warehouse for better customer relationship management and customer service. The company currently has three operational databases: the sales database deals with promotion of new products to their customers; the transaction database deals with customer purchases; and the service database deals with customer complaints about products.

(a) Discuss how to integrate data into the central repository from the source systems.

(b) Describe briefly a possible star schema structure for the data warehouse.

(c) If the sales database contains data about potential customers, what problem may this bring to the data warehouse?

5 For the data in Table 3.7:

(a) If the Salary attribute needs to be discretized into three pay bands, suggest a simple yet sensible solution for the discretization backed with a valid argument.

(b) If Mr Dujevic's salary were unknown and the unknown value needed to be imputed, what is a sensible replacement value and why?

(c) Among the employee records, which record can be considered as an outlier? What harm can an outlier object cause to the understanding of the data set?

6 Use a spreadsheet tool, such as Microsoft Excel, to answer the following questions for the student marks data set in Table 3.5.

(a) Find the minimum, maximum, mean and standard deviation for each homework column and the exam column.

(b) Add an additional column for the average homework mark for each student. If the weighting on the homework average is 25% and that on the examination is 75%, add an additional column for the overall folded mark.

(c) Given the following criteria for grade classification, discretize the overall folded marks to grades. Produce a histogram of the grades.

```
F   between 0 and 39
D   between 40 and 54
C   between 55 and 69
B   between 70 and 84
A   between 85 and 100
```

(d) Construct a correlation matrix of homework and exam variables. What can you conclude from the matrix?

(e) Discuss various ways of treating the missing values in the data set.

7 For the data set in Table 3.5 (found on page 59), produce the following visualizations with a spreadsheet tool:

(a) A pie chart and a histogram for the grades in Exercise 6(c).

(b) A bar chart of the average homework and exam marks for every student.

(c) A scatter plot of points with the average homework marks and the exam marks.

(d) A parallel dimension chart of homework marks and final exam marks

8 Use a text editor to create an ARFF file for the data set in Table 3.5, open it in Weka, and perform the following tasks:

(a) Observe the summary data for the data set and the histograms for all attributes on the Preprocess tab page. Use the Visualize tab page to view the scatter plots between the variables of the data set.

(b) Apply the unsupervised Discretize filter to the exam marks.

(c) Redo Exercise 6(b) using appropriate filters.

(d) Practise filling in missing values in Weka both manually in the Viewer window and by using filters.

9 Principal component analysis (PCA) is a useful tool to reduce dimensionality of a given data set. Weka is equipped with a PCA filter, which can be used on the Select Attribute tab of the Explorer. Open one of the data sets provided in Weka, such as `cpu.arff`. On the Select Attribute tab, press the Choose button and select the PrincipalComponents filter. Press the Start button and observe the output in the Attribute Selection Output window. The window should show the new attributes in eigenvectors, each of which is a linear combination of the original attributes and the ranking among them according to their significance. Discuss your findings.

10 Online analytic processing (OLAP) perceives a data set as a hypercube in a multi-dimensional space. For the data set in Table 3.7, carry out the following exercises:

(a) Draw a diagram of a 3D hypercube using the following attributes: Year of Birth, Status and Salary.

(b) What do the data points inside the cube represent?

(c) Use the cube as an example to discuss the meaning of OLAP operations such as pivoting, slicing and dicing, rolling up and drilling down.

BIBLIOGRAPHICAL NOTES

References for this chapter come from a wide range of sources. Many statistics texts cover the concepts of measurements of data, data types and applicable operations. In their recent book, Taylor and Cihon (2004) discussed issues of accuracy, precision and bias in data measurements. Loftus and Loftus (1988) give an overview of the four domain types as measurement scales and show their permissible transformations. Tan et al. (2006) provide a wide review of different types of data set.

References to data sources are mainly from texts on databases and data warehouses. Join operations over relational tables and concepts of normalized relations are well covered in many database textbooks, such as Silberschatz et al. (2002). Anahory and Murray (1997) provide a short coverage of data warehouse concepts and principles. Schema structures for data warehouses are also discussed in many texts, including Connolly and Begg (2005). The issues of data quality are addressed extensively in the literature. Kelly (1997) defines the quality of data in a data warehouse context and describes how to manage data quality in an organization. *Communications of the ACM* ran a special edition to examine data quality that included a number of articles calling for total data quality management (CACM 1998).

Data pre-processing is again covered by a wide range of sources. Sampling methods appear in almost every statistics text, including Rees (2001). Dimensionality reduction, known as 'multidimensional scaling' in statistics, is studied in some statistics and linear algebra texts. Borg and Groenen (1997) provide an in-depth description of the topic. A well-cited, online tutorial about principal component analysis (PCA) is given by Smith (2002). Feature transformation, feature selection and construction are discussed in Liu and Motoda (1998). A recent comprehensive survey of feature selection algorithms is given by Molina et al. (2002). However, it is generally accepted that feature transformation is related to data background and discipline of study. Discretization has also been extensively investigated in the context of data mining because of the constraints of certain data mining solutions and a desire for better results. Kotsiantis and Kanellopoulos (2006a) present a recent survey on discretization algorithms and methods. Although most statistics texts provide some general coverage of the problem of missing values and the potential effects of data imputation to data distribution, the issue very much depends on an understanding of the missing values and the intended data analysis purposes. Little and Rubin (2002) provide a broad study of this issue. A more recent article by Magnani (2004) surveys some main techniques for dealing with missing values.

Data aggregation and OLAP in this chapter are mainly based on general descriptions given in Connolly and Begg (2005), an early work in attribute-oriented generalization by Cai et al. (1990) and an OLAP model by Agrawal, Gupta and Sarawagi (1995). Thomsen (2002) describes OLAP solutions in a more systematic manner. Exploratory data analysis appears in almost every statistics textbook. All summary statistical figures mentioned in this chapter are well covered. Readers can use any of them as a reference. Data visualization has become widely available with software such as MatLab, SPSS, and Microsoft Excel. Soukup and Davidson (2002) provide a thorough discussion of data visualization within the context of exploratory data mining.

CHAPTER 4

Basic techniques for cluster detection

LEARNING OBJECTIVES

To understand basic concepts of clusters and cluster detection

To study ways of measuring proximity between data objects

To learn how the basic K-means method detects clusters

To learn different variants of the basic K-means method

To learn how the agglomeration method detects clusters

To understand the use and effects of different merging strategies in the agglomeration method

To appreciate the strengths and limitations of the K-means and the agglomeration methods

To gain a fundamental understanding about evaluation of cluster quality

To observe how to use the simple K-means method in Weka

One of the data mining objectives mentioned in Chapter 1 is to describe the general characteristics of a data set. A single data record by itself shows the characteristics of a specific data object through its attribute values. When the data set is small, it may just be manageable to browse manually through individual records in the data set and appreciate common characteristics among the data records. However, this task quickly becomes impractical when the data set is large. One effective way is to automatically partition the records into a set of homogeneous groups according to their similarity. This task is known as *cluster detection, cluster analysis* or simply *clustering data*. After clustering, general features shared by members of each group become easier to study.

This chapter and Chapter 5 address issues of cluster detection and describe solutions for automatically clustering data records in a given data set. This chapter describes the basic approaches and methods and Chapter 5 introduces more advanced clustering solutions. In Section 4.1, the problem of cluster detection is first explained and the requirements for good clustering solutions are outlined. Section 4.2 describes a number of ways of measuring proximity among data objects. Two basic clustering solutions, i.e. the K-means and the agglomeration methods, are then presented in Sections 4.3 and 4.4. The evaluation of the quality of clusters and cluster tendency are discussed in Section 4.5. A cluster detection example using the simple K-means method in Weka is demonstrated in Section 4.6.

4.1   PROBLEM OF CLUSTER DETECTION

The term *cluster* refers to a group of data objects among which there exists a certain degree of similarity. The centre of the group is known as the *centroid* and the data records within the group are known as the *members* of the cluster. Cluster detection is an automatic process of discovering clusters from a given set of data objects, also known as the *data population*.

In essence, a clustering solution must include three essential elements:

■ A sensible measure of similarity among data objects. Using an appropriate similarity measuring function that is applicable to the data concerned is extremely important. After all, clusters are formed according to the results of the measurement. If an inappropriate function is used, the measuring result may not make sense, and data objects that are not so close to each other in reality may be grouped together, making the resulting cluster incorrect with little or no meaning.

■ A 'goodness-of-fit' function to evaluate the quality of the resulting clusters. Intuitively, a clustering result is considered desirable if both similarity among data objects within the cluster and difference with objects in other clusters are maximized. In other words, data objects within a cluster are maximally similar to each other whereas objects from one cluster are maximally different from objects from another cluster. In practice, the result of the goodness-of-fit function determines if a further round of clustering is needed. Indeed, such a function can serve as the stopping criterion of the overall clustering process.

■ An effective clustering algorithm. The algorithm uses the similarity measuring function repeatedly to determine which homogeneous group a data record should belong to. The effectiveness of a clustering algorithm is reflected through *correctness* and *completeness* of the results. Correctness means that the right objects are clustered into the right groups. Completeness refers to the coverage of the data population by the groups. A clustering algorithm that assigns membership of a group to every data record produces a complete result; otherwise it is incomplete.

The major requirements for an ideal clustering algorithm are as follows:

■ *Scalability*. The efficiency of a clustering algorithm is determined by the speed of execution. Efficiency must be assured in order for the algorithm to cope with large data populations.

■ *High dimensionality*. Good clustering algorithms should be able to deal with accurate and sensible measurement of similarity when many attributes are involved. As the dimensionality increases, data tend to become more uniform, making any separation of data according to similarity difficult. Sometimes, similarity may exist only in a subspace of the given high-dimensional space.

■ *Ability to deal with different types of attribute*. The algorithm must use a sensible similarity function that is capable of measuring similarities upon attributes of various data types, not just numerical attributes.

■ *Discovery of clusters of various shapes and densities*. Good algorithms must not only be able to deal with clusters of convex shapes, but also clusters of any complex shape. Algorithms that only produce clusters of convex shapes may have their limitations in certain application areas. Clusters of different densities also affect the working of clustering algorithms (see Chapter 5).

■ *Minimal requirements for domain knowledge to determine input parameters*. Good algorithms do not heavily rely on domain knowledge so that automation of the discovery is maximized and the discovery results are not biased.

■ *Incorporation of user-specified constraints*. A single similarity function cannot normally meet all requirements for all types of application. Good clustering solutions should accommodate user-defined constraints in its measurements of similarities that are specific to an application scenario.

■ *Ability to deal with noise and outliers*. Good algorithms should be able to tell if some objects are noise and outliers so that their existence does not distort the results of the discovery. In other words, good algorithms should be more tolerant of noise and outliers.

■ *Insensitive to order of input records*. Good clustering algorithms should be deterministic and produce the same resulting clusters even when the order of the data records is changed; otherwise, the algorithms produce different groupings for the same set of data in different repeats of the same clustering process.

■ *Interpretability and usability*. Good algorithms must produce interpretable clusters. The number of clusters should stay reasonably small. The features of the clusters must be informative, distinguished between one cluster and another. There is little need to perform clustering if the result of the clustering cannot be understood.

It must be said that this ideal list of requirements may not be completely fulfilled in practice due to the difficulties involved. In some circumstances, it may even be desirable not to meet some of the requirements.

Clustering has a wide range of applications. Possible areas of application for clustering include spatial data analysis, customer profiling, market research, web-log record analysis for websites, pattern recognition, image processing and so on. That is why many clustering solutions have been developed.

Table 4.1 shows 11 subjects and their attribute values. Plotting the subjects according to body height and body weight indicates the existence of two clusters (Figure 4.1). The upper-right cluster

TABLE 4.1	Medical data about subjects				
SubjectID	Body Height (cm)	Body Weight (kg)	Blood Pressure	Habit	Blood Sugar
s1	125	61	high	smoker	high
s2	178	90	normal	nonsmoker	low
s3	178	92	normal	nonsmoker	normal
s4	180	83	normal	nonsmoker	normal
s5	167	85	normal	nonsmoker	normal
s6	170	89	high	nonsmoker	low
s7	173	98	high	smoker	high
s8	135	40	normal	smoker	normal
s9	120	35	high	nonsmoker	normal
s10	145	70	normal	smoker	high
s11	125	50	normal	nonsmoker	high

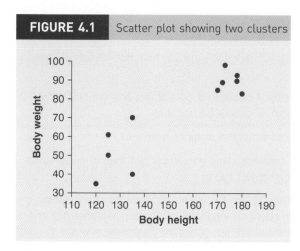

FIGURE 4.1   Scatter plot showing two clusters

appears more tightly organized and hence better quality than the lower-left cluster. Most of the members of the upper-right cluster have normal blood pressure and normal blood sugar. Most of them are also non-smokers.

4.2   MEASURES OF PROXIMITY

Proximity is a generic term that means either similarity or dissimilarity between two data objects. Similarity shows the likenesses whereas dissimilarity illustrates the differences. A proximity function measures the *degree* of the likeness or difference as a numerical amount. The reason for using the term 'proximity' is that sometimes similarity is preferred and at other times difference is better measured.

Proximity can be measured in many different ways, depending on how data records are perceived. If data records are considered as points in a multidimensional space, geometric distance functions such as the commonly used Euclidean function (see Section 4.2.3) can be used. If data records are perceived as vectors, the angle between two vectors can be considered as an indicator of proximity. If data records are viewed as elements in regions, small regions with a high concentration of data elements are considered as a dense region, indicating the existence of a cluster. If data records are representative of time-series signals, more appropriate measures of proximity, such as time-warping, may be best suited. Some of those ways of measuring proximity are explained in this section. Others are introduced in Chapter 5.

Proximity can also be measured in different scales. Sometimes, it is measured in absolute quantity of a numeric amount and sometimes as a fraction. Sometimes, it is measured in a symmetric range between –N and N. There are reasons for the existence of all the scales. It is not always necessary to force the transformation of proximity measures into a single normalized scale, say [0, 1] although it may be desirable to do so. Indeed, if a similarity function S returns 1 as the maximum degree of similarity and 0 as the least degree of similarity, and at the same time a dissimilarity function D returns 0 as the least degree of difference and 1 as the maximum degree of difference, the similarity fraction s by the function S may be transformed into a dissimilarity fraction d by the function D where $d = 1 - s$. In other words, maximizing similarity is in fact the same as minimizing dissimilarity.

In many circumstances, dissimilarity is preferred because it is easier and more direct to measure with a distance function. Measuring a distance between two data objects involves firstly *measuring* differences in values of the individual attributes of the data objects and then *combining* the value differences into a single amount.

4.2.1 Metric Properties of Proximity Functions

A function D with a measurement of distance $d(x, y)$, where x and y are any two data objects, is called a *metric* if it satisfies the following three properties:

- $d(x, x) = 0$ and $d(x, y) \geq 0$ when $x \neq y$: The distance between a data object and the object itself is zero and the distance between any two data objects cannot be negative.

- $d(x, y) = d(y, x)$: the distance from x to y is the same as the distance from y to x.

- $d(x, y) \leq d(x, z) + d(z, y)$: Any direct distance between x and y must be less than or equal to an indirect total distance from x to object z and from object z to y.

In mathematics, all distance functions, for instance the Euclidean distance function, satisfy the properties listed above and hence are metrics. In the data mining literature, the term distance function is much more loosely used. Proximity functions that possess only some of the properties may still be used to measure dissimilarity for clustering purposes. The metric properties are therefore not essential. Nevertheless, understanding the metric properties of a distance function is useful for clustering algorithms: an algorithm may exploit the properties to reduce the amount of memory required and speed up the clustering process.

4.2.2 Value Differences for Different Domain Types

In Chapter 3, attribute domains were categorized into nominal, ordinal, interval and ratio types. Measurement of the difference between values of an attribute is directly related to the domain type of the attribute.

Difference between nominal values   For nominal values, the only operators that are applicable are the Boolean operators $=$ and $\neq$. Two nominal values are either exactly the same or completely different. For instance, for data objects <'Mary', 'secretary'>, <'John', 'manager'> and <'Liz', 'manager'>, John and Liz are *similar* in the status field whereas Mary and Liz are not. Therefore, the numerical difference between two nominal values can be recorded as 0, if the two values are the same, and as ∞, if the two nominal values are different. In practice, when the value difference is measured as a fraction between 0 and 1, ∞ is replaced by 1, the maximum difference.

Difference between binary values   The difference between binary values can be understood in the same way as nominal values: the two values are either the same or different. One widely used numerical notation for Boolean variables is to use 1 representing one value and 0 the other. This representation can directly reflect the meaning of difference between the Boolean values: the difference between two equal Boolean values is 0 (i.e. $0 - 0 = 1 - 1 = 0$) and the difference between two different Boolean values is 1 (i.e. $|0 - 1| = |1 - 0| = 1$), provided that absolute difference between 0 and 1 is always used and no fraction calculation is ever attempted.

Difference between ordinal values   For an ordinal domain, there is a ranking order among the values. For instance, for a domain representing customer status as {bad, OK, good, excellent}, 'excellent' is better than 'good', which is better than 'OK', which is better than 'bad'. To maintain the order among the values, the difference between 'good' and 'excellent' is considered to be less than the difference between 'OK' and 'excellent'. Converting ordinal values to consecutive integers is a normal way of representing them quantitatively, as long as the same order among values is maintained. So our customer status values can be converted to {0, 1, 2, 3}. After the transformation, the same order is maintained and the same understanding over differences is also maintained to a certain extent. The difference between 'excellent' and 'good' is $3 - 2 = 1$, whereas the difference between 'excellent' and 'OK' is $3 - 1 = 2$, which is greater than the former. However, this conversion may give the wrong impression that the categories are measured in the same interval. For instance, d(good, OK) = d(excellent, good) = 1, but in reality, the two differences cannot really be compared. Unfortunately, it appears there is no better option to deal with this problem.

Difference between interval and ratio values   The difference between two interval or ratio values is normally measured as the absolute difference between the two numerical values. However, one should remember that any use of ratio operations such as multiplication and division over interval values in data transformation or normalization does not make much sense since interval data has no reference to an absolute zero; it should not be attempted.

Ideally, the constraints over operations by different domain types must be strictly adhered to. Otherwise, the proximity measure in numerical terms may not reflect the truth. One has to make the best effort in designing a meaningful proximity function, particularly when a clustering solution is developed for a specialized application. In reality, however, sometimes it is difficult to adhere to all domain type constraints when not all relevant information is available. Some of the constraints may be relaxed: a not-so-perfect measure may be better than no measure at all.

One problem in measuring proximity between objects is how to deal with unknown attribute values. Although handling missing values is normally a task for data pre-processing, data records may still contain unknown values after the pre-processing stage either because no suitable data imputation method can be found, or because unknown values themselves convey certain meaning. When there is little or no domain knowledge, a common policy for handling unknown values is as follows. For nominal attributes, we assume an unknown value is maximally different from any other value, even from another unknown value. This means the maximum distance should be recorded. For numeric attributes, the difference between two unknown values is considered to be the maximum. If one value is missing and the other is known, either the size of the known value or the absolute value itself is considered as the difference. This means that if the values are missing, the difference is as large as it can possibly be.

A distance function between data objects combines the value differences of individual attributes into a single numerical measurement. However, how to combine attribute value differences depends on how data objects are perceived.

4.2.3 Distance Functions for Interval and Ratio Attributes

Data objects can be considered as points in a multidimensional space where each dimension represents an attribute. A point signifies the existence of a combination of attribute values, i.e. the data object. A well-known distance function is the *Minkowski* distance metric.

Let $i = <x_{i1}, x_{i2}, \ldots, x_{ip}>$ and $j = <x_{j1}, x_{j2}, \ldots, x_{jp}>$ be two p-dimensional data objects. Suppose that the dissimilarity of the two data objects is measured upon *all* the dimensions. The Minkowski distance between objects i and j is defined as

$$d(i, j) = \sqrt[q]{|x_{i1} - x_{j1}|^q + |x_{i2} - x_{j2}|^q + \ldots + |x_{ip} - x_{jp}|^q}$$

where q is a positive integer. Three versions of the metric are in practical use according to the value of q. When q is set to 1, the metric represents the total sum of the absolute value difference over all dimensions. This version is known as the *Manhattan* or *City-block* distance. When q is set to 2, the metric first calculates the total sum of the squared value differences over all dimensions and then takes the square root of the total sum. This version is known as the *Euclidean* distance. When q is set to ∞, the metric takes the maximum of the absolute value differences among all the dimensions. This version is known as the *Chebyshev* (or *Supremum*) distance.

$$\text{Manhattan distance: } d_1(i, j) = \sum_{t=1}^{p} |x_{it} - x_{jt}|$$

$$\text{Euclidean distance: } d_2(i, j) = \sqrt{\sum_{t=1}^{p} (x_{it} - x_{jt})^2}$$

$$\text{Chebyshev distance: } d_{max}(i, j) = \max_t (|x_{it} - x_{jt}|)$$

The Euclidean distance is normally preferred because it measures direct distance between two points. The Manhattan distance measures the indirect distance between the two points and the Chebyshev distance measures the distance very coarsely: the value difference of a single attribute, that is the maximum, represents the distance between the two points.

To illustrate the use of the Minkowski distance function, the distance between records s1 and s3 in Table 4.1 is measured upon the Body Height and Body Weight dimensions by using the three versions of the function:

$$d_1(s1, s3) = |s1.BodyHeight - s3.BodyHeight| + |s1.BodyWeight - s3.BodyWeight|$$

$$= |125 - 178| + |61 - 92| = 84$$

$$d_2(s1, s3) = \sqrt{(s1.BodyHeight - s3.BodyHeight)^2 + (s1.BodyWeight - s3.BodyWeight)^2}$$

$$= \sqrt{(125 - 178)^2 + (61 - 92)^2} \approx 61.4$$

$$d_{max}(s1, s3) = \max(|s1.BodyHeight - s3.BodyHeight|, |s1.BodyWeight - s3.BodyWeight|)$$

$$= |125 - 178| = 53$$

In the same example, the distance between tuples s1 and s11 is calculated with the Euclidean function as:

$$d_2(s1, s11) = \sqrt{(s1.BodyHeight - s11.BodyHeight)^2 + (s1.BodyWeight - s11.BodyWeight)^2}$$

$$= \sqrt{(125 - 125)^2 + (61 - 50)^2} = 11$$

Since $d_2(s1, s3) > d_2(s1, s11)$, the data point s1 is said to be more similar or closer in location to data point s11 than to data point s3.

4.2.4 Dissimilarity Measurement for Nominal Attributes

Another commonly used method of measuring proximity between two data objects is to see how many features, among all features, that the two data objects have in common. This task becomes particularly simple when the features are represented by a small set of discrete nominal terms. Therefore, a natural way of measuring dissimilarity between two data objects with nominal attributes is the *ratio of mismatched features* (RMF). Given two data objects i and j of p attributes, let m represent the number of attributes in which the attribute values of the two data objects match. The ratio of mismatched features is defined as follows:

$$RMF(i, j) = \frac{p - m}{p}$$

A slightly different way of expressing the ratio of mismatched features can be explained as follows. Given data objects i and j, if their corresponding attribute values match, the difference between the two values is set to 0, i.e. the minimum. If their corresponding attribute values do not match, the difference between the two values is set to 1, i.e. the maximum. Then the 1s and 0s for all attributes are added together into a total sum that is calculated as a ratio of the total number of attributes. The same ratio of mismatched features can now be expressed as:

$$RMF(i, j) = \frac{\sum_{f=1}^{p} d_{ij}^{f}}{p}$$

where $d_{ij}^{f} = 1$ if objects i and j do not match on attribute f; otherwise, $d_{ij}^{f} = 0$.

So far, the rather vague term 'match' has been used. Most of the time, it means that the nominal attribute values concerned must be exactly the same. However, in certain situations, different nominal values may match in the meaning they convey. For instance, 'male' and 'gentleman' may be considered a match although they are two different words.

In Table 4.1, if only the attributes Blood Pressure, Habit and Blood Sugar are considered for measuring dissimilarity, and two values match when they are exactly the same, then the dissimilarity between data objects s1 and s2, and that between data objects s2 and s3 are measured in RMF as follows:

$$RMF(s2, s1) = \frac{3 - 0}{3} = 1$$

$$RMF(s2, s3) = \frac{3 - 2}{3} = \frac{1}{3} \approx 0.33$$

The result of measurement indicates that s2 is more similar to s3 than to s1.

Instead of using the ratio of mismatched features, an alternative way of measuring the proximity of nominal attributes is to replace the nominal values by Boolean values and then use the distance functions for Boolean variables to measure dissimilarity. For a nominal attribute with two possible values, the attribute can be treated directly as a Boolean variable. For a nominal attribute A with n values $\{a_1, a_2, \ldots, a_n\}$, it can be replaced by n Boolean variables each of which takes the value 1 if $A = a_i$ ($1 \leq i \leq n$) for the data object. For instance, the attribute Habit in Table 4.1 can be treated as a Boolean attribute. Attribute Blood Sugar may be replaced by three Boolean variables BS_low, BS_norm and BS_high. For data record s1, BS_low and BS_norm would take the value 0 while BS_high would take the value 1. The problem with this approach is that the dimensionality of the original data set may increase dramatically as a result. A lot of extra 0 values are also introduced. One way to ease the increase of dimensionality is to use a combination of logN instead of N Boolean variables to replace the original nominal attribute. For instance, attribute Blood Sugar may be replaced by two instead of three Boolean variables. A combination of 0s and 1s represents each original nominal value, such as 00 for low, 01 for normal and 10 for high blood sugar levels. However, an increase in dimensionality cannot be completely avoided.

4.2.5 Distance Measurement for Binary Attributes

If two objects i and j have p binary attributes, according to the possible combinations of the Boolean values, a contingency table can be constructed (Table 4.2). In the table, a represents the number of attributes where both objects i and j have the value 1, d the number of attributes where both i and j have

TABLE 4.2	Contingency table for Boolean attributes			
		Object j		
		1	0	total
Object i	1	a	b	$a+b$
	0	c	d	$c+d$
	total	$a+c$	$b+d$	p

the value 0, b the number of attributes where i has the value 1 and j has the value 0, and c the number of attributes where i has the value 0 and j has the value 1.

If both binary values of the attribute are considered equally important, the attribute is called a *symmetric Boolean variable*. If one binary value is considered more important than the other binary value, the attribute is known as an *asymmetric Boolean variable*. If data objects i and j contain only symmetric binary attributes, the distance between the objects can be measured by

$$d(i, j) = \frac{b+c}{p} = \frac{b+c}{a+b+c+d} = RMF(i, j)$$

This distance function measures how many attributes out of the total have values that are different. It is in fact the same as the *RMF* function for nominal attributes. Indeed, a binary attribute can be considered as a special case of nominal attribute.

For asymmetric binary attributes, where the occurrence of values is more important than the absence of the values, a ratio measure known as the Jaccard Coefficient (JC) is used:

$$JC(i, j) = \frac{b+c}{a+b+c}$$

The number of attributes whose values are both 0s, i.e. quantity d, is disregarded from the *JC* measure. The difference between *RMF* and *JC* measures can be demonstrated by the following document search example (see Table 4.3). A document can be represented as vectors of binary attributes. Each attribute value represents the occurrence or absence of a keyword (or term) in the document.

The distance between documents t1 and t2 is measured in *RMF* as:

$$RMF(t1, t2) = \frac{1+0}{1+1+0+5} = \frac{1}{7} \approx 0.1429$$

TABLE 4.3	Documents and keyword occurrences (1s) and absences (0s)						
DocumentID	query	database	programming	interface	usability	user	network
t1	1	1	0	0	0	0	0
t2	0	1	0	0	0	0	0
t3	0	1	1	0	0	0	0
t4	0	1	0	1	0	0	0

The distance measured is measured in *JC* as

$$JC(\text{t1, t2}) = \frac{1+0}{1+0+1} = \frac{1}{2} = 0.5$$

According to the *RMF* measure, the two documents are quite similar. However the similarity reflects mostly the common absence of keywords from the two documents rather than their similarity in containing keywords. The *JC* measure on the other hand does not consider the common absence of keywords, but only the differences and similarities in the words the two documents actually contain. It is therefore more appropriate for the purpose of searching for similar documents.

4.2.6 Cosine Similarity Measures

The Minkowski functions treat data records as points and measure the distance between the points. The attributes of data objects are considered as separate and independent variables. The relativity between the values of different attributes is not considered. For instance, big fish and small fish share similar proportions in their tail length, overall body length and body shape. Baby tigers and adult tigers share similar proportions in their tail length, overall body length and body shapes. Using the Euclidean distance function and ignoring the relativity of the attribute values, baby tigers and small fish may be measured as similar objects and hence put into the same cluster, as illustrated in Figure 4.2(a). This clustering result may have little practical meaning. However, if each data object is represented as a vector and the difference between the vector angles is measured as an indication of proximity, then the difference between small fish and big fish is actually very small, as is the difference between baby tigers and adult tigers. The clustering result therefore shows the fish in one cluster and the tigers in another (Figure 4.3(b)), which is more meaningful than the result obtained by using the Euclidean distance.

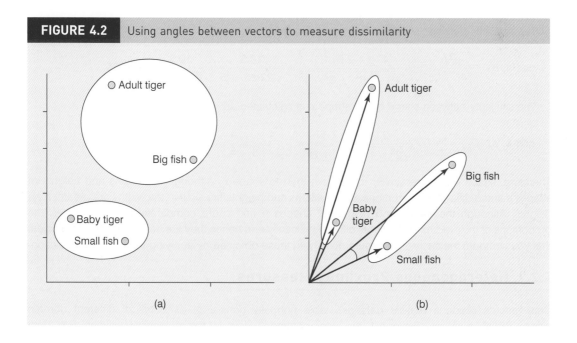

FIGURE 4.2   Using angles between vectors to measure dissimilarity

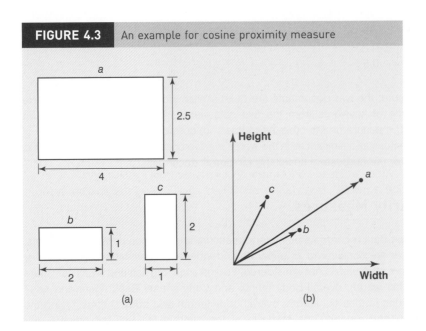

FIGURE 4.3 An example for cosine proximity measure

Vector angles can be measured in a number of ways. The *cosine* function is commonly used to measure similarity between two vectors. Given two data objects $i = <x_{i1}, x_{i2}, \ldots, x_{ip}>$ and $j = <x_{j1}, x_{j2}, \ldots, x_{jp}>$, the cosine function is defined as follows:·

$$\cos(i, j) = \frac{i \bullet j}{\|i\| \times \|j\|} \quad \text{where } i \bullet j = \sum_{k=1}^{p} x_{ik} x_{jk}, \ \|i\| = \sqrt{\sum_{k=1}^{p} x_{ik}^2}, \ \text{ and } \ \|j\| = \sqrt{\sum_{k=1}^{p} x_{jk}^2}$$

Figure 4.3(a) shows three rectangular shapes with width and height attributes. Each shape can be represented as a vector as shown in Figure 4.3(b).

The similarity between shapes a and b is calculated as:

$$\cos(a, b) = \frac{a \bullet b}{\|a\| \cdot \|b\|} = \frac{4 \cdot 2 + 2.5 \cdot 1}{\sqrt{4^2 + 2.5^2} \cdot \sqrt{2^2 + 1^2}} = \frac{10.5}{\sqrt{22.25} \cdot \sqrt{5}} = \frac{10.5}{10.54751} \approx 0.9955$$

The similarity between shape b and shape c is calculated as:

$$\cos(b, c) = \frac{b \bullet c}{\|b\| \cdot \|c\|} = \frac{2 \cdot 1 + 1 \cdot 2}{\sqrt{2^2 + 1^2} \cdot \sqrt{1^2 + 2^2}} = \frac{4}{\sqrt{5} \cdot \sqrt{5}} = \frac{4}{5} = 0.8$$

Therefore, shape b is more similar to shape a than to shape c. Although the widths and heights of shapes a and b differ, the proportions of their widths and heights are similar: the widths are greater than heights. Although the widths and heights of shapes b and c are comparatively much closer, the proportions of their widths and heights differ significantly and hence they are not so similar. We suggest that you compare the similarity measurements with those obtained by applying the Euclidean function.

4.2.7 Heterogeneous Proximity Measures

Data records inside a real-life database table normally consist of attributes of different domain types. Tables such as Table 4.1 are very common. How is the proximity between two data objects i and j measured in this case? The following hybrid function is suggested, based on the principle of the RMF:

$$D(i, j) = \frac{\sum_{f=1}^{p} \delta_{ij}^{f} \times d_{ij}^{f}}{\sum_{f=1}^{p} \delta_{ij}^{f}}$$

where the parameters within the formula are set as follows:

- δ_{ij}^{f} is set to 0, if an attribute value of either i or j is missing, or the attribute f is an asymmetric binary attribute and the corresponding values for the two objects $x_{if} = x_{jf} = 0$. For all other types of attributes, set $\delta_{ij}^{f} = 1$.

- For continuous and ordinal attributes, calculate d_{ij} as the absolute value difference normalized in the range [0, 1].

- For binary and nominal attributes, if the corresponding attribute values are the same, i.e. $x_{if} = x_{jf}$, set $d_{ij} = 0$, the minimum difference; otherwise, set $d_{ij} = 1$, the maximum difference.

In the data set in Table 4.1, suppose that Habit is an asymmetric binary attribute and the values of Body Weight and Body Height are normalized into the range [0, 1]. The distance between s1 and s2 is calculated as follows:

$$D(\text{s1, s2}) = \frac{(1 \times 0.88333 + 1 \times 0.460317 + 1 \times 1 + 1 \times 1 + 1 \times 1)}{(1 + 1 + 1 + 1 + 1)} = \frac{4.343651}{5} \approx 0.86873$$

4.2.8 Attribute Weighting and Scaling

In measuring proximity among objects, it is often necessary to consider weighting some attributes and scaling values of attributes up or down. Adding a weight to certain attributes reflects the different degrees of importance of those attributes. In other words, values of those attributes are more influential than others in the measurement of proximity. For instance, in the league table of UK universities produced by the *Times* newspaper, the attributes Teaching Quality and Research Quality are twice as important as other attributes, such as Graduate Employment Rate.

In a typical proximity function, weight is normally represented as a fraction applied to the calculation of value differences of an attribute. For instance, the weighted Euclidean function can be defined as

$$d_2(i, j) = \sqrt{\sum_{t=1}^{p} w_t (x_{it} - x_{jt})^2}$$

where w_t is the weight assigned to the tth attribute. The weighted version of the combined distance function in Section 4.2.7 may be modified as follows:

$$D(i, j) = \frac{\sum_{f=1}^{p} w^{f} \times \delta_{ij}^{f} \times d_{ij}^{f}}{\sum_{f=1}^{p} \delta_{ij}^{f}}$$

where w^{f} is the weight assigned to the fth attribute. The sum of all weights normally equals 1.

Attribute scaling means that the original attribute values are transformed to new values. It is the same as feature transformation, described in Chapter 3, but is carried out for two specific reasons:

- Data values for the same attribute in different data sources may be measured in different scales. When the data sources are integrated into a single data set, inconsistency among the attribute values occurs. In this case, either all attribute values from both sources must be transformed to a standard scale, or one measurement scale is considered the standard and all values measured in other scales must be transformed to the values of the chosen scale. A simple example is temperature measurements: we must convert all measurements to Fahrenheit, Centigrade, or Kelvin.

- Data values for different attributes may be measured in different scales. Attributes with large measurement values may dominate the computation for proximity, making attributes with small measurement values insignificant (see Exercise 5). As a result, the clusters are largely formed on the basis of the dominant attributes. Normally, attribute scaling is a subject to be dealt with in data warehousing or at the data pre-processing stage.

Attribute values may be scaled up or down to make them more comparable with the values of other attributes or to normalize values of all attributes into the same value range. Many different methods of data normalization exist. One of them is to divide the value of an attribute by the attribute range. Let v_i represent the current value of an attribute A for a data object i. Let $max(A)$ and $min(A)$ represent the maximum value and minimum values for A. Then the new normalized value a_i of the attribute for data object i is

$$a_i = \frac{v_i - min(A)}{max(A) - min(A)}$$

For example, if $v_i = 20$, $max(A) = 30$ and $min(A) = 10$, then the normalized new value is 0.5.

Another commonly used normalization scale is z-score. The z-score reflects variations of the attribute values from the mean. The z-score for the ith value for an attribute f of a domain with n values $\{x_{1f}, x_{2f}, \ldots, x_{nf}\}$ is defined as

$$z_{if} = \frac{x_{if} - \mu_f}{s_f}$$

where μ_f is the mean and s_f is the absolute mean deviation, i.e.

$$\mu_f = \frac{1}{n}(x_{1f} + x_{2f} + \ldots + x_{nf}) \qquad s_f = \frac{1}{n}(|x_{1f} - \mu_f| + |x_{2f} - \mu_f| + \ldots + |x_{nf} - \mu_f|)$$

For example, an attribute with a domain $\{20, 10, 30, 40\}$ can be normalized into an attribute with z-scores $\{-0.5, -1.5, 0.5, 1.5\}$.

We now demonstrate how to calculate the distance between data objects s1 and s2 in Table 4.1 by using the weighted heterogeneous distance function of Section 4.2.7. Suppose that the weights for attributes Body Weight and Body Height are 0.15 (15%), the weights for attributes Habit and Blood Sugar are 0.20 (20%), and the weight for attribute Blood Pressure is 0.3 (30%). Suppose also that binary attributes Blood Pressure and Habit are both symmetric Boolean variables. According to the definition of the distance function, all δ parameters equal 1. Hence,

$$\sum_{f=1}^{5} \delta^f_{s1,\,s2} = 5$$

The normalized value difference between s1 and s2 over Body Height is

$$d^1_{s1, s2} = \frac{|s1.BodyHeight - s2.BodyHeight|}{\max(BodyHeight) - \min(BodyHeight)} = \frac{|125 - 178|}{180 - 120} = \frac{53}{60} \approx 0.88$$

The normalized value difference between s1 and s2 over Body Weight is

$$d^2_{s1, s2} = \frac{|s1.BodyWeight - s2.BodyWeight|}{\max(BodyWeight) - \min(BodyWeight)} = \frac{|61 - 90|}{98 - 35} = \frac{29}{63} \approx 0.46$$

The value differences for attributes Blood Pressure, Habit and Blood Sugar are all set to 1:

$$d^3_{s1, s2} = d^4_{s1, s2} = d^5_{s1, s2} = 1$$

Therefore, the distance between s1 and s2 is calculated as follows:

$$D(s1, s2) = \frac{0.15 \times 0.88 + 0.15 \times 0.46 + 0.3 \times 1 + 0.2 \times 1 + 0.2 \times 1}{5} = 0.1802$$

4.3 THE K-MEANS CLUSTERING METHOD AND ITS VARIANTS

This section introduces a basic clustering algorithm, known as the 'K-means method'. The framework of the method is first outlined and then a K-means algorithm is presented in detail. The algorithm originated in the late 1960s and has been widely used in statistical and data mining tools for various applications.

4.3.1 Overview

The general idea of the K-means method is to divide the data population into K partitions so that each partition can be treated as a separate cluster. The process starts initially with a random partitioning of all data objects into K partitions. Of course, this initial partitioning is unlikely to be precise and hence the resulting partitions should not be taken as the final clusters. In fact, the initial partitions are known as *prototype* clusters. They need to be refined so that some data objects are moved from the wrong partition to the right one. Once all the data objects become the members of the right partitions, there are no more changes of membership. The prototype clusters stabilize and become the final clusters.

During the refinement process, the centre of each prototype cluster, i.e. the centroid, is calculated. The K-means method uses the mean to calculate the centroid: it is a mean vector where each field of the vector is the mean of the values of all members upon that attribute (see Figure 4.4).

Figure 4.4(a) shows the initial partitioning of the data objects into three prototype clusters. The centroid of each prototype cluster is calculated (as indicated by the + points in Figure 4.4(b)). The membership of each data object is checked and reassigned to the nearest centroid: data objects either stay in the same partition or are relocated to a different partition. Figure 4.4(c) illustrates the boundaries of the updated partitions and the locations of the newly calculated centroids. Two data objects have changed partition membership, which in turn influences the locations of the new centroids.

4.3.2 A K-means Algorithm

In this section, a particular algorithm based on the K-means principle is given so that some operational details of the K-means method can be specified. The algorithm takes a typical relational table *DB* with attributes $A_1, A_2, \ldots, A_p$ as an input data set. The output of the algorithm is the original data set with a

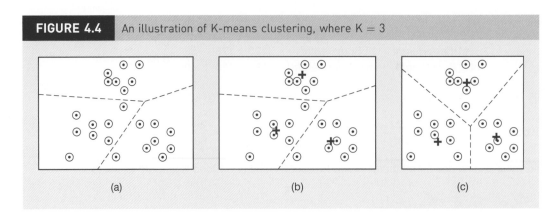

FIGURE 4.4   An illustration of K-means clustering, where K = 3

(a)   (b)   (c)

cluster tag assigned to all data records. Therefore, an additional integer column is added to the input table to store the cluster tags. An integer K is a parameter to the algorithm. It not only represents the total number of clusters, but also enables integers between 1 and K to be used as cluster tags. The parameter f represents a distance function. Making the distance function a parameter makes the algorithm more generic and robust: a suitable distance function can be selected for a specific application. The algorithm is given in pseudo-code as follows:

```
algorithm Kmeans (var DB: data set, K: integer, df: distance function)
   MemberChange : Boolean;
begin
   for every record r in DB do
      r.clusterTag := null;
   for;
   S:= Ø;//empty the seed set S
   for j := 1 to K do
      select at random a record r_j in DB into S;
      r_j.clusterTag := j;
   endfor;
   repeat
      MemberChange := false;
      for every record r in DB do
         for every seed s_i in S do
            calculate df(r, s_i)
         endfor;
         find s in S where df(r,s) = min(df(r,s_1), df(r,s_2)...df(r,s_K));
         If r.clusterTag ≠ s.clusterTag then
            MemberChange := true;
            r.clusterTag := s.clusterTag
         endif;
      endfor;
      S := Ø;//empty the seed set S
      for j := 1 to K do
         collect members of cluster j into C;
         calculate the mean vector a_j = <ā_1, ā_2, ..., ā_p>
```

$$\text{where } \bar{a}_i = \frac{1}{|C|}\sum_{A_i} a_t \text{ for attribute } A_i \ (1 \leq i \leq p) ;$$

```
      save the mean vector a_j as a seed into S;
```

```
        endfor;
    until not MemberChange or other criteria are met;
end
```

The algorithm facilitates the initial partitioning of the data set by selecting, at random, K data records from the data set to serve as seeds or initial centroids. For each data record, the distance between the data record and each seed is measured and compared. The data record has the same cluster tag as its nearest neighbour. The new centroid for a cluster is calculated by selecting the members and then taking the average over the values of all members for each attribute. The clustering process terminates when there is no membership change between the current iteration and the previous iteration. In rare situations, data objects near the border regions between clusters may constantly change membership from one cluster to another due to small imprecisions in distance calculations. The maximum number of iterations is normally used as an additional stopping criterion, to prevent an infinite loop from occurring.

TABLE 4.4	Applying the K-means algorithm: first iteration				
SubjectID	**Body Height (cm)**	**Body Weight (kg)**	**Distance to centroid 1**	**Distance to centroid 2**	**Cluster Tag**
s1	125	61	60.415	23.259	2
s2	178	90			1
s3	178	92	2.000	67.476	1
s4	180	83	7.280	62.241	1
s5	167	85	12.083	55.218	1
s6	170	89	8.062	60.216	1
s7	173	98	9.434	69.340	1
s8	135	40			2
s9	120	35	79.931	15.811	2
s10	145	70	38.588	31.623	2
s11	125	50	66.400	14.142	2

To illustrate the working of the algorithm, Table 4.1 is again used. It is assumed that K = 2; subjects s2 and s8 are selected as the initial centroids of the clusters and the Euclidean distance function is used upon attributes Body Weight and Body Height. The algorithm then calculates the distance from every data record to s2 and s8. The result of the distance calculation is shown in Table 4.4. The record is assigned to cluster 1 or 2 according to whether the record is closer to s2 or s8. After the initial round, all data records are assigned as a member of a cluster, as shown in Table 4.4.

The new centroid for each cluster is then calculated by taking the mean Body Height and Body Weight of all its members. The new centroid for cluster 1 is $C_1(174.333, 89.5)$ and the new centroid for cluster 2 is $C_2(130, 51.2)$. In the next round, the distance from every data record to each new centroid is calculated and the membership of the record is re-assigned if necessary. The resulting cluster tags are shown in Table 4.5. It is clear that there have been no changes in membership between this iteration and the previous one. The clustering process therefore terminates. The process in this example is artificially efficient, due to the sensible selection of the initial centroids.

TABLE 4.5	Applying the K-means algorithm: second iteration				
SubjectID	Body Height (cm)	Body Weight (kg)	Distance to centroid 1	Distance to centroid 2	Cluster Tag
s1	125	61	56.974	11.002	2
s2	178	90	3.701	61.721	1
s3	178	92	4.438	62.997	1
s4	180	83	8.624	59.256	1
s5	167	85	8.604	50.114	1
s6	170	89	4.362	55.035	1
s7	173	98	8.604	63.555	1
s8	135	40	63.224	12.265	2
s9	120	35	76.957	19.038	2
s10	145	70	35.223	24.051	2
s11	125	50	63.198	5.142	2

The final clustering result is that cluster 1 contains subjects s2, s3, s4, s5, s6 and s7 and cluster 2 contains s1, s8, s9, s10, and s11. The centroid of cluster 1 is $C_1(174.333, 89.5)$, and the centroid of cluster 2 is $C_2(130, 51.2)$. The result clusters are in fact the two clusters shown in Figure 4.1.

4.3.3 Performance of the Basic K-means Method

The basic K-means method is sensitive to the selection of the initial centroids. In other words, different initial centroids may yield different clustering results. Clusters tend to converge to a local optimal solution rather than a global optimal solution. This feature is considered a limitation of the basic K-means method. The problem can be reduced by a modification, known as the 'bisecting K-means method' (see Section 4.3.4).

The time complexity of the basic K-means method is estimated as $O(dKN)$ where d is the number of iterations required for cluster convergence and N is the number of data records in the data set. When the initial centroids are spread uniformly, clusters normally converge quickly and, hence, d is not large. For comprehensibility of the result, the value of K is expected to be much smaller than N. This means that the time complexity for the algorithm is close to the linear degree of magnitude, which is considered an important advantage of the method. The requirement for memory resources is also limited. Besides that for the data set itself, the additional memory requirement is $O(N + K)$ for the cluster tags and the centroids.

4.3.4 Variants on the Basic K-means Method

The K-mode method   This works in the same way as the basic K-means method. Instead of using the mean for each attribute of the centroid vector, the mode of the attribute is used. This method is therefore particularly suitable for data objects with categorical attributes where the concept of mean does not exist or is hard to define.

The K-medoid method   In the basic K-means method, most centroids are virtual data points. This method takes the actual data record that is closest to the virtual mean point as the centroid of a cluster.

Although only a small modification to the basic method, it has been reported that this method produces marginally better results than the basic K-means method.

The bisecting K-means method   This was developed to overcome the limitation that different initial centroids may yield different clustering results. K-means clustering is performed many times in order to find the best (and hopefully the only) result. A large partition (initially the entire population) is selected. Several attempts are made to bisect the large partition into two smaller partitions. The *best bisected partitions* are those with the least amount of intra-cluster variation (see Section 4.5). The best bisected partitions are taken as the resulting clusters for the current iteration. This process is repeated for K − 1 iterations and eventually K clusters are obtained.

4.4   THE AGGLOMERATION CLUSTERING METHOD

Unlike partition-based clustering methods, such as the K-means method, that achieve one level of partitioning of the entire data set, some clustering methods store a history of possible partitionings or groupings in a hierarchy. At the leaf level of the hierarchy, every data object is considered a cluster by itself. At the root level of the hierarchy, all data objects are considered to be members of a single cluster. In between, there exist different layers of possible groupings among objects (see Figure 4.5). The final result of clustering is the selection of an appropriate layer of the hierarchy.

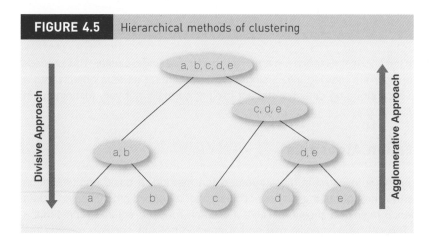

FIGURE 4.5   Hierarchical methods of clustering

To form the hierarchy, there are two different approaches: a divisive approach develops the hierarchy from the root to the leaves by splitting bigger clusters into smaller ones (similar to the bisecting K-means method) and an agglomerative approach develops the hierarchy from the leaf nodes to the root by merging smaller clusters into bigger ones. In general, the agglomerative approach uses fewer resources and is easier to implement than the divisive approach.

4.4.1 Overview

The basic idea of the agglomeration method is simple, as illustrated in Figure 4.6. The process starts by treating each individual data object as a cluster. Then the distance between each possible pair of data objects is measured. The pair of objects that have the shortest distance are merged into a single cluster. Then the distance between the newly merged cluster and all other data objects is

FIGURE 4.6   An illustration of agglomeration clustering

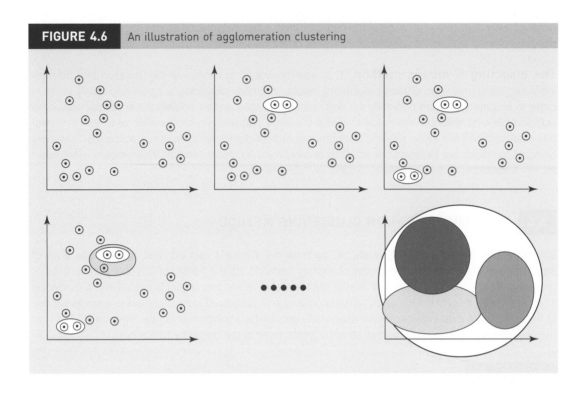

calculated and the pair with the shortest distance are again merged into a single cluster. This process is repeated until all data objects are merged into a single cluster. Merging all data objects into a single cluster is only used as a stopping criterion; the act itself is normally not very meaningful in practical sense.

4.4.2 An Agglomeration Algorithm

To reveal details of computations involved in the agglomeration method, a basic agglomeration algorithm is presented shortly. Throughout the process of clustering, the algorithm maintains a data structure known as a *distance matrix* as shown in Table 4.6. Each row and column represents a data object or a cluster. The cell at a specific row and a specific column position records the distance between a pair of data objects or clusters. The rows and columns of the distance matrix

TABLE 4.6   Distance matrix maintained by agglomeration algorithm

	r_1	r_2	E.	r_N
r_1	$d(r_1, r_1)$	$d(r_1, r_2)$		$d(r_1, r_N)$
r_2	$d(r_2, r_1)$	$d(r_2, r_2)$		$d(r_2, r_N)$
:				
:				
r_N	$d(r_N, r_1)$	$d(r_N, r_2)$		$d(r_N, r_N)$

initially represent individual data objects. As the clustering process continues, two rows and columns are combined into a single row and column to reflect the merging of two data objects or clusters.

The basic agglomeration algorithm is presented in pseudo-code as follows:

```
algorithm AgglomerationBasic (DB: data set, df: distance function): hierarchy
begin
   H := Ø; // empty the hierarchy H initially
   clusterList := record IDs of DB;
   n := |DB|;
   construct distance matrix D with clusterList and df;
   while n > 1 do
      locate entry (i, j) where D(i, j) = min(D(1, 1), D(1, 2), ..., D(n, n));
      record the grouping (i, j) in the hierarchy H;
      modify D by replacing the rows i and j by a new row ij and columns i and j by a
      new column ij;
      calculate the distance between the new entry and each of the existing entries;
      n := n - 1;
   endwhile;
   return(H);
end
```

When implementing the algorithm, some techniques can be exploited to reduce the amount of memory required. For instance, if the dissimilarity function is a metric, then $d(i, i) = 0$ and $d(i, j) = d(j, i)$ and only half of the distance matrix along the diagonal line needs to be maintained. The hierarchy does not need to store all possible clusters but only the groupings of data objects or clusters at each level of the hierarchy for every iteration. The rest of the clusters can be obtained from the previous levels of the hierarchy.

One key step in the agglomeration method is to merge the two clusters with the minimum distance into a larger cluster. How to measure the distance between two clusters becomes an important issue. Given two clusters, the distance between any pair of data points of the two clusters can be obtained. Based on the distances, the following approaches to merging the clusters, also known as *linkage metrics*, can be taken:

■ The *single-link* approach: The distance between the two clusters is defined as the minimum distance, i.e. the distance between the closest pair of points, as illustrated in Figure 4.7(a). The single-link approach is good at discovering non-elliptical clusters. However, it is sensitive to outlier points.

■ The *complete-link* approach: The distance between the two clusters is defined as the maximum distance, i.e. the distance between the two farthest points, as shown in Figure 4.7(b). This approach is less sensitive to outlier points but tends to produce elliptical clusters.

■ The *group-average* approach: The distance between the two clusters is considered as the average of all the distances, as shown in Figure 4.7(c). This approach can be considered as an intermediate approach between the single-link and complete-link approaches. It can be argued that the group average is a reflection of inter-connectivity between the two clusters.

■ The *centroid* approach: The distance between the two clusters is defined as the distance between the two centroids, as illustrated in Figure 4.7(d). This approach is similar to the group-average approach. The difference is in the way 'average' is worked out. In the group-average approach, the final distance is the average of all the pair-wise distances whereas in the centroid approach,

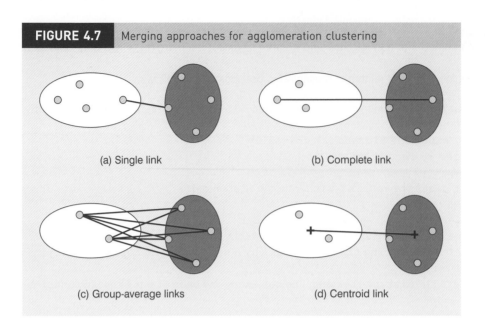

FIGURE 4.7   Merging approaches for agglomeration clustering

(a) Single link

(b) Complete link

(c) Group-average links

(d) Centroid link

TABLE 4.7   Initial distance matrix

Initial matrix	s1	s2	s3	s4	s5	s6	s7	s8	s9	s10
s2	60.42									
s3	61.40	**2.00**								
s4	59.24	7.28	9.22							
s5	48.37	12.08	13.04	13.15						
s6	53.00	8.06	8.54	11.66	5.00					
s7	60.61	9.43	7.81	16.55	14.32	9.49				
s8	23.26	65.95	67.48	62.24	55.22	60.22	69.34			
s9	26.48	79.93	81.32	76.84	68.62	73.59	82.33	15.81		
s10	21.93	38.59	39.66	37.34	26.63	31.40	39.60	31.62	43.01	
s11	11.00	66.40	67.62	64.14	54.67	59.55	67.88	14.14	15.81	28.28

the 'average' points, i.e. the centroids, are worked out first and then the distance between them is measured.

Table 4.1 is again used as an example. Suppose that the Euclidean function upon attributes Body Weight and Body Height is used to measure dissimilarity among data objects. For simplicity, the single-link approach to merging clusters is adopted. The initial 10×10 distance matrix, shown in Table 4.7, records the distance measured between all pairs of data objects, excluding the zero distances from the objects to themselves.

TABLE 4.8	Distance matrix after first iteration								
After first round	s1	s2/s3	s4	s5	s6	s7	s8	s9	s10
s2/s3	60.42								
s4	59.24	7.28							
s5	48.37	12.08	13.15						
s6	53.00	8.06	11.66	**5.00**					
s7	60.61	7.81	16.55	14.32	9.49				
s8	23.26	65.95	62.24	55.22	60.22	69.34			
s9	26.48	79.93	76.84	68.62	73.59	82.33	15.81		
s10	21.93	38.59	37.34	26.63	31.40	39.60	31.62	43.01	
s11	11.00	66.40	64.14	54.67	59.55	67.88	14.14	15.81	28.28

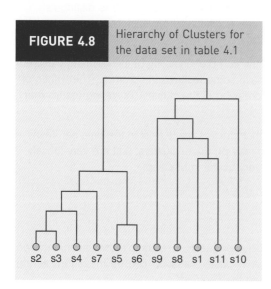

FIGURE 4.8 Hierarchy of Clusters for the data set in table 4.1

s2 s3 s4 s7 s5 s6 s9 s8 s1 s11 s10

As shown in Table 4.7, the minimum distance is that between s2 and s3. The two data objects are grouped into a single cluster, labelled s2/s3. The distances between s2/s3 and all other data objects are updated according to the single-link agglomeration approach. For instance, the distance between s1 and the newly merged cluster s2/s3 is taken as the distance between s1 and s2 because it is less than the distance between s1 and s3. The completely updated distance matrix is shown in Table 4.8, where the highlighted cells indicate the updated distances.

The minimum distance is now that between s5 and s6. The two data objects are merged into a single cluster. The rest of the process is omitted due to space constraints but the complete hierarchy is presented in Figure 4.8.

4.4.3 Performance of the Agglomeration Method

The agglomeration method provides a sequence of possible groupings rather than a single partitioning of the data population space. Unlike the K-means method, there is no need to specify the value of K. All proximities are measured globally, which leads to a globally optimal solution. However, the different levels of cluster groupings cannot be undone. In other words, the groupings are entirely determined by the proximity among objects.

The main drawback of the agglomeration method is its requirement for memory and computational resources. During the clustering process, a proximity matrix as large as N × N must be maintained. If the proximity measure is a metric, the size of the matrix may be reduced to ½N² because of the distance symmetry. The space complexity is therefore $O(\frac{1}{2}N^2)$. Additional memory space $O(N)$ is also required for maintenance of the groupings in the cluster hierarchy. With regards to time, the initial construction of the $N \times N$ proximity matrix requires $O(N^2)$ time. The total number of iterations is $N - 1$. At the ith iteration, two clusters are merged and the proximity matrix is updated. For the merge operation, the matrix of size $(N - i + 1)^2$ needs to be searched for the greatest proximity, and hence the time complexity for the operation is $O((N - i + 1)^2)$. After merging, only $(N - i + 1)$ measures in the proximity matrix need to be updated and hence the time complexity for the updating is $O(N - i + 1)$. The overall time complexity for the basic algorithm is, therefore, $O(N^3)$. With better searching structures for the proximity matrix, the overall time complexity may be improved to $O(N^2 \log N)$. Because of the space and time requirements, the agglomeration method may not be able to deal with very large data sets.

4.5 CLUSTER EVALUATION, VALIDATION AND INTERPRETATION

The problem of cluster detection does not end at obtaining a set of clusters. The results of clustering must be evaluated and interpreted before they become useful information patterns. The issues involved in this 'post-clustering' stage are:

- Cluster quality: This issue is concerned with how good the clusters are and how to distinguish good clusters from bad ones. Good-quality clusters are as different from each other as possible and contain data objects that are as similar as possible.

- Cluster interpretability: This issue is concerned with the comprehensibility of the resulting clusters. Data objects that belong to a specific cluster must have some features in common. The values of those features should assist the explanation or interpretation of the cluster. Clustering results that are difficult to interpret have little practical use.

- Cluster tendency: This issue is concerned with whether clusters really exist in the data set. Many clustering algorithms, such as the K-means method, may produce 'clusters' that are very loosely defined. Such clusters are artificial and may not be very useful in practice.

4.5.1 Cluster Evaluation

Within-cluster variation can be treated as an indicator of cluster quality. It refers to the variation between members and the centroid. Given a cluster C_k, the within-cluster variation can be measured as the average of the squared distances between members and the centroid:

$$wc(C_k) = \frac{1}{|C_k|} \sum_{x \in C_k} d(x, r_k)^2$$

where x is a member and r_k is the centroid of the cluster. Take the clusters in Table 4.5 as an example. Cluster 1 contains subjects s2, s3, s4, s5, s6 and s7, with the centroid C_1 at (174.333, 89.5). Cluster 2 contains subjects s1, s8, s9, s10 and s11, with the centroid C_2 at (130, 51.2). Therefore,

$$wc(\text{Cluster1}) = \frac{1}{6}(d_2(s2, C_1)^2 + d_2(s3, C_1)^2 + d_2(s4, C_1)^2 + d_2(s5, C_1)^2 + d_2(s6, C_1)^2 + d_2(s7, C_1)^2)$$

$$= \frac{1}{6}(13.697 + 19.697 + 74.365 + 74.023 + 19.025 + 74.027) = 45.806$$

and

$$wc(\text{Cluster2}) = \frac{1}{5}(d_2(s1, C_2)^2 + d_2(s8, C_2)^2 + d_2(s9, C_2)^2 + d_2(s10, C_2)^2 + d_2(s11, C_2)^2)$$

$$= \frac{1}{5}(121.040 + 150.440 + 362.440 + 578.440 + 26.440) = 247.760$$

The results above conclude that cluster 1 is better quality than cluster 2 because the within-cluster variation of cluster 1 is lower than that for cluster 2. In other words, members of cluster 1 are much closer to the centroid than their counterparts in cluster 2.

Other measures of within-cluster variations also exist. For instance, instead of measuring the distance from each member to the centroid, distances among members can be measured and added to a total to indicate the within-cluster variation. The overall quality of the resulting clusters can be judged by comparing the distance among objects within clusters against the distance between clusters. As a rough indicator of overall cluster quality, the following ratio may be useful:

$$\frac{BC}{WC}$$

where WC represents the sum of within-cluster variations of all clusters and BC represents the sum of the squared distances between the cluster centroids:

$$BC = \sum_{1 \le j < k \le K} d(r_j, r_k)^2 \text{ and } WC = \sum_{k=1}^{K} wc(C_k)$$

The greater the value of the ratio, the better the quality of the clusters. A value close to 1 indicates a poor clustering result: the distance between clusters is close to the distances within clusters. For the clusters in Table 4.5:

$$BC = d_2(C_1, C_2)^2 = (174.333 - 130)^2 + (89.5 - 51.2)^2 = 3432.305$$

therefore,

$$\frac{BC}{WC} = \frac{3432.305}{45.806 + 247.760} \approx 11.692$$

In some data mining tools such as Weka, the overall quality of clustering is measured for within-cluster variation only, indicating how loosely the clusters are formed. The most used measure for within-cluster variation is the sum of squared errors (SSE), where any amount of variation from the centroid is considered as an amount of *error*. For a data set D and a set of clusters $C = \{C_1, C_2, ..., C_k\}$ with centroids $r_1, r_2, ..., r_k$ respectively, the expression for SSE is given as:

$$SSE(D, C) = \sum_{i=1}^{k} \sum_{x \in C_i} d(x, r_i)^2$$

where d is a distance measure such as the Euclidean distance.

The measure of cluster quality can be used to determine whether another round of clustering is needed. In the K-means method, an outer loop with quality evaluation as the stopping criterion can be added. The loop starts with a small number for K. After K clusters are formed, the quality of the clustering is evaluated with a measure such as SSE. If the quality is not acceptable, the value of K is increased by 1 and another round of clustering is conducted with the new value of K. The process continues until the quality is deemed to be acceptable or we have reached a maximum number of iterations. With the agglomeration method, the concern is to find out which level of the hierarchy is the most appropriate. Therefore, we can start from the root level of the hierarchy and evaluate the quality of the clusters at that level. If the quality is acceptable, the process terminates; otherwise, we move down to the next level in the hierarchy and evaluate cluster quality again. The process continues until the quality is deemed to be acceptable with an appropriate number of clusters or we have reached the leaf level of the hierarchy.

A *scree plot* can be used to highlight where the appropriate number of clusters lies. With the number of clusters as the X coordinate and a quality measure such as SSE as the Y coordinate, a scree plot illustrates the decrease of errors (or improvement of quality) as the number of clusters increases. Figure 4.9 shows the scree plot for a K-means cluster method, with different values of K, applied to the data set in Table 4.1. The SSE values are obtained from Weka. The diagram shows that as the number of clusters increases, the SSE measurements decreases towards zero. However, the greatest reduction occurs when K = 2. After that, although increasing the value of K also reduces the error margin, the reduction is much smaller. This indicates that the appropriate number of clusters is 2.

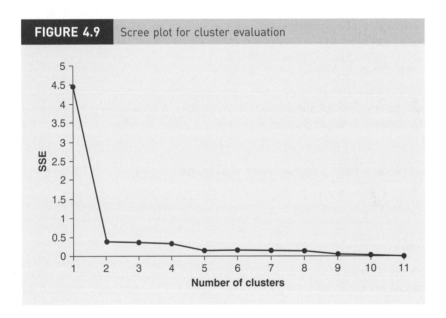

FIGURE 4.9 Scree plot for cluster evaluation

4.5.2 Cluster Tendency Validation

Ideally, cluster tendency is an issue that should be considered at the beginning of a clustering process. It is useful to know whether or not clusters exist before any serious clustering attempt is made. A number of possible methods have been suggested for examining if clusters converge in the given data set. A pilot clustering exercise can be conducted and an overall quality measure, such as BC/WC (mentioned in Section 4.5.1), used to see if the distances between objects within clusters are similar to the distances between clusters, indicating poor convergence. Alternatively, features of the data objects within a cluster can be compared with the features of the whole data set. If there isn't too much difference between each cluster and the whole population, it may well mean that clusters have converged arbitrarily.

A number of statistical measures have been developed for evaluating cluster tendency. A random sample S of n data points is drawn from the data set. At the same time, a randomly generated data set P of n data points is also obtained. For sample S, the distance between each data point p and its nearest neighbour t_p is calculated and summed into a total. Similarly, for the random data set P, the distance between each data point m and its nearest neighbour t_m is also calculated and summed up a total. We can then use Hopkin's statistic to evaluate the cluster tendency. Hopkin's statistic is a ratio defined as:

$$H(P, S) = \frac{\sum\limits_{p,\ t_p \in S} dist(p, t_p)}{\sum\limits_{m,\ t_m \in P} dist(m, t_m) + \sum\limits_{p,\ t_p \in S} dist(p, t_p)}$$

The ratio yields a value close to 0.5 if the sample data points and the randomly generated data points have roughly the same nearest neighbour distances, a strong signal for the data set not having any clusters. If the ratio yields a value close to 1 or 0, then it means there is a cluster tendency in the data set.

Consider the data set in Table 4.1 as a sample of a much larger data set. A random data set P with 11 data points of body weights and body heights within the ranges of the data set in Table 4.1 is also generated (see Table 4.9). The scatter plot of the points generated points is shown in Figure 4.10.

We calculate the distances from each data point to its nearest neighbours using the Euclidean distance function and obtain the following:

$$H = \frac{102.97}{149.34 + 102.97} \approx 0.41$$

TABLE 4.9	A randomly generated data set	
SID	**Height**	**Weight**
r1	156	49
r2	145	66
r3	132	53
r4	158	67
r5	170	42
r6	174	88
r7	177	64
r8	161	78
r9	136	78
r10	139	52
r11	171	70

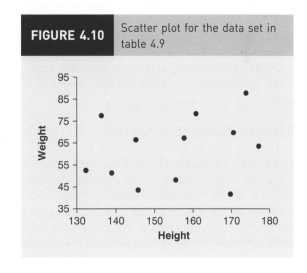

FIGURE 4.10   Scatter plot for the data set in table 4.9

The result indicates that there is a tendency to cluster but that the tendency is quite weak. This example is for illustration only. The small sample size is not realistic, which may in turn have affected the result of the statistic.

4.5.3 Cluster Interpretation

Cluster interpretation, like interpretation of any information pattern discovered from a database, is an important and yet very complex step within the discovery process. Interpretation requires a lot of domain knowledge of the application area and should normally involve domain experts. Generally, data miners can attempt to interpret the meaning of the clusters from the following aspects: within clusters, outside clusters and between clusters.

Within-cluster interpretation This involves summarizing the characteristics of the members of a cluster. The characteristics can be reflected by the distributions of attribute values and therefore should be observed. If necessary, additional summarization of certain attribute values may be added. The focus of understanding is about the commonality of the cluster members. For the data set in Table 4.1, cluster 1 contains members whose body heights are between 167 and 180 centimetres and body weights are between 83 and 98 kilograms. In cluster 2, the body weights and heights of the members are much more diverse.

Outside-cluster interpretation This is meant to discover the abnormality of a small number of data points that stay outside the clusters. These data points are treated as outliers. Understanding them can supplement the understanding of the data points within the clusters. For the data set in Table 4.1, cluster 1 contains members with body heights between 167 and 180 centimetres and body weights between 83 and 98 kilograms. A closer look reveals that two of the six members are somewhat abnormal. Subject s4 is thinner but taller and subject s7 is heavier but shorter. The two subjects may be treated as noise by algorithms such as DBScan (see Chapter 5). Identifying abnormal objects helps the understanding of the norm: body weight increases as height increases for the majority of members of this cluster. Sometimes, our focus of attention is the outlier objects themselves. For instance, fraud detection locates the few data objects that are outside normal boundaries. Some sophisticated clustering algorithms and data mining tools are capable of detecting outlier objects. Weka, for example, has a pre-processing filter to locate outlier objects and instances with extreme values.

Between-cluster interpretation This involves gaining insight into the characteristics of clusters by putting the clusters side by side and comparing the values of important attributes. One specific comparison looks at the distributions of attribute values of each cluster against those of the whole data population. The significant differences between the distributions normally reveal why the cluster is unique. Figure 4.11, for instance, shows the distributions of values for the attributes DURATION and COST, produced by the IBM Intelligent Miner for Data. The shaded bars are for the attribute values of the whole data population whereas the unshaded bars are for the attribute values of the cluster members. The chart shows that, whereas the majority of callers make short and cheap calls, members of cluster 0 (8.03% of all callers) make calls of longer duration that cost much more.

Comparing characteristics of different clusters helps to understand why the clusters are formed. For the data set in Table 4.1, taller and heavier subjects have been grouped in one cluster and lighter and shorter subjects in another. Sometimes, additional attributes can also provide more insight. For instance, one can inspect the values for the attributes Blood Pressure, Habit and Blood Sugar and

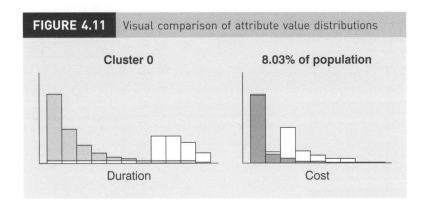

FIGURE 4.11 Visual comparison of attribute value distributions

conclude that members of cluster 2 tend to have normal blood pressure, do not smoke and have low or normal blood-sugar levels; the picture of members of cluster 1 is much less certain. Sometimes, data objects may differ upon clustering attributes but share a degree of similarity upon other attributes; studying those similarities can be useful (see the customer segmentation case study in Section 10.2).

4.6 CLUSTERING USING WEKA

This section demonstrates the general process of using a basic clustering method in Weka. The procedure consists of three stages: selecting attributes, calling a clustering method and collecting results, and visualizing cluster memberships. The data set `iris.arff` is used for its good convergence on clusters.

The selection of clustering attributes is performed on the Preprocess tab. The class attribute is removed from the clustering attribute list so that similarity is measured only upon sepallength, sepalwidth, petallength and petalwidth. It is interesting to observe whether classes of iris flowers correspond to similarities over their descriptive attributes. Figure 4.12 shows the Preprocess tab after the selection of attributes.

Clustering tasks are performed on the Cluster tab. Weka is equipped with a number of clustering solutions. Press the Choose button and select the option SimpleKMeans to apply the basic K-means method with a hybrid distance function based on Euclidean distance. The command for the method and its default parameters are listed in the dialogue box next to the Choose button. Click on the dialogue box to set the *numClusters* parameter, i.e. the value of K, to 3 (because we know that there are three types of iris flower). The random *seed* parameter is left with the default value. Figure 4.13 shows the setting of the parameters and the clustering results in the Cluster output window.

The clustering results include the centroid mean vectors, the standard deviations from the means, the sizes of the clusters, and the evaluation result. Right clicking on the clustering task in the Result list window and selecting the Visualize cluster assignments option brings up a visualization window and shows the assignment of cluster memberships in different colours, as illustrated in Figure 4.14.

You can save the cluster membership for each data object by pressing on the Save button and giving an ARFF file name. The saved file contains an additional column for cluster tags. The assignment of cluster membership to each data object can also be undertaken through the use of the AddCluster filter in the PreProcess tab. Figure 4.15(a) shows the setting of the parameters after the filter is selected and Figure 4.15(b) the creation of the cluster attribute after the filter is applied.

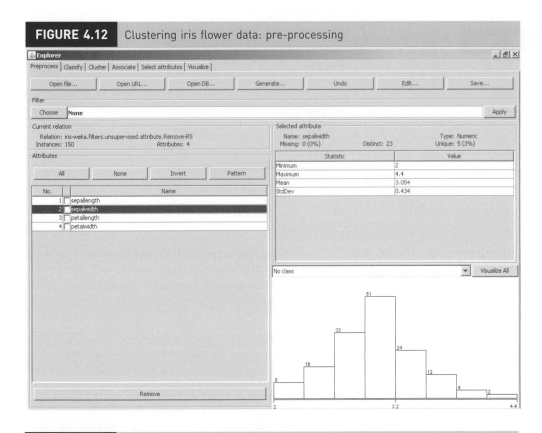

FIGURE 4.12 Clustering iris flower data: pre-processing

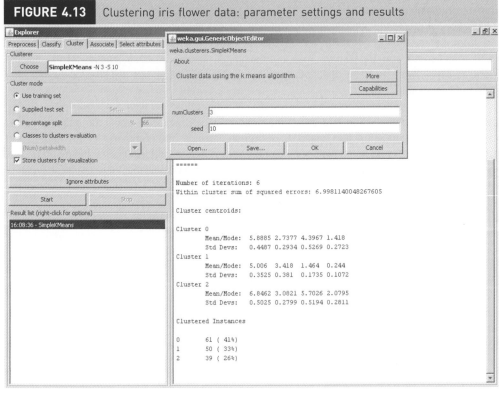

FIGURE 4.13 Clustering iris flower data: parameter settings and results

FIGURE 4.14   Clustering iris flower data: visualizing memberships

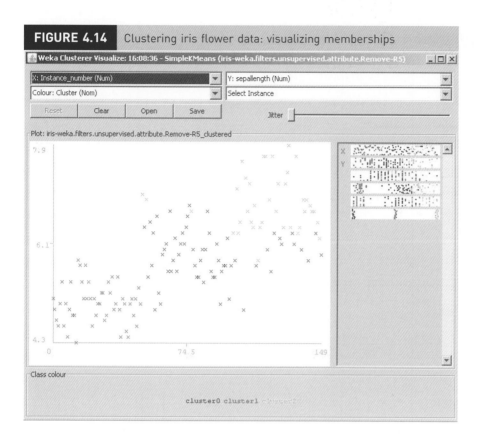

FIGURE 4.15   Clustering iris flower data: assigning cluster memberships

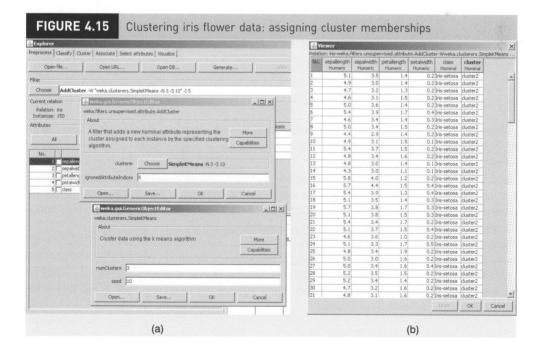

(a)   (b)

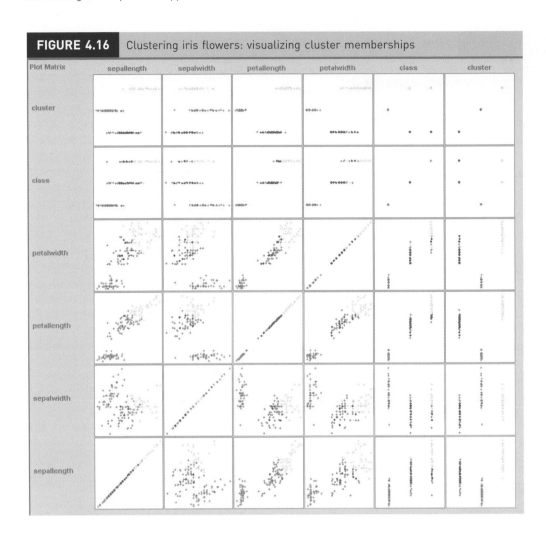

FIGURE 4.16 Clustering iris flowers: visualizing cluster memberships

We have kept the class attribute not for clustering but for reference. It is ignored by the K-means method.

Once membership is assigned, the cluster attribute can be selected as a pseudo-class attribute so that different clusters can be distinguished by different colours in scatter plots on the Visualize tab (Figure 4.16).

The clustering result reveals that there is a strong correspondence between the clusters and the classes of iris flower. All setosa flowers are grouped in one cluster. Out of 50 virginica flowers, 39 are collected into a cluster; the remaining 11 are grouped with the versicolor flowers. Among the descriptive attributes, petal length and petal width are good at separating different types of iris.

For hierarchical clustering, Weka does not provide the basic agglomeration method. Cobweb is an incremental hierarchical clustering method. Using the Cobweb method on the Iris data set with the default parameters yields the result shown in Figure 4.17. The cluster hierarchy can be displayed by selecting the Visualize tree option in the pop-up menu against the clustering task in the Result list window.

FIGURE 4.17   Using Cobweb for clustering

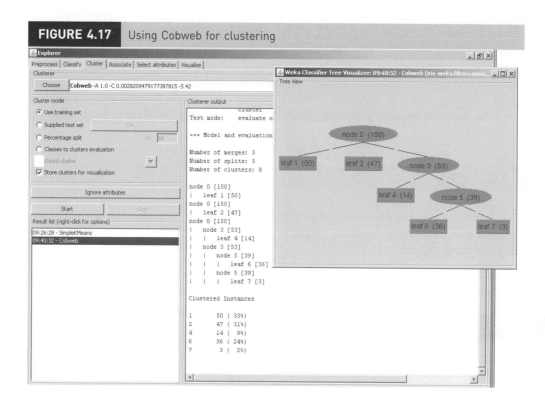

4.7   SUMMARY

This chapter has introduced the basic concepts about clustering. Three fundamental elements of clustering, i.e. a sensible proximity measure, an effective and efficient clustering algorithm and a goodness-of-fit evaluation function, were presented. The chapter also listed an ideal set of requirements for good clustering solutions.

One of the main focal points of the chapter is proximity measurement. A proximity measure function, either a similarity function or a dissimilarity function, defines the closeness of two given data objects in terms of combinations of value differences of attributes. A number of generic measures have been described and their strengths and weaknesses discussed. The chapter also presented a hybrid distance function for heterogeneous data types based on the principle of ratio of mismatched features. How to define closeness is often an issue specific to an application domain. Domain-dependent proximity measures are further discussed in Chapter 5.

Clustering solutions can be classified into hierarchical and non-hierarchical partition-based categories. This chapter presented two basic clustering methods, one partition-based (the K-means method) and one hierarchical (the agglomeration method). Each method is described in terms of its principal ideas, an algorithm and examples. Two variants of the basic K-means method, the K-mode and the K-medoid methods, were introduced. For the agglomeration method, the chapter described four different approaches to measuring the distance between clusters, and the consequent merging mechanisms.

The chapter also described basic concepts of cluster evaluation in terms of cluster quality, cluster tendency and interpretability. Good clustering results require high intra-cluster similarity and maximal inter-cluster distance. The chapter introduced the ratio of inter-cluster measure against intra-cluster measure and the SSE measure for cluster quality. The quality measure can also be used to evaluate cluster tendency. An alternative measure of cluster tendency, Hopkin's statistic, was also introduced. Cluster interpretation assists the understanding of clustering results.

The chapter ended with a demonstration of the use of Weka for clustering. The process includes selection of clustering attributes, selection of cluster method and setting of parameters, assigning cluster memberships and visualizing clusters. We demonstrated the whole process in Weka using the basic K-means method.

4

EXERCISES

1 Discuss the three essential elements of a typical clustering solution. In the context of segmenting customers according to their shopping behaviours, describe the roles that each element plays in such a clustering process.

2 For the data set in Table 4.10, calculate the dissimilarity between any two data records using the Manhattan, Euclidean and Chebyshev metrics.

TABLE 4.10 Data for Exercises 2 and 10

RegNo	Age	Body Weight (kg)	Body Height (cm)
b1	20	65	178
b2	22	70	179
b3	32	75	174
b4	18	68	200
b5	25	60	168
b6	20	67	172
b7	33	80	185
b8	45	90	175
b9	21	62	165

3 In Figure 4.3(a), among three rectangles, b is considered more similar to a than c despite the fact that a is much bigger than c in terms of area. Use the Euclidean distance function to calculate the distances $d_2(b, a)$ and $d_2(b, c)$. Compare the distance measurements with those produced by the cosine distance function. What can you conclude from the comparison?

4 For the data set in Table 4.11, calculate the distance between any two data records using the ratio of mismatched features (RMF) as the distance function.

5 Table 4.12 records the number of house sales and the total revenue generated by branches of an estate agency chain.

   (a) Use the table as an example to discuss the necessity of attribute scaling in any proximity measurement for clustering purposes.

TABLE 4.11	Data for Exercise 4				
Body Weight	Body Height	Blood Pressure	Blood Sugar	Habit	Class
heavy	short	high	3	smoker	P
heavy	short	high	1	nonsmoker	P
normal	tall	normal	3	nonsmoker	N
heavy	tall	normal	2	smoker	N
low	medium	normal	2	nonsmoker	N
low	tall	normal	1	nonsmoker	P
normal	normal	high	3	smoker	P
low	short	high	2	smoker	P
heavy	tall	high	2	nonsmoker	P
low	medium	normal	3	smoker	P
heavy	medium	normal	3	nonsmoker	N

TABLE 4.12	Data for Exercises 5 and 6	
BranchNo	Total Sales Quantity	Total Sales Value
b1	29	£5,500,000
b2	10	£5,000,000
b3	29	£5,000,000
b4	12	£890,000
b5	20	£2,500,000
b6	20	£3,200,000
b7	15	£678,000
b8	29	£5,200,000
b9	30	£5,300,000
b1	29	£5,500,000
b2	10	£5,000,000

(b) Normalize the values of the attributes Total Sales Quantity and Total Sales Value into [0, 1] using the division-by-range method.

(c) Standardize the attribute values using the z-score transformation method.

6 Use the normalized version of Table 4.12 to illustrate the working of the K-means method assuming that K = 3 and b4, b6 and b9 are randomly selected as the initial centroids. Use either the Manhattan or the Euclidean distance function.

7 This exercise is about variants on the basic K-means method.

   (a) Use the steps of the answer for Exercise 6 to illustrate the working of the K-medoid method.

   (b) Use the data set in Table 4.11 to illustrate the working of the K-mode method.

   (c) Use the data set in Table 4.1 to illustrate the working of the bisecting K-means method.

8 Use the WC measure mentioned in Section 4.5.1 to evaluate the quality of each resulting cluster in Exercise 6. Which clusters have better quality than the others?

9 In the K-means algorithm, an alternative termination condition for the clustering process is proposed as follows. Instead of checking whether there are any membership changes, the distances between the existing centroids and their newly created counterparts are calculated and tested. If all the distances are close to zero, it is concluded that there are no longer membership changes. Discuss.

10 During the process of clustering the data set in Table 4.10 using the agglomeration method, a cluster containing b4 and b7 and another cluster containing b5 and b6 are formed. If the Euclidean distance function is used, demonstrate how to measure the distance between the two clusters using the single-link, complete-link, group-average link and centroid link merging strategies.

11 Practise clustering in Weka by using the Cobweb method over the `iris.arff` data set without the class attribute. Observe the output of the method. Pay particular attention to the hierarchy of clusters.

12 In Weka, use the SimpleKMeans method with K = 2, 3, 4 and 5 to cluster the `iris.arff` data set
without the class attribute. Collect the SSE measurements and plot them in a scree plot to show the relationship between the number of clusters and the cluster quality measures.

BIBLIOGRAPHICAL NOTES

Cluster detection has been extensively researched since the 1960s. Early surveys of basic clustering methods include the work by Hartigan (1975). Because of its wide appeal in various areas of application, the subject remains an active area of research and continues to attract interest. More recent surveys of clustering and clustering techniques include Berkhin (2002) and Jain *et al.* (1999). Current research activities concentrate on application-specific clustering in terms of proximity measures, clustering methods and result evaluation.

It is important to appreciate the three essential elements of a clustering solution. This has been echoed by other texts (Han and Kamber 2001; Tan *et al.* 2006). Clustering algorithms are sometimes presented in such a way that a quality evaluation function is treated as part of the termination condition of the clustering process. However, we feel that separating a termination condition based on membership assignments from an evaluation of the cluster quality makes the clustering process clearer. At the same time, it gives a common framework where most (if not all) clustering solutions can be described and compared.

Proximity is measured in a variety of ways. It can be measured according to some degree of 'physical closeness' of data objects or common functional behaviours of the objects, or even some combined forms. The coverage of the proximity measures in this chapter comes from a number of sources in the literature (Han and Kamber 2001; Tan *et al.* 2006). Various distance functions and heterogeneous distance functions are surveyed in an article by Wilson and Martinez (1997). The topic of proximity measures is constantly evolving.

The basic K-means method of clustering was first reported in MacQueen (1967) and later summarized by Hartigan (1975). It has been presented in different styles in numerous texts since. The hierarchical clustering methods are categorized into agglomerative (bottom up) and divisive (top down) in Jain and Dubes (1988) and Kaufman and Rousseeuw (1990). Cluster validity and quality have been discussed in depth in Jain *et al.* (1999) and a range of cluster quality measures are summarized in Berkhin (2002).

CHAPTER 5

Other techniques for cluster detection

LEARNING OBJECTIVES

To appreciate the limitations of basic clustering methods

To gain a broad understanding of the principles of other clustering methods

To understand the principles of density-based clustering and the DBSCAN algorithm

To understand the principles of graph-based clustering and the CHAMELEON algorithm

To understand the principles of mixture model clustering and the EM method

To understand the principles of subspace clustering and the CLIQUE method

To deepen understanding of measuring proximity of data objects

To experience the use of advanced clustering methods in Weka

To appreciate issues regarding clustering applications

Chapter 4 introduced two basic clustering methods. Although the K-means and the agglomeration methods are good for simplicity of implementation, both have severe limitations. This chapter investigates those limitations and studies the principles of clustering algorithms that are designed to overcome them. Some advanced clustering algorithms that are available in Weka are demonstrated.

Clustering has moved from generic groupings of data records to clustering of more complex data objects such as visual images, text documents, sequential signals, biological pathways, etc. The generic proximity measures introduced in Chapter 4 may not be effective in capturing the true proximity of those types of real-life data. This chapter considers some other proximity measures and their effective use.

Clustering has been widely used in different areas of application from text indexing to facial feature extraction and from customer segmentation to identification of living cells. Clustering is an area of extensive research and many algorithms have been developed. This chapter, therefore, also serves as a broad overview of different categories of clustering algorithm.

5.1   LIMITATIONS OF BASIC CLUSTERING METHODS

Clustering is about grouping data objects. The characteristics of data objects must be considered if the grouping is to be meaningful. The basic clustering algorithms described in Chapter 4 give some consideration to characteristics of data such as data types, data value distribution, data value importance, attribute importance, sensibility of different proximity measures, etc. However, not all data characteristics have been taken into consideration and very little attention has been given to the features of the resulting clusters. Between the K-means method and the agglomeration method, the former appears to have more problems than the latter.

5.1.1 Limitations of the K-means Method

The K-means method does not consider the problem posed by the presence of outlier data objects. As indicated in Figure 5.1(a), the centroid of one of the three clusters, marked as +, is very much influenced

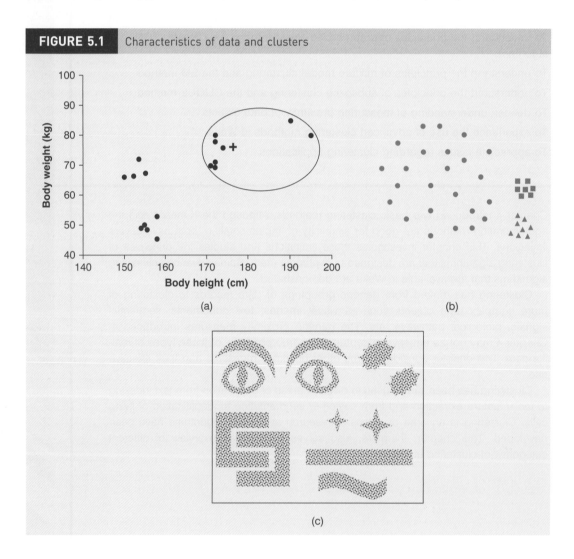

FIGURE 5.1   Characteristics of data and clusters

by the presence of two outlier objects. The problem could be dealt with either by identifying and eliminating the outliers at the pre-processing stage or by finding a better value for K at the post-processing stage. However, identifying outliers itself is not an easy task. Increasing the value of K blindly may lead to undesirable divisions of a natural cluster.

The K-means method often fails to detect clusters of significantly different sizes. Figure 5.1(b) shows two small clusters next to a relatively large cluster. The K-means method tends to divide the large cluster into partitions and merge the small clusters into some of the partitions, resulting in clusters of similar sizes. The cause of the problem is that some data points are closer to the centre of a nearby small cluster than to the centre of their own cluster. This means that the quality and meaningfulness of the clusters are affected. This situation worsens when small, dense clusters are next to a larger, sparser cluster.

The K-means method and the complete-link agglomeration method produce clusters of ellipsoidal convex shapes. However, real-life clusters can be of various shapes. Figure 5.1(c) illustrates a few possible shapes of clusters that may exist in real-life data. For instance, human eyes can be considered as an oval shape, but the eyebrow appears as a concave shape. Virus cells normally have spikes and two mechanical parts may be placed in an interlocked position. A cluster may take the form of a long bar or a thick curve. The K-means method is incapable of identifying clusters of such shapes correctly without breaking them into a number of smaller sub-clusters. This is because of the repeated distance measures to the centres of the clusters. Indeed, the K-means method divides any given data set into K convex regions, whatever value K takes.

5.1.2 Limitations of the Agglomeration Method

The agglomeration method has fewer limitations than the K-means method but they are still major. Although the single-link agglomeration is capable of identifying clusters of arbitrary shapes, the complete-link and centroid-link agglomerations still produce clusters of convex shapes. While the single-link agglomeration can detect clusters of different sizes, the complete-link and centroid-link agglomerations normally cannot. Although the group-average and centroid-link agglomerations are resilient to local noises and artefacts, the single-link and complete-link agglomerations are easily affected by them.

Some researchers have realized two further limitations of the agglomerative methods. They give little consideration to the nature of existing clusters in terms of shape, density and size and they emphasize either interconnectivity or closeness, but not both. These limitations lead to inappropriate decisions over which clusters to merge during the agglomeration process.

Figure 5.2 shows clusters with different natures. In Figure 5.2(a), two pairs of clusters have different densities. If the single-link scheme is used, clusters A and B are merged because the distance between the two closest points for A and B is shorter than that for clusters C and D. However, the resulting cluster contains two clearly separated dense areas. In other words, the merging strategy gives no consideration to the density and homogeneity of the original clusters before merging. On the other hand, distances between the bordering points of C and D are similar to the distances between any points within the two clusters. The resulting cluster after merging C and D has similar features to the two clusters before the merge and, therefore, it is more natural and desirable to merge clusters C and D.

For the clusters in Figure 5.2(b), the group-average scheme merges clusters A and B rather than A and C (the better merge) because it considers interconnectivity between clusters not closeness. Figure 5.2(c) shows two pairs of clusters of similar density but different shapes. The single-link scheme merges clusters A and B instead of C and D. This is because the scheme only considers closeness rather than interconnectivity between two clusters. However, in this case, merging C and D is a better decision because the resulting cluster has connections similar to C and D before merging.

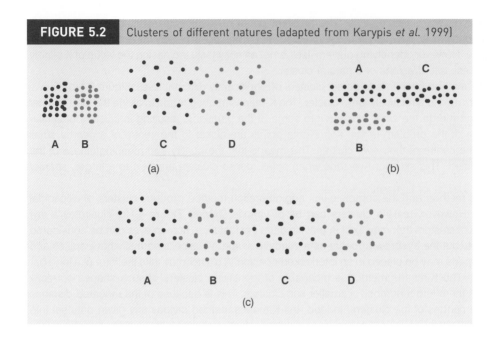

FIGURE 5.2   Clusters of different natures (adapted from Karypis *et al.* 1999)

As well as the limitations mentioned above, the most prohibitive factor for the agglomerative methods is the lack of scalability to cope with large data sets because of the time and space requirements of the methods.

In summary, basic clustering algorithms are insufficient to discover arbitrarily shaped clusters of different sizes and densities without distortion by the presence of noise. Advanced clustering methods are meant to overcome all or some of these limitations.

5.2   OVERVIEW OF OTHER CLUSTERING METHODS

Against the backdrop of the limitations of the basic methods, a large number of more sophisticated clustering methods have been developed. Among them are generic methods that can be used across different application domains and specific methods that are primarily designed for a particular type of application data. There exist different ways of categorizing clustering algorithms in the literature. In general, clustering solutions are divided into *hierarchical* methods that discover sub-clusters and clusters within clusters and *non-hierarchical* methods that discover only one set of disjoint clusters. This categorization is obviously too broad. In this section, the clustering methods are categorized according to their clustering concepts.

■ *Prototype-based* methods form groups of data objects as prototype clusters and modify them throughout the clustering process. Typical methods of this category include partition-based methods, such as the K-means method and its variants, fuzzy clustering methods, such as the fuzzy C-means method, and relationship clustering methods, such as the self-organizing map method.

■ *Density-based* methods use a density function to measure the density of either a region in the multidimensional space of the data set or a neighbourhood of a data point. Clusters are naturally areas where there is a high concentration of data points. Methods of this category include centre-based density clustering methods, such as DBSCAN, subspace clustering methods, such as CLIQUE, and transformation clustering methods, such as WaveCluster.

- *Graph-based* methods consider a given data set as a graph of vertices and links. The vertices represent the individual data points and the links represent the distance or closeness between data points. Clusters are then sub-graphs of vertices where the values attached to the links reflect short distances or high closeness. Typical methods of this category include the minimum spanning tree (MST) method, the optimal partitioning method and the CHAMELEON method.

- *Model-based* methods aim to discover hidden statistical models that best fit the given data set. The model describes the data clusters and probabilistic memberships of data objects to the clusters. One typical method is the expectation-maximization (EM) method, sometimes also known as the Gaussian mixture model (GMM) method when the statistic model is represented in terms of a number of Gaussian distributions.

Because of the sheer number of them, it is not realistic to describe all the known clustering methods or even all those mentioned earlier. This chapter therefore concentrates on one method from each category: the DBSCAN for density-based methods, CHAMELEON for graph-based methods, and EM for model-based methods. We omit the prototype-based category because the K-means method is a typical method for that category and it is covered in Chapter 4. The chapter also presents the CLIQUE algorithm as a typical example for subspace clustering.

5.3 DENSITY-BASED CLUSTERING METHOD: DBSCAN

5.3.1 Overview

DBSCAN is a density-based clustering method. By considering the data objects in a data set as points in a multidimensional space, the method uses a notion of density as the interpretation of object proximity: dense areas where many data points are close to the area centres are naturally clusters. Areas outside clusters are sparse and may contain outlier and noise objects. Although the original algorithm was designed for spatial databases, the principle applies to other types of data.

In DBSCAN, the definition of density is centre-based, i.e. the density of an area is estimated by counting the number of points within a certain radius, known as *Eps*, from the centre point of the area. The *Eps neighbourhood* of a point t, denoted by $N_{Eps}(t)$, refers to a set of points where the distance from each of the points to point t is less than or equal to the value of Eps. With respect to a given Eps, every data point within a given data set can be categorized as one of the following three types:

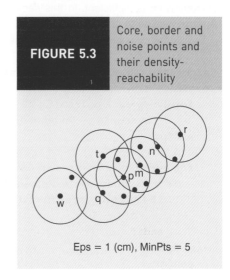

FIGURE 5.3 Core, border and noise points and their density-reachability

- *Core point*: A data point for which the number of neighbouring points within the Eps neighbourhood is greater than or equal to a given minimum threshold known as the *MinPts*. The distance between points is measured with a proximity function. In Figure 5.3, for instance, points p, m and n are core points with respect to the given values of MinPts and Eps whereas points q, w, t, and r are not. Core points normally exist in the interior part of a cluster.

- *Border point:* A point for which the number of neighbouring points within its own Eps neighbourhood is less than that specified by MinPts, but the point

Eps = 1 (cm), MinPts = 5

itself is among the neighbouring points within the Eps neighbourhood of a core point. Border points are located near the border of a cluster. In Figure 5.3, for example, q, r and t are border points with respect to the given minPts and Eps.

■ *Noise Point:* Neither a core point nor a border point, a noise point is outside the Eps neighbourhood of any core point and does not have sufficient neighbouring points within its own Eps neighbourhood. Noise points are not taken into any meaningful cluster. For a complete solution, all noise points can be artificially collected into a special noise group. As illustrated in Figure 5.3, point w is a noise point.

Some properties of the different types of points need to be explained. Any point *a* is said to be *directly density-reachable* from a core point *b* with respect to a given Eps and MinPts if *a* is within the Eps neighbourhood of *b*. More generally, point *a* is *density-reachable* from point *b* with respect to Eps and MinPts if there is a sequence of points *a*, p_2, p_3, ..., p_{n-1}, *b* such that p_{i+1} is directly density-reachable from p_i where $2 \leq i < n-1$. Any point *a* is *density-connected* to a point *b* with respect to Eps and MinPts if there is a core point *c* such that both *a* and *b* are density-reachable from *c*. In Figure 5.3, for instance, point q is directly density-reachable from core point p. Point r is density-reachable from point p via core points m and n. Points q, t and r are density-connected.

Given the understanding of density notions mentioned above, a cluster becomes a maximal set of density-connected points. The framework of the DBSCAN solution can be outlined as follows:

1   The entire data set is scanned record by record and each data record is marked as a core, border or noise point.

2   All noise points are assigned as members of the noise cluster.

3   All core points are scanned and core points that are directly density-reachable with each other are assigned to a separate cluster.

4   All border points are scanned and all density-connected border points are assigned to the cluster of their core point.

5.3.2 The DBSCAN Algorithm

The steps outlined in the previous section require more detailed operations. A direct implementation of the framework is inefficient. In this section, we present a more precise algorithm and discuss some issues in relation to its performance.

The algorithm is presented here in pseudo-code:

```
algorithm DBSCAN(var DB: data set, Eps : real, MinPts: integer)
begin
    for every data point d in DB do
        d.ClusterId := Undefined;
    endfor;
    cid := 0;
    for every data point d in DB do
        if d.ClusterId = Undefined then
            if ExpendCluster(DB, d, cid, Eps, MinPts) then
                cid := cid + 1;
            endif;
        endif;
    endfor;
end;
```

```
boolean ExpendCluster(var DB: data set, Point: data record,
                      ClusterId: integer, Eps: real, MinPts: integer)
begin
   SeedSet := {p | p ∈ DB and dist(p, Point) ≤ Eps};
   if |SeedSet| < MinPts then // Point can be noise or border point
      Point.ClusterId := Noise;
      return (False);
   else // Point is a core point
      for every point t in Seedset do
            t.ClusterId := ClusterId;
      endfor;
      delete Point from Seedset;
      while |SeedSet| > 0 do
         locate a point p in SeedSet;
         Result := {q | q ∈ DB and dist(q, p) ≤ Eps};
         If |Results| ≥ MinPts then
            for every point r in Result do
               if (r.ClusterId = Undefined) or (r.ClusterId = Noise) then
                  if (r.ClusterId = Undefined) then
                     add r into SeedSet
                  endif
                  r.ClusterId := ClusterId;
               endif
            endfor;
         endif
         delete p from SeedSet
      endwhile;
      return True;
   endif
end;
```

5

In the algorithm, it is assumed that the parameter DB represents the input data set, that cluster identifiers are integers, 0, 1, 2, ..., k including special labels *Undefined* and *Noise*, and that a distance function *dist* is already defined. The process starts with any data point in a given data set. If the point does not belong to a cluster, all density-reachable points from this point are collected first. If the point is a core point, then a cluster is formed and all the density-reachable points and the selected point are assigned a unique cluster identifier. If the chosen point is a border point, it does nothing, selects another point from the data set and continues the process. If the chosen point is a noise point, it is labelled as noise and the process continues. The process terminates when all data points either belong to a cluster or are labelled as noise.

All data points in DB are initially assigned as Undefined. In the main loop of the algorithm, the Boolean function ExpendCluster is called to assign the current cluster identifier to the members of the cluster involving the current point before the cluster identifier changes to the next one. Therefore, besides returning true or false, the function has side effects on the input parameter DB, assigning membership of the cluster to a number of data points. When the function is called again, only the points with Undefined membership are considered.

In the ExpendCluster function, the neighbours of a given point within the given Eps are collected. If the number of neighbours is less than the MinPts threshold, the given point is either a noise point or a border point, but it is initially marked as Noise. If the number of neighbours is greater than or equal to the MinPts threshold, the given point is a core point and all its directly density-reachable points are labelled with the same cluster identity. The function then retrieves those points and grows the seed set to include the points that are density-reachable from a point within the seed set. Those further points have the same cluster identity as those in the seed set. Once classified, the points are removed from the seed set. The iterative process ends when the seed set is empty. The border points that were marked as Noise may change their cluster identifiers, if they are density-reachable by other points.

To illustrate the working of the algorithm, we use the data set presented in Table 5.1. The normalized height and weight are calculated using the division-by-range method. For this example, we use the Euclidean distance function. The distance matrix is presented in Table 5.2.

TABLE 5.1	Subject data for analysis with DBSCAN			
SubjectID	Height (cm)	Weight (kg)	Normalized Height (cm)	Normalized Weight (kg)
s1	125	52.7	0.06	0.11
s2	178	90	1.00	0.95
s3	178	92	1.00	1.00
s4	176.4	87.5	0.97	0.90
s5	173.2	85	0.91	0.84
s6	173.2	89	0.91	0.93
s7	170.5	91.7	0.87	0.99
s8	128.4	48.2	0.12	0.01
s9	121.9	47.6	0.00	0.00
s10	127.2	70	0.09	0.50
s11	125	50	0.06	0.05

TABLE 5.2	Distance matrix for data in Table 5.1									
	s1	s2	s3	s4	s5	s6	s7	s8	s9	s10	s11
s1	0.000										
s2	1.264	0.000									
s3	1.295	0.045	0.000								
s4	1.206	0.063	0.105	0.000							
s5	1.126	0.141	0.179	0.080	0.000						
s6	1.186	0.088	0.109	0.066	0.090	0.000					
s7	1.196	0.139	0.134	0.141	0.158	0.078	0.000				
s8	0.118	1.292	1.325	1.231	1.151	1.217	1.234	0.000			
s9	0.127	1.383	1.414	1.323	1.243	1.306	1.318	0.117	0.000		
s10	0.392	1.011	1.032	0.962	0.887	0.925	0.914	0.491	0.513	0.000	
s11	0.061	1.305	1.337	1.246	1.166	1.229	1.241	0.073	0.077	0.452	0.000

Suppose that Eps = 0.08 and MinPts = 3. When the number of points is compared with the MinPts parameter, the centre point itself is included. Initially, all data points are marked as undefined. The algorithm starts with subject s1. Since the only data point within the Eps neighbourhood is s11, s1 is marked as Noise. Point s2 is a core point with s3 and s4 in the Eps neighbourhood. All three points are marked with cluster identifier 0; s3 and s4 are added into the seed set and s2 is removed from the set. Since the seed set is not empty, the algorithm tries to find all density-reachable points of s3 and s4. Point s3 only has s2 as its density-reachable point and therefore s3 is removed from the seed set. Point s4 is a core point with s2, s5 and s6 in its Eps neighbourhood. The membership of s2 is already decided and so it is ignored. Both s5 and s6 are undefined; they are marked with cluster identifier 0 and added to the seed set; s4 is removed from the seed set.

Now the seed set contains s5 and s6 and the algorithm looks for their density-reachable points. Point s5 only has s4 within its Eps neighbourhood and is removed from the seed set. Point s6 is a core point with s4 and s7 as Eps neighbours. Point s4 is already assigned, s7 is marked with cluster identity 0 and is added to the seed. Point s6 is removed from the seed set. Point s7 is the only element in the seed set. Since it only has s6 as its Eps neighbour, it is removed from the seed set and by now the seed set becomes empty.

So far, points s2, ..., s7 are all marked with cluster identifier 0. The cluster identifier now changes to 1. Points s8, s9 and s10 all have insufficient Eps neighbours and are marked as Noise. Point s11 is a core point with s1, s8 and s9 as its Eps neighbours. All four points are stored in the seed set and marked with the cluster identifier 1. Points s1, s8 and s9 are border points that have changed their identifiers. Point s11 is removed from the seed set. Since s1, s8 and s9 all have insufficient Eps neighbours, they are removed from the seed set.

The final result of the DBSCAN clustering is that points s2, s3, s4, s5, s6 and s7 are members of cluster 0 and points s1, s8, s9 and s11 are members of cluster 1. Point s10 remains as a noise point. This result is confirmed by the scatter plot of the original data set in Figure 5.4.

The efficiency of the DBSCAN algorithm is comparable to that of sorting algorithms, which are generally considered to be efficient. Without using any sophisticated search structures, the algorithm has a reported time complexity of $O(N^2)$. If an efficient index structure, such as R*-tree, is used to support region queries for obtaining a seed set and result set in the algorithm, the overall time complexity can be improved further to O(NlogN). This estimate does not include the cost of measuring proximity between data objects, which is determined by the dimensionality of the data. The algorithm does not provide a complete solution: some data records, such as noise objects, do not belong a specific cluster.

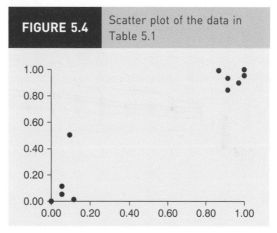

FIGURE 5.4 Scatter plot of the data in Table 5.1

5.3.3 DBSCAN Parameters

The DBSCAN algorithm requires two crucial parameters: the density threshold MinPts and the Eps value. The two parameters are global constants applicable to all clusters. So far no good solutions to automatically determine the values for the two parameters have been reported. The setting of the parameters is left for the user. A heuristic method based on the concept of *thinnest* or least dense cluster has been proposed and is used at the data exploration stage of data mining. Generally, among *k* nearest neighbours of a point, the distance between the point and the *k*th nearest neighbour should not be large if the points belong to the same cluster. However, if either the *k*th nearest neighbour of the point or the point itself is a noise point, the distance is expected to be large. Based on this observation, the following process is repeated to determine the desirable values for the parameters:

1 Choose a fairly small value for *k*.

2 Calculate distances from each data point to its *k* nearest neighbours.

3 Plot the sorted distance to the *k*th neighbour of each data point.

4 Select the value at which there is a sharp increase as the Eps value and the value of *k* as the minPts value.

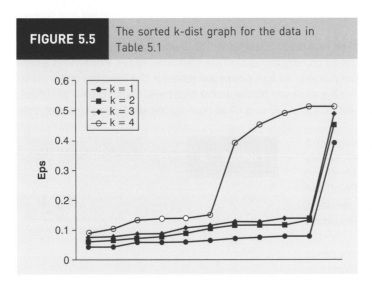

FIGURE 5.5 The sorted k-dist graph for the data in Table 5.1

Figure 5.5 shows the sorted distances between the data points and their *k*th nearest neighbours for the data set given in Table 5.1, when *k* = 1, 2, 3 and 4 respectively. Points to the left of the sharp turn are members of clusters and points to the right of the sharp turn are noise points. From Figure 5.5, we can take the following (Eps, MinPts) pairs without affecting the overall result of clustering: (0.08, 1), (0.141,2), and (0.141, 3). Setting Eps = 0.151 and MinPts = 4 turns too many points into noise. Be aware that the settings are prepared for the least dense clusters that are acceptable as a result.

5.3.4 Strengths and Weaknesses of DBSCAN

The DBSCAN solution uses a centre-based density measure to determine clusters and, hence, it is naturally resistant to noise in the given data set. The method can identify noise data objects that may be of interest for other data mining objectives such as anomaly analysis. Although the solution uses a centre-based proximity measurement scheme, it can still identify clusters of various shapes and sizes when the Eps and MinPts parameters are set properly (see Section 5.8.1 for an example).

The solution also has weaknesses. One major weakness is the fact that there is no automatic way of determining the optimal values for Eps and MinPts. Finding the ideal values for Eps and MinPts may not be easy if the data mining tool does not provide support for the heuristic method mentioned in Section 5.3.3. Another major weakness is the use of global constants for Eps and MinPts. This weakness sometimes causes the solution not to be able to find cluster densities that vary widely from cluster to cluster. Also, the centre-based density measure becomes problematic for high-dimensionality data sets (we return to this issue in Section 5.7).

5.4 GRAPH-BASED CLUSTERING METHOD: CHAMELEON

5.4.1 Overview

CHAMELEON is a graph-based hierarchical clustering algorithm using the principle of dynamic modelling. It uses a combined measure of interconnectivity and closeness to calculate the similarity between clusters and accordingly determine which two clusters are to be merged into a bigger cluster in an agglomeration step. The rationale behind using the combination of two proximity measures is that the merged cluster should have similar characteristics to those of the original two clusters. Proximity based on the balance of interconnectivity and closeness can achieve this objective and overcomes the limitations explained in Section 5.1.

The algorithm is also set to overcome the limitation of the fixed global perception about clusters found in DBSCAN, which uses the same Eps and MinPts for all clusters regardless of their local density variation. In CHAMELEON, however, interconnectivity and closeness of the merged cluster are relative to the internal interconnectivity and closeness of the data points in the original clusters.

Like DBSCAN, the CHAMELEON algorithm is primarily designed for spatial data, but can be applied to data of other applications. The algorithm consists of three major steps in sequence:

1 *Construction:* A *k*-nearest neighbour sparse graph is constructed. The vertices of the graph represent the data points in the data set and the links of the graph represent the proximity between data points. A weight is attached to a link that reflects the proximity between the two points.

2 *Segmentation:* The sparse graph is partitioned into a large number of separate sub-graphs. Each of the sub-graphs forms an initial sub-cluster whose internal interconnectivity and closeness can be measured.

3 *Agglomeration:* The sub-clusters are merged to form bigger clusters. Which sub-clusters should be merged is determined by the measurement of relative interconnectivity and closeness of the sub-clusters. The process continues as long as both the relative interconnectivity and closeness measurements are not below a given threshold.

5.4.2 The CHAMELEON Algorithm

It is necessary to further explain the steps of the CHAMELEON algorithm listed above. The sparse graph construction is a straightforward process. First, the amount of similarity between data points is measured with a chosen similarity function, independent of the CHAMELEON algorithm. For spatial data, the Euclidean distance function is normally used. A similarity matrix that holds the amount of measurement between any pair of data points is created as a result. Then for every data point (vertex), a link to each of its *k* nearest neighbours (NN) is generated. The amount of similarity measurement is assigned to the corresponding link as weight. The value of *k* is directly related to the sparseness of the graph. Also according to the value of k, the sparse graph can be connected or disconnected. Using a sparse graph rather than a fully connected graph saves computation for the algorithm. Figure 5.6 shows examples of nearest neighbour sparse graphs among a set of data points.

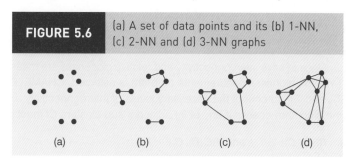

FIGURE 5.6 (a) A set of data points and its (b) 1-NN, (c) 2-NN and (d) 3-NN graphs

(a)   (b)   (c)   (d)

The segmentation step uses an efficient graph-partitioning algorithm known as the *hMETIS* algorithm to partition the sparse graph into a set of sub-graphs. The process starts as if all data points are in the same cluster. It then repeatedly selects among all sub-clusters the largest sub-cluster to partition (similar to the bisecting K-means method). Two parameters control the partitioning process. *Edge cut* refers to the sum of the weights attached to the links that straddle the two resulting partitions. In applying the hMETIS algorithm, the part of the sub-cluster where the edge cut is minimal is bisected. The rationale behind this decision is that links within a cluster should be stronger in similarity than links across clusters and there should be more of such links within a cluster. Minimizing the edge cut means minimizing loose relationships between the resulting partitions.

The *MINSIZE* parameter refers to the size of a sub-graph in terms of the minimum number of vertices. In order to ensure that the measurement of internal interconnectivity and closeness of a sub-cluster is meaningful, there must exist a sufficient number of data points within the sub-cluster. Generally, MINSIZE should be smaller than the size of most expected clusters. Heuristically, MINSIZE is set to a value between 1% and 5% of the total number of data points in the given data set. Figure 5.7 illustrates the partitioning of a larger sub-cluster into two smaller but tighter sub-clusters.

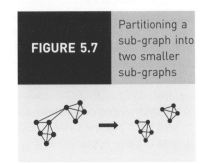

FIGURE 5.7   Partitioning a sub-graph into two smaller sub-graphs

In the agglomeration step, both relative closeness and relative interconnectivity are measured to determine the best pair of sub-clusters to merge. In CHAMELEON, the *relative interconnectivity* is defined as the ratio of the absolute interconnectivity between the two sub-clusters against the average of the internal interconnectivities within two sub-clusters. Given two sub-clusters, C_i and C_j, the absolute interconnectivity between the sub-clusters, denoted as $EC(C_i, C_j)$, is the sum of the weights attached to the links that connect vertices in C_i to those in C_j. In fact, $EC(C_i, C_j)$ is the edge cut between C_i and C_j. The internal interconnectivity, denoted as $EC(C)$, is the minimum edge cut that bisects the sub-cluster C into two roughly equal partitions.

$$RI(C_i, C_j) = \frac{EC(C_i, C_j)}{\frac{1}{2}[EC(C_i) + EC(C_j)]} = \frac{2EC(C_i, C_j)}{[EC(C_i) + EC(C_j)]}$$

Similarly, the *relative closeness* between two sub-clusters is defined as the ratio of the absolute closeness between the two sub-clusters to the average of the internal closeness within the two sub-clusters. Given two sub-clusters C_i and C_j, the absolute closeness between the sub-clusters, denoted here as $\mu EC(C_i, C_j)$, is the average of the weights attached to the links that connect vertices in C_i to those in C_j. This way of measuring closeness reduces the effect of outliers as in single-link agglomeration. The internal closeness, denoted here as $\mu EC(C)$, is the average of the weights attached to the internal links that bisect the sub-cluster C into two roughly equal partitions. The average of the internal closeness of the two sub-clusters is calculated as the weighted sum by the proportional sizes of the two sub-clusters:

$$RC(C_i, C_j) = \frac{\mu EC(C_i, C_j)}{\frac{|C_i|}{|C_i|+|C_j|}\mu EC(C_i) + \frac{|C_j|}{|C_i|+|C_j|}\mu EC(C_j))}$$

Once relative interconnectivity and relative closeness are measured, the best possible pair of clusters (with the highest measurements on both) is selected. CHAMELEON uses two user-defined thresholds T_{RI} and T_{RC} to control the necessary levels of interconnectivity and closeness. For each sub-cluster C_i, the algorithm checks if any of its adjacent sub-clusters C_j meets the requirements:

$$RI(C_i, C_j) \geq T_{RI} \text{ and } RC(C_i, C_j) \geq T_{RC}$$

If such a sub-cluster C_i is located, the two sub-clusters are merged into a bigger cluster. In the situation when more than one adjacent sub-cluster satisfies the conditions above, CHAMELEON merges sub-clusters C_i and C_j such that $EC(C_i, C_j)$ is highest, namely the most connected sub-clusters. The merging can also be repeated as long as both conditions are met. The thresholds are used as a stopping criterion for the agglomeration step: it terminates when either or both measurements are below the threshold. The set of merged clusters at that point is collected as the final clustering result.

The measures of relative interconnectivity and relative closeness can be combined into a single measure and the value should be maximized. The CHAMELEON algorithm proposes the following function that allows the user to place an emphasis on one or both parameters:

$$RI(C_i, C_j) \times RC(C_i, C_j)^a$$

If $a = 1$, both relative interconnectivity and relative closeness are equally important. If $a < 1$, the combined measure emphasizes relative interconnectivity more than relative closeness. If $a > 1$, the combined measure emphasizes relative closeness more than relative interconnectivity.

In terms of the clustering result, it is reported that CHAMELEON outperforms a number of other competitive clustering solutions. Figure 5.8 shows two 2D spatial data sets and the clustering results produced by the CHAMELEON algorithm and the DBSCAN or CURE algorithms. The results show that CHAMELEON can identify spatial entities of various shapes (circles, concaves, lines and rings) and sizes. In contrast, the CURE algorithm fails to detect clusters of any non-convex shapes. While CHAMELEON adapts to the noise and outliers by grouping them as remote members of the clusters the DBSCAN ignores all noise and outlier objects.

FIGURE 5.8   Comparison between CHAMELEON and other algorithms (taken from Karypis et al. 1999 with permission)

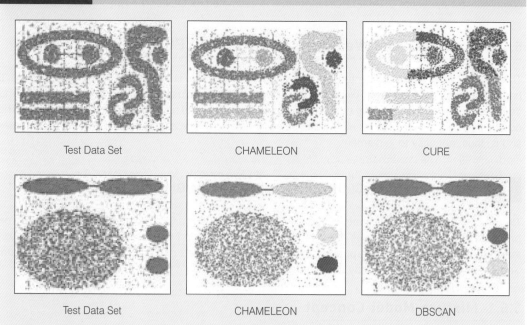

Test Data Set   CHAMELEON   CURE

Test Data Set   CHAMELEON   DBSCAN

Source: Used with permission: George Karypis, Eui-Hong (Sam) Han, Vipin Kumar, "Chameleon: Hierarchical Clustering Using Dynamic Modeling," *Computer*, vol. 32, no. 8, pp. 68-75, August, 1999. IEEE copyright line © **1999 IEEE**

5.4.3 Performance of the CHAMELEON Algorithm

The CHAMELEON algorithm does have higher cost of computation. The first step of the algorithm normally requires a time complexity of $O(N^2)$. If an efficient search structure such as k-d tree is used, the speed of constructing a sparse graph can be improved to the level of $O(NlogN)$, comparable to that of DBSCAN.

The time complexities for the other two main steps of the algorithm depend on the number of initial sub-clusters created by the segmentation step. For the convenience of estimation, it is assumed that the sizes of the initial m sub-clusters are the same and that a pair of clusters is merged at a time. The segmentation step requires the use of the hMETIS algorithm, which can perform one bisection operation in $O(N)$ time. Since the clusters are repeatedly bisected, the whole process requires $O(Nlog(N/m))$ time which is bounded by $O(NlogN)$.

The time complexity of the agglomeration step depends on the time taken to calculate the two proximity measures and the selection of the best pair of sub-clusters to merge. The cost of calculating the proximity measures depends on the cost of calculating the absolute measures between pairs of sub-clusters and the internal measures within each sub-cluster. The time needed to calculate the internal measures is proportional to the size of the sub-cluster, estimated as N/m. Then the time needed to calculate all the internal measures for m sub-clusters is $O(N)$. In the worst case, when all sub-clusters are merged into a single cluster, one at a time, there will be $m-1$ iterations of merging required. Therefore, the total time complexity is $O(Nm)$. Also at each iteration of the agglomeration step, the two proximity measures between any two sub-clusters need to be calculated. Initially, there are m^2 pairs of sub-clusters to be considered. If we store each pair and its measures in a heap-based priority queue, inserting all results into the queue requires $O(m^2logm)$ time. At each merging iteration, the pair with the highest measures is selected and, after merging, the proximity measures between the newly merged cluster and all the other sub-clusters need to be updated. Each update requires $O(mlogm)$ time and there are $m-1$ such updates. Therefore, the total amount of time for this is $O(m^2logm)$. Overall, the time complexity for the entire CHAMELEON algorithm is estimated as $O(NlogN + Nm + m^2logm)$.

5.4.4 Strengths and Weaknesses of CHAMELEON

The CHAMELEON algorithm is intended to overcome some major limitations of the other algorithms. It has advantages over the other clustering algorithms in finding clusters of various shapes, sizes and densities. The algorithm is mainly designed for spatial data sets and has a high cost in computation. The cost is expected to be higher for high-dimensionality data sets. The algorithm is also relatively complex and is, thus, not easy to implement.

5.5 MIXTURE MODEL CLUSTERING METHOD: EM/GMM

This section presents the expectation-maximization (EM) clustering method, which is based on probability and statistical theories. Most of the theories are beyond the scope of this text. The section therefore emphasizes the concept and principles involved instead of every detail of the computation. Some revision of Section 2.7 may be useful.

5.5.1 Mixture Model Concept

Model-based clustering solutions consider a data set as a result of a statistical process. Cluster detection becomes a process of finding a statistical model that best fits the given data set. In the mixture model approach, such a statistical model is represented in terms of a set of k multivariate probability

FIGURE 5.9   Data sets drawn from mixture models

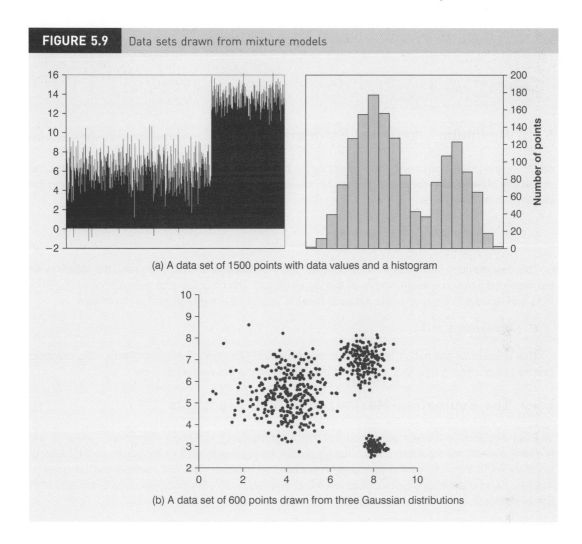

(a) A data set of 1500 points with data values and a histogram

(b) A data set of 600 points drawn from three Gaussian distributions

distributions. Each distribution, known as a *component* and described by a set of parameters, represents an ellipsoidal cluster. A common type of probability distribution is normal, or Gaussian, distribution. For a univariate distribution, the parameters include the mean and standard deviation. For a multivariate distribution, the parameters include the mean vector and the covariance matrix. For simplicity, mixture model solutions normally use distributions of the same type. Mixture models with Gaussian distributions are known as Gaussian mixture models (GMM).

Because of a set of distributions in the mixture model, data objects may belong to more than one cluster. For instance, an object that is 3σ away from the mean of one distribution may also be within 1σ of the mean of another distribution. Therefore, a data object has a probability of belonging to a particular cluster. Figure 5.9(a) shows an example data set of 1500 random values drawn from two univariate Gaussian distributions N(4.5, 2.1) and N(12.5, 1.5) respectively. As well as the actual data values, the histogram of the values is also presented. Figure 5.9(b) shows a separate data set of 600 points drawn from three multivariate Gaussian distributions, forming three different clusters.

Suppose that a mixture model consists of K distributions with parameters θ_1, θ_2, ..., θ_K where θ_j represents the parameters for the jth distribution. The symbol Θ is used to represent all the parameters of the mixture model, i.e. $\Theta = \{\theta_1, \ldots, \theta_K\}$. Given a data set $X = \{x_1, \ldots, x_n\}$, $p(x_i | \theta_j)$ is the probability (in fact the probability density) that data object x_i is drawn from the jth distribution. Let a_j be the probability that the jth distribution is chosen to generate a data object, and $a_1 + a_2 + \ldots + a_K = 1$. Then, the probability that any data object x is generated by the mixture model is expressed as:

$$p(x|\Theta) = \sum_{j=1}^{K} a_j p(x \mid \theta_j)$$

5.5.2 Maximum Likelihood Estimation

Assuming the generation of each data object by the mixture model is an independent random event, the probability of generating the entire data set becomes the product of the probabilities for generating the individual data objects, i.e.

$$p(X \mid \Theta) = \prod_{i=1}^{n} p(x \mid \Theta) = \prod_{i=1}^{n} \sum_{j=1}^{K} a_j p(x \mid \theta_j)$$

This expression is known as the likelihood function, denoted as $L(\Theta|X)$. Normally, the logarithm of the likelihood function is taken, known as the *log likelihood*. The objective is to estimate the parameters in Θ with respect to the given data set such that the value of the log likelihood is maximized, i.e.

$$\hat{\Theta} = \underset{\Theta}{\mathrm{argmax}}\, \log(L(\Theta \mid X))$$

This process of estimation is known as the *maximum likelihood estimation* (MLE). The rationale behind this process is that MLE makes the occurrence of the data set most likely.

5.5.3 The Estimation-Maximization (EM) Algorithm

The EM algorithm is a commonly used method for maximizing likelihood estimation. Similar to the K-means method, the algorithm first randomly decides the initial estimates for the parameters for a set of distributions. It then refines the estimates in an iterative process. The EM method can be used to estimate parameters for any type of distribution (not only Gaussian). The principal steps of the algorithm are as follows:

1 *Initialization:* Estimate the parameters for K distributions randomly.

2 *Expectation:* Based on the estimates for the parameters, calculate the probability that each data object belongs to each of the distributions.

3 *Maximization:* Use the probabilities calculated from Step 2 to find the new estimates for the parameters of the distributions. The new estimates must maximize the likelihood of the distributions fitting the data objects. If the new estimates do not change or the difference between the current estimates and the previous estimates is below a given threshold, the process terminates.

The steps outlined above are quite generic and may be implemented in various ways. For the initialization step, for example, the means for the K distributions can be estimated by selecting K data objects randomly from the data set. Each of the selected objects is treated as the mean vector for one component distribution. The covariance matrix of a component distribution can be guessed, for instance, as the variance for each variable.

The expectation step assigns each data object to each cluster with a probability. For a data object x and a cluster C_j, the probability is calculated according to Bayes rule:

$$p(x \in C_j) = p(C_j \mid x) = \frac{p(C_j)p(x \mid C_j)}{p(x)}$$

where $p(x|C_j)$ can be seen as the probability density function of the distribution describing the cluster C_j. In the iterative process of the algorithm, we use $\Theta^{(t)}$ to represent the estimates of distribution parameters in the current iteration t with regards to the given data set. The probability above can then be calculated as follows:

$$p(x \in C_j) = p(C_j | x, \Theta^{(t)}) = \frac{a_j p(x | \theta_j)}{p(x | \Theta^{(t)})}$$

where, for a Gaussian mixture model, $p(x|\theta_j)$ can be the probability density function of the normal distribution with the current estimated mean vector and covariance matrix, and:

$$p(x | \Theta^{(t)}) = \sum_{j=1}^{K} a_j p(x | \theta_j)$$

To illustrate the expectation step, we continue the example of two univariate Gaussian distributions used at the end of Section 5.5.1. The first distribution, with $\mu_1 = 4$ and $\sigma_1 = 1$, describes cluster C_1 and the second distribution, with $\mu_2 = 8$ and $\sigma_2 = 2$, describes cluster C_2. Suppose that the object x being considered has value 1. The probabilities that the object belongs to cluster C_1 and C_2 respectively are presented as follows:

$$p(1 \in C_1) = \frac{0.6p(1 | \theta_1)}{(0.6p(1 | \theta_1) + 0.4p(1 | \theta_2))} = 0.37136$$

$$p(1 \in C_2) = \frac{0.4p(1 | \theta_2)}{(0.6p(1 | \theta_1) + 0.4p(1 | \theta_2))} = 0.62864$$

Therefore, the object $x = 1$ is more likely to belong to cluster C_2 than cluster C_1.

In the maximization step, the probabilities calculated in the expectation step are used to re-estimate the distribution parameters such that the log likelihood can be maximized. Following on from the previous example, if we assume that there are 1000 data objects in the given data set, the new mean value for cluster C_1 is re-estimated as follows:

$$\mu_1^{new} = \sum_{i=1}^{1000} x_i \frac{p(C_1 | x_i, \Theta)}{\sum_{j=1}^{1000} p(C_1 | x_i, \Theta)}$$

In general, without going through details and relevant theories, the following re-estimates for the three parameters (mean vector μ_j, covariance σ_j and probability a_j) for the distribution for cluster C_j guarantee the maximization of the log likelihood at the current iteration t of the EM process:

$$\mu_j = \sum_{i=1}^{n} x_i \frac{p(x_i \in C_j)}{\sum_{i=1}^{n} p(x_i \in C_j)} = \frac{\sum_{i=1}^{n} p(x_i \in C_j) x_i}{\sum_{i=1}^{n} p(x_i \in C_j)}$$

$$\sigma_j = \frac{\sum_{i=1}^{n} p(x_i \in C_j)(x_i - \mu_j)(x_i - \mu_j)^T}{\sum_{i=1}^{n} p(x_i \in C_j)}$$

$$a_j = \frac{1}{n} \sum_{i=1}^{n} p(x_i \in C_j)$$

The distribution parameters in $\Theta^{(t)}$ are a better fit to the given data than those in $\Theta^{(t-1)}$, and the parameters in $\Theta^{(t+1)}$ are better than those in $\Theta^{(t)}$. Eventually, the differences between the estimates of the previous iteration and those of the current iteration are small enough to terminate the process.

A complete illustrative example is not given here because of the constraints of space. You are encouraged to continue with the partial example given in this section. In Section 5.8.2, we show a practical example of clustering with the EM method over a set of data objects.

One variant factor of the EM algorithm is the value of K. Some implementations of the algorithm treat K in the same way as for the K-means method, i.e. K is a user-defined parameter that can be utilized with respect to cluster quality. Other implementations consider K as another parameter to be estimated within the expectation-maximization process. For instance, one implementation starts with a large value for K. During the expectation-maximization process, a threshold and a goodness-of-fit function is used to decide whether two similar distributions should be treated as the same distribution. This action corresponds to the process of merging two similar clusters into a single cluster.

The time complexity for the EM algorithm is estimated as O(nKD) per EM iteration where n is the size and D is the dimensionality of the data set. The time complexity for the entire algorithm is therefore linear to the number of iterations needed.

5.5.4 Strengths and Weaknesses of EM

The EM method works well for various data sets from different application backgrounds because many data sets are indeed the results of random statistical processes. Clusters of elliptical shapes of different sizes can be discovered. The method uses a small number of descriptors, i.e. mean vector, covariance matrix and percentage, to describe resulting clusters. In many applications, the variance vector replaces the covariance matrix, simplifying cluster description and computation further. The solution is fairly efficient for low-dimensionality data, but can become inefficient when the dimensionality is high.

The solution has its limitations when the data set contains only a small number of data objects for a large number of component distributions. Data sets from some application backgrounds, such as voice signals, require a large number of component distributions to fit the data properly. If there are only a few samples for each component distribution, the estimation is not accurate. Having a value of K is sometimes considered as a weakness, although it is possible to optimize the value of K using the minimum description length principle.

5.6   SUBSPACE CLUSTERING METHOD: CLIQUE

As described before, if data objects are considered as points in a multidimensional space where the dimensions are the attributes, as the dimensionality increases, the data points may become further apart from each other, and fewer and fewer clusters may exist. However, in a *subspace* of the original multidimensional space, clusters may still exist. As shown in Figure 5.10(a), the data points of the example data set are diverse in the given 2D space and do not form clusters. If the data points are projected onto a 1D subspace, three clusters emerge along the horizontal dimension and four clusters along the vertical dimension.

Finding clusters in subspaces can be achieved in two ways. Instead of using all the given attributes, the data analyst can manually select relevant attributes. There are two problems with this approach. First, the data analyst may make a wrong decision over which attributes to select, due to lack of knowledge about the attributes. Second, the number of attributes may be inappropriate even after the manual selection, because the number of selected attributes can be high and any measurement of proximity is still performed over all the selected attributes. Both problems prevent the discovery of possible clusters in the chosen subspace.

The second way to find clusters in subspace is to use automatic dimension reduction methods, such as the principal component analysis (PCA) mentioned in Chapter 3, before clustering. These methods transform the data from the original space to a new space where each dimension is a combination of the original ones. However, the transformation may make the meanings of the new dimensions hard to explain, causing difficulties in cluster interpretation later. Another problem is that clusters in subspaces of different dimensionality may not be discovered because all the significant dimensions, not subsets of them, are considered in the clustering process.

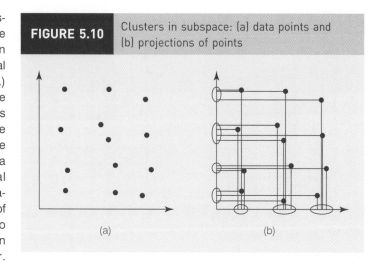

FIGURE 5.10 Clusters in subspace: (a) data points and (b) projections of points

(a)   (b)

CLIQUE is an algorithm purposefully designed to discover clusters in subspaces of a given multidimensional data set. The algorithm aims to find dense regions in the subspaces and describe them in terms of disjunctive normal form (DNF) expressions. The algorithm shares, to a large extent, the same principles as the Apriori algorithm for association rule discovery (refer to Chapter 8).

5.6.1 Problem of Subspace Clustering

Informally, each dimension can be partitioned into a fixed number of equal-length intervals. The multidimensional space and its subspaces are consequently divided into many rectangular cells. Some cells have more data points than others. Those cells that have sufficient data points are dense cells. Connected dense cells then form dense regions and dense regions form clusters. Clusters in different subspaces are collected and described in concise statements.

The problem of subspace clustering is defined as follows. Let S be a d-dimensional space where each dimension A_i ($1 \leq i \leq d$) refers to an attribute with its domain of all permitted values. An input data set V is a set of d-dimensional points, i.e. $V = \{v_1, v_2, \ldots, v_m\}$, and a data point is a vector, i.e. $v_i = <v_{i1}, v_{i2}, \ldots, v_{id}>$, where v_{ij} is a value from the domain for dimension A_j for the data point. Every dimension in S is partitioned into a equal-length intervals where a is a user-defined parameter. The space S is therefore divided into non-overlapping *units*. Each unit is the intersection of one interval from each dimension and is described by the intervals $\{[l_1, u_1), [l_2, u_2), \ldots, [l_d, u_d)\}$ where l_i and u_i are the lower and upper bounds of an interval along the ith dimension.

A data point $v = \{v_1, v_2, \ldots, v_d\}$ is said to be contained in a unit if $l_i \leq v_i < u_i$ for all intervals $[l_i, u_i)$ of the unit. Given a user-defined threshold β, a unit is said to be *dense* if the fraction of the total number of data points contained in the unit is greater than β. Dense units in all k subspaces (where $k < d$) are defined similarly. For simplicity, both a and β are considered as global parameters for all subspaces.

In the entire space S or any subspaces, two k-dimensional units have a *common face* if, for all k dimensions, the corresponding intervals of the two units are the same along $k-1$ dimensions and the upper bound of one unit equals the lower bound of the other unit along one dimension. Two

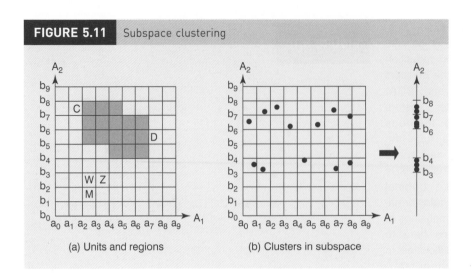

FIGURE 5.11   Subspace clustering

(a) Units and regions   (b) Clusters in subspace

k-dimensional units a and b are said to be *connected* if they have a common face or there exists another unit c where a is connected to c and c is connected to b.

A region in k-dimensional subspace is a union of k-dimensional units. A region r is said to be contained in a cluster C, if $r \subseteq C$. A region contained in a cluster is said to be *maximal* if no superset of the region is contained in the cluster. A cluster can also be said to be the union of maximal regions. A region can be expressed in terms of DNF expressions.

Based on the concepts described above, the problem of subspace clustering can now be described as follows. Given a set of data points and user-defined parameters a and β, the problem of subspace clustering is to discover dense clusters in all subspaces of S and describe them in DNF expressions. Figure 5.11 illustrates the concepts and the problem of subspace clustering. In Figure 5.11(a), in the 2D space, unit W is described by two intervals: $[a_2, a_3)$ and $[b_2, b_3)$. Units W and M are directly connected; whereas M and Z are connected via W. C and D (indicated by the dark shaded areas) are two maximal regions of dense units whose union defines a cluster. The DNF expression $(a_2 \leq A_1 < a_5) \wedge (b_5 \leq A_2 < b_8)$ $\vee (a_4 \leq A_1 < a_7) \wedge (b_4 \leq A_2 < b_7)$ describes the cluster.

In Figure 5.11(b), if the density threshold $\beta = 20\%$, there is no dense unit in the original 2D space. Also, there is no dense unit in the 1D subspace along the horizontal dimension A_1 because the maximum fraction of points within an interval (unit) is 2/12, i.e. 17%, which is below the threshold. In the 1D subspace along dimension A_2, however, there are three dense units (intervals): $[b_3, b_4)$, $[b_6, b_7)$ and $[b_7, b_8)$ because each of them contains three or more data points, above the threshold. Two units are connected, and hence there exist two clusters C_1 defined by $b_3 \leq A_2 < b_4$ and C_2 defined by $b_6 \leq A_2 < b_8$.

5.6.2 The CLIQUE Algorithm

The CLIQUE algorithm decomposes the problem of subspace clustering into three sub-problems that are outlined as follows:

1 Identification of all subspaces that may contain clusters, i.e. subspaces that contain dense units.

2 Identification of clusters among connected dense units in every subspace.

3 Generation of minimum descriptions for the identified clusters in DNF expressions.

Each of the sub-problems above needs an algorithm. For the first sub-problem, CLIQUE exploits the *monotonicity* property among clusters in subspaces in a greedy bottom-up discovery procedure. The monotonicity property states that if a collection of data points forms a cluster in a k-dimensional space, then the collection also forms part of a cluster in any $(k-1)$-dimensional projections of the original space. Based on this property, an Apriori-like algorithm is proposed as follows. First, the data set is scanned and all dense units along every 1D space are discovered and stored in a seed set. Then, the candidate dense units in a k-dimensional space are generated from the dense units discovered from the $(k-1)$-dimensional spaces by using a candidate generation function. Once all k-dimensional candidate dense units are generated, the data set is scanned again to find the actual dense units among the candidates by using the density threshold β. Those dense units are then stored into the current seed set for all k-dimensional subspaces, and used for generating candidate dense units in $(k+1)$-dimensional spaces. The process terminates when the current seed set becomes empty and no more candidates can be generated.

The candidate generation function works as follows. Let $a = \{[l_{a1}, u_{a1}), [l_{a2}, u_{a2}), \ldots, [l_{a(k-1)}, u_{a(k-1)})\}$ and $b = \{[l_{b1}, u_{b1}), [l_{b2}, u_{b2}), \ldots, [l_{b(k-1)}, u_{b(k-1)})\}$ be two dense units in the seed set for all $(k-1)$-dimensional subspaces. The dimensions for unit a are $a_1, a_2, \ldots, a_{k-1}$, and the dimensions for unit b are $b_1, b_2, \ldots, b_{k-1}$. If the following conditions hold:

- $a.a_1 = b.b_1$ and $a.a_2 = b.b_2$ and $\ldots$ and $a.a_{k-2} = b.b_{k-2}$, and there exists a lexicographic ordering relation such that $a.a_{k-1} < b.b_{k-1}$

- $a.l_{a1} = b.l_{b1}$, $a.u_{a1} = b.u_{b1}$ and $\ldots$ and $a.l_{a(k-2)} = b.l_{b(k-2)}$, $a.u_{a(k-2)} = b.u_{b(k-2)}$

a new candidate dense unit $c = \{[l_{a1}, u_{a1}), [l_{a2}, u_{a2}), \ldots, [l_{a(k-1)}, u_{a(k-1)}), [l_{b(k-1)}, u_{b(k-1)})\}$ in a k-dimensional subspace can be then generated. Figure 5.12 shows an example. Assume that an order among dimensions X, Y, Z is enforced such that $X < Y < Z$. Suppose also that there is a dense unit $[x_1, x_2)$ along the X dimension and a dense unit $[y_1, y_2)$ along the Y dimension. A candidate unit $\{[x_1, x_2), [y_1, y_2)\}$ can then be generated in the XY subspace. Suppose further that the unit $\{[x_1, x_2), [y_1, y_2)\}$ is dense and another unit $\{[x_1, x_2), [z_1, z_2)\}$ is also dense. A new XYZ candidate unit $\{[x_1, x_2), [y_1, y_2), [z_1, z_2)\}$ can then be generated.

Once all candidate dense units are generated, if any candidates have at least one subset of size $k-1$ that is not in the seed set for the $(k-1)$-dimensional subspaces, these candidates do not have sufficient data points and therefore are removed from the collection of

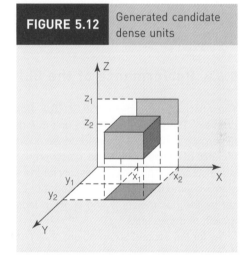

FIGURE 5.12 Generated candidate dense units

all candidates before the data set is scanned to calculate the densities of the candidates. This pruning step may save time by reducing the number of candidate units.

The second sub-problem of finding clusters among dense units can be resolved with a depth-first graph search algorithm. In an iterative process, the current seed set for all k-dimensional subspaces is searched. At the beginning, an arbitrary dense unit is chosen; all its connected dense units are located and marked with the current cluster identifier. An unmarked dense unit is then chosen from the seed set and its connected dense units are located and marked with another cluster identifier. The operation terminates when no dense units in the seed set are left unmarked. At the end of the operation, the clusters within all the k-dimensional subspaces are obtained. The algorithm proceeds to the next seed set to identify clusters in the $(k+1)$-dimensional subspaces.

Suppose there exists a seed set $S_2 = \{\{[x_1, x_2), [y_1, y_2)\}, \{[x_1, x_2), [y_2, y_3)\}, \{[x_0, x_1), [y_1, y_2)\}, \{[y_1, y_2), [z_1, z_2)\}, \{[y_1, y_2), [z_2, z_4)\}\}$. Two clusters C_1 with the dense units $\{[x_1, x_2), [y_1, y_2)\}, \{[x_1, x_2), [y_2, y_3)\}$ and $\{[x_0, x_1), [y_1, y_2)\}$ and C_2 with dense units $\{[y_1, y_2), [z_1, z_2)\}$ and $\{[y_1, y_2), [z_2, z_4)\}$ can be identified.

The third sub-problem of generating a minimum description of the identified clusters is mainly about discovering the minimum number of regions that cover all the dense units of each cluster. CLIQUE takes a two-step approach to solving this problem: a greedy growth algorithm is used to find maximal regions that cover a cluster and a heuristic method is used to remove redundant regions from the collection of the maximal regions for the cluster in order to achieve minimal cover.

The greedy growth algorithm starts with an arbitrary dense unit, grows a maximal region for the unit and saves it in the result set. A dense unit that is not covered by any regions is then selected and the same procedure is repeated. The process continues until all dense units are covered by some maximal region in the result set. The procedure for growing a maximal region of a given unit works as follows. Initially one of the dimensions is randomly selected. Along the chosen dimension, we locate all the connected dense units on the left of the unit and then all the connected dense units on the right as far as the connection within the cluster allows. Eventually, a rectangular region is discovered. The whole rectangular region is then grown on the left as well as on the right along another chosen dimension as far as the connection within the cluster allows. The process continues until all dimensions have been looked at and the resulting region is a maximal region for the cluster.

Once the collection of all maximal regions for the cluster is discovered, a removal heuristic is used: the smallest of the regions whose every dense unit is also contained in some other region is removed. In case of a tie, one such region is chosen arbitrarily. The process is repeated until no more regions can be removed. An alternative heuristic can be used: the cover of the cluster is initially considered as empty; the maximal region that covers the most dense units is located and added to the cover until no more regions can be added.

5.6.3 Performance of the CLIQUE Algorithm

The most expensive step in the CLIQUE algorithm is the bottom-up Apriori-like algorithm for the first sub-problem. The reason is that if a unit in k-dimensions is dense, then all of its projections in the lower-dimension subspaces are also dense and there are $O(2^k)$ subspaces. Therefore, there can be a huge number of dense units to be discovered. Also, for each k dimensionality, the data set needs to be scanned once. The time complexity for the entire step is hence estimated as $O(2^k + mk)$. Some methods of improvement have been reported, but the number of dense units is very much related to the values set for the parameters a and β. As a increases and β decreases linearly, there can be exponential growth of dense units.

As for the second sub-problem, if all clusters in all i-dimensional subspaces need to be discovered by using the ith seed set, the time complexity is estimated as $O(n_i^2)$, where n_i refers to the number of dense units in the seed set, because of the checking for connections between dense units. The solution for the third sub-problem is straightforward. For one cluster, in the worst case, when each region may contain a number of dense units close to n and let us assume the number of regions is p, the time complexity is estimated as $O(np)$.

5.6.4 Strengths and Weaknesses of CLIQUE

The most recognized strength of the CLIQUE algorithm is the capability to find clusters in subspaces of an entire multidimensional space although clusters do not exist in the original entire space. CLIQUE finds clusters within lower-dimensional subspaces without going through the process of data transformation, preserving the meaning of the original dimensions. The algorithm provides minimum length descriptions of clusters in terms of DNF expressions, assisting the comprehension of the resulting clusters.

The most recognized weakness of the algorithm is the potentially huge number of dense units discovered and the possible exponential cost involved. Both are related to the setting of the parameters a and β. Given the fact that for a cluster in a k-dimensional space, all its $(k-1)$-dimensional projects are also part of a cluster in those subspaces, is it really necessary to discover all clusters in all subspaces?

5.7   FURTHER DISCUSSION OF PROXIMITY MEASURES

A number of measures for computing the similarity or dissimilarity between data objects were described in Chapter 4. Based on the values of a set of features (attributes) that may represent structural and functional properties of the data objects, such a measure combines the measurement upon each feature into a single score, indicating the amount of proximity. These measures often become ineffective for data objects of high dimensionality and of non-traditional data types (e.g. multimedia data). In fact, finding a suitable and appropriate proximity function for a given type of data is a challenging and non-trivial task.

In this section, a number of issues regarding similarity measurement are briefly discussed. Readers with a special interest are advised to follow the references given in the Bibliographical Notes.

5.7.1 Shared Nearest Neighbour (SNN) Approach

When the direct measurement of proximity, e.g. the Euclidean distance function and the cosine similarity measure, is undertaken, the data objects involved are treated in isolation: only the proximity of the data objects is measured regardless of the data objects surrounding them. Such a pairwise measurement has two consequences. First, data objects in high-dimensional space are sparse and measurements of similarity between any objects are close. The poor contrast in measurement may lead to poor-quality grouping. Second, natural clusters of different densities may not be detected because the pairwise measurement of similarity between a data object of one group and a data object of another group may be higher than its similarity to its own kind.

The shared nearest neighbour (SNN) approach to similarity measurement is set to resolve the problems. The approach is based on the belief that data objects that have many neighbouring objects in common are likely to be similar to each other. The number of shared nearest neighbours indicates the degree of similarity. The process is straightforward. To measure the similarity between objects X and Y, the k nearest neighbours of X and the k nearest neighbours of Y are found, and then the number of common neighbours is counted. Figure 5.13 presents two situations where the similarity is measured in terms of the shared nearest neighbours. In Figure 5.13(a), no common nearest neighbours are found and hence the level of similarity between objects A and B is measured as 0. In Figure 5.13(b), there are four nearest neighbours in common and the level of similarity between A and B is measured as 4. The similarity can also be measured as a fraction of k. For instance, if $k = 7$, the similarity between A and B in Figure 5.13(b) is measured as $4/7 \approx 0.57$.

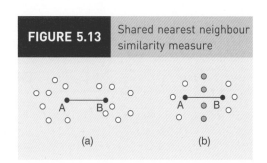

FIGURE 5.13   Shared nearest neighbour similarity measure

(a)   (b)

Adopting the SNN similarity measure in clustering algorithms is quite straightforward. For instance, in a graph-based clustering algorithm, a connected graph of all data objects where the links represent the level of SNN similarity can be constructed first. By setting an appropriate threshold on the similarity, the graph is partitioned by removing links that have values below the threshold. Then, the remaining connected sub-graphs become clusters.

The SNN similarity can also be adopted into density-based clustering algorithms. In a centre-based density approach, such as that for DBSCAN, an SNN connected graph is first constructed. The SNN similarity of each data point with the given Eps is measured. The SNN similarity of a point A with an Eps refers to the number of neighbouring points of A, each of which has an SNN similarity to A equal to or greater than Eps. If the SNN similarity of a point is greater than MinPts, the point is labelled as a core point. For a point whose SNN similarity is less than MinPts, if the point is connected to a core point, it is then a border point; otherwise the point is a noise point. Connected core points become members of the same cluster. Border points are assigned to the cluster of their connected core points. The noise points are removed.

5.7.2 Similarity Measures for Time-series and Sequential Data

In many real-life applications, data of sequential nature are collected. Audio signals, digital images, videos, DNA sequences and text are a few examples of such data. Conventional direct measures of similarity fail to provide a meaningful result.

Figure 5.14 shows two examples. In Figure 5.14(a), two time series are similar in shape. However, a direct measurement of difference between the two sequences at fixed time points with a function such as the Euclidean function indicates that the two sequences are rather different (particularly towards the end of the sequences). An alternative measurement with alignments upon features such as peak, valley, plateau, etc. indicates a strong similarity between the two sequences and makes more sense. Figure 5.14(b) shows two character strings. A direct character-wise comparison yields a matching score of 0. With alignment by inserting a wild card character such as '_' in the right place, the character-wise comparison yields a matching score of three.

Dynamic time warping (DTW) is a method for measuring similarity between two sequences. Let $X = x_1, x_2, \ldots, x_m$ and $Y = y_1, y_2, \ldots, y_n$ represent two sequences where x_i and y_j are data values measured at a time point. Let $d(x_i, y_j)$ represent a distance function (such as the Euclidean function) that measures the distance between x_i and y_j. Then an $m \times n$ distance matrix D can be constructed. Each cell of the matrix, $D(i, j)$, is designated for an alignment between x_i and y_j and contains the value of $d(x_i, y_j)$.

A warping path $W = w_1, w_2, \ldots, w_K$ is a list of cells of the distance matrix D where maximum$(m, n) \leq K < m + n$. Each element of the path $w_t = (i, j)$ where i and

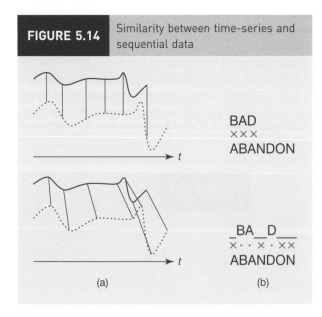

FIGURE 5.14   Similarity between time-series and sequential data

BAD
× × ×
ABANDON

BA_D_
× · · × · × ×
ABANDON

(a)   (b)

j are indices of the corresponding elements of the two sequences. A warping path must satisfy the following constraints:

■ It must start at the beginning of each sequence, i.e. $w_1 = (1, 1)$, and finish at the end of both sequences, i.e. $w_K = (m, n)$.

■ The values of indices in the elements of a warping path must increase monotonically. In other words, given any two elements of a warping path, $w_t = (i, j)$ and $w_{t+1} = (i', j')$, then $i \leq i' \leq i+1$ and $j \leq j' \leq j+1$.

The distance of a warping path W is defined as follows:

$$Dist(W) = \sum_{t=1}^{K} d(w_{ti}, w_{tj})$$

where w_{ti} and w_{tj} refer to points x_i and y_j respectively, and $d(w_{ti}, w_{tj}) = d(x_i, y_j)$. Among many possible warping paths that satisfy the constraints above, the optimal warping path is the path with the minimum distance. Figure 5.15 shows an optimal warping path for two example sequences.

The basic algorithm for finding the optimal warping path (and hence finding the minimum distance between the two sequences) employs the dynamic programming principle: an optimal path of small sub-sequences are first found and then extended to larger sub-sequences until the optimal path is found for the entire sequences. In the first step of the algorithm, the distance matrix D is updated. A cell $D(i, j)$ represents the minimum distance from cell $D(1,1)$ to cell $D(i, j)$, and hence

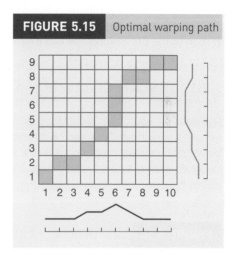

FIGURE 5.15   Optimal warping path

$$D(i,j) = d(x_i, y_j) + \min(D(i-1,j), D(i,j-1), D(i-1,j-1))$$

This updating operation is performed column-wise from the bottom of the matrix to the top. Eventually, cell $D(m, n)$ contains the minimum distance of the optimal warping path.

Once the entire distance matrix is updated, a greedy search can be performed from cell $D(m, n)$ towards the cell $D(1,1)$ in order to locate the optimal warping path. First, (m, n) is pushed onto a stack. At a particular point at position (i, j), the minimum of $D(i-1, j)$, $D(i, j-1)$ and $D(i-1, j-1)$ is found, the corresponding position is added onto the stack, and the search continues from that position. Once cell $D(1, 1)$ is reached, the search is complete. The position $(1, 1)$ and the cell positions popped off the stack form the warping path.

Since the time complexity for computing an optimal warping path is in the order of $O(m \times n)$, the basic method has a serious problem of being applied practically. Much effort has been made to improve the performance of the basic method. For instance, one idea is to constrain the areas of the matrix searched. Instead of searching the entire matrix, areas of the matrix along the diagonal line from the beginning of the path to the end of the path are searched. Far corner areas away from the path, i.e. areas near to $D(m, 1)$ and $D(1, n)$ are not searched. Another idea is to find a concise representation of the original input sequences with many fewer elements but still maintaining features of the original sequences. Then the optimal warping path for the concise representations can be taken as the optimal warping path of the original sequences, or it can be further refined.

5.8 ADVANCED CLUSTERING METHODS IN WEKA

Clustering facilities in Weka are not as extensive as those for classification. By the time this book is published, besides the Simple K-means and Cobweb methods mentioned in Section 4.6, Weka will provide the EM and DBSCAN algorithms but is yet to support the CHAMELEON and CLIQUE methods described in this chapter. Weka also offers a recent sequential information Bottleneck algorithm known as sIB for document clustering and a cluster analysis method, OPTICS, for identifying cluster structures. In addition, Weka is equipped with two meta-clustering tools for users to select and combine a clustering solution with a specific similarity function or various filters for pre-processing the data before clustering.

In this section, the focus of attention is concentrated on demonstrating the DBSCAN and EM methods within Weka. Interested readers could try the other clustering facilities mentioned above after studying the related literature in the Bibliographical Notes. We use a data set that comes with the downloadable demonstration software for CHAMELEON to demonstrate DBSCAN. For the demonstration of the EM method, we use a synthesized data set.

5.8.1 DBSCAN Clustering in Weka

The data set used here is provided with the CLUTO software (see the Bibliographical Notes for the website where the data set can be downloaded). Originally named `t4.8k.dat`, the data file contains the XY co-ordinates of 8000 spatial data points. For this example, an extra subjectID field is introduced to identify each data point, and the file is then converted into an ARFF file. Figure 5.16 shows the scatter plot of the data points before clustering.

FIGURE 5.16   Scatter plot of the CLUTO data set

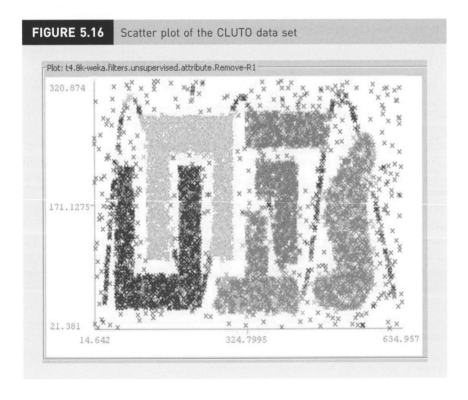

The data set contains clusters of different shapes and noises. The objective is to examine the effectiveness of DBSCAN in identifying the correct clusters. We load the data set and, on the Preprocess tab, deselect the subjectID field so that only the XY co-ordinates take part in proximity measurement. On the Cluster tab, the DBSCAN method is chosen from the pop-up list by clicking the Choose button. We keep the default setting for the Euclidean distance function, because it is appropriate for measuring spatial distances.

Weka does not provide a direct tool to assist in the heuristic estimation of the optimal settings for Eps and MinPts. After a number of trials, we realize that if the Eps is too large and MinPts is too small, nearly every point becomes a core and hence all the data points tend to belong to a single big cluster. If the Eps is too small and MinPts is too large, there are many small clusters. Therefore, the following trial-and-error approach is taken. Eps is initially set to a small value, which is gradually increased while the MinPts is adjusted (with the help of data visualization) so that the number of clusters becomes appropriate. After a number of trials, optimal settings of Eps = 0.0225 and MinPts = 15 are found. Figure 5.17(a) presents the clustering summary, which shows that seven clusters of different sizes are detected and 564 data points are treated as noise. Figure 5.17(b) shows the visualization of cluster memberships. The result demonstrates that DBSCAN has identified all the differently shaped clusters within the data set. However, the parameter settings have allowed an extra small cluster to be found, indicating the difficulty of optimizing Eps and MinPts.

5.8.2 EM Clustering in Weka

A synthesized data set is used to demonstrate the use of the EM method in Weka. The data points within the data set have three continuous variables X, Y, and Z, and are generated by a mixture of three normal distributions. The parameters for the distributions are listed in Table 5.3. The data set is obtained by using the random number generation facility (with different random seeds) of the data analysis toolkit in Microsoft Excel. The data set is converted into an ARFF file using Weka and can be found in the web resource accompanying this book...this book, (www.cengage.co.uk/du).

Figure 5.18 shows a 3D scatter plot of the data points. By using a data set for which the distributions are known, we can test the effectiveness of the EM method.

In Weka, the EM method is the default option for clustering. The command for the method can also be selected in the usual way by clicking on the Choose button and selecting the EM option from the pop-up menu. The EM method in Weka has a number of parameters that can be altered by the user. The most important are *maxIteration* and *numClusters*. The maxIteration parameter specifies the maximum number of iterations; it is set to 100 by default. The numClusters parameter specifies the number of clusters to be discovered. For instance, we can set it to three for our synthesized data set. When the numClusters parameter is set to -1, the EM method determines the number of clusters by cross-validation.

Initially, the number of clusters is set to 1. At every iteration of a repeated process, the data set is divided randomly into 10 folds. Data points in one fold are left out and those in the remaining folds are used in the EM process. Therefore, the EM process is repeated 10 times with different parts of the data set. The resulting 10 log likelihood measures are averaged at the end of that iteration. If the average log likelihood is greater than that in the previous iteration (initially this is assumed to be the case), the number of clusters is increased by 1 and another iteration of the process starts. The process ends when the average log likelihood measure in the current iteration is not greater than that of the previous iteration. Then the existing number of clusters is taken as the optimal number (readers can find more information about cross-validation in Chapter 6).

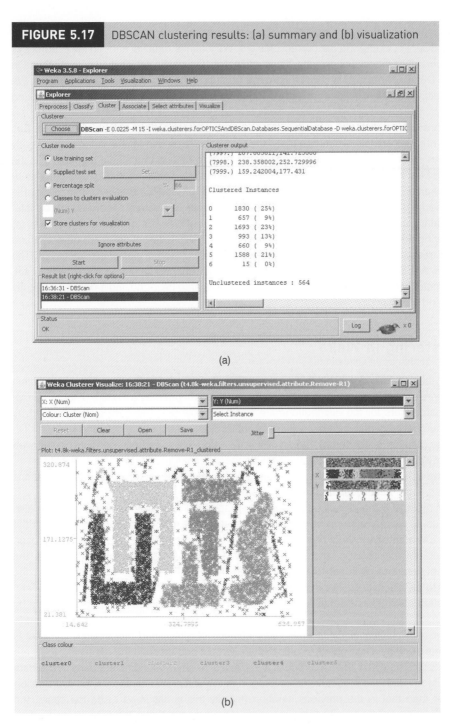

FIGURE 5.17 DBSCAN clustering results: (a) summary and (b) visualization

Figure 5.19 shows the clustering results with numClusters set to −1. From the Cluster output window (Figure 5.19(a)), it is clear that the EM method performs well in discovering the three clusters embedded in the data set. The estimated distribution parameters are close to the distribution parameters used to generate the data points in the data set. Figure 5.19(b) shows the cluster members projected on the XY plane.

TABLE 5.3	Distribution parameters for the synthesized data set			
Distributions	X(μ, σ)	Y(μ, σ)	Z(μ, σ)	No. of Data Points
1	(4, 1.5)	(8, 1.5)	(3, 1.5)	250
2	(3, 0.5)	(3.5, 0.6)	(4, 0.5)	200
3	(9, 1)	(5, 1)	(7, 1.5)	150

5.9   CLUSTERING IN PRACTICE

5

Clustering is a common type of data mining. Sometimes, it is the only type of data mining that can be performed upon a given data set when little prior knowledge exists about the data set. In this section, the tasks of a typical clustering project are outlined. How to choose an appropriate clustering solution is also discussed.

5.9.1 Clustering Project Procedure

A typical clustering project normally involves the following major steps.

Preparation of data Typical tasks include selecting features to be involved with the measurement of proximity, normalizing data values and weighting the selected attributes. Other tasks for data pre-processing, such as data transformation and handling missing values, may also be undertaken if necessary. The original data values may need to be sensibly transformed in order to make it appropriate for the measurement of similarity.

Selection of sensible proximity function In most clustering algorithms, the similarity or dissimilarity function is independent of the

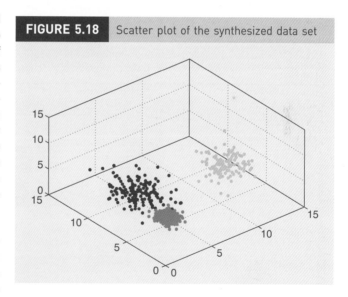

FIGURE 5.18   Scatter plot of the synthesized data set

algorithm, enabling the user to select the right function for the right data. However, only a limited number of software tools allow the user to do so within the capacity of the software itself. It is the data miner's responsibility to check what proximity function is used and whether it is appropriate for the intended data. If a choice is available, the data miner must select the most suitable function. In extreme situations, because of the lack of sound proximity functions in existing software, specially tailored software tools may have to be built to cluster the data.

FIGURE 5.19 EM clustering results

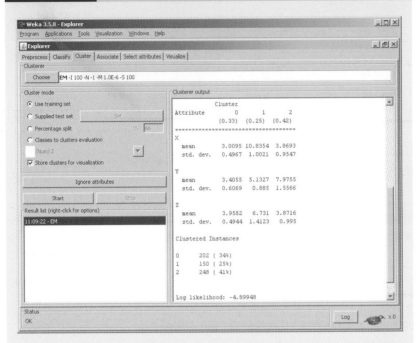

(a)

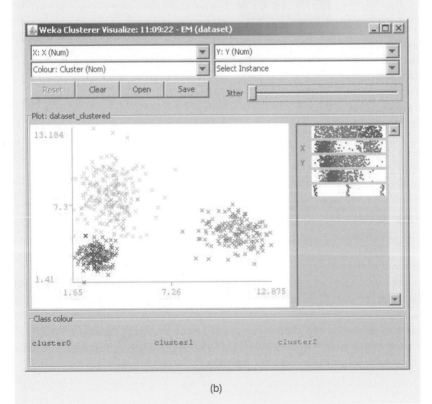

(b)

Selection of clustering solutions Since many clustering solutions exist, the practitioners should be careful to choose the right solution for the right task. Failing to select the right solution may lead to unsatisfactorily poor results. Selection of a clustering solution is discussed in more detail in Section 5.9.2.

Conduct of clustering Clustering, like many other data mining tasks, is normally an iterative process where different settings for relevant parameters may need to be tried in order to gain the best outcome. For instance, the ideal settings for Eps and MinPts parameters for DBCAN in Section 5.8.1 were the result of a number of trials. The repetition is normally determined by evaluation of the clustering results.

Evaluation of cluster quality Most clustering software tools are equipped with cluster evaluation functions, such as SSE, that indicate the quality of the resulting groups. Depending on the evaluation results, the practitioners decide whether the current result of clustering is acceptable or whether another round of clustering with refined parameter settings is needed. A single evaluation result after one round of clustering is hardly useful. The evaluation results of a number of clustering runs can be compared and the best resulting clusters can be located.

Interpretation of clusters Cluster interpretation can be achieved via different means. The summarization of clusters (such as the mean and variance) assists a general understanding of each group. Visualization of cluster membership can also help the understanding of clusters and their coverage. Weka visualizes the cluster memberships of data points against any pair of chosen attributes, allowing the observation of attributes that best separate the clusters. IBM Intelligent Miner for Data provides a comparative view of how the values of an attribute are distributed within the cluster against the distribution of the attribute values for the entire data set. This visualization helps practitioners to locate the most distinct clusters. Some clustering methods, such as CLIQUE, provide a descriptive statement about every cluster that makes the understanding easier. However, such a level of understanding is often basic. Sometimes, further post-processing may be needed. It requires sophisticated thinking to turn clustering results into plausible actions.

A good case study about customer segmentation is given in Chapter 10. Readers are advised to read through this section again after reading the case study.

5.9.2 Choosing a Clustering Solution

Another practical issue relating to clustering is the selection of clustering method to use. Although Section 4.1 summarizes the requirements for a good clustering solution, not all the requirements can be met by a single clustering solution and hence a single clustering solution may not be appropriate for various application backgrounds. This section summarizes a number of considerations to be given when selecting a clustering solution based on the strengths and weaknesses already described in this chapter and Chapter 4. The summary very much echoes that in the text by Tan *et al.* (2006).

A clustering solution can be selected with respect to clustering results, characteristics and descriptions of clusters, characteristics of data and algorithmic concerns. The 'clustering result' here is concerned with complete coverage of all clusters, complete coverage of all data and complete coverage of attributes. The complete coverage of all clusters means whether a complete taxonomy of clusters (i.e. clusters of clusters) or one layer of the taxonomy (i.e. clusters of data) is required. The complete coverage of all data means whether every data record must be assigned as a member of a cluster. The complete coverage of all attributes refers to whether clusters are formed in the entire multidimensional space of all attributes or in a subspace of some of the attributes. Hierarchical clustering algorithms, such as the agglomeration method, result in a taxonomy of clusters whereas the simple K-means method gives a partition-based result. While the result of CHAMELEON covers all data completely, that of DBSCAN does not. The CLIQUE algorithm finds clusters in subspaces when there may be no clusters in the entire space. Data analysts should consider which types of clustering result are desirable for the intended application.

Characteristics of clusters include cluster size, shape, density, etc. Some clustering algorithms, such as the K-means and EM methods, produce clusters of convex or globular shapes whereas others, e.g. CHAMELEON and DBSCAN, can find clusters of arbitrary shapes. Whereas most clustering solutions mentioned in this chapter can find clusters of different sizes, the K-means method and the CURE algorithm tend to identify clusters of similar sizes. Some understanding of the characteristics of desirable clusters during the data exploration period should help in selecting the right clustering solution.

Two forms of cluster description are normally provided as part of the output of a clustering process: the cluster memberships of individual records and a descriptive summary of each cluster (group). All clustering solutions should provide the first kind of description, but the second kind of description varies from solution to solution. Partition-based methods normally provide the cluster centroids; mixture models offer means and covariance; and graph-based methods describe clusters by their members. The CLIQUE algorithm depicts the resulting clusters in terms of logical expressions. It is the description of the clusters that assists in understanding the clusters, and hence it can become a decisive factor in the selection of a cluster solution. The size of the description can also be an important concern. For instance, the European Union's SecurePhone project in the author's department demanded that all cluster descriptions are fitted onto a single SIM card with limited memory resources because of information security concerns.

Characteristics of the data set can also affect the selection of clustering solutions. Besides the issue of suitable distance functions regarding the data types of the attributes involved, the presence of noise and outlier objects, the size of the data set and the number of attributes involved can all be relevant. It is already known that the presence of noise and outliers can severely distort the clustering result if algorithms such as the K-means method are used. Algorithms such as DBSCAN can tolerate the presence of noise and outliers. The size of a data set may prohibit use of certain solutions but favour others. As the number of attributes increases, the performance of some clustering solutions may also deteriorate in terms of time and quality of the resulting clusters.

Besides those mentioned above, there are also considerations regarding clustering algorithms. For instance, the K-means algorithm may produce a non-deterministic result if the initial random partition is different. However, the cluster memberships of most data objects are not affected. If the centroids of the resulting clusters are the main concern, the non-deterministic nature can be tolerated. On the other hand, it cannot be tolerated when the correct membership of every data object becomes the main concern. Some algorithms can determine the number of clusters automatically whereas others can not. In some applications, such as cell identification from a microscopic image, automatic determination of clusters is essential. In other applications, such as facial feature extraction from scanned images, the number and even the whereabouts of facial clusters such as eyes, nose, lips, etc. are more or less known, and therefore automatic determination of the number of clusters may not be needed. Most clustering algorithms require the setting of a number of parameters. Can the optimal setting be determined automatically or manually? Many clustering algorithms use a goodness-of-fit function to decide the quality of the resulting clusters. Does the function always reflect the application objective? In other words, the best clusters found by an algorithm may not always be the best outcome from the application's point of view. For instance, the SSE measure favours dense clusters rather than the sparse cluster in Figure 5.1(b) although the sparse cluster is meaningful too.

The selection criteria described above may help to narrow down the candidate list of clustering solutions, but it does not mean the selection is a trivial process. There may be still a number of solutions that fit all the requirements of the criteria, but sometimes there may be no solution to suit the criteria completely. Existing solutions may need to be tailored or new solutions may have to be developed. Whenever possible, data analysts often use more than one clustering solution over the same data set in order to consolidate the resulting clusters.

5.10 SUMMARY

This chapter has presented a number of more advanced clustering algorithms of different categories. Based on the evaluation of limitations of the basic K-means and agglomeration methods, density-based, graph-based and model-based clustering approaches were broadly described. For each approach, a specific algorithm was studied: the DBSCAN algorithm for density-based methods, the CHAMELEON algorithm for graph-based methods, and the EM algorithm for model-based methods. In addition, the CLIQUE algorithm designed for subspace clustering was also explained against the backdrop that clusters may not exist in high-dimensional spaces. For each algorithm, the chapter broadly described and illustrated its process, discussed its performance and outlined its strengths and weaknesses. Some of the algorithms described in the chapter are also available in Weka and we demonstrated the use of these methods.

Due to their complex nature, the descriptions of some of the algorithms, such as CHAMELEON, are kept brief and only small examples were used for illustrative purposes. The theories behind some algorithms such as the EM/GMM method are also kept to the minimum to appeal to most readers. To achieve more thorough understanding of the algorithms, readers are recommended to read the reference materials given in the Bibliographical Notes.

Proximity between data objects is a broad concept and can be interpreted differently in different circumstances and for different types of data. Taking a meaningful measure of proximity during a clustering process determines the success or failure of the process. Because of the importance of the issue, this chapter further explored how to measure similarity between data objects according to the principles of commonly shared nearest neighbours and the time-warping measure for sequential data records.

Clustering projects have their own unique procedures and issues for consideration. The chapter therefore outlined general principles for conducting clustering tasks. Applying the right solution to the right data is also essential for clustering and the chapter explained how to select a clustering solution.

EXERCISES

1 Use the random number generation facility of either Weka or Microsoft Excel to create an artificial set of 200 uniformly distributed data records. Then use the simple K-means method in Weka to appreciate the limitations of the method in the following aspects:

    (a) Artificial clustering results even though there is no tendency towards clusters in the data set.

    (b) Different clustering results when the random seed for the initial centroid selection is changed. Observe this by saving cluster memberships for different calls of the method and comparing any changes in memberships.

    (c) Convex clusters. Observe this by using the visualization facility in Weka.

2 Discuss, with suitable examples, the major limitations of the agglomeration method.

3 Describe the working principles of the following categories of clustering solution:

  (a) density-based methods;

  (b) graph-based methods;

  (c) model-based methods.

4 The minimum spanning tree (MST) of a given graph is a sub-graph where every vertex is connected to its nearest neighbouring vertex. The data structure and algorithm for finding an MST are common topics of courses in computer science, such as courses on data structures and algorithms. Extend an MST algorithm into a clustering algorithm and provide a description of the algorithm in pseudo-code. What is the time complexity of the algorithm?

5 In density-based clustering, what is the difference between a centre-based density measure and a grid-based density measure? Which one is used in the DBSCAN and CLIQUE algorithms?

6 This exercise requires using the DBSCAN method in Weka on the data set mentioned in Section 5.8.1. You can obtain the data set by downloading the CLUTO software. In the DBSCAN algorithm, the settings of the parameters Eps and MinPts are crucial for the clustering result. Use different values for Eps and MinPts to conduct clustering over the data set and observe the clustering result in the outcome window. For each test run, note the number of clusters and the number of data points being categorized as noise. Explain the reasons behind the differences.

7 Describe the working principle of the CHAMELEON algorithm. Explain how the concept of 'edge cut' is used in its measurement of relative interconnectivity and closeness. Give an example to illustrate this.

8 Describe the working principle of the EM algorithm. In a number of software tools that support the EM algorithm, the covariance matrix is replaced with a variance vector. Discuss the pros and cons of such a replacement.

9 CLUSTER (Bouman 2005) offers a downloadable EM/GMM package solution for clustering and classification. Different from many other EM toolkits, this standalone executable automatically determines the number of clusters. The software can be run in both UNIX and Windows environments. Download and install a copy of the software from the website provided in the Bibliography and observe the software working over the data set provided.

10 Refer to the example in Section 5.8.2. Use a tool such as Microsoft Excel to generate a random data set of 1000 records and two attributes (e.g. body weight and body height). You can assume that the data follow four normal distributions with their respective means and standard deviations that you decide yourself. Use the EM algorithm in Weka to discover four clusters. Then check the size, means vector and standard deviations of each cluster against the original parameters and conclude on the effectiveness of the method.

11 Use the diagram in Figure 5.1(b) as an example to illustrate the principle of the SNN similarity measure. Explain why the SNN approach to similarity measurement is particularly applicable in a situation like this. Describe, in pseudo-code, a basic clustering algorithm based on the SNN similarity measurement.

12 Given two time-series sequences A = 1, 1, 1, 2, 2, 3, 2, 1 and B = 1, 2, 2, 3, 3, 2, let us assume that the Euclidean function is used for measuring the distance between two elements of the sequences at a specific time point:

  (a) Use the basic algorithm to find the optimal warping path.

  (b) Suggest one way of improving the basic algorithm and illustrate your point with examples.

BIBLIOGRAPHICAL NOTES

Han and Kamber (2001) and Tan *et al.* (2006) are among the most useful texts for this chapter. The survey papers that have been referred to most are papers by Jain, Murty and Flynn (1999), Fasulo (1999) and Berkhin (2002). Research papers on the subject include Ester *et al.* (1996) for DBSCAN, Karypis *et al.* (1999) for CHAMELEON and Agrawal *et al.* (1998) for CLIQUE. Coverage of the estimation-maximization (EM) method is extensive. A number of more recent articles such as Verbeek *et al.* (2003) and Bouman (2005) are referred to.

The limitations of basic clustering solutions are well recognized in the clustering literature. In particular, Karypis *et al.* (1999) presents a good survey of the limitations of basic hierarchical clustering solutions with different merging schemes with regard to shape, size, density and similarity of clusters. The survey papers mentioned present an adequate summary of clustering approaches.

As for the algorithms, DBSCAN has generated interest in solutions of the same type. Ester *et al.* (1998) developed an incremental version of the algorithm. Sander *et al.* (1998) generalized the original algorithm into the GDBSCAN algorithm to cope with more general types of data and distance measures. Ertöz *et al.* (2003) developed a similar SNN algorithm with a notion of proximity based on nearest neighbours. The CHAMELEON algorithm was well explained in the original paper. The same research team developed a clustering software toolkit, known as CLUTO, to accompany the algorithm. The software toolkit comes with a collection of test data sets that can be downloaded from Karypis (2006). The CLIQUE algorithm was a continuation of the work on association rules by Agrawal's team at IBM and has prompted a number of follow-up works. The ENCLUS algorithm (Cheng *et al.* 1999) follows a similar procedural framework to CLIQUE but uses entropy to measure coverage, density and correlation, based on the principle that subspaces with clusters have less entropy than subspaces without clusters. The MAFIA algorithm (Nagesh 1999; Nagesh *et al.* 2000) aims to improve on the efficiency and cluster quality of the original algorithm. Parsons *et al.* (2004) give a systematic review of recent works on subspace clustering. The EM algorithm can be found from many sources. It is worth noting that two software toolkits are available and free to download. Torch (Collobert *et al.* 2002) is a modular machine-learning software library from which a Gaussian mixture method can be called. CLUSTER (Bouman 2005) provides a standalone executable that automatically determines the number of clusters.

The SNN similarity measure was first introduced by Jarvis and Patrick (1973). Tan *et al.* (2006) also give a comprehensive explanation of the topic. The SNN density-based clustering and its applications can be found in Ertöz *et al.* (2003). Time-warping methods have been extensively described in the literature. This text mainly refers to the articles by Salvador and Chan (2007) and Keogh and Pazzani (2001). Similarity measurement is an active research area in its own right and much research has been done, particularly into the use and fusion of multiple similarity functions. Wu and Chang (2004) present a scheme to fuse distance measurements of multiple views of sequential data. Aggarwal (2003) describes a framework to fuse parameterized distance functions systematically. Vlachos *et al.* (2003) develop an efficient indexing structure for applying multiple distance functions.

5

CHAPTER 6

Decision tree induction for classification

LEARNING OBJECTIVES

To gain a general understanding of classification by decision tree induction

To appreciate issues of concern with decision tree induction

To gain a broad understanding of decision tree induction algorithms

To gain an in-depth understanding of the ID3 algorithm

To understand and appreciate the purpose of attribute selection measures

To appreciate the problem of model overfitting in decision tree induction

To understand how tree pruning methods work

To understand how to evaluate the performance of a decision tree

To learn how to conduct classification tasks using decision tree methods in Weka

One of the data mining objectives mentioned in Chapter 1 is to determine the class of an unseen data record. Classification has a wide range of applications and many data mining tasks are classification by nature. It is therefore important to study the classification problem and its solutions and to understand practical issues in relation to classification.

As described in Chapter 2, the classification problem is typically resolved in two stages: constructing a classification model and adapting and applying the model to classify data records whose classes are unknown. According to model representations, a number of different approaches have been proposed. This chapter introduces one approach known as *decision tree induction*. Chapter 7 overviews other alternative approaches and techniques.

This chapter is organized as follows. First, the principles of classification by decision tree induction are described. A common procedural framework for inducing a decision tree is outlined. The issue of attribute selection and its effect on the decision tree structure is highlighted. Then, the ID3 algorithm is introduced in detail. An attribute selection measure, known as *information gain*, is described and its rationale discussed. After that, other decision tree induction techniques, particularly other attribute selection measures are reviewed. The chapter then discusses the problem of model overfitting and how the problem is addressed by the decision tree induction approach. The chapter then introduces methods and measures for evaluating the performance of a resulting tree. The chapter concludes with examples of classification by decision tree induction in Weka.

6.1   DECISION TREES AND THE DECISION TREE INDUCTION APPROACH

6.1.1 The Classification Process

In order to develop a reliable model that makes fewer errors in classification, the available population of data examples, whose classes are already known, is normally divided into two subsets: a *training set* and a *test set*. Examples from the training set are used to *induce* a model whereas examples from the test set are used to *evaluate* the accuracy of the model. The accuracy is measured by the error rate of classification when the model is used to classify the examples in the test set. Normally, a number of attempts is made to develop a number of classification models by using different parts of the available population of examples as training and test sets. A model with a significantly better accuracy is then selected as the final model. We return to this issue later in the chapter.

Using a limited number of examples to develop a classification model has a problem that cannot be avoided, known as *the problem of model overfitting*. The model fits well and perhaps *too* well to the examples in the training set, but not so well to the examples in the test set or data at large. When the model is used in practice, it causes unnecessary errors in classification: records of one class are misclassified as records of another. This problem is discussed in more detail later. In order to reduce the effect of model overfitting, the training set is normally further divided into *training* and *validation examples*. The training examples are used to *build* an initial model, and the validation examples are then used to *refine* the initial model, hoping that the resulting model is more robust with a better accuracy. Figure 6.1 illustrates the roles of the different subsets of data.

FIGURE 6.1   Roles of training, validation and testing examples

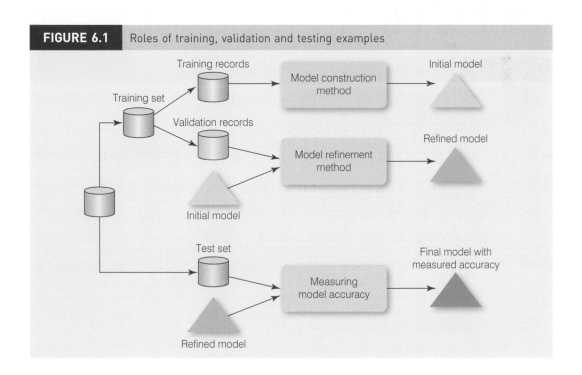

As illustrated in Figure 6.1, computational objectives for the different data subsets are different, and therefore different computational solutions are required. Because of the highly regular structure of a tree, most of the solutions are recursive in nature.

Given a population of examples, there seems to be no general consent regarding how to divide the population into the three different subsets. The issue is also related to how many data records are available. Most data mining tools leave this matter for data analysts and data miners to decide and specify as a parameter of the mining task. For example, some data miners may use half of the population for training and the other half for testing. Others use two thirds for training and one third for testing. Among the training examples, some data miners use two thirds as training examples and one third as validation examples.

There exists some confusion over the use of the terms 'training example' and 'testing example' in the literature. Examples that are used for model refinement and examples for model evaluation have both been called *test* or *testing* examples. Indeed, testing examples for model refinement may well be used for model evaluation too. However, to limit the potential for bias, each subset must and should play a single role at a time. It is therefore felt that the training–validation–testing partition of the available data population is most appropriate and is used by this book. Another potential confusion also exists with the term *classifier*. Some texts use classifier to refer to the classification model, whereas others use it to refer to the classification technique used in developing the model. In this text, attempt is made not to use this ambiguous term.

6.1.2 Decision Tree Induction Approach to Classification

Let us first review the concept of decision tree approach to classification that was briefly described in Chapter 3. A typical decision tree consists of leaf nodes, internal nodes and links. A leaf node represents a class label. An internal node represents the name of an attribute. The link from a parent node to a child node represents a value of the attribute of the parent node. The decision tree approach for classification *induces*, from a set of training examples, a decision tree as the classification model.

Figure 6.2(a) shows a weather condition table that can be used as the training set. A decision tree construction technique such as the ID3 algorithm can be applied to the data set to induce a decision

FIGURE 6.2   From training examples to a decision tree

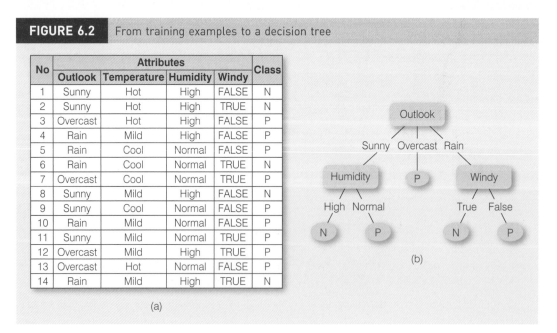

No	Outlook	Temperature	Humidity	Windy	Class
1	Sunny	Hot	High	FALSE	N
2	Sunny	Hot	High	TRUE	N
3	Overcast	Hot	High	FALSE	P
4	Rain	Mild	High	FALSE	P
5	Rain	Cool	Normal	FALSE	P
6	Rain	Cool	Normal	TRUE	N
7	Overcast	Cool	Normal	TRUE	P
8	Sunny	Mild	High	FALSE	N
9	Sunny	Cool	Normal	FALSE	P
10	Rain	Mild	Normal	FALSE	P
11	Sunny	Mild	Normal	TRUE	P
12	Overcast	Mild	High	TRUE	P
13	Overcast	Hot	Normal	FALSE	P
14	Rain	Mild	High	TRUE	N

(a)

(b)

tree such as the one in Figure 6.2(b). The decision tree can then be used to decide if a data record with certain outlook, temperature, humidity and windiness should be of class P or N.

Some important points regarding decision tree induction must be mentioned. First, more than one decision tree can be induced from the same set of training examples. This may be the result of applying different tree construction algorithms and attribute selection measures. Even when the same algorithm is used, the possible non-deterministic nature (randomness) of an algorithm may still result in the construction of different trees.

Second, the structure of a decision tree directly affects the performance of the classification model. With a decision tree, determining the class of a data object involves a sequence of tests from the root node of the tree towards a leaf node, one at each internal node on the path. According to the result of the test, a decision regarding which branch of the tree should be followed to the next level is made. Therefore, the speed of classification is directly related to the number of levels of the tree. The more levels the decision tree has, the more tests need to be conducted, and the longer the classification takes. The crucial question here is how to construct a tree that has a minimal number of levels such that it classifies as many examples as early, at the highest levels of the tree, as possible.

Third, accuracy of classification by a decision tree is a paramount concern. A high degree of accuracy means a high level of confidence in the classification decision by the classification model, making the model more interesting. Sufficiency of accuracy normally depends on the intended application. For instance, the level of accuracy in predicting whether it rains the next day may be less important than the level of accuracy required for predicting the likelihood of a terrorist attack. Even for the same application, certain aspects of accuracy are more desirable than others. For instance, we might be more interested in knowing that someone is a terrorist suspect than that he or she is not.

All these issues are discussed throughout this chapter.

6.1.3 Constructing a Decision Tree

As a major approach to classification, decision tree induction has received a great amount of attention from researchers over the last two or three decades. As a result, a number of decision tree induction methods have been developed. Looking closely at those methods, it is realized that all of them share a similar procedural framework, which can be outlined as follows:

1 If the training set is empty, create a leaf node and label it as NULL. It means that there are no examples in the training set to determine the class outcome and hence the class is considered unknown.

2 If all examples in the current training set are of the same class, create a leaf node and label it with the class label. This means that the label of the leaf node determines the class for those examples.

3 If the examples in the current training set are of different classes, the following operations need to be performed:

(a) Select an attribute to be the root of the current tree;

(b) Partition the current training set into subsets according to the values of the chosen attribute;

(c) Construct a subtree for each subset;

(d) Create a link from the root of the current tree to the root of each subtree, and label the link with appropriate value of the root attribute that separates one subset from the others.

The key step of the entire framework is step 3(a). It uses a formal measure, known as the *attribute selection measure,* to determine which attribute is the most suitable to be used as the root of the current

FIGURE 6.3 A decision tree constructed by random selection of attributes

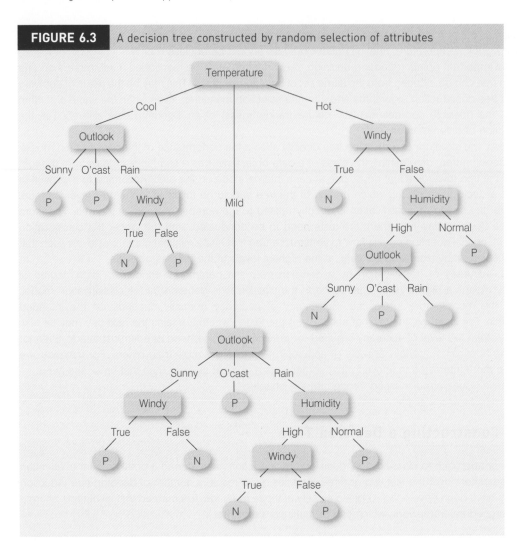

tree. A number of different attribute selection measures (such as information gain) have been developed. What is the significance of those different attribute selection measures? Instead of using a formal measure, could an attribute be selected randomly? In other words, is the use of a formal attribute selection measure really necessary?

Figure 6.3 shows a decision tree that is constructed from the table in Figure 6.2(a) by selecting attributes randomly. The tree in Figure 6.3 is much more complex than the decision tree in Figure 6.2(b), with more branches and more levels. More branches and levels mean not only that more memory resources are required for maintaining the tree but also that more tests are needed in the classification stage and hence a longer time is needed before a classification decision is made. Another more serious problem is that decision trees of complex structures are more likely to overfit, and hence are more likely to make errors and be pruned later.

The decision tree in Figure 6.2(b) is much smaller, more robust and efficient with fewer levels. The tree also indicates that not *every* attribute is needed in the decision-making. For instance, attribute Temperature does not appear in the tree. This means the attribute has very little to do with determining the class outcome.

6.2   THE ID3 ALGORITHM AND INFORMATION GAIN MEASURE

One well-established algorithm, known as ID3, was developed in the early 1980s by the Australian researcher, Ross Quinlan. It follows almost the exact steps of the general framework outlined in Section 6.1.3 and uses information gain as a measure to select an attribute. The algorithm is presented in pseudo-code as follows:

```
algorithm constructTreeID3 (C : training set) : decision tree;
begin
  Tree := Ø; // empty the tree initially
  if C is empty then
    Tree := a leaf node labelled NULL;
    return(Tree)
  else
    if C contains examples of one class then
      Tree := a leaf node labelled by the class tag
    else
      for every attribute A_i (1 ≤ i ≤ p) do
        calculate information gain Gain(A_i)
      endfor;
      select attribute A where Gain(A) = max(Gain(A_1), Gain(A_2), ..., Gain(A_p));
      partition C into subsets C_1, C_2, ..., C_w by values of A;
      for each C_i (1 ≤ i ≤ w) do
        t_i := constructTreeID3(C_i);
        Tree := a tree where node A as root and t_1, t_2, ..., t_w as subtrees;
        label the links from A to the roots of the subtrees with values of A
      endfor;
    endif;
  endif;
  return(Tree);
end;
```

The algorithm first selects the attribute with the highest information gain as the root of the entire tree and then builds a subtree for each subset of the original training set partitioned by the values of the selected attribute. Once the subtrees are built, a link with the partitioning attribute value as the label is created and connected to the root of each subtree. So what is 'information gain'? Why does the ID3 algorithm select an attribute with the highest gain as the root?

6.2.1 Information Gain

In order to fully appreciate the rationale behind the information gain measure, some concepts of information theory must be understood. Although these concepts may sound mathematical, the ideas behind them are quite straightforward. Readers who may not be very comfortable with mathematical formulae and notations should rely on the examples used throughout this section.

The concept of information gain originates in probability and information theory. The purpose is to quantify and measure the amount of information when random events occur. Before explaining what information gain is, we first introduce the concept of an information system. In information theory, an *information system S* is a system about sample space that consists of a set of events $E_1, E_2, .., E_n$ with associated probabilities of event occurrences $P(E_1), P(E_2), ..., P(E_n)$. Suppose M is the size of the sample space and N_k is the number of outcomes that convey the event E_k, then the probability that E_k occurs is calculated as

$$P(E_k) = \frac{N_k}{M}$$

For a training set of examples, each attribute can be considered as an information system. For instance in the weather condition table in Figure 6.2(a), the attribute Class is a system with two probable events: the class being positive and the class being negative. The associated probabilities for the two events are respectively 9/14 and 5/14. The sum of the two probabilities equals 1. In other words, the table contains examples that are either of positive or negative class.

For an information system S, the amount of *self-information* of an event E_k $(1 \leq k \leq n)$ of S is defined as

$$I(E_k) = \log_q \frac{1}{P(E_k)} = -\log_q P(E_k)$$

when $P(E_k) = 0$, $I(E_k)$ is set to 0. The logarithm in the definition can be thought of as a rescaling of the raw probability values that may be sparse and skewed. The logarithm transformation makes the values more evenly distributed and separated out. The base q of the logarithm defines the *unit* of measure for the amount of information. If base 2 is used, the amount is measured in *bits*. If base 10 is used, the amount is measured in *digits*. This is similar to weight being measured in either the metric scale or the imperial scale.

The definition of self-information states that if event E_k always happens, then $P(E_k) = 1$ and $I(E_k) = 0$. In other words, the occurrence of an event that always happens gives no information. For instance, the event 'the sun rises from the east' always happens, the occurrence of this everyday event therefore conveys no information. If E_k frequently happens, $P(E_k)$ is close to 1 and $I(E_k)$ is close to 0, i.e. the occurrence of a frequently occurring event conveys very little information. For instance, earthquakes happen quite often in Japan and people there are quite used to them. Such an event has little value as news. If E_k hardly happens, $P(E_k)$ is close to 0 and $I(E_k)$ is very large, which means that the actual occurrence of the event conveys a large amount of information. As an example, earthquakes hardly happen in the United Kingdom and a small tremor normally becomes headline news. If E_k never happens, the amount of information should be infinite. To avoid this useless situation, the self-information is forced to zero.

Based on self-information of individual events, the *average* information, also known as *entropy*, of the whole information system S is defined as the weighted sum of self-information of all events in S. The weights are the probabilities of the events of S.

$$H(S) = \sum_{k=1}^{n} P(E_k) \cdot I(E_k) = -\sum_{k=1}^{n} P(E_k) \cdot \log P(E_k)$$

For the table in Figure 6.2(a), the self-information of the event that class is positive and the average information of the attribute Class are respectively:

$$I(Class = P) = -\log_2 P(Class = P) = -\log_2 \frac{9}{14} = 0.637 bits$$

$$\begin{aligned} H(Class) &= -P(Class = P) \cdot \log_2 P(Class = P) \\ &\quad -P(Class = N) \cdot \log_2 P(Class = N) \\ &= -\frac{9}{14} \log_2 \frac{9}{14} - \frac{5}{14} \log_2 \frac{5}{14} = 0.94 bits \end{aligned}$$

The entropy of an information system S of N events indicates the degree of uncertainty. If there is an absolute certainty that one event in S always occurs, the probability of that event is 1 and the probabilities of all other mutually exclusive $N - 1$ events ought to be 0. Then, each term in the entropy expression equals 0 and hence $H(S) = 0$. On the other hand, when every event of S has equal probability $1/N$, the system is most uncertain, and $H(S) = \log N$, the maximum. Most of time, $0 \leq H(S) \leq \log N$.

Given two information systems S_1 and S_2, the conditional self-information of event E_k of S_1 given that event F_j of S_2 has occurred, is defined as

$$I(E_k \mid F_j) = \log_q \frac{1}{P(E_k \mid F_j)} = -\log_q P(E_k \mid F_j) = -\log_q \frac{P(E_k \text{ and } F_j)}{P(E_k)}$$

This definition is almost the same as that for the self-information of a single event, except that the conditional probability of event E_k given event F_j is used. For the table in Figure 6.2(a), the conditional self-information of the event that the class is positive, given the Outlook is sunny, is calculated as follows:

$$I(Class = P \mid Outlook = sunny) = -\log_2 P(Class = P \mid Outlook = sunny)$$

$$= -\log_2 \frac{P(Class = P \text{ and } Outlook = sunny)}{P(Outlook = sunny)} = -\log_2 \frac{2}{5} = 1.322 bits$$

The average conditional information, also known as the *expected information*, of system S_1 of n events at the presence of system S_2 of m events is the weighted sum of the conditional self-information over all pairs of events in S_1 and S_2:

$$H(S_1 \mid S_2) = \sum_{i=1}^{n} \sum_{j=1}^{m} P(E_i \text{ and } F_j) \cdot I(E_i \mid F_j) = -\sum_{i=1}^{n} \sum_{j=1}^{m} P(E_i \text{ and } F_j) \cdot \log_q \frac{P(E_i \text{ and } F_j)}{P(F_j)}$$

When a decision tree is being constructed, two information systems are present at a time: the attribute A and the attribute Class. $H(Class)$ represents the average information of Class system *before* the attribute A is considered as the root of the decision tree while $H(Class \mid A)$ represents the expected information of Class system *after* the attribute A is chosen as the root. The information gain over the attribute A, denoted as $G(A)$, is the difference between $H(Class)$ and $H(Class \mid A)$, i.e.

$$G(A) = H(Class) - H(Class \mid A)$$

It is important to understand what information gain actually represents. As mentioned previously, $H(S)$ signifies a degree of uncertainty. Then, $H(Class)$ and $H(Class \mid A)$ must reflect respectively the degrees of uncertainty *before* and *after* attribute A is selected. Then information gain $G(A)$ represents a *reduction* of uncertainty over the choice of A. The attribute that has the highest information gain is the one that reduces the degree of uncertainty the most. In other words, the ID3 algorithm selects the attribute whose values *influence* the outcome of the class the most, ensuring the classification of as many examples as close to the root of the tree as possible.

6.2.2 Calculating Information Gain

In a set of training examples, suppose that there are p positive and n negative examples, and there are p_i positive and n_i negative examples whose attribute A has the value a_i. Then $p + n$ is the total number of examples and $p_i + n_i$ is the total number of examples having the attribute value a_i. The figures are listed in a contingency table, Table 6.1.
Therefore,

$$H(Class) = -\frac{p}{p+n} \log \frac{p}{p+n} - \frac{n}{p+n} \log \frac{n}{p+n}$$

TABLE 6.1 Contingency table

Attribute A	Classes		Total
	Positive	Negative	
a_1	p_1	n_1	$p_1 + n_1$
a_2	p_2	n_2	$p_2 + n_2$
E	E	E	E
a_v	p_v	n_v	$p_v + n_v$
Total	p	n	$p + n$

and

$$H(Class \mid A) = \sum_{i=1}^{v}\left(-\frac{p_i}{p+n}\log\frac{p_i}{p_i+n_i} - \frac{n_i}{p+n}\log\frac{n_i}{p_i+n_i}\right)$$

$$= \sum_{i=1}^{v}\frac{p_i+n_i}{p+n}\left(-\frac{p_i}{p_i+n_i}\log\frac{p_i}{p_i+n_i} - \frac{n_i}{p_i+n_i}\log\frac{n_i}{p_i+n_i}\right)$$

$$= \sum_{i=1}^{v}\frac{p_i+n_i}{p+n}H(Class \mid A = a_i)$$

where $(p_i + n_i)/(p + n)$ is the probability of attribute A taking the value a_i, and $H(Class|A = a_i)$ is the average information of Class when the value of attribute A of the examples equal to a_i. Now we are ready to show the calculation of the information gain for attribute Outlook of the table in Figure 6.2(a):

$$H(Class) = -\frac{9}{14}\log_2\frac{9}{14} - \frac{5}{14}\log_2\frac{5}{14} = 0.94 bits$$

Since:

$$H(Class \mid Outlook = sunny) = -\frac{2}{5}\log_2\frac{2}{5} - \frac{3}{5}\log_2\frac{3}{5} = 0.971 bits$$

$$H(Class \mid Outlook = overcast) = -\frac{4}{4}\log_2\frac{4}{4} = 0 bits$$

$$H(Class \mid Outlook = rain) = -\frac{3}{5}\log_2\frac{3}{5} - \frac{2}{5}\log_2\frac{2}{5} = 0.971 bits$$

$$\therefore H(Class \mid Outlook) = \frac{5}{14}H(Class \mid Outlook = sunny) + \frac{4}{14}H(Class \mid Outlook = overcast)$$

$$+ \frac{5}{14}H(Class \mid Outlook = rain) = \frac{5}{14}\times 0.971 + 0 + \frac{5}{14}\times 0.971 = 0.694 bit$$

Therefore:

$$Gain(Outlook) = H(Class) - (H(Class \mid A) = 0.94 - 0.694 = 0.246 bits$$

Similarly, the information gains over the other attributes of the table are as follows: Gain (Temperature) $\approx$ 0.029 bits, Gain(Humidity) $\approx$ 0.151 bits and Gain(Windy) $\approx$ 0.048 bits.

6.2.3 Creating a Decision Tree in ID3

It is clear from the information gain results in the previous section that attribute Outlook has the highest information gain and therefore should be chosen as the root of the entire decision tree. The values of the attribute, i.e. sunny, overcast and rain, are then used to partition the original training set into three subsets as shown in Figure 6.4. Each subset contains only examples that have the same attribute value for the attribute Outlook.

For the subset in Figure 6.4(a), the process of calculating information gains on the remaining attributes is repeated. Among the attributes, Humidity has the highest gain and hence is selected as the root of the subtree for that subset. The two values of the root, high and normal, partition the subset further into two smaller subsets. Each of the smaller subsets contain examples of only one class (N when Humidity = high and P when Humidity = normal). Therefore, two leaf nodes, one labelled N and the other P, are created. Then two links labelled with appropriate attribute values are created from the root node of the subtree to the leaf nodes, as shown in Figure 6.5(a). All examples in the subset in Figure 6.4(b) are of positive class. This means that only a leaf node with label P needs to be created as the tree for the entire subset as shown in Figure 6.5(b). Similarly, for the subset in Figure 6.4(c), the attribute Windy has the highest gain and hence is chosen as the root of the subtree for the subset. The subset is further partitioned into two smaller subsets according to TRUE or FALSE, and each of them contains examples of the same class (P for FALSE and N for TRUE), and therefore two leaf nodes are created and a subtree with Windy as the root is formed as shown in Figure 6.5(c). Finally, links with appropriate labels from the root of the entire tree to the roots of the subtrees are added and the complete decision tree shown in Figure 6.5(d) is obtained.

FIGURE 6.4   Subsets partitioned from the original training set

Temperature	Humidity	Windy	Class
Hot	High	FALSE	N
Hot	High	TRUE	N
Mild	High	FALSE	N
Cool	Normal	FALSE	P
Mild	Normal	TRUE	P

(a) Outlook = sunny

Temperature	Humidity	Windy	Class
Hot	High	FALSE	P
Cool	Normal	TRUE	P
Mild	High	TRUE	P
Hot	Normal	FALSE	P

(b) Outlook = overcast

Temperature	Humidity	Windy	Class
Mild	High	FALSE	P
Cool	Normal	FALSE	P
Cool	Normal	TRUE	N
Mild	Normal	FALSE	P
Mild	High	TRUE	N

(c) Outlook = rain

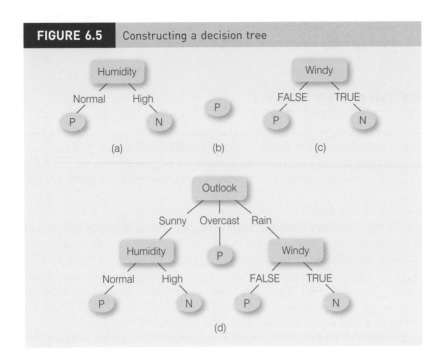

FIGURE 6.5 Constructing a decision tree

6.3 ATTRIBUTE SELECTION MEASURES IN OTHER DECISION TREE METHODS

As well as the information gain, other attribute selection measures also exist, normally as a part of a decision tree induction algorithm. Algorithms such as C4.5 and C5 use the information gain ratio, the CART algorithm uses the Gini index of impurity, and the CHAID algorithm uses a measure known as the chi-square statistic. All measures serve the same purpose: to find the best attribute for separating classes.

6.3.1 Information Gain Ratio in the C4.5 and C5 Algorithms

The *information gain ratio* is defined as the ratio of the information gain over attribute A against the average information of the attribute, i.e.

$$Gain\ Ratio(A) = \frac{Gain(A)}{H(A)}$$

The gain ratio *normalizes* uncertainty across different attributes in order to avoid bias towards attributes with more distinct values. For the attribute Outlook in Figure 6.2(a):

$$H(Outlook) = -\frac{5}{14}\log_2\frac{5}{14} - \frac{4}{14}\log_2\frac{4}{14} - \frac{5}{14}\log_2\frac{5}{14} = 1.577 bits$$

$$Gain\ Ratio(Outlook) = \frac{Gain(Outlook)}{H(Outlook)} = \frac{0.246}{1.577} \approx 0.156$$

Similarly, we have GainRatio(Temperature) ≈ 0.019, GainRatio(Humidity) ≈ 0.151, and GainRatio (Windy) ≈ 0.019. Although the three-value attribute Outlook is still chosen as the root, its gain ratio is much closer to the two-value attribute Humidity. Experimental studies have shown that the information gain ratio has marginally better performance than the information gain in terms of classification accuracy of the resulting tree. That is why the successors of ID3 (C4.5 and C5) have adapted this measure of attribute selection.

6.3.2 Gini Index of Impurity in the CART Algorithm

Instead of information-based attribute selection measures, algorithms such as CART, SLIQ and SPRINT, consider the training set as an impure set of examples of different classes. Constructing a decision tree is a process of splitting the data set into purer and purer partitions where examples of one class overwhelm examples of the others. Suppose that a training set has w classes $C1, C2, \ldots, Cw$. A function that measures the level of impurity of the data set, known as the *Gini impurity function*, under a given condition t is defined as:

$$Gini(t) = 1 - \sum_{i=1}^{w} P(C_i \mid t)^2$$

where $P(C_i \mid t)$ is the fraction of a specific class under the condition t. The level of impurity of a training set can be measured initially without any conditions as follows:

$$Gini(Class) = 1 - \sum_{i=1}^{w} P(C_i)^2$$

If the training set has two classes and each class is equally probable, the level of impurity is $1 - 0.5^2 - 0.5^2 = 0.5$, the most impure. If the training set contains examples of only one class, the level of impurity is 0, the least impure.

When constructing a decision tree, we are searching for an attribute whose values (the condition t) split an impure set into a number of partitions. The partitions have fewer degrees of impurity than the original impure set before partitioning. To construct an effective tree, the attribute whose values reduce the levels of impurity the most, are selected as the root of the decision tree. The *Gini index* of impurity over an attribute A of m values is defined as

$$GiniIndex(A) = Gini(Class) - \sum_{j=1}^{m} P(a_j) \cdot Gini(A = a_j)$$

where $P(a_j)$ is the probability of $A = a_j$. For the table in Figure 6.2(a), since the number of P class is 9 and the number of N class is 5, the level of impurity of the data set is measured as:

$$Gini(Class) = 1 - \left(\frac{9}{14}\right)^2 - \left(\frac{5}{14}\right)^2 \approx 0.459$$

and

$$Gini(Outlook = sunny) = 1 - P(Class = P \mid Outlook = sunny)^2 - P(Class = N \mid Outlook = sunny)^2$$
$$= 1 - \left(\frac{2}{5}\right)^2 - \left(\frac{3}{5}\right)^2 = 0.48$$

$$Gini(Outlook = overcast) = 1 - P(Class = P \mid Outlook = overcast)^2 - P(Class = N \mid Outlook = overcast)^2$$
$$= 1 - \left(\frac{4}{4}\right)^2 - \left(\frac{0}{4}\right)^2 = 0$$

FIGURE 6.6   Gini index of impurity for the weather condition table

Class	Humidity		Windy		Outlook			Temperature		
	High	Normal	TRUE	FALSE	Sunny	Overcast	Rain	Hot	Mild	Cool
P	3	6	3	6	2	4	3	2	4	3
N	4	1	3	2	3	0	2	2	2	1
Gini	0.367		0.438		0.343			0.440		
GiniIndex	0.092		0.021		**0.116**			0.019		

(a)

Class	Outlook		Outlook		Outlook		
	Sunny	{Overcast, rain}	Overcast	{Sunny, rain}	{Sunny, overcast}	Rain
P	2	7	4	5	6	3
N	3	2	0	5	3	2
Gini	0.394		0.357		0.457	
GiniIndex	0.065		**0.102**		0.002	

(b)

$$Gini(Outlook = rain) = 1 - P(Class = P \mid Outlook = rain)^2 - P(Class = N \mid Outlook = rain)^2$$

$$= 1 - \left(\frac{3}{5}\right)^2 - \left(\frac{2}{5}\right)^2 = 0.48$$

therefore,

$$GiniIndex(Outlook) = 0.459 - \left(\frac{5}{14} \cdot 0.48 + \frac{4}{14} \cdot 0 + \frac{5}{14} \cdot 0.48\right) \approx 0.116$$

Figure 6.6(a) lists the number of examples of positive and negative classes before and after partitioning with each attribute, together with the measures of impurity and GiniIndex to illustrate the different degrees of impurity reductions. Among all the attributes, Outlook has the highest Gini index value. That means the attribute reduces the level of impurity the most, and hence is chosen as the root of the decision tree. This decision is the same as that made on the basis of information gain.

The CART algorithm primarily produces binary trees. That means a two-way split is required instead of multi-way splits from parent node to child nodes of the tree. In this case, the algorithm seeks the best two-way split: the one that reduces the impurity the best. Figure 6.6(b) illustrates the various two-way splits of Outlook and their corresponding values of GiniIndex. When Outlook = overcast, the split has the highest Gini index value and therefore this test is used as the root of the tree.

6.3.3 Chi-square statistic in the CHAID Algorithm

The chi-square (χ^2) statistic is a measure for the degree of association or dependence between two variables. For classification, the statistic can be used to measure the degree of dependence between a given attribute and the class variable. Given a set of N examples of w classes, $C_1, C_2, \ldots, C_w$, and an attribute A of v values, $a_1, a_2, \ldots, a_v$, the χ^2 function is defined as follows:

$$\chi^2 = \sum_{j=1}^{v} \sum_{i=1}^{w} \frac{(x_{ij} - E_{ij})^2}{E_{ij}}$$

where x_{ij} represents the actual frequency that examples have attribute value a_j and class C_i, and E_{ij} represents the expected frequency. Under the null hypothesis that the class and the attribute are not dependent on each other, $E_{ij} = n_i \times n_j/N$. The chi-square statistic calculates the difference between the actual frequencies of classes in an attribute with the expected frequencies when no association between that attribute and class is assumed. The greater the difference, the stronger the association between the class and the chosen attribute. For the attribute Outlook in Figure 6.2(a):

$$\chi^2(Outlook) = \left(\frac{\left(2 - \left(\frac{5 \times 9}{14}\right)\right)^2}{\left(\frac{5 \times 9}{14}\right)} + \frac{\left(3 - \left(\frac{5 \times 5}{14}\right)\right)^2}{\left(\frac{5 \times 5}{14}\right)} \right) + \left(\frac{\left(4 - \left(\frac{4 \times 9}{14}\right)\right)^2}{\left(\frac{4 \times 9}{14}\right)} \right)$$

$$+ \left(\frac{\left(3 - \left(\frac{5 \times 9}{14}\right)\right)^2}{\left(\frac{5 \times 9}{14}\right)} + \frac{\left(2 - \left(\frac{5 \times 5}{14}\right)\right)^2}{\left(\frac{5 \times 5}{14}\right)} \right) \approx 29.653$$

Similarly, $\chi^2(Temperature) \approx 7.985$, $\chi^2(Humidity) \approx 39.2$ and $\chi^2(Windy) \approx 13.067$. Of course, the level of significance of the association should also be tested. Provided the level of association is significant, the CHAID algorithm appears in favour of Humidity as the root of the decision tree. It has been reported that the chi-square test has to be used with care: it should not be used when the expected frequency is low and the size of the training set is small.

6.4 SOLVING THE PROBLEM OF OVERFITTING

6.4.1 Review of the Problem

All algorithms for classification face the model overfitting problem: the classification model built from a limited set of training examples is too representative of the training examples themselves rather than general characteristics of the data. In decision tree induction, a fuller and more complex tree with extra branches and levels tends to be built as a consequence. The problem worsens when the number of training examples at a leaf node is very small. The resulting trees tend to have low accuracy in classification when they are used in practice.

The problem of model overfitting can be caused by the presence of noise records in the training set, lack of representative examples in the training set and the repeated attribute selection process of a model construction algorithm. The presence of noise records increases the peculiarity of the data, increasing the chances of additional subtrees being built to accommodate the few peculiar noise examples. If the training data records were de-noised before a model is built, this cause of the problem would be avoided. However, most of the time, we have little or no idea which examples are noises. In fact, building a decision tree helps to identify those peculiar examples, but doing so is not really the solution.

The repeated process of attribute selection can also cause the problem of overfitting. As we explained earlier, the process of building a tree is the same as splitting the training set into subsets where class purity is improved. For one attribute, dividing its range into segments may improve the purity by a certain threshold. In the tree construction, a number of candidate attributes are evaluated at a time for class purity improvement. There are more chances that one of the attributes achieves the threshold requirement and the decision tree continues to grow. The question here is how much the threshold should be for the improvement to be considered significant.

Lack of representative examples in the training set can also cause the problem of model overfitting. In this case, the resulting model does not reflect all aspects of all data, but all aspects of some data. For instance, a student performance model built using only home student records may *overfit* to home students and may not work well in predicting the performance of an overseas student.

There are a number of ways of reducing the effect of the problem of model overfitting depending on the causes of the problem. If there is a lack of representative examples, the only sensible way to solve the problem is to ensure the inclusion of the right examples in the training set. For the other two causes, the problem is solved via *tree pruning*.

6.4.2 Tree Pruning

The act of 'pruning' a tree is to replace a subtree by a leaf node, making the tree smaller, more robust and less prone to error. A pruning method is used to determine which part of a decision tree to prune and how to prune it. There are two types of tree pruning methods: pre-pruning and post-pruning. Pre-pruning means that the pruning takes place while the decision tree is being built. In other words, during the construction of a tree using the training examples, a decision is made as to whether a further subtree along a branch should be built or not. For instance, a minimum information gain threshold can be introduced. If the threshold is not reached when the information gains for candidate attributes are calculated, no further subtree is built, which results in a smaller and more robust tree. The problem here is to decide what the appropriate minimum threshold should be. Some decision tree algorithms, such as C4.5, make full use of the available training examples to estimate the number of generalization errors that the tree may make to unseen records based on certain assumptions about the data distribution. Some algorithms use the principle of Occam's razor to penalize trees with extra complexity. The principle states that plurality should not be applied without necessity. In other words, the simplest explanation is normally the best explanation. The algorithms then select a tree with less complexity and the least expected number of errors to be the final tree. This is the only sensible approach when the number of training examples is extremely limited.

Post-pruning means that pruning is conducted after an entire tree is fully grown. Most post-pruning methods, if not all, require the use of an independently sampled set of validation examples. The validation examples are used to test how well the unpruned tree and the pruned tree perform in classifying the examples. Experimental studies have shown that post-pruning methods produce more robust and accurate trees than pre-pruning methods. In the case where useful examples for training are scarce, however, post-pruning can be problematic.

Several post-pruning methods have been developed. They include reduced-error pruning, cost-complexity pruning, pessimistic pruning, production-rule simplification, path-length pruning and cross-validation pruning. We shall concentrate on the principal idea of the *reduced-error pruning* method. The Bibliographical Notes point out references for the other methods.

6.4.3 Reduced-Error Pruning Method

The reduced-error pruning method is outlined as follows:

1 Classify all examples in the validation set using the tree. Note down, at each non-leaf node, the type and number of errors.

2 For every non-leaf node, count the number of errors if the subtree where the node is the root were to be replaced by a leaf node with *the best possible class* label.

3 Prune the subtree that yields the largest reduction of the number of errors.

4 Repeat steps 2 and 3 until further pruning increases the number of errors.

Two further points need to be clarified about Step 3 in the method outline above. First, a subtree may be pruned even when there is a zero rate of error reduction, to reduce the complexity of the tree. Second, there may be a number of subtrees with the same error reduction. In this case, the largest subtree is pruned. This description, however, raises several further concerns. First, it is unclear whether the pruning is done in an iterative fashion in which all subtrees (big or small) are considered for pruning and the bigger subtrees are pruned or in a single-sweep bottom-up fashion in which each subtree is examined from the bottom to the top, i.e. we do not prune a bigger tree until smaller trees that reduce the number of errors are pruned first. Second, it is unclear how to determine the best possible leaf label for a subtree to be pruned. Should only the validation examples, only the training examples, or both be considered when a decision is made? Third, certain parts of the decision tree may not be used at all when testing examples are classified. Pruning these parts of the tree, as far as the validation examples are concerned, does not increase the number of errors in the pruned tree. According to the principle above, these parts should be pruned, but is this strategy correct? After all, this act may increase the number of errors as far as the training examples are concerned.

The most recent research results address these uncertainties as follows. Iterative pruning may lead to the pruning of a bigger subtree and even the pruning of its smaller subtrees may lead to an increase of errors. Such a decision tree may not be able to maintain good accuracy. It is *over generalized*. Therefore, it is suggested that the pruning should be done in a single sweep, bottom-up approach. The decision tree should be traversed in post order, i.e. all subtrees of a parent node must be dealt with first before considering the tree with the parent node as the root.

For the second concern, the best possible leaf for a subtree that may be pruned should be determined by *validation examples only*. A number of reasons justify this decision. First, training examples should not be used to determine which parts to prune. The tree is built with these examples and will, therefore, make no or very few errors with them. The problem of overfitting therefore remains unsolved. Second, using both training and validation examples may sound logical, but in practice, there are normally more training examples than validation examples. If the training and validation examples were used together, there would be more use of training examples than validation examples. The pruned decision tree would, therefore, favour the training examples and it would nullify the idea of using an independent set of validation examples to modify the tree.

For the third concern, it is believed that the existing strategy of pruning parts of a decision tree that are not used by testing examples complies with the principle of overcoming effects of overfitting; these parts of the tree are in facts the parts that represent the overfitting from training examples. They reflect the particularities of the training examples. If testing examples are truly sampled independently, the data set should represent features of the data in general. Hence the arguments justify the removal of these parts. The best possible leaf label can be determined by looking at whether there are more positive training examples than negative training examples, if we have information on the counts of training examples at each leaf node. Otherwise, if we have equal numbers of positive and negative classes, the label can be determined with consideration of the training examples.

With those clarifications, we are now ready to show an example of pruning a decision tree using the reduce-error pruning method. Figure 6.7(a) shows a set of training examples and Figure 6.7(b) shows a separate set of validation examples that contain data records about motor vehicle drivers. The decision tree that is built from the training examples is presented in Figure 6.7(c). The decision tree has 100% accuracy as far as the training examples are concerned. How is this tree pruned in the light of the set of validation examples?

The process starts by using the decision tree to classify every example from the validation set and recording the number of errors made via each internal node of the decision tree. In order to help determine the best label for the leaf node for a pruned subtree, the number of positive and negative validation examples arrived at each leaf node is also recorded in the positive/negative format. Figure 6.8(a) shows the results of counting the errors.

FIGURE 6.7	Training and validation examples and an unpruned decision tree

AgeGroup	Gender	Married	YearsOfLicence	Class
Teen	Male	No	1	P
Teen	Male	Yes	1	P
Teen	Female	No	2	N
Adult	Male	No	2	P
Adult	Female	Yes	2	N
Adult	Male	Yes	1	N
Teen	Female	Yes	2	N
Teen	Male	No	3	N
Adult	Female	Yes	1	P
Senior	Male	Yes	2	N
Senior	Female	Yes	2	N
Senior	Male	No	3	P

(a) Training examples

AgeGroup	Gender	Married	YearsOfLicence	Class
Teen	Male	No	2	P
Teen	Male	Yes	3	P
Teen	Female	No	2	P
Teen	Female	No	2	P
Adult	Female	Yes	3	N
Adult	Female	Yes	3	N
Adult	Female	Yes	2	N
Teen	Female	No	1	P
Senior	Male	Yes	1	N
Senior	Female	Yes	1	N
Senior	Female	Yes	3	N
Adult	Male	No	2	N

(b) Validation examples

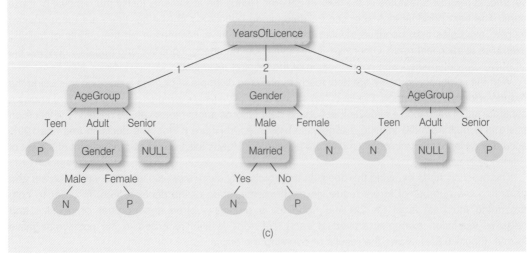

(c)

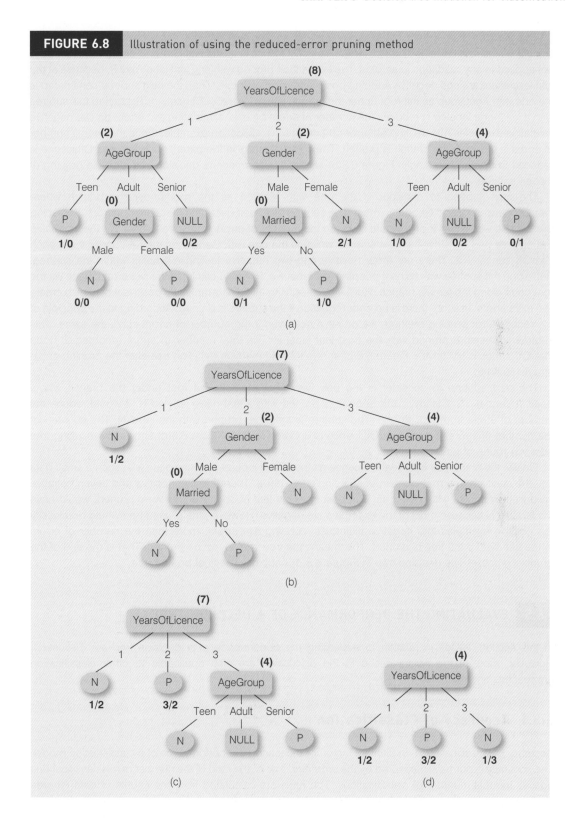

FIGURE 6.8 Illustration of using the reduced-error pruning method

The decision tree is then traversed in post order. The first subtree encountered is the one with Gender as the root under the branch where YearsOfLicence = 1 and AgeGroup = adult. This subtree is not applied to any validation examples. The tree is then pruned with any leaf label, say P, because at the leaf level there are one negative and one positive training example. Then the next subtree considered is the one with AgeGroup as the root under the branch where YearsOfLicence = 1. Replacing this subtree with a leaf node labeled N reduces the number of errors by one, eliminating two errors on two negative validation examples but creating an error on one positive validation example. Since the overall number of errors is reduced, the branch is pruned. The count of errors in the parent node, i.e. YearOfLicence is reduced to seven accordingly. Figure 6.8(b) shows the intermediate decision tree after the pruning of the left subtree.

The next subtree to consider is the one with Married as the root under the branch where YearOfLicence = 2 and Gender = male. The subtree has been used and there are no errors. Replacing this subtree with either P or N would increase the number of errors from zero to one. We therefore skip this subtree and consider the next subtree which is the one with Gender as the root under the branch YearOfLicence = 2. There are three positive and two negative testing examples within the subtree. Replacing the subtree with its best possible leaf label, i.e. P, would eliminate the two errors made via the root node along the female branch. However, classifying all five examples as positive would also create two extra errors. In short, there is no error reduction if the subtree is pruned. According to the principle of the reduce-error pruning method, we prune a tree even if the number of errors stays the same. This subtree is therefore pruned with the best leaf label P. The total number of errors recorded at node YearOfLicence is still seven. Figure 6.8(c) shows the intermediate decision tree after the pruning of the middle subtree.

The next subtree to consider is the one with AgeGroup as the root under the branch where YearOfLicence = 3. Clearly, if this subtree is pruned with a leaf node labeled N, it would reduce the number of errors from four to one. The subtree is therefore pruned with the label N. The counter for the number of errors at node YearOfLicence is updated to four. Figure 6.8(d) shows the resulting tree after this round of pruning.

Finally, the entire tree with YearOfLicence as the root is looked at. Quite often with such a small data set, the decision tree may contain only a single leaf node. There are five positive and seven negative validation examples within the tree. The best possible leaf node, if the tree were pruned, would have the label of N because most of the examples are negative. However, the pruned tree would misclassify the positive examples into negative examples, creating five errors, more than the number of errors in the tree before the tree is pruned. This means the tree should not be pruned. That is the end of the pruning process. The decision tree in Figure 6.8(d) becomes the final pruned tree.

6.5   EVALUATING THE PERFORMANCE OF A DECISION TREE

In this section, issues in relation to evaluating the performance of a decision tree are discussed. However, most of the points raised in the discussion are also applicable to other classification approaches and methods.

6.5.1 Accuracy of Classification

Accuracy of classification is an ultimate factor for measuring the performance of a classification model. The accuracy is normally measured by the *error rate,* that is, the ratio of the number of misclassifications against the total number of classifications. The rates are calculated from the counts of data records correctly and incorrectly classified by the model. The counts can be presented in a tabular form known as a *confusion matrix*. Table 6.2 shows the general structure of a confusion matrix for two-class situations and Table 6.3 shows a confusion matrix for a decision tree induced from the data set in Figure 6.2(a).

In the confusion matrix:

TABLE 6.2	Structure of a confusion matrix		
		Predicted Classes	
Confusion Matrix		**Positive**	**Negative**
Actual Classes	**Positive**	TP	FN
	Negative	FP	TN

- True Positive (TP) refers to the number of actual positive examples classified as positive. In Table 6.3, eight out of nine positive examples are classified as positive.

- True Negative (TN) refers to the number of actual negative examples classified as negative. In Table 6.3, four out of five negative examples are classified as negative.

- False Negative (FN) refers to the number of actual positive examples classified as negative. In Table 6.3, one out of nine positive classes are classified as negative.

TABLE 6.3	Confusion matrix for the weather data decision tree		
		Predicted Classes	
		P	**N**
Actual Classes	**P**	8	1
	N	1	4

- False Positive (FP) refers to the number of actual negative examples classified as positive. In Table 6.3, one out of five negative examples are classified as positive.

Then the overall error rate of a classification model *T* is calculated as:

$$errorRate(T) = \frac{FP + FN}{TP + FN + FP + TN}, \text{ and } accuracyRate(T) = 1 - errorRate(T)$$

For the confusion matrix in Table 6.3, the overall error rate of the decision tree induced is calculated as $2/14 = 0.143$.

Although the overall error rate is a good indicator of how accurate the classification model is, the TP, TN, FN and FP indicators are more detailed and can be more useful for certain applications. For instance, for a face verification system where entry to a sensitive area is granted according to the analysis of a scanned face image, false acceptance (the equivalent of FP) is a more serious error than false rejection (the equivalent of FN). Therefore, classification models with a low error count for the FP indicator would be more acceptable than ones with a lower overall error rate. It is therefore desirable to look at the confusion matrix for the right understanding of accuracy instead of referring to a single overall error rate.

6.5.2 Methods for Evaluating Accuracy

In the previous section, it is not clear what data are used to measure the error rate of a decision tree. Obviously, if the error rate is measured against the training examples from which the decision tree is built, the error rate should be very low, and hence the accuracy rate should be very high: artificially and unrealistically high. That is why classification methods rely on the use of a separate set of testing examples to measure accuracy. Accuracy of a decision tree that is measured upon unseen data is more unbiased and hence more realistic.

There are a number of methods for evaluating the performance of a classification model when a set of testing examples is available. The *holdout* method divides the available data set into two partitions. One is used as the training set and the other as the test set. There is no general agreement regarding the proportion of data for the two sets. Most of the time, a 50–50 or 2/3–1/3 division is adopted by data analysts. The main problem is that getting the right balance between the training examples and testing examples can be difficult. The more examples for training means that fewer examples are available for measuring accuracy and the less reliable the measurement of accuracy may become. The fewer examples we use for training means the induced model from those training examples is less applicable and consequently makes more errors. Another possible problem is that class representation in one partition may be different from another when not-so-random sampling methods are used. The problem again can affect the accuracy of the resulting classification model. As an improvement of this method, *random subsampling* repeats the holdout method several times when different examples are selected for the two separate sets. Accuracy of the produced model is measured each time. In the end, the average of the accuracy measures for all iterations is calculated and treated as the accuracy of the final model.

Bootstrap is also a method of dividing the whole data set available into two separate sets. In this method, however, instead of sampling without replacement, as in the holdout and random subsampling methods, sampling with replacement is adopted when the training examples are selected. The final accuracy is the average of the accuracy measurements of a number of bootstrap trials. This means that examples used for training can also be used as testing examples. Therefore the accuracy on testing examples can be improved.

Cross-validation is another method for evaluating classification performance. It is based on the idea that each example should be used as a testing example once. The basic principle of *k-fold* cross-validation is to divide the data population available into *k* folds, i.e. *k* equal-sized partitions. In each run of decision tree induction, one partition is used for testing and the rest of the partitions are used for training. The process is repeated *k* times. The errors are averaged across the iterations and the average is used as the final error rate.

Two specific cross-validation variations are worth mentioning. Two-fold cross-validation divides the data set into two equal partitions. One fold is used to build a decision tree and the other to evaluate the accuracy. After that, the two folds swap their roles. This time, the second partition is used to build a decision tree and the first partition is used to evaluate the accuracy. The final accuracy of the better model can be estimated as the average of the two model accuracies. In N-fold cross-validation, N refers to the number of data records in the available data set. Known as *leave-one-out*, this version takes one example as the test example and the rest for training. However, this version can be computationally expensive when N is large. Experimental work reveals that 10-fold cross-validation appears to produce optimal results.

All the evaluation methods are meant to achieve a realistic estimation of accuracy. However, accuracy at the model development stage is not a true indicator of actual accuracy in the model used in practice. Indeed, this accuracy may prove inadequate in practical trials, justifying a need to develop new models.

6.6   DECISION TREE CLASSIFICATION IN WEKA

Weka is well equipped with classification techniques. For the decision tree induction approach, Weka provides a range of tree construction methods, ranging from sophisticated ID3 and J48 to random tree and manual construction. In this section, the ID3 method is used to illustrate the process. Then we provide an overview of some other decision tree methods available in Weka.

6.6.1 Decision Tree Induction Using ID3

The data set in the file named `weather.nominal.arff` is used for the demonstration because of its simplicity in terms of a few nominal descriptive attributes and a class variable of only two class labels. You are quite familiar with the data set because it has been used for illustrations throughout the chapter. Figure 6.9 shows the Preprocess tab after the data set is loaded. The default class attribute is the attribute Play. The currently highlighted attribute is Outlook. It can be seen from the visualization of the attribute that one value (overcast) of the attribute can best separate the classes.

In Weka, classification is performed on the Classify tab. The page is divided into three main parts. The Classifier block contains a Choose button and a textbox. As on the Cluster tab, the Choose button is used to select a classification method and the textbox displays the method with its parameters, which can be modified in the generic object editor popped up when the command is clicked. To select the ID3 method, press Choose and select the method ID3 from a folder named trees in the pop-up window. The ID3 method in Weka does not have any parameters and produces an unpruned tree with the data set as the training set.

In the Test options block Weka provides four essential options:

- Use training set allows the decision tree to be evaluated on the training examples for accuracy.

- Supplied test set allows data analysts to locate a separate test set. Click the Set... button to locate and load the test data set file.

- Cross-validation with 10 folds is the default option. Data miners can change the number of folds. Therefore, this option includes the holdout and leave-one-out methods.

- Percentage split enables the data analyst to split the loaded data set into two partitions by a proportion indicated in the % field. The specified percentage (66% by default) of the loaded data set is held back as test examples.

For this exercise, the default 10-fold cross validation is selected. Press the Start button to execute the ID3 program and the result is displayed in the Classifier output pane of the screen, as shown in Figure 6.10.

FIGURE 6.9 The loaded data set for decision tree induction

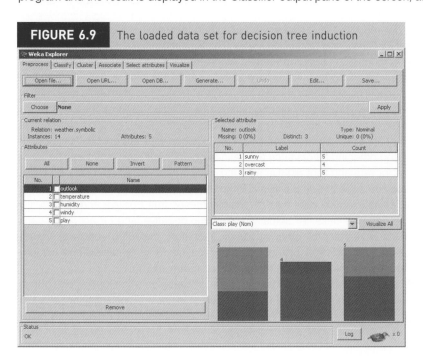

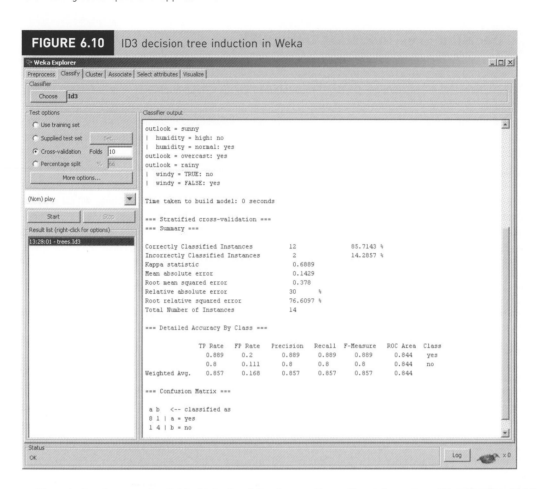

FIGURE 6.10 ID3 decision tree induction in Weka

The window is normally divided into the following sections: Run Information, Classification Model, Summary, Detailed Accuracy By Class, and Confusion Matrix. The Run Information section summarizes the data set, the classification technique used and the test mode (option) adopted. The Classification Model section shows the classification model built from the training set (in this case, a decision tree) and the time taken to build the model. The Summary section lists ways of evaluating the overall accuracy of the classification model. The list may vary slightly among different classification approaches. It includes the overall accuracy rate and error rate (e.g. 85.7143%) as defined in Section 6.5.1, a kappa statistic that indicates agreement between observed classes and predicted classes with corrections for random chance in the classification, and other indicators such as mean absolute error rate, root mean squared error rate, relative absolute error rate and root relative squared error. The Detailed Accuracy By Class section lists details of accuracy in terms of true positive (TP) and false positive (FP) for each class. For the positive class of the two-class example data set, TP actually means true positive and FP actually means false negative. For the negative class, TP actually means true negative, and FP actually means false positive. Weka also lists a number of other accuracy indicators including precision, recall, F-measure, etc. The Confusion Matrix section provides a confusion matrix of predicted and actually observed classes; Figure 6.10 shows the content of the confusion matrix in Table 6.3.

The Result list block lists the classification tasks that have been undertaken. Highlighting one brings back the result of that classification task in the main Classifier output window. This facility enables the operator to browse through the data mining tasks that have been performed and make some quick comparisons across them.

FIGURE 6.11 Results of ID3 with different test options

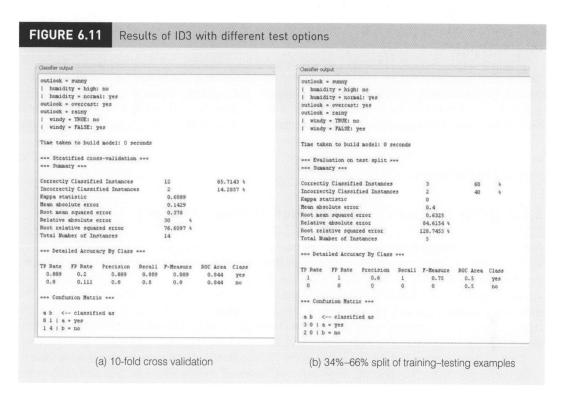

(a) 10-fold cross validation

(b) 34%–66% split of training–testing examples

The decision tree shown in the Classifier output window in Figure 6.10 is the same tree as the one in Figure 6.2(b). To show that accuracy may be affected by different test options, Figure 6.11 lists the accuracy summary for the default 10-fold cross-validation alongside that for a 34%–66% split of training–testing examples.

Once the decision tree is built and the accuracy rate is acceptable, the classification model can then be used to determine the classes of unseen records. In Weka, this is done indirectly with the Supplied test set option and the visualization facility. First, an ARFF file that contains a list of unseen records must be prepared. Figure 6.12(a) shows the content of such a file where the unknown class labels are marked

FIGURE 6.12 Classifying unseen records with a classification model

```
@relation weather.symbolic

@attribute outlook {sunny,overcast,rainy}
@attribute temperature {hot,mild,cool}
@attribute humidity {high,normal}
@attribute windy {TRUE,FALSE}
@attribute play {yes,no}

@data
overcast,hot,high,FALSE,?
sunny,hot,normal,TRUE,?
sunny,mild,high,FALSE,?
rainy,mild,normal,FALSE,?
rainy,mild,high,TRUE,?
```

```
@relation weather.symbolic_predicted

@attribute Instance_number numeric
@attribute outlook {sunny,overcast,rainy}
@attribute temperature {hot,mild,cool}
@attribute humidity {high,normal}
@attribute windy {TRUE,FALSE}
@attribute predictedplay {yes,no}
@attribute play {yes,no}

@data
0,overcast,hot,high,FALSE,yes,?
1,sunny,hot,normal,TRUE,yes,?
2,sunny,mild,high,FALSE,no,?
3,rainy,mild,normal,FALSE,yes,?
4,rainy,mild,high,TRUE,no,?
```

(a)

(b)

as '?', the 'unknown' symbol for ARFF file format. Click on the Supplied test set option and click the Set... button to locate and load the file.

When you press Start, all examples from the data set are classified, but the messages displayed in the Classifier output window are misleading. Ignore the messages and continue the operation by right-clicking the classification task in the Result list section and selecting Visualize classifier errors. This action brings up the visualization page. Set both X and Y dimensions to Instance_number(Num) and press Save to save the classification results into a file. Figure 6.12(b) shows the content of the saved file. You can see that Weka has changed the description of the file with the '_predicted' phrase, added an extra attribute named 'predictedplay' with 'yes' and 'no' as values, and has assigned each record in the data section a class label.

6.6.2 Other Decision Tree Induction Methods in Weka

A tree induction method known as J4.8 is similar to ID3. J4.8 is Weka's Java implementation of the C4.5 algorithm that can generate pruned or unpruned trees with both categorical and numeric attributes. To demonstrate the use of the algorithm, we use the data set in `weather.arff`. The Temperature and Humidity attributes of this data set are measured in interval and ratio scales respectively. Load the data file and select the J48 algorithm from the list of decision tree induction methods. Use the default setting of the parameters and perform the classification task. The unpruned tree is displayed in Figure 6.13(a).

Click on the command in the textbox next to the Choose button. The parameter *unpruned* is used to switch on and off J4.8's own pruning. As an exercise, we switch this parameter to True and perform the classification task. The same tree as in Figure 6.13(a) is obtained. This means that J4.8 has decided not to prune any part of the tree. The parameter *reducedErrorPruning* enables the use of the reduced error pruning method instead. To enable the pruning, the *numFolds* parameter must be set to divide the training set into a number of folds. Among the folds indicated by the value, one fold is used as the validation records for pruning a tree and the rest are used as training records to build the tree. For instance, the parameter is set to 10. A pruned tree is shown in Figure 6.13(b). The pruned tree has only one leaf node predicting every data record as P.

For some decision induction methods (not all), the resulting decision tree can be visualized by selecting the Visualize tree option from the pop-up menu against an entry in the Result list block.

FIGURE 6.13 (a) Unpruned and (b) pruned trees from the J48 method

```
J48 unpruned tree
------------------

outlook = sunny
|   humidity <= 75: yes (2.0)
|   humidity > 75: no (3.0)
outlook = overcast: yes (4.0)
outlook = rainy
|   windy = TRUE: no (2.0)
|   windy = FALSE: yes (3.0)

Number of Leaves :    5

Size of the tree :    8
```

(a)

```
J48 pruned tree
------------------
: yes (10.0/4.0)

Number of Leaves :    1

Size of the tree :    1

Time taken to build model: 0 seconds

=== Stratified cross-validation ===
=== Summary ===

Correctly Classified Instances          9
Incorrectly Classified Instances        5
```

(b)

Figure 6.14 shows the visualization of the decision tree in Figure 6.13(a). The visualized tree is more natural in appearance than the text-based presentation.

Other decision tree induction methods are also available in Weka. ADTree is a method that generates a decision tree enhanced with boosting nodes. BFTree is a method that builds a tree based on a best-first strategy. NBTree constructs a decision tree with naïve Bayes classifiers as the leaf nodes. REPTree generates either a decision tree or a regression tree with or without reduced-error pruning. RandomTree produces a decision tree by randomly selecting attributes. RandomForest produces a number of random trees. Due to constraints of space, we cannot explain them all in detail. You are encouraged to try some of them as an exercise.

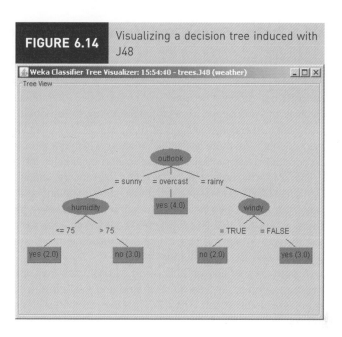

FIGURE 6.14 Visualizing a decision tree induced with J48

6.7 RELATED ISSUES OF DECISION TREE INDUCTION

Decision tree induction is a complex process that involves a number of related issues. In this section, some of those issues are briefly discussed in order to deepen understanding of the decision tree induction approach for classification.

6.7.1 Deriving Classification Rules from a Decision Tree

One of the main advantages of the decision tree induction approach is that a set of classification rules of 'IF..THEN' form can be derived from a given tree. A classification rule has a conjunction of Boolean tests upon attributes in the IF part and the class variable taking a specific class value in the THEN part, explaining why the decision about the class outcome is made. The way of deriving rules is straightforward: every path of the tree is traversed from the root node towards a leaf node. During the traversal, the names of the attributes together with their values attached to links are collected and transformed into Boolean tests in the IF clause of the rule, and the final class label forms the expression in the THEN clause of the rule.

For the decision tree in Figure 6.2(b), the following classification rules can be derived:

```
IF outlook = overcast THEN class = P;
IF outlook = sunny and humidity = high THEN class = N;
IF outlook = sunny and humidity = normal THEN class = P;
IF outlook = rain and windy = true THEN class = N;
IF outlook = rain and windy = false THEN class = P.
```

6.7.2 Order, Shape and Iterative Construction of Decision Trees

As explained so far, most decision tree induction methods produce multi-way split decision trees where the internal nodes are attribute names and the branches are attribute values. However, algorithms such as CART can produce two-way split binary trees. An internal node of such a tree is a Boolean test that involves an attribute and a specific attribute value. The labels for the two branches from an internal node represent true and false outcomes of the test. Binary trees tend to be simpler in their representations in memory but have more levels than multi-way split decision trees. However, the total number of tests to be conducted when making a classification decision is the same.

Not only is the order of a decision tree relevant, the shape of the decision tree may also be of interest. Computationally, certain tree structures, such as balanced trees, are desirable for indexing because all searching actions take the same amount of time. However, this may not be the case for decision trees. A decision tree that classifies most data records with a few tests (few levels) and uses more tests for a few records with a particular set of attribute values is more desirable than a balanced tree where every decision takes the same number of tests.

A decision tree can be built using all examples from the training set. However, if there are many training examples, in order to save time and resources, a subset of the training set can also be used in an iterative approach. The ID3 algorithm promotes an iterative framework that can be outlined as follows:

1 Select a subset, called a *window*, of the training examples.

2 Construct a decision tree based on the training examples in the window with a tree construction algorithm such as ID3.

3 Apply the resulting decision tree to the rest of the examples in the training set.

The examples that the decision tree classifies incorrectly are collected and added into the window. A new decision tree is then built. This process continues until all the examples in the training set are classified correctly by the decision tree.

The iterative approach has the advantage of saving system resources and hence can be used in resource-restricted circumstances.

6.7.3 Other Issues Regarding Attribute Selection Measures

In the previous sections, we have shown induction of decision trees for data sets that involve discrete or categorical attributes. How does an algorithm calculate the amount of attribute selection measurement for a continuous attribute? In general, this problem is dealt with through a repeated process of iterations. At each iteration, a candidate threshold value for the attribute is introduced. The threshold value divides the value range for the attribute into two segments. The attribute selection measure is then calculated using the partitions. At the end of the process, the measurement amounts for all iterations are compared and either the maximum or the minimum measure is used to represent the amount of measurement for the attribute. For instance for the data set in Figure 6.2(a), if the humidity is measured as a percentage, we may find that the level of impurity measured by the Gini impurity function is at the lowest level when Humidity = 75% for sunny weather conditions. Then, attribute Humidity is chosen as the root of the subtree and the two branches of the node are labelled '≤75' and '>75'.

During the decision tree construction with an algorithm such as ID3, it may be the case that more than one attribute has the maximum information gain. Which attribute in this case should be chosen as the root of the decision tree? A simple way is to select randomly. However, this simple act may lead to a non-deterministic result. The tree created using one random choice may be different from a tree with a different random choice. Of course, one can fix the random seed such that the same random choice can be repeatedly made. Alternatively, other attribute selection measures can be used as a second-line selection measure. For instance, if two attributes have the same information gain, their dependence to the class variable can be measured by the chi-square test. The attribute with the highest measure result is chosen as the root of the decision tree.

Attribute selection measures can also serve to rank attributes according to their relationships with the class variable. Constructing a decision tree reveals which attribute is most related to the class outcome in a certain condition. For instance, the information gain, gain ratio and Gini index of impurity have all ranked the attributes for the data set in Figure 6.2(a) in the same order: Outlook, Humidity, Windy and Temperature. However, this does not necessarily mean that all measures *always* produce the same order.

6.7.4 Noise Handling in Decision Trees

Many decision tree induction solutions accommodate facilities to deal with noise data in training examples. Noise here refers to erroneous attribute values or classes. A training set with noise can cause the following problems:

- *Inadequate attribute*: Two training examples may have exactly the same values for all descriptive attributes, but different class tags. This problem is normally caused by wrong values on descriptive attributes. In this situation, values of the descriptive attributes cannot distinguish the examples of two different classes.

- *Spurious complexity:* Wrong descriptive attribute values also distort the distribution of values and hence affect the selection of attributes as roots of subtrees. Wrong class names have the same effect. Then, the decision tree built on the examples is likely to have extra complexity, i.e. more branches and more levels. The unnecessary complexity of the tree reflects added particularities, making the tree more overfitting.

A possible solution to the first problem is to attach the class label of a leaf node with a likelihood ratio of the class. Given there are p positive and n negative examples at the leaf, the likelihood ratio for being positive is calculated as $p/(p+n)$ and for being negative as $n/(p+n)$. A leaf node with a positive class label indicates that there are more positive examples than negative examples at the leaf. The same happens to negative leaf nodes. Of course, instead of keeping the likelihood ratio, two counters, p and n, can simply be kept at each leaf. If $p > n$, the leaf is labelled as positive. If $n > p$, the leaf is labelled as negative. If $p = n$, the node label can be marked as NULL, meaning that the class cannot be determined due to equal numbers of examples of the two classes.

The problem of spuriously complex trees was discussed in the context of model overfitting and tree pruning. The ID3 algorithm uses a pre-pruning strategy to deal with the problem. The algorithm eventually conducts a chi-square test between the attribute with the highest information gain and the class variable to decide whether to further build a subtree instead of using a minimum information gain threshold.

6.7.5 Strengths and Weaknesses of Decision Tree Induction

The strengths of the decision tree induction approach include the following:

- A decision tree not only assigns a class label to an unseen record, but also explains why the decision is made in terms of an easy-to-understand classification rule.

- A decision tree classifies unseen records efficiently. The classification time depends on the number of levels of the tree, not the number of examples in the training set.

- Decision tree induction methods can handle both categorical and continuous attributes although most of them work better with categorical attributes.

- The attribute selection measures used by decision tree induction methods are capable of indicating the most *important* attribute in relation to class.

  The main weaknesses of decision tree induction methods can be highlighted as follows:

- Decision trees have high error rates when the training set contains a small number of instances of a large variety of different classes due to the problem of model overfitting.

- Single attribute splitting results in rectangular class boxes. The algorithms may not work well on data sets where class distributions of any other shape exist.

- Decision trees are computationally quite expensive to build. Algorithms such as ID3 are recursive in nature. At each recursive call, the algorithm must calculate information gains over all remaining descriptive attributes before one of them can be selected as the root of the current tree. This means every example within the current training set or subset must be searched. Overall, the time complexity is roughly $O(|L| \cdot |C| \cdot |A|)$ where $|L|$ refers to the number of internal nodes in the decision tree, $|C|$ refers to the size of the training set and $|A|$ refers to the number of attributes. The actual time complexity is expected to be lower than the rough estimate because $|C|$ and $|A|$ decrease as we move down the levels of the decision tree.

6.7.6 Decision Trees in Practice

Like many other data mining projects, classification using a decision tree follows the procedure of data preparation, mining, evaluation, etc. We highlight a number of points directly related to decision tree mining. In order to build a decision tree, the follow data preparation tasks need to be conducted. First of all, the class variable needs to be defined. The class variable may be an existing attribute or a new attribute that is introduced, normally by the domain expert. If a new class variable needs to be introduced, the class value for each example must be assigned carefully and accurately. One must ensure that the data set contains examples of all classes. For good quality results, one should also ensure that a sufficient number of examples of each class are present. Next, all descriptive attributes must be identified. The inclusion of the descriptive attributes must be treated cautiously. Manual selection of attributes is possible but attribute selection in the classification model should normally be a matter that is left to the attribute selection measure of the learning algorithm to decide.

A decision tree induction method needs to be chosen and its parameter settings determined. After that, the evaluation options must be decided. This task includes determining the sizes and split of the training and testing examples, whether to use cross-validation or not, and even selecting training examples and testing examples to ensure that coverage of class labels and attribute values is sufficient. After that, the decision tree induction and evaluation of the decision tree performance can start. The final classification model is chosen to be a classification model with a high accuracy with the testing data that is statistically significant. The model is then delivered and used in practice.

Over the years, many data mining tools have adopted well-known decision tree induction algorithms into their data mining toolkits. See5 is a single-purpose decision tree induction tool that uses the C4.5 algorithm. The IBM Intelligent Miner for Data uses the CART algorithm and the statistical software tool SPSS Clementine endorses the CHAID algorithm.

6.8 SUMMARY

In this chapter, one important classification approach, the decision tree induction was introduced. The chapter first gave an overview of general decision tree induction and the different roles that data examples play in the process. It then explained decision tree construction in terms of a generic procedural framework for the construction process and the roles that an attribute selection measure plays in tree construction. One attribute selection measure, the information gain, was described in detail. The rationale behind the measure was explained. To enable a full understanding of the ID3 algorithm, an example was used to illustrate the entire process of constructing a decision tree. The chapter also surveyed a number of attribute selection measures used by other algorithms, i.e. information gain ratio, Gini index of impurity and chi-square test. Like the information gain, what each measure represents and how it is calculated were explained. Attempts were made to ensure that the explanation is as intuitive as possible.

The problem of model overfitting was explained and how the decision tree induction approach deals with the problem. The use of a specific pruning method, i.e. the reduced-error pruning method, was demonstrated. Model overfitting is a problem not only for decision trees but also for all classification approaches and techniques.

A lot of effort was made to describe and discuss issues in relation to the measurement of accuracy of a decision tree. A number of different measures of accuracy and approaches to estimating true accuracy for a classification model with limited data were explained. Based on the relevant fundamental knowledge of statistics from Chapter 2, the confidence interval for true accuracy with the observed measures of accuracy was discussed. A related issue over how to compare two classification models by evaluating their estimated accuracies was also investigated. The basic idea is to select a classification model whose estimated accuracy is significantly better than others. In the case where the difference between accuracies is not significant, other factors, such as structure simplicity, speed of classification etc., should be taken into consideration. This very issue will be revisited in Chapter 7.

This chapter also summarized a number of related issues with decision tree induction. The purpose of discussing those issues is to gain a broader understanding of decision trees and the induction process. At the end of the chapter, decision tree induction in Weka was demonstrated with some simple examples. Weka offers a wide range of decision tree induction methods and evaluates the performance of the resulting trees with a number of evaluation measures. To this extent, Weka is sufficient. However, classifying unseen records in Weka is not straightforward and can be tedious.

EXERCISES

1 Use decision tree induction as an example to illustrate the two stages of classification, i.e. development of a classification model and use of the model. In the same context, describe the roles that training, validation and testing examples play.

2 Algorithms such as CART produce binary decision trees as the classification model. Describe clearly the composition of such a binary decision tree. What does a binary tree look like for a training set such as the weather condition table in Figure 6.2(a)?

3 The data set in Table 6.4 contains data about heart disease and its conditions. The class label P means that heart disease is present and the class label N that the disease is absent. Suppose that the data set is used as a training set.

(a) Calculate the information gain over the attribute Blood Pressure.

TABLE 6.4	Data set for Exercises 3, 4 and 5				
Body Weight	**Body Height**	**Blood Pressure**	**Blood Sugar Level**	**Habit**	**Class**
heavy	short	high	3	smoker	P
heavy	short	high	1	nonsmoker	P
normal	tall	normal	3	nonsmoker	N
heavy	tall	normal	2	smoker	N
low	medium	normal	2	nonsmoker	N
low	tall	normal	1	nonsmoker	P
normal	medium	high	3	smoker	P
low	short	high	2	smoker	P
heavy	tall	high	2	nonsmoker	P
low	medium	normal	3	smoker	P
heavy	medium	normal	3	nonsmoker	N

(b) Given the information gains over the other descriptive attributes as follows:

- gain(BodyWeight) = 0.0275 bits
- gain(BodyHeight) = 0.2184 bits
- gain(BloodSugarLevel) = 0.1407 bits
- gain(Habit) = 0.0721 bits

Which attribute should be chosen as the root of the decision tree by the ID3 algorithm?

4 Given the training set in Table 6.4, the partial decision tree in Figure 6.15 has been constructed with the ID3 algorithm. Complete the construction of the remaining part of the tree. Discuss what to do if two attributes have the same amount of information gain.

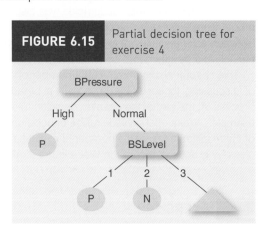

FIGURE 6.15	Partial decision tree for exercise 4

5 Use the training set in Table 6.4 to calculate the Gini index of impurity and the chi-square test score upon every descriptive attribute. Which attribute should be selected as the root of the tree according to each of the two measures?

6 Use the decision tree constructed in Exercise 4 to classify the unseen records in Table 6.5.

TABLE 6.5	Data set for Exercises 6 and 8				
Body Weight	**Body Height**	**Blood Pressure**	**Blood Sugar Level**	**Habit**	**Class**
heavy	medium	high	1	smoker	
heavy	medium	normal	3	smoker	

TABLE 6.6	Data set for Exercise 7				
Body Weight	**Body Height**	**Blood Pressure**	**Blood Sugar Level**	**Habit**	**Class**
heavy	short	high	2	smoker	P
heavy	tall	normal	1	smoker	N
heavy	medium	normal	3	smoker	N
low	short	normal	3	smoker	N
low	medium	high	1	nonsmoker	N
low	medium	high	3	nonsmoker	P

7 The validation examples in Table 6.6 are available.

(a) Use the reduced-error pruning method to prune the decision tree obtained from Exercise 4.

(b) Suppose that we mix the examples from the training set in Table 6.4 and the validation set in Table 6.6 to form a test set. Estimate the overall accuracy of the pruned tree obtained from part (a) and compare the accuracy with the unpruned tree.

(c) Construct a confusion matrix for the unpruned tree obtained from Exercise 4, assuming that the combination of training and validation examples forms the test set.

8 Use the data set in Table 6.4 as a training set and perform the following tasks in Weka:

(a) Use the ID3 algorithm to construct a decision tree under each of the test options. Use the validation data set in Table 6.6 as a test set for the Supplied test set option.

(b) Use the decision tree obtained from (a) to determine the classes for the unseen data records in Table 6.5.

9 Perform decision tree induction in Weka using different decision tree induction algorithms (RandomTree, ID3, J48 and REPTree). Compare the resulting trees and the measures of accuracy. Switch the pruning parameter on and off to observe the unpruned and pruned trees.

10 HouseMove is a successful estate agency that wants to extend its house sale business to a new city. The company wants to conduct a data mining project in order to better understand the local housing market of the city before setting up a new branch office there. They are particularly interested in what kinds of houses sell quickly, what kinds of houses do not, and why. A possible source of information is the local newspaper that is freely distributed to most of the households in the city and the surrounding areas each week. The newspaper has a property section in which houses are advertised. A typical advertisement describes the number of bedrooms, the facilities (garage, bathrooms, utility room, study, etc.), the selling price and the location. The number of bedrooms of a house can be 2, 3, 4 or 5. The selling prices of the houses are in the region of £100,000 to £300,000. The location of a house is represented by the first part of its postcode. The company has been monitoring the appearance of house advertisements and the periods of the appearances in the newspaper for the past two months and has accumulated a database of around 2000 records. Houses that are sold within two weeks of the first appearance of the advertisement are considered to be quick sales; otherwise, they are slow sales. A data mining software tool equipped with decision tree induction techniques is available for the project.

(a) Describe any data preparation tasks and any data preprocessing tasks that need to be performed before data mining starts.

(b) Suppose that decision tree induction techniques are to be used and describe related data mining activities and tasks for obtaining a decision tree.

(c) Explain the use of the k-fold cross-validation in model construction, model selection and estimation of error rate for the chosen model.

BIBLIOGRAPHICAL NOTES

Most references for this chapter originate from the machine-learning domain of artificial intelligence. The general process of classification is described in most data mining texts (Berry and Linoff 1997; Han and Kamber 2001; Tan *et al.* 2006). The roles that examples play were highlighted by Berry and Linoff (1997) and they used the terms *training*, *testing* and *evaluation* examples, which might cause some confusion with the general understanding of training and testing sets in the community. This chapter uses the more accepted terms of *training*, *validation* and *testing* examples.

The general procedural framework described in this chapter is also known as Hunt's algorithm. We emphasize this generic feature so that the procedure for building a decision tree and the attribute selection measure can be separated. Indeed, such a separation has enabled a comparison among attribute selection measures (Du *et al.* 2000).

The attribute selection measures described in this chapter were introduced by various researchers in developing decision tree induction algorithms (Breiman *et al.* 1984; Hart 1984; Quinlan 1986). These measures are surveyed and compared by Mingers (1989). The comparative study sparks a debate over a claim that Mingers made: random selection of attributes followed by pruning is as good as any other attribute selection measure in terms of accuracy. This claim was overturned by Liu and White (1994), who have shown beyond reasonable doubt that attribute selection measures are more important in delivering a robust and accurate decision tree than random selections.

The main focus of this chapter is around Ross Quinlan's work on the ID3 algorithm (Quinlan 1986). The information gain measure originates from the concept of mutual information between two information systems. Jones (1979) gives a comprehensive but brief explanation of the concept and the properties of entropy. Quinlan (1987) presents a comprehensive survey of various tree pruning methods in dealing with the problem of model overfitting.

The issue of accuracy has also been addressed in a number of data mining texts (Tan *et al.* 2006; Witten and Frank 2005). A number of methods, such as holdout and cross-validation, have been proposed, but the best approach to developing classification models and evaluating accuracy is still not clear.

CHAPTER 7

Other classification techniques

LEARNING OBJECTIVES

To broaden views on classification approaches and methods

To understand the general principles of the nearest neighbour approach and the PEBLS algorithm

To understand the general principles of the rule-based approach and the sequential covering algorithm

To understand the general principles of the Bayesian classifier approach and the Naïve Bayes classifier

To be aware of the basic concepts of artificial neural networks and how they are used for classification purposes

To gain a comparative understanding of different classification approaches

To be aware of other related issues with classification

To learn how to use a range of classification methods and compare their performance in Weka

As stated in Chapter 2, as well as decision tree induction (introduced in Chapter 6), other classification approaches, such as rule-based, nearest neighbour, Bayesian classifiers and artificial neural networks, also exist. These approaches are categorized according to the form in which the classification model is represented. Many classification methods under each category have been developed. Given that many data mining tasks in real-life applications are classification tasks in nature, awareness of a wide range of classification techniques is very useful.

The overall objective of this chapter is to gain a broad understanding of the different classification approaches and methods. Due to limited space, it is impossible to cover all classification methods for every approach. The chapter therefore shows one particular algorithm in each approach category. Issues of concerns in the different approaches are summarized and discussed. At the end of the chapter, a number of examples demonstrate how to use classification methods in Weka. This chapter also introduces the Experiment module of Weka for comparing the performance of different classification methods.

7.1 THE NEAREST NEIGHBOUR APPROACH

The nearest neighbour classification approach, also known as *case-based reasoning* or *memory-based reasoning*, considers a classification model as a memory space of representative examples. Each example is perceived as a point in this memory space whose dimensions are descriptive attributes. The representative examples come directly from the training set. There is *no* training! The training examples are taken from the training set, saved in the memory space (sometimes known as exemplars) and called upon when classifying an unseen record. Sometimes, examples may be attached with a weight indicating their sphere of influence in the classification decision-making.

To classify an unseen record, the nearest neighbouring examples are located. The class of the record is determined by the class of the neighbours. The motto behind the approach is very much that 'If something walks like a duck, quacks like a duck, and looks like a duck, it probably *is* a duck'.

Delaying computation of input data till the time when it is necessary is known as a *lazy* approach. The nearest neighbour approach is certainly lazy: the classification decision is delayed to the classification stage rather than building a classification model in advance.

7.1.1 A Generic *k*NN Algorithm

A generic *k*-nearest neighbour (*k*NN) algorithm for classification (not for construction of a classifier) is given here in pseudo-code:

```
algorithm k-NearestNeighbour (Tr: training set; k: integer; var r: data record)
begin
   for each training example t in Tr do
      calculate distance d(t, r) upon descriptive attributes
   endfor;
   Select into D k nearest neighbours of r according to their distances to r;
   r.Class := majority class in D
end;
```

The algorithm first measures the proximity between the record to be classified and each of the training examples and then selects the nearest *k* neighbours of the record. The class of the record is determined by the majority class of the *k* neighbours.

To illustrate the working of the algorithm, we use the data set in Figure 7.1(a) giving the height, weight and gender of subjects. The Gender attribute is the class attribute with two values (F for female and M for male). The data points are plotted in Figure 7.1(b). From the scatter plot, it is clear that there exist some correlations between the gender and body weight and height: the majority of males, represented by squares, are heavier and taller than the majority of females, represented by triangles.

Suppose that an unseen record has a body height of 168 cm and a body weight of 84 kg as indicated by a circle in figure 7.1(b), and $k = 3$. After calculating the distance between the record and every training example using the Euclidean distance function, it is found that s2, s5 and s6 are the three nearest neighbours. Points s2 and s5 are males and s6 is a female. According to the majority vote principle of the algorithm, the record is classified as a male.

The voting criterion adopted in the generic algorithm is very simple and can be further modified. The actual distance from each nearest neighbour to the record can be taken into consideration when the majority voting takes place. In the example above, s6 is the closest neighbour to the record and could

FIGURE 7.1   An example data set for demonstrating the *k*NN algorithm

SubjectID	Body height (cm)	Body weight (kg)	Gender
s1	125	61	F
s2	176	90	M
s3	177	92	M
s4	178	83	M
s5	167	85	M
s6	170	89	F
s7	173	98	M
s8	135	40	F
s9	120	35	M
s10	136	70	F
s11	125	50	F

(a) Training examples   (b) Training examples in memory space

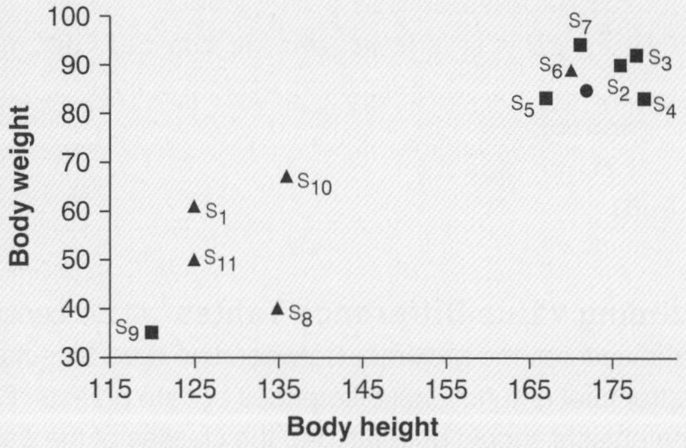

have a greater say in the class of the record whereas s5 and s2 are farther away and could have a lesser say in the classification. However, using *k* nearest neighbours is to reduce the effect of the presence of noise points. A number of neighbours making a decision is considered better than a single neighbour making a decision.

The nearest neighbour approach in classification is close to the way a human mind works. Lawyers make a court appeal on the basis of past cases. Help-desk technicians resolve customer problems based on their experiences with similar problems.

The *k*NN algorithm has a wide range of applications. For instance, template-based iris recognition systems use the algorithm to verify a human's identity. Besides classification, the *k*NN algorithm can also be used to estimate the value of a continuous output variable. For instance, the average of the output values of the *k* nearest neighbours of a house record may be taken as a good estimate of the house price for the record. In many situations when other classification techniques fail, the *k*NN algorithm may still work as long as there is a sensible proximity measure.

7.1.2 A Weighted Nearest Neighbour Algorithm: PEBLS

The generic *k*NN algorithm is very simple, but quite naïve too. This section presents the PEBLS algorithm, which is based on the same principle but has made three further changes to the generic algorithm. First, a class-based *similarity* measure is used instead of a simple distance function. Second, each example is attached with a performance-related weight that influences the selection of the nearest neighbour. Third, training examples are used to classify each other to gain understanding about their performance. The pseudo-code description of the algorithm is as follows:

```
algorithm PEBLS (Tr: training set; Ts: validation set): exemplar space
begin
    Space := Ø; //empty the memory space initially
    construct value difference table for each descriptive attribute of Tr;
    for each instance e in Tr do
        add e into Space with weight = 1;
        calculate the distance between e and each exemplar in Space;
```

```
        find the nearest neighbour exemplar e' of e;
        adjust the weight of e' according to classification of e by e';
    endfor;
    for each instance e in Ts do
        adjust the weight of the nearest neighbour exemplar e' according to
            classification of e by e';
    endfor;
    return(Space)
end;
```

Building Value Difference Tables   At the centre of a nearest neighbour algorithm is the function that measures the proximity between two data objects. For clustering, any measure of proximity relates to structural or functional differences of data objects. For classification, the proximity of feature values of data objects should be related to the classes of the data objects. The difference between feature values and consequently the distance between data objects must be redefined on the basis of proximity over classes. The PEBLS algorithm proposes a distance function that is based on the posterior distribution of classes to measure the difference between two values of an attribute.

For a set of training examples, let $a_1, a_2, \ldots, a_m$ be the m values of attribute A and $c_1, c_2, \ldots, c_n$ be the n classes. Let c_{ij} represent the number of examples in the training set that have the value a_i and belong to class c_j. The sum C_{ai} represents the total number of examples in the training set that have the value a_i, and the sum C_{cj} represents the total number of examples that belong to class c_j. The difference between two values a_i, and a_j of A is defined as

$$d(a_i, a_j) = \sum_{t=1}^{n} \left| \frac{c_{it}}{C_{ai}} - \frac{c_{jt}}{C_{aj}} \right|^K$$

where K is a constant, set to 1 by the algorithm. Intuitively, the difference between two values of an attribute can be understood as the sum of differences in posterior probabilities of belonging to each of the classes between the two values. For the attribute Outlook in the weather condition table in Figure 6.2, $c_{\text{sunny P}} = 2$, $c_{\text{sunny N}} = 3$, $c_{\text{overcast P}} = 4$, $c_{\text{overcast N}} = 0$, $C_{\text{sunny}} = 5$, and $C_{\text{overcast}} = 4$. The value difference between sunny and overcast is defined as follows:

$$d(sunny, overcast) = \left| \frac{2}{5} - \frac{4}{4} \right| + \left| \frac{3}{5} - \frac{0}{4} \right| = \frac{3}{5} + \frac{3}{5} = \frac{6}{5} = 1.2$$

In general, a contingency table for a training set is built (see Figure 7.2(a)). Based on the value difference definition, a *value difference table* for attribute A contains pairwise value differences as shown in Figure 7.2(b). Once the value difference tables for all descriptive attributes have been built, they are stored in memory for reference when the distance between two data objects is measured. The value difference tables for the descriptive attributes for the weather condition table are shown in Figure 7.2(c).

Distance between Two Data Objects   Let $X = (x_1, x_2, \ldots, x_m)$ and $Y = (y_1, y_2, \ldots, y_m)$ be two data examples. Let w_X and w_Y be the weights associated with X and Y. The distance between X and Y is defined as

$$D(X, Y) = w_X w_Y \sum_{i=1}^{m} d(x_i, y_i)^r$$

FIGURE 7.2	From contingency table to value difference table

(a) Contingency table (b) Value difference table

Value difference table for outlook

	Sunny	Overcast	Rain
Sunny	0	1.2	0.4
Overcast	1.2	0	0.8
Rain	0.4	0.8	0

Value difference table for temperature

	Hot	Mild	Cool
Hot	0	0.33	0.5
Mild	0.33	0	0.33
Cool	0.5	0.33	0

Value difference table for humidity

	High	Normal
High	0	0.857
Normal	0.857	0

Value difference table for windy

	True	False
True	0	0.5
False	0.5	0

(c) Value difference tables for the weather condition data set

where r is a constant, set to 2, and m refers to the number of attributes. As an example, the distance between rows 1 and 3 of the table in Figure 6.2 is calculated as follows, assuming that the weights attached to the rows are set to 1:

$$D(row1, row3) = d(row1_{outlook}, row3_{outlook})^2 + d(row1_{temperature}, row3_{temperature})^2 +$$

$$d(row1_{humidity}, row3_{humidity})^2 + d(row1_{windy}, row3_{windy})^2$$

$$= d(sunny, overcast)^2 + d(hot, hot)^2 + d(high, high)^2 + d(false, false)^2$$

$$= 1.2^2 + 0 + 0 + 0 = 1.44$$

The weight of an example reflects its performance in classification. In the PEBLS algorithm, the weight is defined as a ratio according to the performance of the example in classifying other data objects. Let T denote the total number of uses of an example X and C represent the total number of correct uses of the example. The weight of X, W_X, is a ratio defined as follows:

$$w_X = \frac{T}{C}$$

Both T and C are initialized with value 1 when the example is first projected as an exemplar into the memory space, in order to avoid division by zero and the deeming of an example as unfit for ever. In general, a weight is always greater than or equal to 1. Well-performing exemplars have weights near to or equal to 1. Not-so-well-performing ones have weights slightly greater than 1. Unreliable exemplars have weights much bigger than 1. Acting like a repelling force, a heavier weight drives any data object away from the exemplar. The bigger the weight is, the longer the distance from the exemplar to an example, the less likely the exemplar is selected as the nearest neighbour, and hence the less likely it is involved in classification.

The Working of the Algorithm The table in Figure 6.2(a) is again used to illustrate the working of the PEBLS algorithm. The algorithm first constructs the value difference tables for all descriptive attributes as shown in Figure 7.2(c). The algorithm then projects the training examples one by one as an exemplar with the default weight of 1 into the memory space. Every time a new example is added, the distance between the new example and each of the existing exemplars in the memory space is calculated. The nearest neighbour exemplar is then located. If the class of the nearest neighbour is the same as the class of the new example, the weight of the nearest neighbour is 'tuned down' by increasing both the total number of use and the total number of correct use by 1. If the classes are not the same, the weight of the nearest exemplar is 'tuned up' by only increasing the total number of use. The process continues until all training examples are projected into the space.

The algorithm then uses validation examples one by one to further tune the weights of the exemplars in the memory space. The weight of the nearest exemplar is modified according to its decision to classify a validation example, just as with training examples. The difference is that the validation examples are not projected into the memory space. Eventually, a final memory space with training examples that have appropriate weights is returned as the classification model (see Figure 7.3).

Classification by the PEBLS algorithm is the same as with the kNN algorithm, except that the value of $k = 1$. When an unseen record is classified, the distance between the record and every exemplar in the memory space is calculated with reference to the value difference tables, and the nearest neighbour is located. The class of the nearest neighbour is considered to be the class of the record. In Figure 7.3, distances between the unknown record and the 14 exemplars are calculated. The nearest neighbour is row 3, and the class for the record is therefore determined as P.

FIGURE 7.3 Using the final exemplar space in the PEBLS algorithm

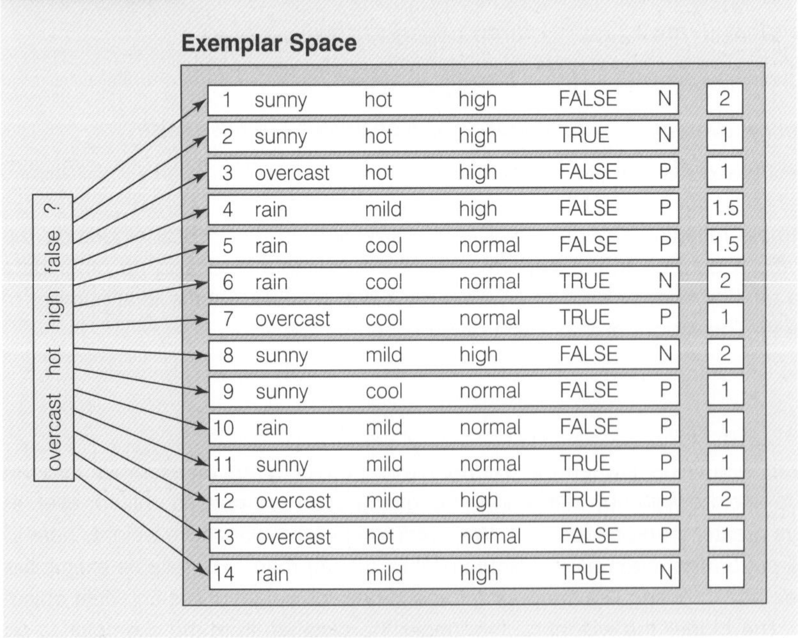

Exemplar Space

1	sunny	hot	high	FALSE	N	2
2	sunny	hot	high	TRUE	N	1
3	overcast	hot	high	FALSE	P	1
4	rain	mild	high	FALSE	P	1.5
5	rain	cool	normal	FALSE	P	1.5
6	rain	cool	normal	TRUE	N	2
7	overcast	cool	normal	TRUE	P	1
8	sunny	mild	high	FALSE	N	2
9	sunny	cool	normal	FALSE	P	1
10	rain	mild	normal	FALSE	P	1
11	sunny	mild	normal	TRUE	P	1
12	overcast	mild	high	TRUE	P	2
13	overcast	hot	normal	FALSE	P	1
14	rain	mild	high	TRUE	N	1

overcast hot high false ?

7.2 THE RULE-BASED APPROACH

Rule-based classification methods construct a sequence of rules from a training set of examples. When classifying an unseen record, the rules are searched until a rule that *covers* the record is found. The rule is then *fired* and the class of the record is determined by the consequent part of the rule statement.

Such rules can be discovered directly or indirectly. The direct approach discovers the rule statements directly from the training examples, whereas the indirect approach first discovers a model in another form and translates it into rules. An example of the indirect approach is to induce a decision tree from a training set and then translate the tree into a sequence of classification rules, as explained in Chapter 6. This chapter concentrates on the direct rule-based approach.

7.2.1 Classification Rules

A classification rule takes the form of *Antecedent* → *Consequent*. The antecedent is composed of a conjunction of comparisons of attributes and their values, and the consequent is a single statement: the class takes a specific class label. The rule statement structure is formally presented as follows:

$$(A_1 \, op_1 \, v_1) \land (A_2 \, op_2 \, v_2) \land ... \land (A_m \, op_m \, v_m) \rightarrow class = y_j$$

where A_i is an attribute name, v_i is an attribute value, op_i is a comparison operator ($<, >, =,$ or $\neq$), and y_j is a class label. For instance, a rule that states 'a game of golf is played if the outlook is sunny and humidity is normal ($\leq$75%)' is presented as follows:

$$(\text{Outlook} = \text{sunny}) \text{ and } (\text{Humidity} \leq 75\%) \rightarrow \text{Class} = \text{Play}$$

A rule *covers* a data record if the attribute values of the record match the condition listed in the antecedent of the rule. The quality of the rule is measured by *coverage* and *accuracy*. Given a training set, let D represent the number of examples in the training set and A represent the number of examples covered by a rule. Let B_c represent the number of examples covered by the rule that have a specific class label c. Then the coverage and accuracy of a rule r are defined as follows:

$$\text{coverage}(r) = \frac{A}{D} \qquad \text{accuracy}(r) = \frac{B_c}{A}$$

For the weather condition training set and the example rule given above, $D = 14$, $A = 2$ and $B_c = 2$. Therefore, the rule has coverage of $2/14 \approx 14\%$ and accuracy of $2/2 = 100\%$.

7.2.2 Rule-based Classification Models

A rule-based classification model consists of a set of rules. The rules may be listed as an *ordered* list or an *unordered* set. Ideally, the rules should be mutually exclusive and exhaustive. Rules are *mutually exclusive* if no more than one rule is triggered by a record. Rules are *exhaustive* if each combination of attribute values is covered by at least one rule. The mutual exclusivity is desirable to avoid conflicts in class predictions by different rules that are fired by the same record. The exhaustiveness is to ensure that all combinations of attribute values are covered by existing rules so that a classification decision can always be made for any given unseen record. In practice, however, enforcing mutual exclusivity across all rules may not always be possible. As a consequence, more than one rule may be fired at the same time. If the rules are unordered, all applicable rules are fired. The class of the record is determined by some voting principle among the predicted classes. For instance, the majority voting can be adopted to determine the final class outcome. If the rules are ordered, the fired rules can be listed in order of priority and the class determined by the rule at the top of the priority list.

The exhaustiveness feature is normally achieved via the introduction of a default rule. The default rule has no antecedent:

$$() \rightarrow y_j$$

where class label y_j normally refers to the majority class of training records not yet covered by the existing rules. The default rule is listed at the end of a rule list and is only applied when all other rules have been tried and falsified.

Ordered and Unordered Rules   In an ordered rule list, rules are tested in a sequence from the beginning of the classification model. A rule is not applied unless all rules before it have been tested and fail. If a rule covers a record, the rule is fired to determine the class for the record and no other rules are tested.

In a classification model where rules are not ordered, the rules need to be self-contained, in the sense that the validity of the rule should not depend on the falsification of any previous rule. When used, all rules that cover the records are to be triggered. Figure 7.4 shows a list of unordered rules and a list of ordered rules for the weather condition table used in Chapter 6.

As shown in Figure 7.4, unordered rules must have all necessary terms in the antecedent in order to be self-contained, whereas some later rules in the ordered list can be simplified with the understanding that the previous rules are negated. However, the understanding of the ordered rules must take the negation of previous rules into account otherwise the interpretation can be incorrect. Moving towards the end of the ordered list, more and more previous rules are negated and it becomes increasingly harder to understand the current rule. The default rule makes more sense as the last rule in the situation of ordered rules.

Order-by-Rule vs Order-by-Class   There are alternative approaches to ordering rules within a model: order-by-rule or order-by-class. The order-by-rule approach lists the rules in descending order of a quality measure. With the quality measure, the *best* applicable rules are listed at the beginning and *not-so-good* rules are listed towards the end. There are various measures for measuring rule quality. Rule coverage, rule accuracy, and total length (in terms of conjuncts involved) of rule description can all be a candidate for this measure.

The order-by-class approach groups the rules according to class labels in the consequent part. In this case, the classification model consists of an ordered list of classes but each class has a collection of

---

FIGURE 7.4   A rule-based classification model

Outlook = overcast → class = P Outlook = sunny **and** Humidity = high → class = N Outlook = sunny **and** Humidity = normal → class = P Outlook = rain **and** Windy = true → class = N Outlook = rain **and** Windy = false → class = P

(a) Unordered rules

1. Outlook = overcast → class = P 2. Outlook = sunny **and** Humidity = high → class = N 3. Outlook = sunny → class = P 4. Windy = true → class = N 5. () → class = P

(b) Ordered rules

FIGURE 7.5 | Rule ordering schemes

1. Outlook = overcast → class = P 2. Outlook = sunny **and** Humidity = high → class = N 3. Outlook = rain **and** Windy = false → class = N 4. Outlook = sunny → class = P 5. () → class = N

Outlook = overcast → class = P Outlook = sunny **and** Humidity = normal → class = P Outlook = rain **and** Windy = false → class = P Outlook = sunny **and** Humidity = high → class = N Outlook = rain **and** Windy = false → class = N

(a) Ordered by rule   (b) Ordered by class

---

unordered rules. Figure 7.5(a) lists the classification rules for the weather conditions following the order-by-rule scheme using coverage as the quality measure. Figure 7.5(b) lists the rules following the order-by-class scheme.

Both approaches have advantages and disadvantages. The advantage of order-by-rule is that the ordering is based on the applicability of the rules. The best rules are applied first. The biggest disadvantage of the approach is that the negation of all previous rules makes it hard to understand rules towards the end of the list. The advantage of the order-by-class scheme is that rules are easier to interpret. However, inferior rules may be applied to the record because of lack of order among rules of the same class. The two schemes can be combined, producing a class-dependent sequence of rules among which rules for the same class are ordered according to a quality measure. However, it should be noted that measures of quality are not unique. Different measures may exist that rank the rules in different orders. As discussed in Chapter 2, the issue of interestingness and its measures is yet to be settled.

7.2.3 Extracting Rules from Training Examples

Rules can be extracted from a training set by employing rule extraction algorithms. One simple method, known as the basic *sequential covering* algorithm, is outlined as follows:

```
algorithm SequentialCover (Tr: training set; Y: classes): list of rules
begin
   R := ∅; //empty the rule list initially
   A := the set of all attribute value pairs {(Ai, vj)};
   determine the default class yk;
   for each class y in Y - {yk} do
      repeat
         r := learn_one_rule(Tr, A, y);
         append r at the end of the rule list R;
         remove training examples in Tr covered by rule r;
      until a stopping condition is met
   endfor;
   append rule {} → yk to the end of the rule list R;
   return(R);
end;
```

The algorithm can be explained briefly as follows. It takes a training set Tr and a class list Y as inputs and returns a rule list R as the output. The algorithm first constructs a list of attribute–value pairs for all attributes. The algorithm then extracts rules for every class except the chosen default class. During the rule extraction process, all examples of class y are considered as *positive* and examples of other classes as *negative*. For each class, one rule at a time is extracted from the training examples until a stopping condition is met. The rule must be the *best possible rule* that can be extracted from the training examples available at the time. (The extraction of a single rule is discussed later.) Once a rule is extracted, it is added at the end of the rule list so that an order among the resulting rules (best first) is enforced. The training examples covered by the new rule, positive or negative, are then removed from the training set, leaving behind those examples that are not covered by the rules so far. The algorithm then starts extracting another rule from the remaining examples of the training set. The next rule may cover another collection of positive examples in the training set. Once all possible rules for the class have been extracted, the algorithm moves on to the next class and repeats the process until all classes except the default class have been tried. After all rules are extracted, a default rule classifying the remaining examples into the default class is added at the end of the rule list.

Figure 7.6 illustrates the process of the sequential covering algorithm. The training set contains examples of three classes shown as triangles, squares and circles. The class marked with triangles is taken as the default class. The diagrams in Figure 7.6 demonstrate the complete process of extracting a rule that covers the positive training examples and removing the covered examples.

The default class is normally the majority class in order to keep the final rule list simple. The algorithm searches for rules on a class-by-class basis, but it does not specify in which order among the classes that rule extraction is conducted. An algorithm, known as RIPPER, that is derived from the basic sequential covering algorithm specifies the order according to the frequencies of the classes: the least frequent class is listed at the beginning and the most frequent class is listed at the end and taken as the default class.

FIGURE 7.6   Using the sequential covering algorithm

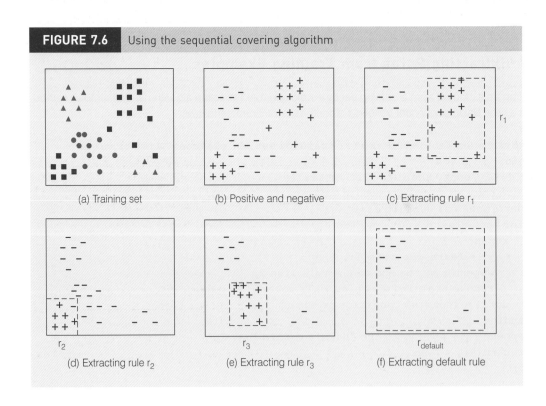

(a) Training set

(b) Positive and negative

(c) Extracting rule r_1

(d) Extracting rule r_2

(e) Extracting rule r_3

(f) Extracting default rule

A rule is considered desirable if it covers most positive examples and very few or no negative examples. Therefore, a rule evaluation criterion relating to rule quality should be embedded in the learn_one_rule operation.

The repeat loop of the basic algorithm should be controlled by a termination condition that stops the process of extracting rules from the training examples for a class. A rule performance threshold is normally employed. If the performance of the most recent rule falls below the threshold, the process is terminated, indicating that no more good rules can be found from the remaining training examples.

7.2.4 Generalization vs Specialization Approaches for Learning a Rule

The *learn_one_rule* operation may find an optimal rule in the following fashion: an initial prototype rule is generated and refined until a certain evaluation criterion is met. There are two approaches for doing this: generalization and specialization. With the generalization approach, a positive example is randomly selected and converted to a specific rule that only covers the record itself. The conversion is straightforward: all attribute–value pairs in the record are conjuncts in the antecedent and class $= y$ is added in the consequent. For instance, a training example (overcast, high, false, P) can be converted into a rule:

```
Outlook=overcast and Humidity = high and Windy = false → class = P
```

Then, one of the conjuncts in the antecedent is chosen and removed from the rule so that the rule covers more positive examples. This process can be repeated until the rule starts to cover negative examples. For instance, for the rule above, the conjuncts Windy = false and Humidity = high can be removed while maintaining class = P.

With the specialization approach, an empty rule () $\rightarrow y$ for class y is first defined. Then, the best possible attribute–value pair from list A is added into the antecedent. This process continues until the rule performance measure cannot improve further. In an algorithm, known as PRISM, that is a variant on the basic algorithm, rule accuracy is used as the performance measure. The attribute–value pair that maximizes the accuracy $P(y|A_i = v_i)$ is selected and added to the antecedent. For instance, the attribute–value pair Outlook = overcast may be selected because of its accuracy $P(\text{class=P}|\text{Outlook=overcast}) = 100\%$. The conjunct is inserted into the antecedent part, creating the following rule:

```
Outlook = overcast → class = P
```

Accuracy may not always yield the best applicable rules. For instance, a rule with 90% accuracy but covering 10% of all training examples should be better than a rule with 100% accuracy but only covering 0.5% of all training examples. Other possible measures for rule quality evaluation have been proposed. These measures combine rule accuracy with coverage. The likelihood ratio statistic, Laplace measure and FOIL information gain are a few examples. Details of these measures are beyond the scope of this text. Interested readers may consult the references given in the Bibliographical Notes.

7.2.5 Rule Pruning

The extracted rules may be further modified to improve their generality. Similar to tree pruning, *rule pruning* further removes or generalizes attribute–value pairs in the antecedent parts of rules. Rule pruning is normally conducted in the presence of a set of validation records. If the pruned rule increases coverage of the right class and reduces coverage of the wrong class, the pruned rules substitute the original rules. In general, rule pruning can be considered as a way to solve the problem of overfitting in the rule-based approach to classification.

Different understandings regarding when rule pruning should take place seem to exist. Similar to post-pruning of decision trees, rule pruning can take place after the classification model, i.e. the complete rule list, is constructed. Each rule is examined in the presence of a validation set. Some algorithms suggest rule pruning when the rule is extracted (similar to the pre-pruning of trees). In other words, the rule performance upon validation records becomes part of the rule evaluation criteria. The RIPPER algorithm, for instance, embeds the maximum error rate upon validation examples (50%) as part of its evaluation criterion, which is primarily based on the minimum description length principle.

7.3   THE BAYESIAN CLASSIFIER APPROACH

In many real-life situations, classification is fundamentally probabilistic: it is uncertain to which class a record should belong. We only know that the record is relatively more likely to belong to class A than to class B. This may be due to the presence of noisy data or, more importantly, many factors that are not even present in the data set for model development. For instance, when a doctor examines the symptoms of a patient, quite often the doctor needs to make a decision over a number of possible (sometimes competing) explanations. To handle problems of this kind, classification models that describe probabilistic relationships between attribute values and a class outcome are needed, and so are techniques to induce such models. The *Bayesian classifier* approach is for this purpose.

Bayesian classification is based on the Bayes theorem: the posterior probability of the class that a record belongs to is approximated using prior probability drawn from the training set. The classification model estimates the likelihood of the record belonging to each class. The class with the highest probability becomes the class label for the record.

7.3.1 The Bayes Theorem

The Bayes theorem can be explained as follows. Given two random variables X and Y, each of them taking a specific value corresponds to a random event. A conditional probability $P(Y|X)$ represents the likelihood of events for Y to happen when events for X have already occurred. As described in Chapter 2,

$$\because P(X \mid Y) = \frac{P(X \cap Y)}{P(X)}, \qquad \therefore P(X \cap Y) = P(X \mid Y) \cdot P(Y)$$

$$\therefore P(Y \mid X) = \frac{P(X \mid Y) \cdot P(Y)}{P(X)}$$

The equation above is known as the *Bayes theorem*. The theorem states that the posterior probability of Y given X, i.e. $P(Y|X)$, can be estimated by the prior probability of Y, i.e. $P(Y)$. To illustrate the use of the theorem, take two badminton players A and B competing in world tournaments as an example. Suppose that there are two world tournaments, the world cup (Cup) and the world championship (Champ). A is overall a better player having won 70% of the matches between the two. However, B performs well at world championships having 80% of wins in that tournament whereas only 30% of A's wins come from the world championship. Which player is more likely to win the next world championship?

Let X represent a world tournament and Y represent the winning player. From the information given above, it is understood that:

$$P(Y = A) = 0.7, \ \ P(Y = B) = 1 - 0.7 = 0.3,$$
$$P(X = Champ \mid Y = A) = 0.3$$
$$P(X = Champ \mid Y = B) = 0.8$$

We need to find the results of $P(Y = A \mid X = Champ)$ and $P(Y = B \mid X = Champ)$.

According to the Bayes theorem,

$$P(Y = A \mid X = Champ) = \frac{P(X = Champ \mid Y = A) \cdot P(Y = A)}{P(X = Champ)} = \frac{0.3 \times 0.7}{P(X = Champ)}$$

and

$$P(Y = B \mid X = Champ) = \frac{P(X = Champ \mid Y = B) \cdot P(Y = B)}{P(X = Champ)} = \frac{0.8 \times 0.3}{P(X = Champ)}$$

since

$$
\begin{aligned}
P(X = Champ) &= P(X = Champ \cap (Y = A \cup Y = B)) \\
&= P((X = Champ \cap Y = A) \cup (X = Champ \cap Y = B)) \\
&= P(X = Champ \cap Y = A) + P(X = Champ \cap Y = B) \\
&= P(X = Champ \mid Y = A) \cdot P(Y = A) + P(X = Champ \mid Y = B) \cdot P(Y = B) \\
&= 0.3 \times 0.7 + 0.8 \times 0.3
\end{aligned}
$$

Therefore,

$$P(Y = A \mid X = Champ) = \frac{0.3 \times 0.7}{0.3 \times 0.7 + 0.8 \times 0.3} = 0.46667$$

$$P(Y = B \mid X = Champ) = \frac{0.8 \times 0.3}{0.3 \times 0.7 + 0.8 \times 0.3} = 0.53333$$

It is concluded that player B has a higher chance of winning the world championship.

7.3.2 Bayesian Theorem as a Classification Model

In the Bayes theorem, if Y represents a class attribute and X represents a collection of descriptive attributes, $P(X|Y)$ is called the class-conditional probability, $P(Y)$ the prior probability of the class and $P(X)$ the probability of an *evidence* record being classified. In other words, the likelihood of an evidence record belonging to a class can be estimated by the class-conditional probability, prior probability of the class and the evidence probability. In particular, we want to predict the likelihood of a record X belonging to each of the classes, i.e. $P(y_1|X)$, $P(y_2|X)$, ..., $P(y_k|X)$. Based on the likelihood measurements, we can conclude which class the record belongs to, i.e. the class with the highest likelihood.

Among the terms of the Bayes theorem, $P(Y)$ can be calculated from the training set. $P(X)$ is given as evidence but can be ignored when comparing the different predicted probabilities. This is because the same $P(X)$ is used as the common denominator for all class probabilities, $P(y_1|X)$, $P(y_2|X)$, ..., $P(y_k|X)$. The class-conditional probability $P(X|Y)$ needs to be estimated from the training examples. There are different ways of estimating $P(X|Y)$. Naïve Bayes and the Bayesian belief network are two alternative methods. The next section describes the naïve Bayes method. Readers who are interested in the Bayesian belief network can follow the references given in the Bibliographical Notes.

7.3.3 The Naïve Bayes Method

The naïve Bayes method makes the assumption that descriptive attributes are conditionally independent of each other given the class label is known. In fact this may well not be the case. That is why the approach is called *naïve* Bayes. It is understood from the basic statistics described in Chapter 2 that if a set of events are independent, the probability that all of them happen at the same time equals the *product* of the probabilities for the individual events. Therefore, the class-conditional probability $P(X|Y = y)$ is estimated as the product of all conditional probabilities $P(X_1|Y = y)$, $P(X_2|Y = y)$, ..., $P(X_d|Y = y)$:

$$P(X \mid Y = y) = \prod_{i=1}^{d} P(X_i \mid Y = y)$$

Therefore,

$$P(Y = y \mid X) = \frac{P(Y = y)\prod_{i=1}^{d} P(X_i \mid Y = y)}{P(X)}$$

When comparing the probabilities of variable Y taking different classes with $P(X)$ cancelled out as the common denominator, the following expression is used most of the time:

$$P(Y = y \mid X) = P(Y = y)\prod_{i=1}^{d} P(X_i \mid Y = y)$$

For categorical attributes, $P(X_i|Y = y)$ is estimated as the fraction of training examples of class y that take the attribute value X_i. For a continuous attribute, it is assumed that the attribute values follow a normal distribution. The probability $P(X_i|Y = y)$ is then estimated by using the Gaussian probability density function based on the mean and the variance of the fraction of training examples for the class.

The weather condition table in Figure 6.2 is used again, to illustrate the working of the naïve Bayes method. First, the probabilities $P(\text{Class} = P)$ and $P(\text{Class} = N)$ are calculated. The data set is then divided into two subsets: one for examples of class P and the other for examples of class N. All probabilities for the two classes are presented in Table 7.1.

TABLE 7.1	Values for Bayesian theorem parameters for the weather condition data set
$P(\text{Class} = P) \approx 0.643$	$P(\text{Class} = N) \approx 0.357$
$P(\text{Outlook=sunny} \mid \text{Class=P}) = 2/9 \approx 0.222$	$P(\text{Outlook=sunny} \mid \text{Class=N}) = 3/5 = 0.6$
$P(\text{Outlook=overcast} \mid \text{Class=P}) = 4/9 \approx 0.444$	$P(\text{Outlook=overcast} \mid \text{Class=N}) = 0/5 = 0$
$P(\text{Outlook=rain} \mid \text{Class=P}) = 3/9 \approx 0.333$	$P(\text{Outlook=rain} \mid \text{Class=N}) = 2/5 = 0.4$
$P(\text{Temperature=hot} \mid \text{Class=P}) = 2/9 \approx 0.222$	$P(\text{Temperature=hot} \mid \text{Class=N}) = 2/5 = 0.4$
$P(\text{Temperature=mild} \mid \text{Class=P}) = 4/9 \approx 0.444$	$P(\text{Temperature=mild} \mid \text{Class=N}) = 2/5 = 0.4$
$P(\text{Temperature=cool} \mid \text{Class=P}) = 3/9 \approx 0.333$	$P(\text{Temperature=cool} \mid \text{Class=N}) = 1/5 = 0.2$
$P(\text{Humidity=high} \mid \text{Class=P}) = 3/9 \approx 0.333$	$P(\text{Humidity=high} \mid \text{Class=N}) = 4/5 = 0.8$
$P(\text{Humidity=normal} \mid \text{Class=P}) = 6/9 \approx 0.667$	$P(\text{Humidity=normal} \mid \text{Class=N}) = 1/5 = 0.2$
$P(\text{Windy=true} \mid \text{Class=P}) = 3/9 \approx 0.333$	$P(\text{Windy=true} \mid \text{Class=N}) = 3/5 = 0.6$
$P(\text{Windy=false} \mid \text{Class=P}) = 6/9 \approx 0.667$	$P(\text{Windy=false} \mid \text{Class=N}) = 2/5 = 0.4$

After collecting the theorem parameters from the training examples, the theorem is now ready to be used for classifying an unseen record. Given a record X with Outlook = overcast, Temperature = mild, Humidity = normal and Windy = false, the theorem is used to calculate P(Class = P | X) and P(Class = N | X) and then determine which probability is higher.

$$
\begin{aligned}
P(X \mid \text{Class} = \text{P}) \;=\;\; & P(\text{Outlook} = \text{overcast} \mid \text{Class} = \text{P}) \times \\
& P(\text{Temperature} = \text{mild} \mid \text{Class} = \text{P}) \times \\
& P(\text{Humidity} = \text{normal} \mid \text{Class} = \text{P}) \times \\
& P(\text{Windy} = \text{false} \mid \text{Class} = \text{P}) \\
=\;\; & 0.444 \times 0.444 \times 0.667 \times 0.667 = 0.0877 \\[6pt]
P(X \mid \text{Class} = \text{N}) \;=\;\; & P(\text{Outlook} = \text{overcast} \mid \text{Class} = \text{N}) \times \\
& P(\text{Temperature} = \text{mild} \mid \text{Class} = \text{N}) \times \\
& P(\text{Humidity} = \text{normal} \mid \text{Class} = \text{N}) \times \\
& P(\text{Windy} = \text{false} \mid \text{Class} = \text{N}) \\
=\;\; & 0 \times 0.4 \times 0.2 \times 0.4 = 0 \\[6pt]
P(\text{Class} = \text{P} \mid X) \;=\;\; & P(X \mid \text{Class} = \text{P}) \times P(\text{Class} = \text{P})/P(X) = (0.0877 \times 0.643)/P(X) \\
P(\text{Class} = \text{N} \mid X) \;=\;\; & P(X \mid \text{Class} = \text{N}) \times P(\text{Class} = \text{N})/P(X) = (0 \times 0.357)/P(X) \\
& \text{so } P(\text{Class} = \text{P} \mid X) > P(\text{Class} = \text{N} \mid X)
\end{aligned}
$$

Therefore the unseen record is more likely to be of class P than of class N.

The Naïve Bayes method is robust to isolated noisy data: any peculiar noisy values are averaged out in the estimation of conditional probabilities. The method can also cope with null values, i.e. null values are ignored during the calculation of average, variance and probabilities. The classifiers are also robust against irrelevant attributes. This is because the class-conditional probabilities of irrelevant attributes are almost uniformly distributed and, hence, have very little impact on the final estimates. Because of these advantages, the naïve Bayes method is widely used for different applications. Interested readers are recommended to follow the referred texts in the bibliographic notes for thorough coverage of this important subject.

7.4 THE ARTIFICIAL NEURAL NETWORK APPROACH

An artificial neural network (ANN) is a connected network of artificial neuron nodes, emulating the network of biological neurons of the human brain. Artificial neural networks have been used successfully in various application areas. One important area is classification: it remains as one of the most important approaches to classification and it would, therefore, be inappropriate not to mention it. However, the subject is too big to be accommodated in one chapter, let alone a section within a chapter. This section covers the fundamental concepts and principles of ANN and concentrates on the use of ANN for classification.

7.4.1 Concepts of Artificial Neural Networks

An artificial neural network normally consists of layers of neuron nodes. A neuron node normally takes as input data values produced from nodes on the previous layer and outputs a single value. Figure 7.7(a) illustrates such a node where w_1, w_2, and w_3 are the weights attached to the links through which the input values i_1, i_2 and i_3 are fed into the node and y is the output value of the node.

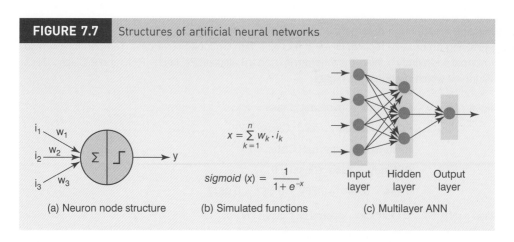

FIGURE 7.7   Structures of artificial neural networks

(a) Neuron node structure

(b) Simulated functions

$$x = \sum_{k=1}^{n} w_k \cdot i_k$$

$$sigmoid\ (x) = \frac{1}{1 + e^{-x}}$$

(c) Multilayer ANN

Input layer   Hidden layer   Output layer

A node combines two functions: a sum function and a transformation function. The sum function summarizes the input values to the node and the transformation function transforms the summary result into the output value of the node. The most commonly used sum function is the weighted sum and one of the most commonly used transformation functions is the sigmoid function, as shown in Figure 7.7(b). Step functions and linear functions can also be used as transformation functions.

An artificial neural network normally consists of layers of artificial neuron nodes that are connected via links, as shown in Figure 7.7(c). The *input layer* is where nodes receive attribute values as input from outside. The *output layer* is where nodes produce final output values from the network. In between are layers known as the *hidden layers* where nodes receive values from the nodes in the previous layer and produce output values to be used as input by the nodes in the next layer. Networks with links from lower layers *only* to upper layers are known as *feed-forward* networks, whereas networks with links between nodes of the same layer or links to previous layers are known as *recurrent* networks. A simple one-node network is known as a *perceptron*.

Some useful properties of artificial neural networks are summarized as follows:

- Although a neural network can have several hidden layers, for most applications one layer is usually sufficient.

- The more nodes a hidden layer has, the more capacity for pattern recognition the network has, but the more specific to the training examples the network becomes (model overfitting).

- Different transformation functions can be employed for nodes in different layers. However, doing so increases the complexity of the network.

- Constants known as bias factors can also be fed into the nodes in the hidden and output layers as inputs. Normally, the constant amount of the bias is deducted from the weighted sum before the transformation function is called.

To illustrate how a neural network works, a perceptron (as shown in Figure 7.8(a)) is used with an example data set (shown in Figure 7.8(b)). The input nodes let the input values pass through directly without applying any functions. A step function is used as the transformation function in this example. It takes the value 1 if the sum function result is greater than 0, otherwise, -1. A bias factor a is subtracted from the sum function result. The example data set contains three Boolean variables and a class variable. The class takes the value of $+1$ if two of the three Boolean variables take the value 1 and -1 if two of the three Boolean variables take the value 0.

FIGURE 7.8	The working principles of ANN

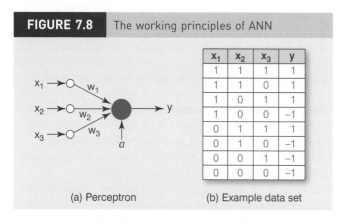

(a) Perceptron

x_1	x_2	x_3	y
1	1	1	1
1	1	0	1
1	0	1	1
1	0	0	−1
0	1	1	1
0	1	0	−1
0	0	1	−1
0	0	0	−1

(b) Example data set

Suppose that the initial weights are set randomly to $w_1 = 0.8$, $w_2 = 0.1$ and $w_3 = 0.1$ and constant $a = 0.3$. When the attribute values of the first training example, i.e. $x_1 = 1$, $x_2 = 1$ and $x_3 = 1$ are fed into the perceptron, the result of the sum function is:

$$x = 0.8 \times 1 + 0.1 \times 1 + 0.1 \times 1 - 0.3 = 0.7 > 0$$

The output of the network, y, takes the value 1, the same as the actual class value in the table. In this case, the weights stay unchanged. However, when the values of the fifth training example, i.e. $x_1 = 0$, $x_2 = 1$ and $x_3 = 1$ are fed into the perceptron, the result of the sum function is:

$$x = 0.8 \times 0 + 0.1 \times 1 + 0.1 \times 1 - 0.3 = -0.1 < 0$$

Then the output of the network y takes the value of −1, different from the actual class value 1. In this case, the weights need to be updated. A simple formula is outlined as follows:

$$w_j^{(k+1)} = w_j^{(k)} + \lambda(y - \hat{y}^{(k)})x_j$$

where $w_j^{(k+1)}$ and $w_j^{(k)}$ are respectively the new weight and current weight for attribute j, λ is called the *learning rate* with a value in [0,1], y is the actual class value of the current training example and x_j is the value of the jth attribute of the example. Suppose that $\lambda = 0.5$. Then the new weights are:

$$w_1 = 0.8 + 0.5 \times (1 - (-1)) \times 0 = 0.8$$
$$w_2 = 0.1 + 0.5 \times (1 - (-1)) \times 1 = 1.1$$
$$w_3 = 0.1 + 0.5 \times (1 - (-1)) \times 1 = 1.1$$

This example shows that when the prediction of the class is correct, little or no changes are made to the weights. When the prediction is wrong, the weights need to be increase or decreased to compensate for the prediction errors. In this example, since the wrong prediction has a negative value, the weights should be increased to compensate for the error in the prediction.

7.4.2 Developing an Artificial Neural Network as a Classification Model

In the artificial neural network approach to classification, a trained network with the right weights attached to the links is taken as the classification model. Developing a neural network model involves the definition of a network topology and the training of the defined network.

Defining the Network Topology The definition of network topology consists of defining the number of nodes in the input layer, the number of nodes in the output layer, the number of hidden layers and the number of nodes in each hidden layer, together with the choice of the type of network.

The number of nodes in the input layer is determined by the number and data types of the descriptive attributes. For continuous and binary attributes, one node is needed for each attribute. For a categorical attribute, since the attribute has a number of discrete labels, either the labels are converted into numeric values, or the attribute is replaced by a number of binary attributes. If the conversion is possible and sensible, one node is needed for the attribute. Otherwise, the attribute of k labels, at least $\log(k)$ binary attributes and therefore $\log(k)$ nodes are needed to replace the categorical attribute.

The number of nodes in the output layer is determined by the number of classes. For a two-class situation, one node is sufficient. For a k-class situation, at least $\log(k)$ nodes are needed.

The number of hidden layers and the number of nodes in each hidden layer are more difficult to decide. There seems to be no good solution here. Heuristics can help in determining the number of layers. Performance factors of the network may help in determining the number of nodes in each layer.

Training the Defined Network Like other classification approaches, a neural network is trained over a set of training examples. Each training example may be used many times and many training examples may be needed. However, training is resource intensive, so the number of training examples must be restricted. The training examples must be prepared because a neural network only takes continuous values as input and normally produces continuous values as output. The descriptive attribute values are either normalized or converted to binary attributes.

The objective of training a neural network is to ensure the outputs produced by the network are as close as possible to the actual classes of the training examples by assigning the best possible weights on the input links of each node. The following pseudo-code algorithm outlines the principle behind training a network:

```
algorithm trainingNetwork (Tr: training set, var R: ANN)
begin
  // R is initial network with a particular topology
  w := a vector of all weights;
  w⁽⁰⁾ := w with randomly generated weights;
  repeat
    for each training example t = <xᵢ, cᵢ> in Tr do
      compute the predicted class output ĉ⁽ᵏ⁾
        for each weight wⱼ⁽ᵏ⁾ in the weight vector w⁽ᵏ⁾ do
          update the weight wⱼ⁽ᵏ⁾ to wⱼ⁽ᵏ⁺¹⁾
        endfor;
    endfor;
    k := k + 1;
  until a stopping criterion is met
  modify R with the updated w;
end;
```

The updated weight for the jth attribute must reflect the difference between the actual class value and the predicted class value. The bigger the difference, the more modification needs to be made to the new weight. The value for the learning rate λ also affects the updated weight. Normally, at early iterations when weights are heavily influenced by random values, the value of λ is big indicating that the weights need to be modified with a bigger amount. As the process continues, the value of λ can be gradually reduced, indicating that learning is less influenced by random effects.

For general neural networks with hidden layers, the updating of weights becomes more difficult. This is because, for a node in a hidden layer, it is not clear what would be the expected 'actual' class value and therefore it is difficult to calculate the difference between the actual class value and the node output value. One technique for solving the problem is known as *back-propagation*. The idea of the technique is to update the weights in a backward fashion: the weights between the last hidden layer and the output layer are updated before the weights between the hidden layers and the weights between the first hidden layer and the input layer are updated. Calculation about errors in the output layer helps in estimating errors in the last hidden layer, the errors in the last hidden layer help in estimating errors in the previous hidden layer, etc.

7.4.3 Using an Artificial Neural Network for Classification

Once the network is trained, the network may be fine-tuned with validation examples in order to reduce the effect of model overfitting. Similar to the nearest neighbour approach, a validation example is used for the tuning of the weights of links in the network even further. Finally, the trained and tuned network is used to predict the class of a given unseen record. For estimation applications, the output of a neural network may need to be converted to a sensible output value range. For the purpose of classification, an output value closer to one end of the output range indicates one class.

One strength of the artificial neural network approach to classification is that neural network methods handle a wide range of problems of different kinds. Neural networks can be used not only for classification, but also for estimation, clustering, etc. Neural network methods also produce good results, which means that a classification model normally has good accuracy.

The most obvious weakness of neural networks is that they do not offer any explicit explanation of the classification results. Neural networks may sometimes converge prematurely to an inferior solution.

7.5 RELATED ISSUES

7.5.1 Comparison of Classification Approaches

In Chapter 6 and this chapter, the main approaches to classification have been introduced. Each approach is good at certain aspects, but not so good at others. In this section, all the classification approaches are brought together and compared upon a list of factors in order to appreciate the strengths and weaknesses of each. The comparison factors include model interpretability, model maintainability, training cost and classification cost. Model interpretability refers to the ease of understanding the model's classification decisions. Model maintainability refers to the ease of modifying the classification model upon the presence of new training data. The training cost means the computational cost of building a classification model, which includes the initial training cost and the modification cost. The classification cost refers to the computational cost in classifying an unseen record using the classification model. The comparison results are in Table 7.2.

In terms of model interpretability, decision tree and rule-based techniques produce classification models whose classification decisions are clearly explained. Models produced by the nearest neighbour methods are also comprehensible: the data object is of a particular class because it is most similar to the examples known about that class. The interpretability of a naïve Bayes model is rather mixed. On the one hand, the model description merely consists of numerical representations of the Bayes theorem parameters. On the other hand, the classification decision-making is made on clear grounds: given the same record, how probable it is for the record to belong to each of the classes. An artificial neural network comes to a classification result through a sequence of numeric calculations. It is difficult for the model to explain how the decision is made.

TABLE 7.2	Comparison of classification approaches			
Classification Approach	**Model Interpretability**	**Model Maintainability**	**Training Cost**	**Classification Cost**
Decision tree	High	Low	High	Low
Nearest neighbours	Medium	High	Low	High
Rule-based	High	Low	High	Medium
Bayesian classifier	Medium	Medium	Medium	Low
Artificial neural network	Low	Low	High	Low

In terms of maintainability, the nearest neighbour approach scores high because the model, i.e. the exemplar space, is fully adaptive and dynamic. The memory space can evolve over time by taking out old exemplars, adding in new ones and tuning the weights. As for the naïve Bayes method, adding and deleting training examples means that all parameters must be recalculated. However, the cost involved is not very high. Therefore it is still adaptive to change. Decision trees and neural networks on the other hand are much more rigid and static. When there are changes in the training set, a new decision tree has to be rebuilt because the likely change of attribute values may alter the selection of root nodes for subtrees. Although changing training examples may not necessarily change the topology of a neural network, the new examples must be used to retrain the network. The rule-based classification approach is similar to that for decision trees and neural networks.

Regarding training cost, the nearest neighbour methods have the least amount of training. The basic *k*NN algorithm has no training cost at all and the PEBLS algorithm has a very minimal amount of training, i.e. the construction of value difference tables, which can be achieved with linear time complexity. The naïve Bayes method also has a small amount of training cost, i.e. the calculation of the theorem parameters, with linear time complexity. The training cost for decision tree methods and rule-based methods can also be relatively high. The training cost of neural networks is even higher because of repeated use of training examples. As indicated in the basic sequential covering algorithm, for each class the training set is searched for an optimal rule. Although the training set gets smaller as the learning continues, the repeated search for optimal rules can still be costly.

Once built, decision trees and neural networks can perform efficiently in classifying data records. The speed is determined by the number of levels of the tree or the number of layers of the network. As for an exemplar space, the class of a data object cannot be determined until the distance from the data object to every exemplar is calculated. The more exemplars there are in the space, the longer it takes to find the neighbours, and hence the longer it takes to make a decision. For rule-based models, the classification speed is determined by the number and order of the rules because the rules must be searched sequentially. The more rules there are, the longer it takes to make a decision. However, the number of rules is normally fewer than the number of training examples. Therefore, searching through the rules should take less time than searching through the training set for the nearest neighbours. The estimation of likelihood of classes in Bayesian classifiers also takes time, but it is related to the number of classes and the number of descriptive attributes.

The most important issue regarding classification is accuracy. However, there is no clear winner as to which classification approach produces more accurate models than others. Comparison works reported in the literature are often either too limited or inconclusive. The situation, to a certain extent, explains why all approaches are still in use and why there is a need for ensemble classification methods.

7.5.2 Ensemble Methods for Classification

So far, the classification procedure outlined in Figures 2.2 and 6.1 has been followed. A *single* classification model is induced from a set of training examples. The model accuracy is measured with a set of test examples. The single model is then used to predict the class of an unseen record. Instead of a single model, can a number of classification models, say, a set of decision trees, be used to classify an unseen record? Does accuracy improve in most cases? The answers to both questions are positive. This section briefly describes a type of classification method that induces a number of classification models and combines or fuse the class predictions from the different models. The methods are known as *ensemble methods* for classification.

The principle behind ensemble methods is quite straightforward. The ideal is to draw a number of different versions of the training set, induce a classification model known as the *base model* from each version, and use the base models to predict the class of the unseen record by majority voting. A general procedural framework in terms of two separate algorithms are presented here in pseudo-code:

```
algorithm ensembleTraining(Tr: training set, k: integer): model set
begin
    for i := 1 to k do
        draw a subset Tr_i from Tr;
        develop a base model M_i from Tr_i;
    endfor;
    M := M_1 ∪ M_2 ∪ ... ∪ M_k;
    Return M;
end;


algorithm ensembleClassifying(M: model set, var r: data record)
begin
    for i := 1 to k do
        use model M_i in M to predict the class label C(r)_i for data record r;
    endfor;
    r.Class := the majority of C(r)_1, C(r)_2, ..., C(r)_k;
end;
```

When a version of the original training set is drawn, certain methods may be employed to manipulate the examples to be included in the sample. *Bagging* is a technique that draws a sample from the original training set using the sampling with replacement method. The sample has the size of the original set and, on average, contain about 63% of the examples of the original set. Experimental results show that bagging in general improves the accuracy of prediction by reducing variance in the predictions.

Boosting is a technique that assigns and changes the weight of each training example at each iteration of the training process so that more copies of the examples with heavier weights are drawn into the sample for the subsequent iteration of the process. Examples with heavy weighting are normally those that are incorrectly classified by the base models. For instance, one boosting ensemble method initially assigns an equal weight to each training example so that all have an equal chance of being selected into the first sample. The method then uses the classification model induced from the sample to classify all the original training examples and measures the total weighted errors. The measurement of errors is then used to increase or decrease the weight attached to each example according to whether the example is classified correctly or incorrectly.

In the situation when there are a large number of redundant attributes, different samples of the training set may contain different descriptive feature attributes. A set of attributes can be randomly selected when the sample is drawn by sampling with replacement. One ensemble method, known as the *Random Forest*, selects the attributes randomly and uses decision trees as the base models.

In a situation in which there exists a large number of classes at an iteration of the training process, the classes can be randomly divided into two groups. The training examples are superimposed with the group identity (e.g. 0 and 1) of the group to which the classes of the examples belong. A sample is then drawn as described before and a classification model that predicts the group identity outcome is built. During the classification phase, the group identity of an unseen record is predicted. The classes in the predicted group all receive a vote. At the end of the classification phase, the votes are counted. The class that receives the most votes is assigned as the class of the unseen record.

The general framework in the algorithm above does not indicate what base models should be developed. In practice, the base models can be homogeneous or heterogeneous. For instance, in the Random Forest method, a set of decision trees are developed as the base models. We can also have a mixture of decision trees, rule-based models and neural networks. When developing base models, a weighting system can also be introduced to the models according to their performance on the original training set or a set of validation examples so that models with better accuracies of prediction have a greater say in the final decision of the class.

7.5.3 Multiple Classes and Class Imbalance

This chapter and Chapter 6 used examples of classes whose representations in the training set are more or less balanced. In practice, however, it may often be the case that more than two classes may be present in the training set. In some situations, the number of examples of each of the classes is not similar or even close.

Most classification methods and techniques can readily be adapted to deal with multiple classes. For instance, decision tree induction algorithms such as ID3 are capable of computing the information gain of attributes over multiple classes. The k nearest neighbour methods simply apply the majority voting strategy to multiple classes. However, some classification techniques aim at primarily binary situations, and the classification models can only handle two possible classes. For these classification techniques, an ensemble strategy can be adopted: a number of binary classification models are developed and majority voting is applied. One approach is to take one of the original classes as the *positive* class and the others as the *negative* class and build a binary model. Similarly, each of the other classes can be treated in the same way. Another approach is to take pairs of specific classes and build a binary model with training examples of only the two classes. In both cases, all binary models are then applied to an unseen record at the classification stage and the class that receives the most votes is the one for the record.

The class imbalance problem poses a major challenge to existing classification methods. Many existing methods do not cope well with the *rare class*. The rare class is often ignored in class predictions and is sometimes even treated in the same way as noise. As a consequence, many classification models cannot correctly predict the rare class although they may have very high overall accuracy rate. For instance, a decision tree trained with 99 examples of the majority and one example of the rare class may still have an accuracy rate of 99% although the test record is of the rare class.

In Section 6.5.1, a number of measures of accuracy, i.e. true positive (TP), true negative (TN), false negative (FN) and false positive (FP), and the overall error rate were described. In the class imbalance situation, different measures of accuracy need to be used. Precision and recall are two measures that are defined as follows:

$$precision = \frac{TP}{TP + FP} \qquad recall = \frac{TP}{TP + FN}$$

Precision refers to the ratio of the number of true positive predictions to all positive predictions made by the model. *Recall* is the ratio of the number of true positive predictions to the total number of actual true positive examples. High precision means few negative examples being predicted as positive. High recall means few positive examples being predicted as negative. Depending on the objective of discovery, data analysts can decide whether to aim at better precision or recall or both when the rare class is considered as the positive class.

Besides using a more realistic accuracy measure to reflect the performance of a classification model with a rare class, the presentation of the rare class can be increased with sampling to cope with class imbalance problems between positive and negative classes during the training stage. Suppose there exists a training set that consists of 200 examples of the rare class and 1000 examples of the majority class.

■ *Under-sampling* selects fewer majority class examples to make the presentation of the classes more balanced in the training set. For instance, 200 examples of the majority class may be selected to form a sample of 400 examples with the rare class examples. The problem with this method is that the majority class may be under-represented in the sample, and hence an inferior model may be induced. To solve this problem, an ensemble method of classification can be adopted so that different samples of the majority class can be selected for developing the classification models.

■ *Over-sampling* increases the number of examples of the rare class by creating duplicates perhaps with some embedded noise variants. For instance, the 200 examples of the rare class may be duplicated to 1000 examples that combine with the 1000 examples of the majority class into a training set of 2000 examples. Over-sampling may run the risk of creating overfitting models when the few original rare class examples contain noise. Through over-sampling, the effects of noise are increased by duplication.

In practice, both over-sampling and under-sampling can be used in preparing a sample of the training set. For instance, instead of over-sampling to 1000 examples, the existing 200 examples of the rare class may be increased to 500 by duplication. At the same time, the 1000 examples of the majority class may be reduced by sampling to 500. Then the 500 examples of each class can form a training set of 1000 examples.

7.6 CLASSIFICATION IN PRACTICE

7.6.1 Performing a Classification Task

To conduct a classification task, the steps below should be followed:

1 A sufficient number of examples must be collected for the purposes of training, validation and testing. The collected examples should cover all class labels and all possible domain values of the descriptive attributes. Ideally, there should be a sufficient number of examples for the combination of each class label with each attribute domain value. This may not always be practicable but effort in that direction must be made at this stage. If the objective cannot be achieved, the data analysts must note that it may influence decisions in the other steps of the mining process.

2 The collected data must be prepared. Data preparation for classification involves the selection of descriptive attributes from the given data set, the identification or definition of the class attribute, and sampling of training, validation and testing examples. When selecting the examples for different purposes, the spread and coverage of the classes and descriptive attribute values in each subset must be ensured. Other data preparation work may include data transformation, noise removal and handling of missing data. Depending on the method chosen, additional preparation work, such as data normalization, may be needed.

3 A classification method must be chosen. Selecting a suitable method is influenced by a number of concerns including the suitability of the method to the data, the accuracy of the model, and the need for any additional classification information. For instance, if the user wants to know not only the predicted classes for unseen records but also why the classification decisions are made, then rule-based or decision tree methods are preferred to neural network methods. In practice, it is often the case that more than one method is used so that all concerns can be evaluated and a suitable and efficient classification model with a high level of accuracy can be developed.

4 The classification task must be defined. Here, we let the chosen software construct a classification model and then fine-tune it and evaluate it. If the model is not acceptable, the process of classification needs to be restarted. If all resulting models of a specific kind are not acceptable, one should consider whether the initial choice of classification solution is appropriate. Further evaluation of classification models (such as complexity, comprehensibility, etc.) may also be needed. This evaluation effort may again influence the process and may involve a new iteration from Step 3.

5 Once they are satisfied with the model evaluation, the data analysts can deliver the model and test it in a real environment. They can further modify the model if necessary. This step is an initial use of the final model in practice. Of course such a use should be carefully controlled in order to avoid expensive failures.

Besides the general framework, specific tasks particularly relevant to a chosen classification approach or method should be taken into consideration. For the nearest neighbour approach, care should be taken in choosing training examples and determining a sensible distance function. We choose the training examples carefully to ensure that correct and desirable training examples are included in the training set. Noise, i.e. examples with wrong attribute values or wrong class tags, need to be avoided. After all, the training examples become the exemplars in the memory space of the model. Determining a sensible distance function for finding the nearest neighbour or neighbours is to ensure that the measure of similarity or dissimilarity is meaningful in the context of the data and for the purpose of classification. This task may not always be possible with some data mining software tools.

For the neural network approach, besides ensuring the coverage of values of the descriptive attributes and classes, any input values, whether continuous numeric values of numeric attributes, discrete ordered values for ordinal attributes, or discrete values for categorical attributes, must be normalized into the numeric range [0, 1]. The output class value produced by an artificial neural network is a real number between 0 and 1. Such a value must also be converted to a meaningful class label. Modern neural network solutions embed both the transformation for the input and for the output as part of the solution. However, the normalization of input can still be done as part of data preparation. Generally, training a neural network is an expensive process. It requires feeding the training examples many times through the network. Although a large number of training examples produce more accurate classification models, the demand on resources can limit the number of training examples that can be used in reality.

Decision tree induction methods work better with categorical or discrete attributes. This means that some supervised discretization at the data pre-processing stage may help to produce better performing models. The same can be said for rule-based methods. Naïve Bayes methods work fine with any types of attribute but expect a great degree of independence between attributes. If attributes are highly correlated, with a great degree of information redundancy, techniques for dimension reduction, such as PCA, should be used at the data pre-processing stage to transform the original attributes into a set of more independent attributes before the classification is attempted.

7.6.2 Estimating the Accuracy Confidence Interval

Once the accuracy of a classification model is measured, does the measurement reflect true accuracy when the model is used in practice? Maybe not, but a confidence interval within which the true accuracy lies may be obtained. Confidence interval estimation was discussed in Chapter 2.

Statistically, testing whether the model assigns the correct class label to N testing examples can be seen as a random experiment with two outcomes: success and failure. Given a random variable X representing the number of correctly classified test examples, the values of X follow a binomial distribution with pN as the mean and $p(1-p)N$ as the variance where p represents the true accuracy rate. The actual accuracy measure $f = X/N$ is an estimate of p. According to the central limit theorem, explained in Chapter 2, if the experiment has a large number of trials, the accuracy measures from different trials follow a normal distribution with the true accuracy p as the mean and $p(1-p)/N$ as the variance. Therefore,

$$P(-Z_{a/2} \le \frac{f-p}{\sqrt{p(1-p)/N}} \le Z_{a/2}) = 1 - a$$

where $Z_{a/2}$ is the two-tailed t value of the t-distribution. Solving the inequality, we obtain the following expression for the confidence interval for p at the confidence level $1 - a$:

$$\frac{\left(f + \frac{Z_{a/2}^2}{2N} - Z_{a/2}\sqrt{\frac{f}{N} - \frac{f^2}{N} + \frac{Z_{a/2}^2}{4N^2}}\right)}{\left(1 + \frac{Z_{a/2}^2}{N}\right)} \le p \le \frac{\left(f + \frac{Z_{a/2}^2}{2N} + Z_{a/2}\sqrt{\frac{f}{N} - \frac{f^2}{N} + \frac{Z_{a/2}^2}{4N^2}}\right)}{\left(1 + \frac{Z_{a/2}^2}{N}\right)}$$

When N is large (measured in hundreds), at a confidence level of 95% (i.e. $a = 0.05$), $Z_{a/2} = 1.96$. For a classification model with $f = 85\%$ from a test set of size $N = 1000$, the confidence interval is [82.65%, 87.08%]. Similarly, for a test set of size $N = 100$, at the same confidence level, the confidence interval is [76.72%, 90.69%]. As shown in this example, the bigger the test set, the more accurate and closer the actual measurement of accuracy to the true accuracy.

7.6.3 Comparison and Selection of Classification Models

Building a classification model can be an iterative process. A number of possible models may be generated. How should we select among the candidates the right model to be the final model? Is the model with the highest accuracy automatically the best model to choose?

Given two models M_1 and M_2, let e_1 represent the error rate of M_1 when it is tested on the test set D_1 and e_2 the error rate of M_2 when it is tested on the test set D_2. Determining if the difference between e_1 and e_2 is statistically significant involves conducting a hypothesis test. The null hypothesis states that the difference is not significant while the alternative hypothesis states that it is. When D_1 and D_2 contain a large number of examples, the error rates are normally distributed and so are the differences between the error rates. The normal distribution for the error differences has the true difference d_t as the mean and the following variance σ^2:

$$\sigma^2 \approx \frac{e_1(1-e_1)}{|D_1|} + \frac{e_2(1-e_2)}{|D_2|}$$

Then the confidence interval for d_t at confidence level $1-a$ can be calculated as:

$$|e_1 - e_2| - Z_{a/2} \cdot \sigma \le d_t \le |e_1 - e_2| + Z_{a/2} \cdot \sigma$$

If the interval includes 0 in its range, the difference is not significant; otherwise, it is. For instance, if we have two models with $e_1 = 0.1$ from a test set of size 50 and $e_2 = 0.15$ from a test set of size 2000, Then

$$\sigma \approx \sqrt{\frac{0.1 \cdot (1-0.1)}{50} + \frac{0.15 \cdot (1-0.15)}{2000}} \approx 0.0432$$

Therefore,

$$|0.1 - 0.15| - 1.96 \cdot 0.0432 \le d_t \le |0.1 - 0.15| + 1.96 \cdot 0.0432$$
$$-0.03467 \le d_t \le 0.1347$$

Since zero appears in the range, the difference is not statistically significant. In other words, the 5% difference in percentage between the two error rates is insignificant. In a separate experiment, when the size of the test set for the first model is 1000 examples instead of 50, the confidence interval at the confidence level of 95% is [0.0257, 0.0743]. Since the range does not span zero, the 5% difference between the two models is considered to be statistically significant. The first decision tree has significantly better accuracy than the second tree and it is taken as the final model.

7.7 CLASSIFICATION METHODS IN WEKA

Besides decision tree induction methods, Weka is equipped with many classification methods that follow the approaches described in this chapter. Pressing the Choose button on the Classify tab reveals a list of folders. The nearest neighbour, rule-based, Bayesian and neural network methods are listed, respectively, in the *lazy*, *rules*, *bayes* and *functions* folders. Some of those methods are now demonstrated with the data sets in `iris.arff` and `weather.nominal.arff` files.

7.7.1 Lazy Methods

In the *lazy* category folder, Weka provides two nearest neighbour methods: IB1 and IBk. The IB1 method uses the Euclidean distance function to find the nearest neighbour training example. If more than one training example has the same distance, the first example is taken as the nearest neighbour. The method does not require any input parameters. Figure 7.9 shows a test run of the method on the iris data set. The overall accuracy rate is more than 95% for the data set, which is comparable to other classification methods for this good-quality data set.

The IBk method has a number of input parameters. The parameter kNN allows the user to specify the value of k. When the parameter crossValidate is set to true, the value of k between 1 and the value set for the kNN parameter is determined automatically with leave-one-out cross-validation. When the k nearest neighbours vote for the class of the unseen record, the distances between the examples and the record may also be considered. Therefore, in the distanceWeighting parameter, the user can select 'No

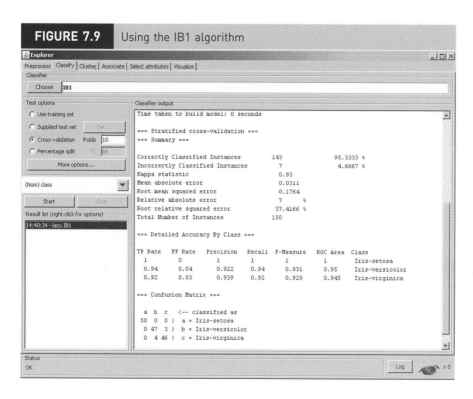

FIGURE 7.9 Using the IB1 algorithm

distance weighting', 'Weighting by 1/distance' (division by the distance) or 'Weighting by 1-distance' (subtracting the distance). The IBk method also allows the user to specify the eventual number of training examples remaining in the model's memory space (windowSize). The most significant feature of the method is that it enables the user to select a nearest neighbour search algorithm (press the Choose button associated with the nearestNeighbourSearchAlgorithm parameter) and a distance function for measuring similarity (click on the command line for nearestNeighbourSearchAlgorithm and then on the Choose button associated with the distanceFunction parameter) as shown in Figure 7.10. Three versions of the Minkowski distance functions are available.

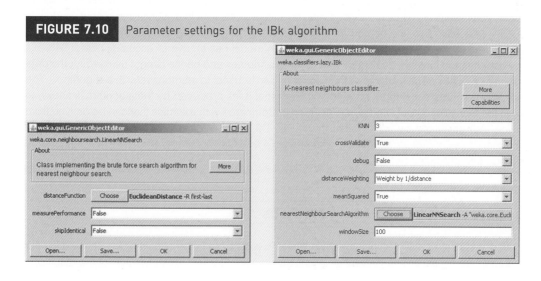

FIGURE 7.10 Parameter settings for the IBk algorithm

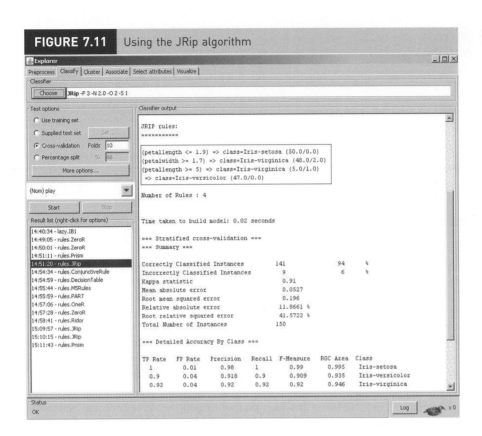

FIGURE 7.11 Using the JRip algorithm

7.7.2 Rule-based Methods

In the *rules* folder, Weka provides a number of learning methods of different levels of sophistication. JRip is a Java implementation of the Ripper algorithm. It is an incremental rule induction algorithm with pruning that works for both categorical and numeric attributes. A test run of the algorithm using the iris data set produces three ordered rules plus a default rule, as shown in the box in the Classifier output window in Figure 7.11. After each rule, the number of examples of the class and the number of examples of other classes covered by the rule are listed. The classification model has an overall accuracy rate of 94%.

The Prism method in Weka deals only with nominal attributes and hence cannot be used for the data set from `iris.arff`. The weather condition data set is used to demonstrate this algorithm. The method does not require any input parameters. The list of rules produced by the algorithm is shown in the box in the Classifier output window in Figure 7.12. Compared with the rules that can be derived from a decision tree produced by an algorithm such as ID3, the rule-based model produced by Prism contains more rules of greater complexity with only a 64% overall accuracy, which is lower than that of the decision tree produced by ID3.

7.7.3 Bayesian Classification Methods

Weka offers a variety of naïve Bayes solutions. NaiveBayesSimple is the simple naïve Bayes classifier where numeric attributes are modelled by normal distribution. Figure 7.13 shows part of the result of a

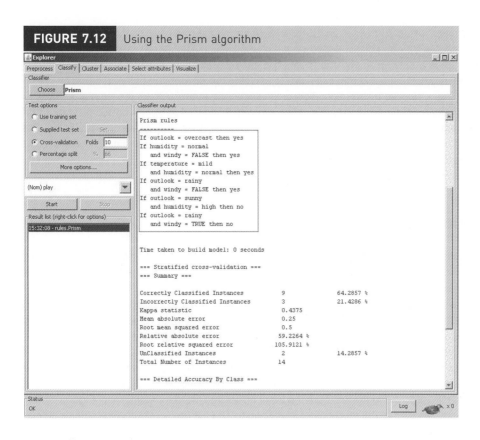

FIGURE 7.12 Using the Prism algorithm

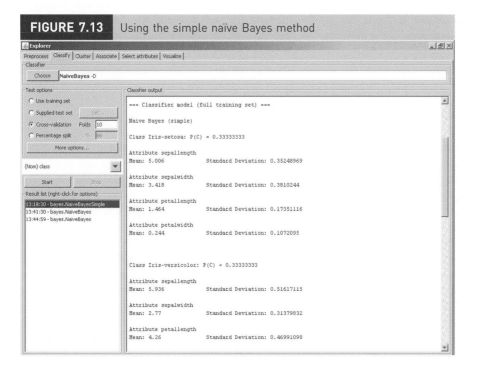

FIGURE 7.13 Using the simple naïve Bayes method

test run using the method over the `iris.arff` data set. It shows the means and standard deviations of the descriptive attributes for each class, based on which the likelihood of each class is calculated. The overall accuracy rate is above 95%, not bad for such a naïve system.

The NaiveBayes method uses a *kernel estimator* to estimate the distribution of the numeric attributes rather than assuming a normal distribution. The estimator locates and utilizes the *normal kernels* to represent the data distribution more accurately. A test run with the kernel estimator turned on shows that the overall accuracy rate is increased to nearly 97%, higher than the result produced by the *NaiveBayesSimple* method. Other variants of the naïve Bayes approach in Weka are not discussed here due to space constraints.

7.7.4 Artificial Neural Network Methods

Weka offers an artificial neural network solution in the *functions* folder. Known as *MultiLayerPerceptron*, the method takes a set of input parameters and produces a trained network of neuron node solutions using back-propagation.

The parameters include settings for the number of hidden layers and the nodes on each hidden layer, transformation of nominal attributes to binary, normalization of attribute values, the training time in terms of the number of epochs (the number of times the entire training set is swept through), the learning rate and any possible learning decay, etc.

The topology of the network, the weights attached to links, and the performance measures are described in a textual format and displayed in the Classifier output window in Figure 7.14(a). The input nodes and the weights attached to the link from the input nodes are listed for each node. Figure 7.14(b) is the graphical representation of the topology of the network. The accuracy rate is 96%, comparable to those of other classification methods.

Weka offers a graphical user interface for the neural network solution, which the user can access by setting the GUI parameter to True. Through the interface, the user can add and delete neuron nodes and so modify the topology of the network. The user can also set some input parameters and start the training process.

7.7.5 Ensemble Methods

Weka offers a whole set of ways to enhance the performance of base models. In fact, the current version of Weka provides no less than 29, among which are the bagging and the boosting methods mentioned in Section 7.5.2. To use the bagging method, select Bagging from the method list in the *meta* folder. The user can specify the bag size (which defaults to 100%) with regard to the size of the training set, the number of iterations or the number of base models (default 10) and the type and parameter setting of the base models.

Figure 7.15 shows an example of selecting the boosting method AdaBoostM1 for the iris data set. The base model type is selected as an unpruned REPTree, a decision tree produced by an algorithm similar to C4.5. The number of iterations is set to 10. The resulting base models and performance evaluation details are listed in the output window. This ensemble method manages to achieve similar accuracy over the data set as many other techniques. However, it does not particularly show the strength of the ensemble methods in combining the powers of multiple classification models.

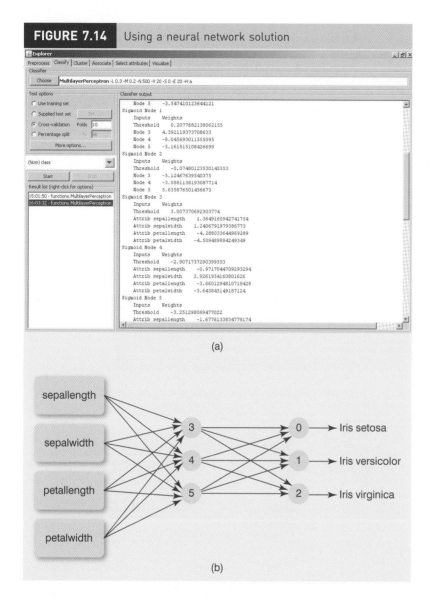

FIGURE 7.14 Using a neural network solution

(a)

(b)

7.8 COMPARING THE POWER OF CLASSIFICATION TECHNIQUES

Weka provides a system module called Experimenter for comparing the performance of classification solutions. The subsystem allows the user to set up experiments with different techniques and different parameter settings over a number of data sets. The performance data are then collected and comparisons are made of the statistical significance in differences of the accuracy rates of the classification models produced by the techniques. The experiments are performed in a batch-processing fashion: the experiment details are set up, the computational task is configured and the machine (or machines) is left to complete the experiment. The interface of the subsystem has three tabs: Setup, Run and Analysis.

In the Setup tab (see Figure 7.16), the user creates a new experiment by pressing the New button. The Open and Save buttons allow the user to save an experiment and then open and edit it later. This also means that an experiment can be repeated if necessary. In the Experiment Type block, the user can

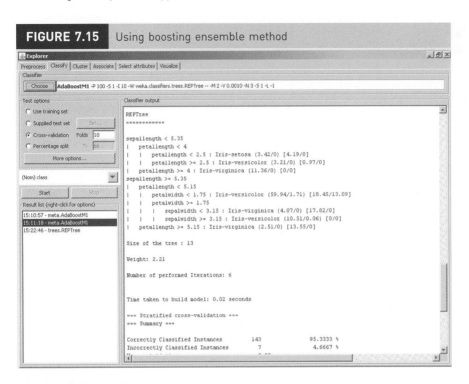

FIGURE 7.15 Using boosting ensemble method

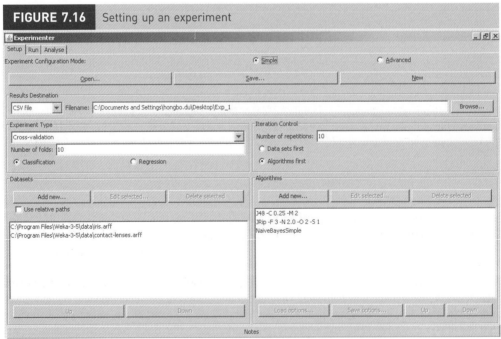

FIGURE 7.16 Setting up an experiment

specify the nature of the experiment (classification or regression) and choose a test option (e.g. cross-validation). In the Iteration Control block, the user can also specify the number of times that one algorithm is repeated on one data set, and whether the experiment results are grouped by algorithm or by data set. In the Data sets area, the user can add and remove data sets. The Edit selected button allows the user to

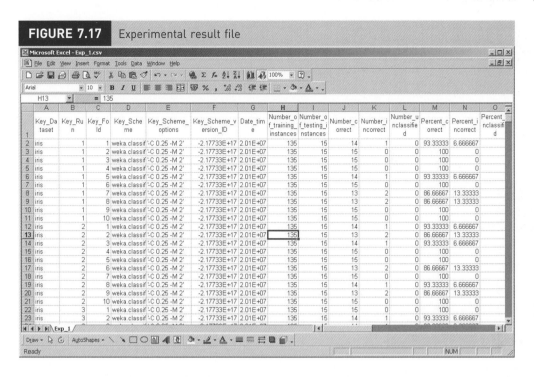

FIGURE 7.17 Experimental result file

open the data viewer and browse the selected data set. In the Algorithms area, the user can add algorithms, edit the parameters of a selected algorithm, or remove an algorithm. Figure 7.16 shows the setting up of a trial experiment with two data sets and three algorithms with their default parameter settings. The experiment type is set as 10-fold cross-validation and each classification is repeated 10 times.

In the Results Destination block, the user specifies the location and name of a file to store the results of the experiment. The file stores detailed result data, including the experiment configuration data (data set name, run number, the fold number in cross-validation, the classification algorithm and the algorithm parameter settings) and the performance data (the numbers of correctly and incorrectly classified examples, the percentages of correctly and incorrectly classified examples, etc.). Figure 7.17 presents part of the experiment result file Exp_1.csv. From this result file, significance analysis is conducted and reported.

The Run tab provides the control buttons for starting (Start) and stopping (Stop) an experiment. The Log panel displays log messages about the running status of the experiment, indicating if the experiment completes successfully or is aborted. The Status panel displays run-time text messages about the progress of the experiment.

The Analyse tab consists of two main panels: Configure test allows the user to configure the analysis settings and Test output displays the results. By default, the results of the current experiment are analyzed when the user presses the Experiment button. The analysis result is displayed in the Test output panel when the user presses the Perform test button.

Figure 7.18 shows the analysis result for the experiment in Figure 7.16 by taking all default settings. Pair-wise t-tests are conducted between the baseline algorithm (J48) and either JRip or NaiveBayesSimple with the percentage of correct classification as the comparison field when significance is set to 0.05. The result generally states that the average accuracy rates by the classification techniques for each of the two data sets are similar and the differences in the accuracy rates are statistically insignificant.

In Figure 7.18, in the analysis result table, '(100)' represents the number of tests for each algorithm on each data set. An algorithm is repeated 10 times; for each run, 10 randomly divided folds are created and used to test accuracy, resulting in 100 tests. The percentage of correct classifications listed is in fact the

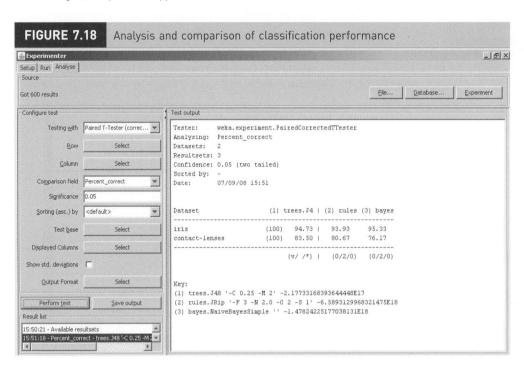

FIGURE 7.18 Analysis and comparison of classification performance

average. The user can choose to list the standard deviation with the average by selecting the 'Show std. deviations' checkbox. At the bottom of the analysis table are listed triple counters in (x/y/z) format, showing the number of times the algorithm is statistically better than, the same as and worse than the baseline algorithm. For instance, the triple (0/2/0) below the 'rules' column indicates that JRip produces the same levels of accuracy as J48 for the two given data sets. If the triple were (0/1/1), it would mean that JRip produces the same level of accuracy as J48 for one data set, but a statistically worse level of accuracy than J48 for another data set. The symbol '*' is placed after the worse accuracy measure, and the symbol 'v' is used after the better. The triple (v/ /*) below the baseline algorithm serves as a reminder of the two symbols.

Weka provides other configuration facilities for tests. For instance, the user can choose a different 'Comparison field', for example 'Percent_incorrect' to compare error rates instead of accuracy rates. The user may also specify another algorithm as the baseline algorithm by pressing the Select button for the 'Test base' parameter.

The Experimenter can be very useful in practice. It allows the user to compare a number of classification techniques and draw conclusions on which classification technique delivers a better model on the basis of statistical significance.

7.9 SUMMARY

This chapter has given a broad overview of four major classification approaches in addition to decision tree induction. The approaches differ from each other over the form of classification model they produce. The nearest neighbour approach uses the training examples themselves as the classification model and determines the class of an unseen record by the majority of the closest training examples to the record. From the training examples, the rule-based approach induces a list of rules and determines the class of an unseen record by firing the rules that cover the record. The naïve Bayes methods use the knowledge about prior probability of class from the training examples to predict the posterior likelihood of a record belonging to a class. The artificial neural network approach uses training examples to tune weights attached to the links within a network of artificial neurons. The trained network calculates via a sequence of layers of neurons the class of an unseen record. All approaches and methods mentioned in this chapter are feasible classification solutions. One is not meant to replace the others. Each approach has its own features, strengths and weaknesses, which are summarized in Section 7.5.1.

The chapter has explained the general principles of each approach and described some specific algorithms with examples. Most of the algorithms and solutions mentioned in the chapter are also available in Weka, making Weka a rich source of classification solutions. It is a useful exercise to practise using these solutions in Weka.

The chapter also briefly mentioned the ensemble methods for classification. Many researchers from different application backgrounds have recognized the power of fusing multiple classification techniques when one classification technique is insufficient to achieve the level of accuracy required.

This chapter also explained how to estimate the interval for accuracy of classification based on the confidence interval estimate in chapter 2, and how to choose a classification model with significant better accuracy also based on the hypothesis testing in chapter 2. Although it sounds somewhat too theoretical, such an understanding on the basis of statistical significance is too important to ignore. The understanding should also help readers to understand what how Weka selects a model to present and how accuracy is estimated when cross validation is chosen as the test option.

EXERCISES

1 Use the weather condition table in Figure 6.2(a) as an example to illustrate the classification models produced by algorithms of the following classification approaches:

(a) decision tree;

(b) nearest neighbour;

(c) rule-based;

(d) naïve Bayes;

(e) artificial neural network.

2 Load the weather condition data set from `weather.nominal.arff` into Weka. Select one algorithm from each classification approach listed in Exercise 1 to induce a classification model of each type. Observe the models and compare their performance in terms of accuracy of classification.

3 Given the training examples in Table 7.3 and assuming that $k = 3$, demonstrate the use of the basic kNN algorithm in determining the class of the unseen record in Table 7.4. (Choose a suitable similarity measure yourself.)

4 Given the data set in Table 7.3, perform the following exercises on the PEBLS algorithm:

(a) Construct a value difference table for attributes Blood Pressure and Habit.

(b) Use the PEBLS distance function to calculate the distance between any two rows in the data table, assuming the weight for each row is initialized as 1.

(c) Discuss the training and validation processes proposed by the algorithm.

(d) Discuss the rationale behind the weighting scheme of the algorithm. How does the algorithm use the weighting to 'punish' or 'reward' exemplars that have been chosen as the nearest neighbour?

(e) Explain how the unseen record in Table 7.4 is classified.

(f) The algorithm appears biased against early exemplars in the memory space. Suggest a way of reducing such a bias.

5 Given the data set in Table 7.3, perform the following exercises on the basic sequential covering algorithm:

(a) Illustrate the whole process of sequential covering.

(b) Use some rows to demonstrate the construction of a rule by generalization and specialization.

TABLE 7.3 Data set for Exercises 3, 4, 5 and 6

Body Weight	Body Height	Blood Pressure	Blood Sugar Level	Habit	Class
Heavy	Short	High	3	Smoker	P
Heavy	Short	High	1	Nonsmoker	P
Normal	Tall	Normal	3	Nonsmoker	N
Heavy	Tall	Normal	2	Smoker	N
Low	Medium	Normal	2	Nonsmoker	N
Low	Tall	Normal	1	Nonsmoker	P
Normal	Medium	High	3	Smoker	P
Low	Short	High	2	Smoker	P
Heavy	Tall	High	2	Nonsmoker	P
Low	Medium	Normal	3	Smoker	P
Heavy	Medium	Normal	3	Nonsmoker	N

TABLE 7.4 Unseen data for Exercises 3, 4, 5 and 6

Body Weight	Body Height	Blood Pressure	Blood Sugar Level	Habit	Class
Heavy	Medium	High	1	Smoker	

(c) Illustrate the firing of a rule when the unseen record in Table 7.4 is classified.

(d) Derive classification rules from the decision tree in Figure 6.15. Compare the rules with the rules derived in part (b). Explain any differences.

6 Given the data set in Table 7.3, construct a classification model using the simple naïve Bayes method. (Treat the Blood Sugar Level as discrete rather than continuous.) Use the model to classify the unseen record in Table 7.4.

7 Summarize and compare how the main classification approaches mentioned in this chapter and Chapter 6 solve the problem of model overfitting.

8 In Weka, load the data set from `soybean.arff`. Perform classifications using the following methods:

(a) NaiveBayesSimple;

(b) IB1 and IBk (with different *k* values);

(c) JRip;

(d) MultilayerPerceptron;

(e) Bagging (with different classifiers).

9 In Weka, perform an experiment that compares the performance (in terms of accuracy level) of the classification algorithms mentioned in Exercise 8 against that of J48 over the data set in

soybean.arff. Observe and explain the analysis results. The experiment may take some time because of the involvement of the MultilayerPerceptron algorithm.

10 Assume a decision tree T with an error rate of 15% is tested on a set of 1000 examples. If the confidence level is set to 95%, estimate the confidence interval for the accuracy of the decision tree T.

11 Two decision trees, T_1 and T_2, are tested over the same test set D of 300 test examples. T_1 has an error rate of 15% and T_2 has an error rate of 17%. Is the difference in the error rates statistically significant? In this case, how should we decide which tree to take as the final classification model?

BIBLIOGRAPHICAL NOTES

References for this chapter come from a variety of sources. Existing texts such as Han and Kamber (2001), Tan *et al.* (2006) and Witten and Frank (2005) all cover the main approaches mentioned in this chapter. The many previous attempts to survey classification approaches and methods from the machine-learning perspective include Michie *et al.* (1994).

The nearest neighbour approach has long been considered a simple yet powerful approach to classification and hence has been widely used in a range of applications from text categorization to face recognition. As a result, many different versions of the basic algorithm have been used although an exhaustive survey of them does not appear to exist. The exact origin of the basic *k*NN algorithm is unclear. The PEBLS algorithm was developed by Cost and Salzberg (1993) to apply the principle of *k*NN to categorical attributes. Although the article was published a long time ago, the treatment of data object proximity and the weighting scheme are quite unique.

Methods for rule-based classification largely follow the sequential covering principle. The RIPPER algorithm was developed by Cohen (1995) and the PRISM algorithm was developed by Centrowska (1987). Methods that apply the same principles as RIPPER but use different rule quality measures include CN2 (Clark and Boswell 1991) and AQ (Michalski *et al.* 1986). One simple method that is worth mentioning is Holte's one-rule (1R) algorithm, which derives a single best-fit rule (Holte 1993). Despite its simplicity, the algorithm achieves the same level of accuracy as a decision-tree method for a good-quality data set such as iris.arff.

Naïve Bayes classification techniques have been reviewed by a number of sources. Langley *et al.* (1992) gave an early survey and Lewis (1998) gave a summary for the information retrieval community. Despite the naïve assumption regarding feature independence, the Naïve Bayes classifiers have worked very well and hence have been widely used in a range of applications.

There is a vast amount of literature regarding neural networks. A comprehensive coverage of neural networks can be found in (Aleksander and Morton 1995). More recently, a textbook by Haykin (2008) offers a systematic review of the subject. Most data mining texts contain only general coverage of the subject because of its vast scope. This text follows the same tradition and keeps the coverage even shorter because the subject can only be studied properly through a separate course module. You are advised to refer to the bibliography in Han and Kamber (2001) for sources of information regarding the back-propagation algorithm, dynamic adjustment of a network topology and rule extraction from a neural network.

Classification is a vast area of data analysis. Many other classification methods, such as support vector machines (Vapnik 1998), various regression analyses (Mendenhall and Sincich 2003), and hidden Markov models (HMM) (Rabiner 1989), have not been included in this chapter. Some general understanding of them is bound to be beneficial.

CHAPTER 8

Techniques for mining Boolean association rules

LEARNING OBJECTIVES

To understand basic concepts of association rules, particularly Boolean association rules

To decompose the problem of mining Boolean association rules

To learn how the Apriori algorithm discovers frequent itemsets

To learn how the Apriori algorithm generates Boolean association rules

To appreciate the strengths and limitations of the Apriori algorithm

To learn how the FP-Growth algorithm discovers frequent itemsets

To understand how to evaluate the strength of an association rule

To appreciate practical issues in relations to association rule mining

To learn and observe how to mine Boolean association rules in Weka

Association rule mining is concerned with the discovery of significant associations among data items. Such associations are expressed in the form of co-occurrences of a number of data items in a given data set, or in the form that occurrences of some data items imply the occurrences of other data items with a certain measure of likelihood. In a typical supermarket, for instance, *milk* may occur with *sugar* in more than 50% of all customer transactions. It may be the case that customers who purchase milk are 98% likely to buy sugar as well. Association rules of this kind have many areas of application, including retail data analysis, bioinformatics, text mining, etc. Consequently, association rule mining has attracted a great deal of attention from researchers and practitioners in the last decade or so.

In this chapter, the problem of mining a particular type of association rule, known as Boolean association rules, is investigated. First, some basic concepts about data input are introduced. Based on the concepts, the problem of mining Boolean association rules is properly defined. The task of mining Boolean association rules is decomposed into two main tasks: mining of frequent itemsets and generation of rule expressions.

This chapter presents two algorithms for mining frequent itemsets. First, a greedy approach, known as the Apriori algorithm, is described. Both the algorithm for mining frequent itemsets and the algorithm for generating rule expressions are shown. Then, an alternative algorithm, known as FP-Growth, is presented to overcome some of the limitations of the Apriori approach. Possible ways of measuring the strengths of association rules are also discussed. The process of mining Boolean association rules using Weka is demonstrated. Some practical application issues concerning association rule mining are discussed at the end of the chapter.

8.1 PROBLEM DESCRIPTION AND DECOMPOSITION

8.1.1 Transaction Database, Itemset and Support

Before association rules are formally defined, a number of terms that will be frequently used should be explained. The input data set for Boolean association rule mining takes the form of a *transaction database*. Informally, a transaction database is a table of two columns, where each row is a single transaction. The first column represents a unique transaction identifier and the second column represents a list of 'purchased' items in the transaction. In a real-life retailing context, the transaction identifier can be thought of as a payment card number concatenated with the date and time when the transaction is made. An item can refer to the product name or its barcode number. Figure 8.1(a) shows an example transaction database of four transactions and five items.

The table in Figure 8.1(a) is not really a relational table because the second column contains a collection of items. The transaction database can be represented in a relational table where a row corresponds to a transaction and a column corresponds to one individual item. The value of a column is 1 for a row if the item occurs in the corresponding transaction, or 0 otherwise, as shown in Figure 8.1(b). In practice, however, because most transactions contain only a few items, such tables

FIGURE 8.1 Representations of a transaction database

TID	Items
100	Apple, Coke, DVD
200	Bread, Coke, Egg
300	Apple, Bread, Coke, Egg
400	Bread, Egg

(a)

TID	Apple	Bread	Coke	DVD	Egg
100	1	0	1	1	0
200	0	1	1	0	1
300	1	1	1	0	1
400	0	1	0	0	1

(b)

TID	Item
100	Apple
100	Coke
100	DVD
200	Bread
200	Coke
200	Egg
300	Apple
300	Bread
300	Coke
300	Egg
400	Bread
400	Egg

(c)

can be very sparse, i.e. there can be many zeros. An alternative way is to use a table of two columns: the first column denotes the transaction identifier and the second column represents a single item that the transaction contains, as shown in Figure 8.1(c). Both columns form a composite primary key for the table. For simplicity of solutions, items within each transaction are assumed to be sorted in the same order.

Given a set of all possible items, any non-empty subset of this *global* set of items is known as an *itemset*. An itemset that contains *k* items is referred to as a *k-itemset*. In Figure 8.1, for example, the global set of all items is {Apple, Bread, Coke, DVD, Egg}. {Apple, Coke} is a 2-itemset. {Bread} is a 1-itemset. Given a transaction database, a transaction is said to *support* an itemset, if every item in the itemset appears in the transaction, i.e. the itemset is a subset of items in the transaction. The support for an itemset by the transaction database refers to the fraction of all transactions in the transaction database that support the itemset. Normally, the support is expressed as a percentage but sometimes, for convenience, it is represented as the total count of transactions that support the itemset. For instance, the 2-itemset {Apple, Coke} has the support of two transactions or 50% of transactions in the database in Figure 8.1.

8.1.2 Boolean Association Rules

A Boolean association rule is represented as an implication expression $X \Rightarrow Y$ where X and Y are itemsets. The itemset X on the left hand side, i.e. the antecedent of the rule, should have no items in common with the itemset Y on the right hand side, i.e. the consequent of the rule. This constraint is set in order to avoid mining apparent associations between the same items. The rule $X \Rightarrow Y$ is said to hold in a given transaction database D with support s and confidence c, if s% of transactions in D contain items in X or Y, and c% of transactions in D that contain items in X also contain items in Y. The precise definitions of support s and confidence c are given as follows:

$$s(X \Rightarrow Y) = \frac{|\{t \mid t \in D \wedge (X \cup Y) \subseteq t.Items\}|}{|D|} \times 100$$

$$c(X \Rightarrow Y) = \frac{|\{t \mid t \in D \wedge (X \cup Y) \subseteq t.Items\}|}{|\{t \mid t \in D \wedge X \subseteq t.Items\}|} \times 100$$

where t represents a transaction and $t.Items$ refers to the collection of items in the transaction.

Support and confidence together show, to some degree, the strength of a rule. The support indicates the scope of coverage of the rule whereas the confidence indicates the level of belief of truth in the rule. An example rule from the transaction database in Figure 8.1 is {Egg} $\Rightarrow$ {Bread, Coke} with 50% support because two out of four transactions contain the items Bread, Coke and Egg, and 67% confidence because out of the three transactions that contain Egg, two of them also contain Bread and Coke. Another example rule is {Bread} $\Rightarrow$ {Egg}, which has support of 75% and confidence of 100%. That means customers who purchase Bread definitely buy Egg as well. The second example rule appears stronger than the first example rule both in support and in confidence. In reality, however, it is common that rules either have high support and low confidence or low support and high confidence. The strength of a rule cannot be represented by only one of the two factors.

8.1.3 The Problem of Mining Boolean Association Rules

The purpose of mining Boolean association rules is to find *all* possible rules from a given transaction database that have support and confidence greater than or equal to minimum support and confidence thresholds. Both thresholds are defined by the user before the mining starts. In the transaction database in Figure 8.1, if the minimum support threshold is 50% and the minimum confidence threshold is 90%, the rule {Bread} ⇒ {Egg} is accepted because it has sufficient support and confidence. The rule {Egg} ⇒ {Bread, Coke} is dropped because it has only 67% confidence even though the level of support is sufficient.

The task of mining association rules can be decomposed into two sub-tasks:

1 Find all itemsets from the input transaction database that have support greater than or equal to the *minimum support* threshold. Such itemsets are called *frequent* itemsets.

2 Using the frequent itemsets, generate rule expressions that have confidence greater than or equal to the *minimum confidence* threshold. Rules with such a property are called *strong* rules.

The solution of the second sub-task can be straightforward: a subset of a frequent itemset is taken as the antecedent of a rule and the rest of the items from the same frequent itemset as the consequent of the rule, and the confidence of the rule is then calculated. If the confidence is above or equal to the minimum confidence threshold, the rule is accepted into the result set; otherwise, it is dropped. This operation is attempted for all possible combinations of items in the itemset. Due to the number of combinations of items, the execution time for this process can be lengthy.

The first task is comparatively more challenging. Many research activities therefore have concentrated on solving this problem of finding all frequent itemsets. A brute-force approach is to enumerate all possible subsets of items as *candidate* itemsets, scan through the transaction database and count the support to each candidate, and then remove infrequent itemsets and keep the remaining frequent itemsets as the result. This brute-force approach has the following problems:

- For a transaction database of k items, there are $2^k - 1$ non-empty subsets. For instance, if the transaction database has five items, there are 31 non-empty subsets. If the transaction database has eight items, there are 255 non-empty subsets. As k increases, the number of subsets grows exponentially. This means that the number of candidate itemsets is potentially huge, and hence it is impossible for the main memory to hold them all. Storing candidate itemsets on disk further slows down the processing speed.

- The database must be searched as many times as the number of candidate itemsets. If the number of candidate itemsets is huge, the database has to be scanned a huge number of times.

- Transaction databases are normally big and reside on disk. Scanning such a database for counting the support to a large number of candidates is slow.

Therefore, the brute-force approach of finding all frequent itemsets is not practical.

All possible combinations of items from a transaction database form a lattice structure. Figure 8.2 shows the structure for the transaction database in Figure 8.1. In order to save space, an item is represented by the first letter of the item name. The lattice has 32 nodes. The shaded nodes are the frequent itemsets in the transaction database when the minimum support threshold is set to 50%.

Except in extremely rare circumstances, only a small part of the lattice structure is required. Most nodes of the structure represent infrequent itemsets that are not useful. The challenge is therefore to develop an optimal solution to locate all nodes that represent the frequent itemsets while traversing as little as possible of the rest of the lattice. This can be understood to be the same as reducing the number of candidate itemsets before we count and deciding whether they are frequent or not.

Two closely related facts, known as the Apriori principles, are established:

- If an itemset is frequent, all its non-empty subsets are also frequent.

- If an itemset is infrequent, all its extensions or supersets are bound to be infrequent.

FIGURE 8.2   Lattice structure of candidate itemsets

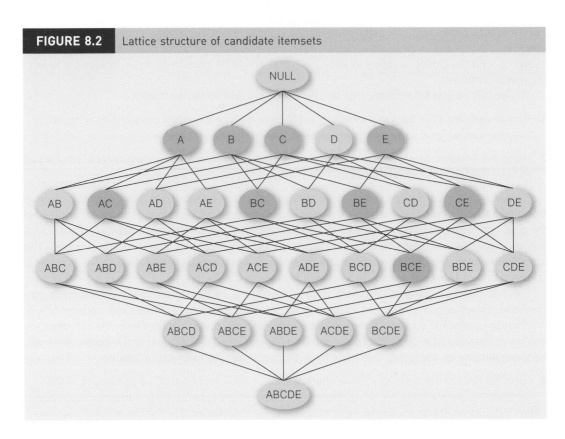

The first principle is based on the fact that the chance of two events happening together simultaneously is less than or equal to the chance of the two events happening separately. If an itemset is frequent, a sufficient number of the transactions contain all the items of the itemset and they must also contain subsets of the itemset. Therefore, the subset itemsets must also be frequent. The second principle can be proved by contradiction. If an itemset is infrequent and an extension of the itemset is assumed to be frequent then, according to the first principle, the original itemset, that is a subset of the extension, must also be frequent, which directly contradicts the original assumption that the itemset is infrequent. Therefore, the assumption that an extension of an infrequent itemset is frequent cannot be true.

Based on those principles, the underlying framework of the Apriori approach for finding all frequent itemsets is clear: frequent items or itemsets are used to generate new candidate itemsets and infrequent candidate itemsets are abandoned during the process. This greedy approach can be summarized as follows:

1 List all individual items in the transaction database. Count the support to each item. Select and maintain only the frequent items. Ignore the infrequent items.

2 Use the frequent items or itemsets of the previous round to create new candidate itemsets. Count the support to each of the new candidates. Save the frequent candidates as frequent itemsets and ignore the infrequent ones.

3 If the current collection of frequent itemsets is not empty, go back to Step 2 and continue the process; otherwise, collect all frequent itemsets found at each round and terminate the process.

8.2 FINDING ALL FREQUENT ITEMSETS: THE APRIORI ALGORITHM

The Apriori algorithm for finding all frequent itemsets was developed by the QUEST project group at the IBM research centre in Almaden, California in the early 1990s. It has been adopted in the data mining software tool named IBM Intelligent Miner for Data. A pseudo-code description of the algorithm is as follows:

```
algorithm Apriori (DB : Database; MS: support threshold): set of itemsets;
begin
    I := all items in DB;
    F₁ := {i | i ∈ I and i.count ≥ MS}; //First seed set
    k := 2;
    while F_{k-1} ≠ Ø do // as long as the previous seed set is not empty
        C_k := apriori_gen(F_{k-1});
        for each transaction t in DB do
            C_t := subset(C_k, t);
            for each candidate itemset c in C_t do
                c.count := c.count + 1;
            endfor;
        endfor;
        F_k := {c | c ∈ C_k and c.count ≥ MS};
        k := k + 1;
    endwhile;
    return (F₁ ∪ F₂ ∪ . . . ∪ F_k)
end;
```

The algorithm takes a transaction database *DB* and the minimum support threshold *MS* (in terms of support count rather than support fraction) as inputs and returns a set of all frequent itemsets as output. It is assumed that each item or itemset has an attached support counter. The algorithm first collects an initial seed set F_1 of frequent items, i.e. frequent 1-itemsets, from the global set *I* of all items in the transaction database. Then the algorithm starts a repeated process of generating candidate itemsets and collecting frequent itemsets. At a particular iteration *k* of the process, as long as the current seed set is not empty, the algorithm calls the apriori_gen function to generate new candidate *k*-itemsets, C_k, based on the frequent $(k-1)$-itemsets stored in the seed set F_{k-1} of the previous round. The exact detail of the operation of the apriori_gen function is explained in Section 8.2.1.

The algorithm then searches the database, transaction by transaction. For each transaction, the algorithm uses the subset function to locate the newly generated candidates that are supported by the transaction in the set C_t. Then, the counters of those candidates are all increased by 1. After scanning the entire database, the algorithm selects those candidate *k*-itemsets with sufficient support, i.e. the frequent *k*-itemsets, into a new seed set, ready for the next round of mining. Finally when the loop terminates, the algorithm collects all frequent *k*-itemsets in all the seed sets, F_1, F_2, ..., F_k, together with their supports into the final result collection.

8.2.1 Generating New Candidate Itemsets: Apriori_gen

The apriori_gen operation in the Apriori algorithm consists of two steps: merging and pruning. The merging step constructs a candidate itemset whereas the pruning step determines and eliminates the candidate itemset if it is bound to be infrequent. There are a number of possible ways of merging frequent itemsets into a new candidate. For instance, a frequent $(k-1)$-itemset can be merged with a single frequent item to generate a new candidate k-itemset. However, this means that two sets of seeds have to be maintained. For simplicity and convenience, the Apriori algorithm uses a method that constructs a new candidate k-itemset based on two frequent $(k-1)$-itemsets both from the current seed set.

Suppose that $p = \{i_1, i_2, \ldots, i_k\}$ and $q = \{j_1, j_2, \ldots, j_k\}$ are two frequent k-itemsets in the current seed set. The two frequent itemsets can be merged into a new candidate $(k+1)$-itemset $\{i_1, i_2, \ldots, i_k, j_k\}$, if the following two conditions are met:

$$i_1 = j_1, \ i_2 = j_2, \ \ldots, \ i_{k-1} = j_{k-1}$$
$$i_k < j_k$$

For instance, frequent 3-itemsets $\{1, 2, 3\}$ and $\{1, 2, 5\}$ in a seed set can be merged into a new candidate 4-itemset $\{1, 2, 3, 5\}$ whereas frequent 3-itemsets $\{1, 3, 4\}$ and $\{1, 4, 5\}$, and $\{1, 3, 4\}$ and $\{2, 3, 5\}$ cannot. To generate candidate 2-itemsets from frequent items, only condition 2 is applied. For instance, frequent 1-itemsets $\{1\}$ and $\{2\}$ merge into a new candidate 2-itemset $\{1, 2\}$. Both conditions are necessary to avoid duplicate candidate itemsets being generated. Although item identifier numbers are used in the example earlier, the same idea works for categorical item names too. An artificial order, such as alphabetical order, is enforced among the names. Condition 2 can therefore be applied.

The merge operation can also be expressed in a dynamically constructed SQL statement as follows:

```
SELECT p.i₁, p.i₂, . . ., p.iₖ₋₁, p.iₖ, q.jₖ
FROM Lₖ p, q
WHERE p.i₁ = q.j₁ and p.i₂ = q.j₂ . . . and p.iₖ₋₁ = q.jₖ₋₁ and p.iₖ < q.jₖ
```

The apriori_gen operation guarantees the completeness of the resulting collection of candidates. This can be illustrated by the following example. There is no need to merge frequent itemsets $\{1, 3, 4\}$ and $\{1, 4, 5\}$ to get the new candidate $\{1, 3, 4, 5\}$. This is because the new candidate should have been generated already by frequent itemsets $\{1, 3, 4\}$ and $\{1, 3, 5\}$ earlier in the process. If the new candidate does not exist, this must mean that at least one of $\{1, 3, 4\}$ and $\{1, 3, 5\}$ is infrequent and hence absent from the seed set. In this case, the new candidate $\{1, 3, 4, 5\}$ is bound to be infrequent.

The apriori_gen operation limits the use of different seed itemsets to generate the same candidate: only one combination of seeds is attempted to generate the new candidate. Any other combinations generate the same candidate and, hence, are not needed. The operation therefore ensures the use of a small part of the lattice structure and avoids generating duplicate itemsets.

The second step of the apriori_gen operation is to prune away newly generated candidate itemsets that are bound to be infrequent before searching the database to count their support. The idea is that for every newly generated candidate k-itemset, all its subsets of $k-1$ items must be in the current seed set. If any of the subsets is not in the seed set, it means that the subset is infrequent and the new candidate, as an extension of the subset, is bound to be infrequent. Therefore, there is no need to count the support to the candidate in the transaction database. For instance, suppose that the seed set shown in Figure 8.3 exists.

A new candidate itemset $\{1, 2, 3, 4\}$ can be generated from frequent itemsets $\{1, 2, 3\}$ and $\{1, 2, 4\}$. However, some of the 3-item subsets of the new candidate,

FIGURE 8.3 Sample seed set

Itemset	Support
$\{1, 2, 3\}$	2
$\{1, 2, 4\}$	3
$\{2, 3, 5\}$	2
$\{2, 3, 6\}$	2
$\{2, 5, 6\}$	3
$\{3, 5, 6\}$	2

i.e. {1, 3, 4} and {2, 3, 4}, are not in the seed set. Hence the new candidate must be infrequent. For a new candidate {2, 3, 5, 6} generated from {2, 3, 5} and {2, 3, 6}, since all of its 3-item subsets, i.e. {2, 3, 5}, {2, 3, 6}, {2, 5, 6} and {3, 5, 6}, are already in the seed set, the new candidate has a chance of being frequent and it should be kept.

The pruning step does not affect the correctness of the apriori_gen operation, but it improves the speed of support counting by reducing the number of unnecessary candidates. In practice, the pruning operation can eliminate many spurious candidate itemsets. Most of the time, unless in some extreme situation, all newly created candidates are held in the main memory. Therefore, the time overhead for the pruning operation may still be worth the effort, compared to counting support for spurious candidates by scanning transactions on disk.

8.2.2 Locating Candidate Itemsets Supported by a Transaction

The subset function in the Apriori algorithm takes the newly created collection of all candidate k-itemsets and a single transaction from the transaction database as inputs and returns all candidate itemsets that are contained in the transaction. A straightforward way of implementing this function is to scan through the entire collection of candidates. For each candidate, the function then has to decide whether it is a subset of the transaction's items. The best time complexity for a check is linear to the size of the candidate. However, since the number of candidates can be large, this method can still be slow, particularly when the function is called repeatedly when scanning the database.

In order to speed up the function, the implementation of the algorithm can adopt some efficient data structures such as a hash tree for storing newly created candidate k-itemsets. The exact details of using such a data structure are not of interest here. The general idea is to enumerate items within the transaction and check the existence of the corresponding candidate k-itemsets within the structure. If the candidate itemsets exist, their support counters are incremented.

8.2.3 An Illustration of the Apriori Algorithm

To illustrate the running of the Apriori algorithm, the transaction database in Figure 8.1 is used. The minimum support threshold is set to 50%. Since the database contains four transactions, the minimum support threshold equates to two transactions.

The process is illustrated in Figure 8.4. First, all individual items in the database are collected as 1-itemsets in C_1 and the support to each is counted. The frequent 1-itemsets, i.e. {Apple}, {Bread}, {Coke} and {Egg}, are saved in the first seed set F_1. Based on the seed set, the apriori_gen operation generates new candidate 2-itemsets and stores them in C_2. The support to each new candidate is then counted by searching through the database. After obtaining the total support to each candidate, frequent 2-itemsets, i.e. {Apple, Coke}, {Bread, Coke}, {Bread, Egg} and {Coke, Egg}, are saved in the new seed set F_2. From this seed set, only one new candidate 3-itemset {Bread, Coke, Egg} can be generated according to the conditions of the apriori_gen operation. Since all its 2-item subsets, i.e. {Bread, Coke}, {Bread, Egg} and {Coke, Egg}, exist in F_2, the new candidate is kept in C_3. The support to the candidate is then counted. The candidate is indeed frequent and is therefore copied into the new seed set F_3. Since there is only one entry in F_3, no more candidates can be made and hence no more frequent itemsets can be found. The process therefore terminates. F_1, F_2 and F_3 make up the final collection of all frequent itemsets.

Both frequent itemsets and their supports are used in the second sub-task of mining association rules.

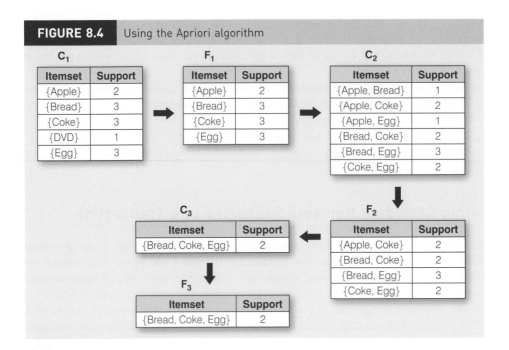

FIGURE 8.4   Using the Apriori algorithm

8.3   GENERATING ASSOCIATION RULES: THE APRIORI APPROACH

Once frequent itemsets are found, they and their supports are taken as inputs by the rule generation step. Since the confidence of a rule can be calculated from the supports of the frequent itemsets, there is no need to scan through the transaction database.

A brute-force rule generation method is as follows:

```
for all frequent itemsets j where |j| ≥ 2 do
   for all non-empty proper subset jj of j do
      conf := support(j) / support(jj);
      if conf ≥ Minimum Confidence then
         output rule jj ⇒ (j - jj)
      endif;
   endfor;
endfor;
```

Starting from a frequent 2-itemset, a rule expression is formed by taking one item of the itemset to the left-hand side and the other to the right-hand side of the rule. The confidence of the rule is then calculated. The rule is kept if the confidence is greater than or equal to the minimum confidence threshold; otherwise, the rule is dropped. The same procedure is repeated for all frequent 2-itemsets. For other frequent k-itemsets ($k > 2$), all possible non-empty proper subsets of each k-itemset are attempted to be located on the left-hand side and the rest on the right-hand side of a rule, and confidences are measured. Again, any confident rules are kept and not-so-confident ones are dropped.

Given a frequent itemset Y, for any proper non-empty subset X of Y, a rule in the form of $X \Rightarrow Y - X$ can be created. For any k-itemset, there are $2^k - 2$ possible rules. For instance, for a frequent itemset $\{1, 2, 3\}$, there are six possible rules: $\{1, 2\} \Rightarrow \{3\}$, $\{1, 3\} \Rightarrow \{2\}$, $\{2, 3\} \Rightarrow \{1\}$, $\{1\} \Rightarrow \{2, 3\}$, $\{2\} \Rightarrow \{1, 3\}$, and $\{3\} \Rightarrow \{1, 2\}$. Most of these rules may have insufficient confidence and hence are dropped.

Generating all these rules and later dropping them is a real waste of effort. After investigating the nature of the problem, the following theorem is found:

Theorem: if a rule $X \Rightarrow Y - X$ does not satisfy the minimum confidence threshold, any rules $X' \Rightarrow Y - X'$ where $X' \subseteq X$, will not satisfy the minimum confidence threshold.

The proof of this theorem is beyond the scope of the book, but the actual use of it is significant. A single item or a small subset of a frequent itemset can be located on the right of the rule and then the confidence of the rule is calculated. As soon as the rule's confidence level is below the minimum confidence threshold, any remaining rules with a subset of items from X on the left-hand side should not be attempted because they will not have sufficient confidence. The way of creating a subset of the frequent itemset as the right-hand side of the rule can follow the process of the apriori_gen operation: it starts with single items and then merges them into larger subsets, and any items or subsets that make a weak rule are dropped. The process of generating rules for a given frequent itemset terminates when this collection of subsets becomes empty. This Apriori algorithm for rule generation is:

```
algorithm Apriori_RuleGen(F: set of itemsets, mf: confidence threshold)
begin
    for each f_k (k≥2) in F do
        H_1 := {{i} | i∈f_k};
        call ap_genrules(f_k, H_1, mf)
    endfor;
end;
procedure ap_genrules(f_k: frequent itemset, H_m: set of consequent itemsets,
                      mf: confidence threshold)
begin
    if k ≥ m + 1 then
        for each h in H_m do
            cf := support(f_k) / support(f_k - h);
            if cf ≥ mf then
                output rule: f_k - h ⇒ h with support(f_k) and cf
            else
                delete h from H_m
            endif;
        endfor;
        H_{m+1} := apriori_gen(H_m)
        call ap_genrules(fk, H_{m+1}, mf)
    endif;
end;
```

For the transaction database in Figure 8.1, all frequent itemsets, obtained by using the Apriori frequent itemset mining algorithm, and their support are listed as follows:

F = { ({Apple}, 2), ({Bread}, 3), ({Coke}, 3), ({Egg}, 3), ({Apple, Coke}, 2), ({Bread, Coke}, 2), ({Bread, Egg}, 3), ({Coke, Egg}, 2), ({Bread, Coke, Egg}, 2) }.

With the Apriori rule generation algorithm, the following rules that have minimum support of 50% and minimum confidence of 90% are derived:

{Apple} ⇒ {Coke}	confidence = 100% and support = 50%
{Egg} ⇒ {Bread}	confidence = 100% and support = 75%

```
{Bread} ⇒ {Egg}            confidence = 100% and support = 75%
{Coke, Egg} ⇒ {Bread}      confidence = 100% and support = 50%
{Bread, Coke} ⇒ {Egg}      confidence = 100% and support = 50%
```

Because those rules have both sufficient support and sufficient confidence, they are considered strong association rules.

8.4 IMPROVING THE APRIORI ALGORITHM

8.4.1 Limitations of the Basic Apriori Algorithm

The Apriori algorithm for finding frequent itemsets is a greedy algorithm that follows a generate-and-test approach. The algorithm has some major limitations listed as follows:

- The time complexity of Apriori is $O(|C|*|DB|)$ where $|C|$ stands for the number of candidate itemsets generated and $|DB|$ represents the number of transactions in the database. $|C|$ is related to the minimum support threshold. Linear reduction of the threshold leads to exponential growth of the number of candidate itemsets generated.

- Although the algorithm already employs ways of controlling the number of candidate itemsets generated in the apriori_gen operation, many candidates are still generated; the number of the candidate 2-itemsets is potentially huge and can become a bottleneck.

- The algorithm scans through the database many times to count support. The number of database scans increases when frequent itemsets contain a large number of items. Searching the database on disk is a slow process due to the speed of disk access.

- The algorithm relies heavily on the use of memory resources during the generation and maintenance of candidate itemsets, particularly at the beginning when 2-itemsets are mined.

Because of the limitations listed above, researchers have been working on how to improve the efficiency of the basic Apriori algorithm. The main areas of improvement include the representation of frequent itemsets, the representation of data sets, traversal of the itemset lattice and reducing the size of the database.

8.4.2 Exploiting Maximal and Closed Itemsets

Not all frequent itemsets need to be explicitly discovered and stored. In fact many frequent itemsets can be derived from others. Two concepts are introduced here. A frequent itemset is a *maximal frequent itemset* if all of its immediate supersets with one item extra are infrequent. For instance, itemsets {Apple, Coke} and {Bread, Coke, Egg} are the two maximal frequent itemsets in the final list of all frequent itemsets in Section 8.2.3. In fact, from these two maximal itemsets, all other frequent itemsets can be derived although not all levels of support can be.

A frequent itemset is a *closed frequent itemset* if none of its immediate supersets has exactly the same levels of support as itself. Again, in the final list of all frequent itemsets in Section 8.2.3, {Bread}, {Coke}, {Egg}, {Apple, Coke} and {Bread, Coke, Egg} are closed frequent itemsets. It is from the closed frequent itemsets that the support levels of all the non-closed frequent itemsets can be derived.

The understanding of these two properties of frequent itemsets is important. It means that the basic Apriori algorithm can be improved by discovering only maximal and closed frequent itemsets which are much fewer than those discovered by the basic Apriori algorithm. Details on how this is done are beyond the scope of this book.

8.4.3 Horizontal vs Vertical Representation of a Data Set

The representation of the data set is an issue regarding how the input transaction database is represented before the mining starts. Normally, the data set is represented in a horizontal fashion: each transaction is a list of items. However, the transaction database can also be represented vertically: the data set contains a list of records and each record represents an item and a list of identifiers of the transactions that contain the item. This can be achieved easily by performing an SQL query upon the table in Figure 8.1(c), grouping the rows according to the item name. The pre-computation can be done at the data preparation stage.

If the input data set is represented in this fashion, counting support is much easier: any combination of items, i.e. an itemset, requires the set intersection of their transaction lists. If the transaction identifiers are sorted in the same order, this intersection operation can be performed with a merge method that possesses linear time complexity $O(N)$.

8.4.4 Bottom Up vs Top-Down Lattice Search

The itemset lattice can be traversed in different fashions. The Apriori algorithm takes a typical breadth-first search strategy: frequent items make candidate 2-itemsets, frequent 2-itemsets make candidate 3-itemsets and so on, signifying a traversal of the itemset lattice layer by layer from the top. Researchers have realized that a depth-first search along a particular branch is a better strategy in locating maximal frequent itemsets; generally smaller parts of the lattice need to be traversed. Coupled with the idea of locating maximal frequent itemsets outlined in Section 8.4.2, the speed of the basic algorithm can be improved.

Another issue regarding lattice traversal is whether to start the traversal from the top, known as *general-to-specific*, or from the bottom, known as *specific-to-general*. This very much depends on the length of transactions in the transaction database. If most transactions are relatively short, i.e. with a few items in each, then traversal from the top of the lattice is recommended because many deeper layers are likely to contain infrequent itemsets. On the other hand, if most of transactions are relatively long with many items, then a traversal from the bottom will quickly capture many maximal frequent itemsets.

8.4.5 Reducing Database Size

Not all the transactions are useful during the process of finding frequent itemsets. For instance, some transactions may contain only k items. After counting the support to candidate k-itemsets, such transactions are no longer useful for counting the support of larger itemsets, and hence can be dropped from the database. Removing unnecessary transactions from the database makes the database smaller and quicker to search when counting supports to larger itemsets, making the later iterations of the algorithm run faster.

The researchers who developed the basic Apriori algorithm also thought about such an improvement to the basic Apriori algorithm. A modified version of Apriori, known as *AprioriTid*, has also been developed. This modified algorithm updates the transaction contents with the candidate itemsets they support and then, at a later iteration, certain transactions are removed from the database.

8.5   FINDING ALL FREQUENT ITEMSETS: THE FP-GROWTH ALGORITHM

Although various ideas for improvement have been suggested in Section 8.4, the basic principle of generating candidates and selecting frequent itemsets remains the same. This section introduces another algorithm that discovers frequent itemsets without generating candidate itemsets.

8.5.1   Principle of the FP-Growth Algorithm

Over the years since the Apriori algorithm was developed in 1993, researchers have been working on alternative algorithms for finding frequent itemsets. The most noticeable is the FP-Growth algorithm by Han, Pei and Yin, which was developed in 2000. The algorithm takes a completely different approach from the generate-and-test approach of Apriori, by constructing a representation of the input transaction database as a tree (called an FP-tree) and extracting frequent itemsets directly from the tree. In other words, the algorithm consists of only two main steps:

1   Construct a tree representation of the input database.

2   Extract all frequent itemsets from the tree.

   This algorithm avoids generating candidate itemsets. The construction of the tree needs only two scans through the transaction database at the beginning and then the database is no longer needed. The second step of extracting frequent itemsets does not need to scan the database either, saving time spent on accessing disks. The tree is a compact representation of the database and hence can fit in main memory.

8.5.2   Constructing an FP-Tree

FP-tree stands for *frequent pattern* tree. It consists of a root node labelled as *null* and child nodes, each of which comprises an item name, a support counter, the parent-link pointer and a node-link pointer. The *parent-link* pointer refers to the parent of the current node and the *node-link* pointer refers to a sibling node.

   The FP-tree for the transaction database in Figure 8.1 is shown in Figure 8.5. A solid line represents a parent-link pointer and a dashed arrow refers to a node-link pointer. As well as the tree, a header table is constructed to serve as an index to the FP-tree. An entry in the header table consists of the frequent item name, the actual count of support for the item and a pointer to the head (first node) of a linked list for the item. The entries of the header table are listed in descending order of the support of the items. In other words, the entry for the most frequent item is listed at the top and the entry for the least frequent item is listed at the bottom of the table. The header table is useful when the FP-tree is traversed for frequent itemsets.

FIGURE 8.5   An FP-tree and its header table

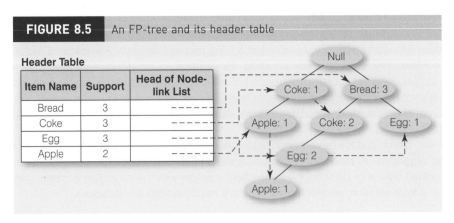

Header Table

Item Name	Support	Head of Node-link List
Bread	3	
Coke	3	
Egg	3	
Apple	2	

The algorithm for constructing a FP-tree is as follows:

```
algorithm FPTree_Construct(DB: database, ms: support threshold): FPTree
begin
    T :=∅; //empty the tree initially
    collect the list of all single items into set C and count the support to each;
    F := {i | i ∈ C and support(i) ≥ ms};
    sort items in F in descending order of support and save into header table L;
    create a root of tree T and label it "null";
    for each transaction t in DB do
        sort t.Items in the same order as in L and represent t = {h|Tail};
        call insert_tree(t, L, T);
    endfor;
    return T with L;
end;

Procedure insert_tree({h|Tail}, L, T)
begin
    if T has a child node N and N.itemName = h.itemName then
        N.counter := N.counter + 1;
    else
        create a new node N;
        N.counter :=1;
        create a parent-link to T;
        create a node-link pointer to N from the last node in the node-linked list for
                the item in L;
    endif;
    if Tail ≠ ∅ then
        call insert_tree(Tail, L, N)
    endif;
end;
```

The algorithm first scans through the transaction database, collects all items in the database and counts their support. Only the frequent items are then selected and saved into the header table in descending order of their support. The algorithm then scans through the transaction database again and attempts to insert frequent items in each transaction into the FP-tree on a path. The recursive procedure insert_tree either updates the support counter of an item node on an existing path or creates a new item node. At the same time, the header table entry may be updated with a pointer to the newly created node.

From the FP-tree construction algorithm, it is clear that the paths of the FP-tree represent overlapping transactions in the transaction database. The more overlapping among transactions, the fewer paths there are in the FP-tree, and hence the more compact the tree becomes. A node-link list, whose header pointer is located in the entry for a frequent item in the header table, allows counting of the total support to the item by adding counter values of the nodes along the list.

We now illustrate the construction of the FP-tree shown in Figure 8.5 in some detail. At the beginning, all frequent items are collected from the transaction database in Figure 8.1 and stored in the header table in the descending order of their supports as shown in Figure 8.6(a).

The root node of the FP-tree is then constructed and marked as *null*. The database is searched again transaction by transaction. For the first transaction, the frequent items in the transaction, i.e. Apple and

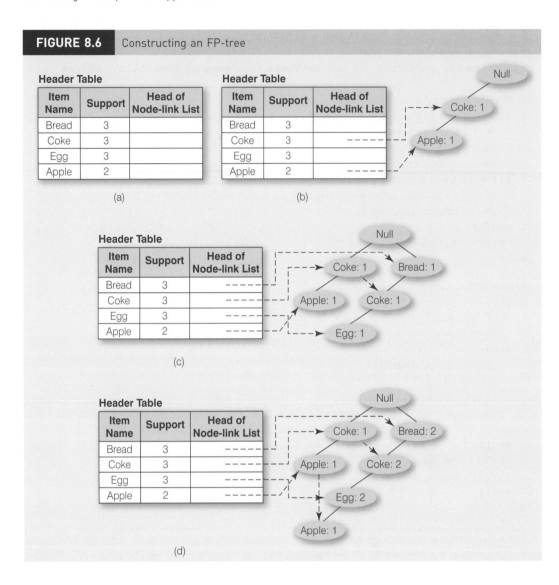

FIGURE 8.6   Constructing an FP-tree

Coke, are sorted in the same order as entries in the header table and inserted into the FP-tree. That means that item Coke is inserted into the tree before item Apple. Since there are no nodes other than the root, a new node for Coke is created below the root and the support counter in the new node is set to 1. Similarly, a new node for item Apple is created as the child node of the node for Coke and the support counter of the new node is also set to 1. After setting the parent link (solid line) and node link (dashed line) pointers, the FP-tree takes the shape shown in Figure 8.6(b).

For the second transaction, the frequent items are Bread, Coke and Egg. Since there is no existing node for Bread under the root node, a new node for the item is created under the root. Similarly, a new node for Coke is created under the node for Bread, and a new node for Egg under the node for Coke. The support counters for all the new nodes are set to 1. After setting the parent links among the new nodes along the newly created path, a node-link pointer is set from the node for Coke in the path created for the first transaction to the node for Coke for the second transaction, as in Figure 8.6(c).

When the frequent items in the third transaction, i.e. Bread, Coke, Egg and Apple, are inserted into the FP-tree, since the nodes for items Bread, Coke, and Egg already exist, there is no need to create new nodes for the items. The values of the support counters for the items are increased by 1. It is necessary to create a new node for item Apple in the transaction as the child of the node for item Egg and set the counter for this node to 1. After updating the node link list for item Apple, the FP-tree is as shown in Figure 8.6(d).

Similarly, for the last transaction in the database, the support counter in the node for the frequent item Bread is increased by 1. A new node for item Egg is created under the node for Bread with the support counter set to 1. A node-link pointer is set from the node for Egg for the previous transaction to the new node for Egg for the current transaction. The final FP-tree obtained is the one shown in Figure 8.5.

8.5.3 Extracting Frequent Itemsets from an FP-Tree

The FP-Growth algorithm is developed to directly extract frequent itemsets from a constructed FP-tree. The basic idea is to find a frequent item from the header table first, and then use the item to find all frequent itemsets that take the item as the *suffix*. The algorithm is recursive in nature:

```
algorithm FP-Growth(T: FPTree, var f: itemsets): set of itemsets
begin
   F := Ø; // empty the result set initially
   if T contains a single path P then
      for each combination β of nodes in path P do
         generate itemset i: <β∪f, s> where s = minimum support of nodes in β;
         F := F ∪ {i};
      endfor;
   else
      for each item a in the header table L of T do
         generate itemset i: <β, s> where β = a∪f and s = a.support;
         F := F ∪ {i};
         construct a conditional FP-tree Tβ for β;
         if Tβ is not empty then
            call FP-Growth(Tβ, β)
         endif
      endfor;
   endif;
   return (F);
end;
```

In the FP-Growth algorithm, the parameter *f* is used to store temporarily the suffix of frequent itemsets. It is set to {} when the algorithm is first called. The algorithm states that if the current FP-tree has only one path, then any combination of the items represented by the nodes along the path with the items in parameter *f*, i.e. suffix items, forms a frequent itemset whose support is set as the minimum of all the items involved. It must be said that this does not mean that all frequent itemsets of different sizes concerning the items on the path are obtained. Only those frequent itemsets with the items in the parameter *f* as the suffix are obtained. Frequent itemsets ending with other items, represented by the nodes on the path, are collected later when frequent itemsets using those items as the suffix are considered.

In the likely situations where the FP-tree has more than one path, the algorithm computes all frequent itemsets recursively by taking each item listed in the header table as the suffix item for frequent itemsets. In a typical bottom-up fashion, that item at the bottom of the header table is used first. The frequent item with support is first added into the result set *F* and then into the suffix item list. Another temporary FP-tree, known as the *conditional* FP-tree of the suffix item, is then constructed. A conditional FP-tree is a temporary tree that has the same structure as a general FP-tree. The only difference is that a conditional FP-tree is constructed by treating the paths of the previous FP-tree that end with the suffix item as *virtual* transactions. The counter values for all items on such a path must be set to the value for the suffix item because that value indicates how many actual transactions support all the items including the suffix item. Since the tree is a conditional tree of the suffix item, the suffix item itself is not included when the tree is constructed.

The FP-tree in Figure 8.5 is used as an example to demonstrate the working of the algorithm. At the beginning, the algorithm checks if the given FP-tree has a single path. Since the tree has more than one path, the item in the last entry in the header table, i.e. Apple, is taken to generate a frequent itemset <{Apple}, 2> and added into the result set *F*. The FP-tree has two paths that terminate with item Apple: {Coke:1, Apple:1} and {Bread:3, Coke:2, Egg:2, Apple:1}, as shown in Figure 8.7(a). The counters for

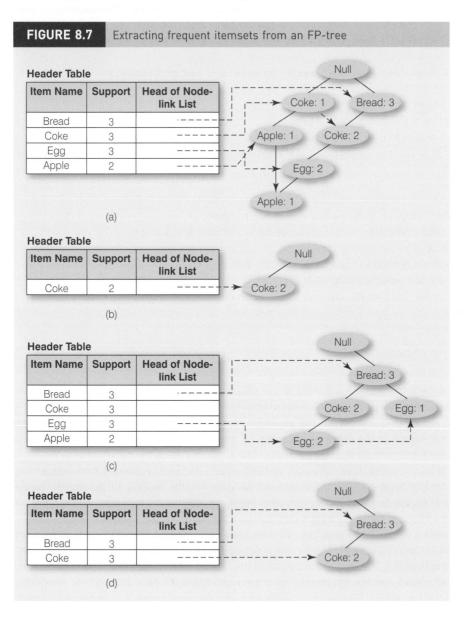

FIGURE 8.7   Extracting frequent itemsets from an FP-tree

all the items in the second list should be set to the counter value for Apple, i.e. 1, because only one transaction supports the entire list. Therefore, the two lists become {Coke:1, Apple:1} and {Bread:1, Coke:1, Egg:1, Apple:1} after the update. The end item Apple is moved to suffix parameter *f* and the two lists without the final item, i.e. {Coke:1} and {Bread:1, Coke:1, Egg:1} can be treated as two virtual transactions. From these two transactions, a conditional FP-tree for Apple and an associated header table can be constructed. The new header table has item Coke with support = 2 as the only entry because it is the only frequent item. The constructed conditional FP-tree is shown in Figure 8.7(b). Since the new conditional FP-tree has only one path from the root, a new frequent itemset {Coke, Apple}, that combines the item Coke on the single path with the suffix item Apple is extracted. The support of the newly extracted frequent itemset is set to the minimum of the two items, i.e. 2. This new frequent itemset <{Apple, Coke}, 2> is then added to the final collection *F*.

The algorithm then moves to the second item from the last in the original header table, i.e. item Egg, and immediately generates a frequent itemset <{Egg}, 3>. Again there are two paths ending with item Egg, i.e. {Bread:3, Coke:2, Egg:2} and {Bread:3, Egg:1}, as indicated in Figure 8.7(c). The support for item Bread in the first list is reduced to the level of support for item Egg, i.e. 2, and the support for item Bread in the second list is reduced to the level of support for item Egg in that path, which is 1. The updated paths are now {Bread:2, Coke:2, Egg:2} and {Bread:1, Egg:1}. Again taking the two updated paths without the suffix item Egg as virtual transactions, a header table and a conditional FP-tree for item Egg are constructed and illustrated in Figure 8.7(d). Since there is only one path in the conditional FP-tree, we attempt all possible combinations of the items on the path and the suffix item Egg, and extract the frequent itemsets <{Bread, Egg}, 3>, <{Coke, Egg}, 2> and <{Bread, Coke, Egg}, 2>.

The next item in the original header table is Coke. By following the node-link pointer, a frequent itemset <{Coke}, 3> can be generated. There are again two paths with item Coke as the suffix: {Coke:1} and {Bread:3, Coke:2}. After modifying the counter for item Bread in the second path and constructing the conditional FP-tree for Coke as we did for the other items, the tree has one only path with item Bread. This means that another frequent itemset <{Bread, Coke}, 2> can be generated.

Finally, for item Bread, the first entry in the original header table, it is realized that the part of the FP-tree referred to by the node-link pointer for the item has only one path, with only one node on the path. Therefore only one frequent itemset <{Bread}, 3> can be generated. The final collection *F* contains all frequent itemsets that are listed in the order they are generated as follows:

```
F = {<{Apple}, 2>, <{Apple, Coke}, 2>, <{Egg}, 3>, <{Bread, Egg}, 3>, <{Coke,
Egg}, 2>, <{Bread, Coke, Egg}, 2>, <{Coke}, 3>, <{Bread, Coke}, 2>, <{Bread}, 3>}.
```

It is clear that, except for the order, the list is the same as the result list produced by the Apriori algorithm.

8.5.4 Strengths and Weaknesses of the FP-Growth Algorithm

The strengths of the FP-Growth algorithm can be summarized as follows. First, there is no need to scan the database many times. The algorithm only scans the database twice during the construction of the FP-tree. Second, the FP-tree offers a compact representation of the input transaction database. When many transactions share the same items, the tree contains very few common prefix paths and very few branches. Third, the support for frequent itemsets are calculated from the support for items stored in the FP-tree, hence there is no need to search through the database to count them. According to some empirical studies, test results show that the FP-growth algorithm is several times faster, on average, than the basic Apriori algorithm in many real-life situations.

The FP-Growth algorithm has a number of weaknesses too. First, the FP-tree is big when the database is sparse. In this case, many branches are created in the tree. Second, the algorithm requires extra memory resources due to its recursive nature. Third, the algorithm is much more complex than the Apriori algorithm. Despite those weaknesses, the FP-Growth algorithm is a novel and efficient solution. There have been reports that the algorithm has been adopted in a number of data mining software tools.

8.6 EVALUATION OF ASSOCIATION RULES

Support and confidence have been the only two parameters that we have used to measure the strength of association rules. The higher the support, the wider the coverage of the rule. The higher the confidence, the more certain is belief in the association. However, support and confidence alone have their own limitations. The support threshold can prevent interesting rules being found if it is not set appropriately. If the support level is set too low, a massive number of association rules can be found and looking for an interesting rule can be a prohibitive task. If the support level is set too high, very few associations are found. Some rules may be found at the end, but those rules tend to be overly general and of hardly any practical use.

TABLE 8.1	Data set for tea and coffee drinkers		
	Coffee	No coffee	Total
Tea	150	50	200
No tea	650	150	800
Total	800	200	1000

High support and high confidence can also be misleading. Table 8.1 shows tea and coffee drinkers among 1000 subjects investigated. The association rule {tea}⇒ {coffee} has support of 15% and confidence of 75%. It can be considered as a strong rule. Does the rule really tell us something important? Is the rule interesting? A further investigation reveals that 80% of the subject group are coffee drinkers regardless of whether they drink tea or not. Knowing they are tea drinkers does not add more confidence than not knowing. In fact, the confidence reduced from 80% to 75%. This example demonstrates the insufficiency of support and confidence parameters alone.

In practice, an additional measure called *lift* is normally used with support and confidence. Lift is defined as the ratio of the rule's confidence to the support to the rule's consequent:

$$lift(X \Rightarrow Y) = \frac{c(X \Rightarrow Y)}{s(Y)} = \frac{s(X \cup Y)}{s(X) \cdot s(Y)}$$

where $s()$ represents the support as a fraction. It is interesting to interpret the meaning of this measure. The value of lift equals 1 when X and Y are considered *statistically independent*. This is based on the concept that the probability of two events occurring together equals the product of the probabilities of the events occurring separately. This means that X and Y occur together by chance! The value of lift is greater than 1 when X and Y are *positively* correlated, i.e. X and Y occur more often together. The value of lift is less than 1 when X and Y are *negatively* correlated, i.e. the presence of X and absence of Y occur more often. For the data set in Table 8.1:

$$lift(\textbf{tea} \Rightarrow \textbf{coffee}) = \frac{s(\textbf{tea}, \textbf{coffee})}{s(\textbf{tea}) \times s(\textbf{coffee})} = \frac{0.15}{0.2 \times 0.8} = 0.9375$$

The result indicates that the association between tea and coffee almost happen by chance and, in fact, the two items are slightly negatively associated.

Lift alone also has limitations. It does not consider the absolute support level of the rule. In practice, therefore, support, confidence and lift are often used together to measure the strength of an association rule. Other measures of interestingness of association rules have also been proposed, including correlation, IS measure, J-measure, etc. Coverage of these measures is beyond the scope of this book.

8.7 MINING BOOLEAN ASSOCIATION RULES IN WEKA

Although Weka provides a number of association rule solutions, it directly supports only quantitative association rule mining, not Boolean association rule mining. This is because Weka only accepts relational tables as input data format. It does not directly read a transaction database file. Boolean association rules have to be discovered indirectly. The following method is proposed.

First, a transaction database is transformed, outside Weka, into a relational table format. The transformed table takes transactions as rows and items as columns. The occurrence of an item in a transaction is represented by a Boolean value, say, 1 or Y. The absence of an item is depicted by a missing value, the character '?' in the ARFF file format. Then, associations are mined as if they are quantitative association rules. Boolean association rules are those where every attribute involved takes the value 1 or Y.

The transaction database in Figure 8.1 is now used to demonstrate the mining of Boolean association rules in Weka. First, an ARFF file for the transaction database is created, as in Figure 8.8(a). Then the data set is loaded from the Preprocess tab in the Explorer. After loading, the tranID is removed and class attribute unspecified. By default, all attributes representing items should be taken as nominal types. If Weka treats them as numeric, the NumericToBinary filter must be used to ensure that 1s in the table are treated as binary values. Figure 8.13(b) shows the Preprocess tab with the data set open in a viewer window.

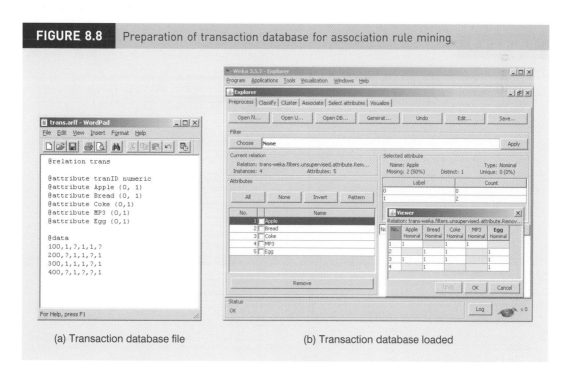

FIGURE 8.8   Preparation of transaction database for association rule mining

(a) Transaction database file   (b) Transaction database loaded

The mining of association rules is performed on the Associate tab. Press the Choose button to select an association rule mining method. In this demonstration, the Apriori method is selected. The command and the default settings of its parameters is listed next to the Choose button. Weka's implementation of the Apriori algorithm is slightly different from the basic version presented earlier. It starts mining of association rules with high support levels and gradually reduces the level of support until the minimum support threshold is reached or the maximum number of rules has been achieved. The algorithm also tries to accommodate the function for mining classification rules via association. Therefore, a number of parameters should be set. The lowerBoundMinSupport refers to the minimum support threshold. The parameter delta refers to the fraction of support to be iteratively reduced from the maximum level, specified against the parameter upperBoundMinSupport towards the minimum lowerBoundMinSupport. The minimum confidence is set as a fraction against the parameter minMetric after selecting Confidence for the parameter metricType. Instead of confidence, other metrics such as lift, leverage, etc. can also be used. Other parameters are either obvious in meaning or are related to classification.

For this demonstration, the upper bound of the minimum support is set to 1, the lower bound to 0.5 and delta to 0.1, as in Figure 8.9(a). The minimum confidence is set to 0.9. The maximum number of rules in the numRules parameter is set to as many as 10. Press the Start button to run the program and five rules appear in the Associator output window (Figure 8.9(b)).

Remember *item* = 1 in a rule indicates the existence of the item. The integer after the antecedent of a rule refers to the actual level of support for the itemset in terms of absolute number of transactions. The integer after the decedent of a rule refers to the support of the rule. For instance, in rule 4, integer 2 after Coke = 1 and Egg = 1 indicates that the support for {Coke, Egg} is 2 transactions (50%). The integer 2 after Bread = 1 shows that the support for {Bread, Coke, Egg} is 2 transactions (50%). The set of rules is the same as those listed at the end of Section 8.3.

Through the demonstration, it appears that mining Boolean association rules in Weka is possible, but only when the input data set is expressed in the format shown in Figure 8.1(b). Mining association rules in general is a weak spot for Weka. Another data mining tool, IBM Intelligent Miner for Data, makes Boolean association rule discovery simpler. A data set is expressed in the format shown in Figure 8.1(c).

FIGURE 8.9   Mining Boolean Association with Apriori in Weka

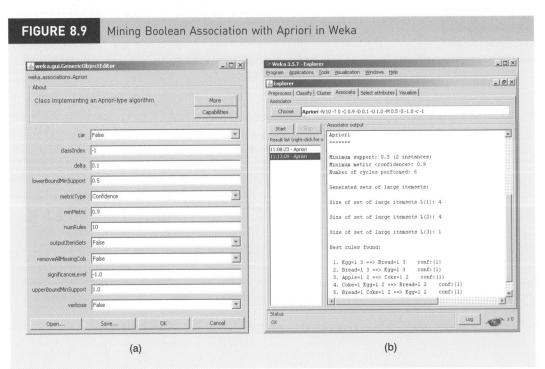

(a)   (b)

The data miners only need to specify which attribute or combination of attributes in the input table should be used as the transaction identifier and which attribute should be treated as the item attribute such that associations between different values of the attribute can be found. The rules are expressed in the form described earlier in this chapter.

8.8   ASSOCIATION RULE MINING IN PRACTICE

In this section, a number of issues concerning the practical application of association rule discovery solutions are raised for discussion.

8.8.1 Performance Issues

As mentioned earlier, the time complexity of the Apriori algorithm is $O(|C|*|DB|)$, and the total number of candidate itemsets is directly related to the minimum support threshold. For the transaction database in Figure 8.1, if the minimum support threshold is reduced to one transaction (i.e. 25%), then all combinations of items, i.e. $2^5 - 1 = 31$ of them, will become frequent. If there are 10,000 items, which is quite common in real-life supermarkets, there will be $2^{10,000} - 1$ itemsets to be created! Of course, this estimate is the worst-case scenario. Nevertheless, it clearly shows the scale of the problem. In general, association rule mining is a combinatorial problem and the search space can be huge, depending on the level of the support threshold.

Possible ways of improving performance of the algorithms include the following:

- *Implementation techniques:* This includes the use of good data structures and fast implementation of basic operations, such as apriori_gen in the Apriori algorithm. However, there is a limit on what can be achieved.

- *Algorithm improvements:* Finding algorithms that are more efficient is challenging (see Section 8.4). Since the problem of mining association rules is to find *all* rules that satisfy the threshold requirements, there is again a limit on what can be done.

- *Use of parallel processing:* This may be the only possible way forward. Parallel processing uses a number of processors and memory units on the same motherboard to share out the workload that is traditionally taken by a single processor. More detailed description of mining association rules in a parallel processing environment are given in Chapter 9.

- *Sampling the transaction database:* From the previous sections, we realize that one factor affecting the speed of mining is the size of the transaction database. Reducing the database size results in fewer iterations when counting the support to items and itemsets. Sampling is an effective way of reducing the number of transactions prior to discovery. According to some research results, sampling can reduce the size of the transaction database without too much loss of association rules. Based on the statistical estimation of binomial distribution, the probability that the support to itemsets is affected is very low for a sample of a certain size. One report claims that a sample of 3000 transactions from a database of millions of transactions gives 93% coverage of all association rules. If this claim is substantiated, it means the speed of mining of association rules can be greatly improved at the expense of losing a small number of rules.

8.8.2 Interactive Discovery

In association rule discovery, the user plays an important role in the process. The discovery of association rules can be an iterative process in which the user is responsible for setting the initial minimum support and minimum confidence thresholds. During the discovery, the user may decide to further fine-tune the thresholds based on the understanding of the rules being discovered and the number of the rules found. The user can also use the lift measure to determine the level of interestingness of the rules.

The user can specify what items are to appear on either or both sides of the resulting rules. Such association rules are known as *template* association rules. For instance, the user may decide that the item nappies should appear on the right-hand side of all resulting rules, i.e. $\{X\} \Rightarrow \{nappies\}$, with confidence 95% and support 20%. This means that the user wants to know what other items occur with nappies in 20% or more of the transactions, and what other items that customers purchase so that they are 95% likely to purchase nappies too. If the user specifies that nappies should appear on the left-hand side of all resulting rules, the question then becomes 'what other items are the customers likely to purchase if they buy nappies?' If the user specifies that beer should appear on the left-hand side and nappies should appear on the right of all resulting rules, the existence of such rules will test a hypothesis that states 'customers who purchase beer are also 95% likely to purchase nappies'.

The user can exploit a category hierarchy of some kind among items to roll up rare items into a category where the support for the category is comparable to the support for other items. For instance, in a typical supermarket setting, purchases of books, newspapers and magazines can be below the minimum support threshold. However, when those items are categorized as 'reading material', the support for the category can be sufficient. The use of categories of items is investigated further in Chapter 9.

8.8.3 Associations of Various Kinds

From the application point of view, there are different kinds of association rules that can be discovered from a real-life database. The useful associations tend to suggest some course of action. For instance, if it is found that many customers buy beer and nappies together on Thursdays, the two items can be put side by side to improve the customer throughput in the store. Trivial associations state existing facts but do not suggest any course of action. For instance, if it is known that most customers normally purchase large appliances with a maintenance agreement at an extra cost, an association rule that customers who purchase large appliances also purchase extended maintenance agreements merely states the known fact. The rule does not lead to a course of action to be taken. Inexplicable associations have meanings that are not easy to explain and no clear course of action can be taken. An example is that 'one of the most commonly sold items is an MP3 player'. No explanation (association with others) can easily be given for why this happens and almost no action can be planned for the future.

Most of the time, discovery of association rules is anonymous: we do not know and we do not want to know which transactions support the rules. In practice, however, for promotion purposes, the discovery of association rules can also be signature based: we not only know the rules but also which people comply with the rules. Of course, legal issues regarding the use of information must be addressed before such mining is permitted.

Besides the Boolean association rules discussed in this chapter, there are other types of association rule. Generalized association rules are concerned with items and categories of items occurring in transactions. For instance, we may be interested in finding not only associations between Coke and Bread but also associations between Soft Drinks and Bakery Products. Quantitative association rules describe associations between values of different attributes of a relational table. For instance, we may find a strong association between being married with children and living in a semi-detached house. Sequential association rules are concerned with association over time. For instance, there may exist a sequential purchase pattern that states customers who buy TVs later buy appliance insurance. All those kinds of association rule are topics of Chapter 9.

8.9 SUMMARY

This chapter has investigated the problem of mining Boolean association rules. It has shown that associations might exist among items in a transaction database. The strength of an association rule is normally measured in terms of support and confidence. The interestingness (or importance) of the rule can be indicated by the lift factor. The problem of mining association rules can be decomposed into two sub-tasks: finding frequent itemsets and generating the rules. The first sub-task is more challenging and most of the effort in association rule mining is concentrated on this sub-task.

The Apriori algorithm for finding frequent itemsets has been studied in depth. How candidate itemsets are made and how support for candidate itemsets is counted have been explained and illustrated with examples. The Apriori algorithm for generating Boolean association rule expressions has also been studied. Using the Apriori theorem, the algorithm controls and reduces the number of possible rules that do not meet the requirement of the minimum confidence threshold.

An alternative method of finding frequent itemsets, the FP-Growth algorithm, has also been studied in depth. The FP-Growth method uses an FP-tree to represent the input database in a compact form and derive frequent itemsets from the tree when needed. A typical feature of the method is to avoid generating a potentially huge number of candidate itemsets.

The evaluation of association rules is an important issue. The strengths and weaknesses of some major evaluation parameters, such as support, confidence and lift, have been discussed. The main problem with mining association rules is that there may be a huge number of association rules. Searching through those rules for something interesting remains a challenging task. The Lift parameter provides an additional measure of the interestingness of a rule, besides support and confidence. However, it has its own limitations.

At the end of the chapter, a number of practical issues relating to association rule mining were raised briefly. The purpose is to draw attention to those situations in which association rule mining is practised. To illustrate association rule mining practically, we used the Weka data mining software tool.

EXERCISES

1 In the context of a typical supermarket, explain what it is meant by {milk} ⇒ {sugar, flour} with support = 20% and confidence = 75%.

2 Why are the association rules described in this chapter called Boolean association rules? In the discovery process of this type of association rule is the quantity of an item in a transaction significant?

3 Other than the retail industry, find some real-life application scenarios where association rules can be useful.

4 A simple transaction database is given in Table 8.2. Suppose that the minimum support threshold is set to 40% and the minimum confidence threshold to 90%.

   (a) Use the basic Apriori algorithm for finding frequent itemsets to discover all frequent itemsets that have sufficient support.

   (b) Use either the brute-force method or the Apriori algorithm to generate strong association rules.

   (c) Calculate the lift for the association rule {4, 5} ⇒ {2}. Compare the lift value with that for the association rule {3} ⇒ {2}. Discuss the strengths and interestingness of the rules.

TABLE 8.2	Data set for Exercises 4, 5 and 8
TranID	**Items**
100	1, 3, 4
200	2, 4, 5
300	1, 2, 4, 5
400	1
500	1, 2, 3, 4, 5
600	1, 5
700	1, 3

5 Use the FP-tree construction algorithm to build an FP-tree for the transaction database in Table 8.2. Discuss the strengths and weaknesses of the FP-tree representation of a transaction database.

6 Use the FP-Growth algorithm to find all frequent itemsets with support $\geq$ 40%. Discuss the strengths and weaknesses of the FP-Growth algorithm in comparison with the Apriori algorithm.

7 A public library provides the general public with a wide range of books in various categories, such as gardening, IT, fiction, history, etc. The books are stored on shelves located in different areas within the library building. The library possesses a database that records details on which readers have borrowed which books over different dates. The library issues a library card with a unique ID number for each reader, which helps the library to track the books being borrowed. The book-borrowing details are recorded in a single table that consists of the reader's card number and the book title, category, and borrowing date. The chief librarian of the library wants to analyze the data in the database and discover what categories of books are frequently borrowed together so that book locations can be re-arranged to make it easier for readers to find their favourite books.

(a) Describe how to transform the database table for borrowing details into a suitable transaction database for Boolean association rule mining. In the transformation, you must consider what attributes of the original table should be used as a transaction identifier and what attributes should be used as items, by considering the objectives of the intended data analysis.

(b) If the chief librarian is interested in associative patterns in different seasons, what additional data preparation work is needed and how should it be conducted?

(c) Describe some example frequent itemsets and example association rules that should meet the aims of the chief librarian's investigation.

8 It is understood that the number of frequent itemsets increases exponentially as the minimum support threshold decreases linearly. Given the transaction database in Table 8.2, count the number of actual frequent itemsets discovered when the minimum threshold is set to 6, 5, 4, 3, 2 and 1 transactions. Plot the results on a graph using a spreadsheet tool, such as Microsoft Excel, and observe the trend of increase in the number of frequent itemsets. (You must be patient with this exercise – the end result and understanding justify the effort.)

9 A transaction database can be represented in a vertical fashion as explained in Section 8.4.3. For instance, the transaction database in Table 8.2 is represented vertically in Table 8.3. Develop a version of the Apriori algorithm for mining frequent itemsets for vertical transaction databases.

TABLE 8.3	Data set for Exercise 9
Item	**TranIDs**
1	100, 300, 400, 500, 600, 700
2	200, 300, 500
3	100, 500, 700
4	100, 200, 300, 500
5	200, 300, 500, 600

TABLE 8.4	Data set for Exercise 11
TransID	**Items**
100	Apple, Bread, Butter, Egg, Orange_Juice, Sugar
200	Bread, Butter, Coke, Egg, Sugar
300	Apple, Butter, Ketch_up, Potato_Chip, Sugar
400	Apple, Coke
500	Bread, Butter, Coke, Egg, Sugar
600	Coke, Ketch_up, Orange_Juice, Potato_Chip, Sugar
700	Egg, Sugar
800	Coke, Egg, Orange_Juice
900	Bread, Butter, Egg, Ketch_up, Potato_Chip, Sugar

10 [Optional exercise for computer science students] Use of efficient data structures is essential for improving an algorithm's speed at the implementation stage. With your knowledge of programming languages, discuss the use of built-in language data structures for storing a collection of candidate k-itemsets for the Apriori algorithm and for storing the FP-tree for the FP-Growth algorithm.

11 Table 8.4 contains transactions for item purchases.

(a) Follow the steps outlined in Section 8.7 and conduct a mining task for Boolean association rules using the Apriori algorithm in Weka.

(b) Set different parameters and observe the association rules discovered.

(c) Weka provides association evaluation parameters other than support, confidence and lift. Observe the evaluation results by those evaluation parameters of example rules.

BIBLIOGRAPHICAL NOTES

Association rule mining started in the early 1990s, in the QUEST project team at IBM's Almaden research centre and the research team at Helsinki University. Because of the complexity of the problem and the wide application potential of solutions, association rule mining has attracted a great amount of attention in research communities and industry. The association between beer and nappies has become the most frequently used example to explain to beginners what data mining is about.

The main sources of reference for this chapter are the original papers published during the 1990s and early 2000s by Agrawal's research team at IBM. The references to the basic concepts of association rules and the Apriori algorithm for mining frequent itemsets are based on Agrawal et al. (1993) and Agrawal and Srikant (1994). The description of the Apriori algorithm for generating association rule expressions is based on Agrawal et al. (1996). For the FP-tree algorithm, we referred to the original paper by Han et al. (2000). The evaluation of association rules is widely discussed in a number of texts. Tan et al. (2006) provide a systematic summary of all known evaluation parameters. Berry and Linoff (2004) discuss extensively issues in relation to mining association rules in practice.

There has been extensive research into association rule mining. Recent surveys include the report by Zhao and Bhowmick (2003) and the article by Dunham *et al.* (2000). Tan *et al.* (2006) have given a thorough overview of research works and a systematic categorization of the works on association rule mining. Interested readers should read the bibliographic notes in Chapter 6 of that book. Maximal frequent itemsets and closed frequent itemsets have been studied in a number of articles (Gunopoulos *et al.* 1997; Pasquier *et al.* 1999; Zaki and Orihara 1998), and have also been summarized in Tan *et al.* (2006).

8

CHAPTER 9

Mining techniques for other types of association

LEARNING OBJECTIVES

To understand different types of association rule

To study an adapted Apriori algorithm for mining generalized association rules

To study an adapted Apriori algorithm for mining quantitative association rules

To understand issues regarding redundant rules in the context of generalized and quantitative associations

To study an adapted Apriori algorithm for mining sequential patterns

To observe and practise mining association rules in Weka

To briefly consider online incremental solutions for mining association rules

To briefly consider parallel solutions for mining association rules

Besides Boolean association rules among values of a single attribute (i.e. items), a variety of other types of association rule also exist. Most of those association rules have their origin in business, commerce and industry. It is therefore very useful to understand those associations and study the techniques of mining them.

This chapter concentrates on three types: generalized associations, quantitative associations and sequential patterns. Many solutions have been developed for mining these types of associations. The chapter focuses on effective adaptations of the basic Apriori principles for mining Boolean associations that were presented in the last chapter. Some issues regarding rule redundancy in the context of mining generalized and quantitative association rules also need to be addressed. This chapter demonstrates the use of mining techniques to discover quantitative association rules in Weka.

The change of database content and the size of search space during the discovery of association patterns also cause concerns. This chapter attempts to address those concerns by introducing incremental methods and parallel solutions for association rule mining.

9.1   GENERALIZED ASSOCIATION RULES

9.1.1 Description

Compared to item-level associations in Boolean association rules, generalized association rules are concerned with *multilevel* associations among items and categories of items. The data inputs include a category hierarchy, i.e. a *taxonomy,* and a transaction database. The taxonomy may be the specification of domain knowledge. It serves as a multilevel categorization of items: a category at a higher level is a *generalization* of a group of items or categories at a lower level and an item or category at a lower level is a *specialization* of a category at a higher level. All categories of an item or category are called the *ancestors* of that item or category.

Figure 9.1 shows a transaction database and a taxonomy that defines that apple and pear belong to the fruit category, fruit and potato belong to Fruit & veg category and baguette and loaf bread belong to the bakery category.

In this context, the term *item* includes category and an *itemset* is therefore a set of items and categories. A transaction t is said to support a generic item x if $x \in t.items$ or x is an ancestor of item i and $i \in t.items$. A transaction is said to support an itemset if it supports every item or category in the itemset. For the example in figure 9.1, transaction 200 supports not only items apple and loaf bread, but also categories fruit, Fruit & veg and Bakery. In the case where a transaction contains a number of items of the same category, the transaction support to the category is only counted as 1 because it is the appearance of the category in the transaction rather than the number of appearances that is of interest.

Like Boolean association rules, a generalized association rule, also known as a *multilevel* association rule, takes the form of $X \Rightarrow Y$ where X and Y are itemsets. In general, either side of a generalized association rule can be items, categories or a mixture of the two. However, the constraint $X \cap Y = \emptyset$ must still be satisfied. In addition, no items in Y are ancestors of items in X. The additional constraint limits the creation of trivial rules such as 'if customers purchase apple they also purchase fruit' which always has a confidence of 100%. The rule $X \Rightarrow Y$ is said to hold in an input transaction database DB with support s and confidence c if s fraction of the transactions in DB supports $X \cup Y$ and c fraction of the transactions that support X also support Y. An example generalized association rule discovered from the transaction database in Figure 9.1 is {Loaf bread} $\Rightarrow$ {Fruit}. The rule has 50% support and 100% confidence.

Some facts about generalized association rule mining are worth noting. First, if an item has sufficient support, so has its ancestors. If the support for an item is insufficient, the support for its ancestor may still be sufficient. However, if the support for an ancestor is insufficient, all descendants of the ancestor

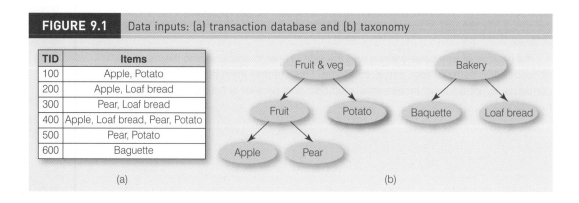

FIGURE 9.1   Data inputs: (a) transaction database and (b) taxonomy

TID	Items
100	Apple, Potato
200	Apple, Loaf bread
300	Pear, Loaf bread
400	Apple, Loaf bread, Pear, Potato
500	Pear, Potato
600	Baguette

(a)

(b)

do not have sufficient support. For instance in Figure 9.1, the support for loaf bread is 50%, but the support for bakery is 67%. If the 67% support for bakery is considered insufficient, the 17% support for baguette and the 50% support for loaf bread are both insufficient. Second, given two rules {Apple} $\Rightarrow$ {Potato} and {Pear} $\Rightarrow$ {Potato}, the support level for {Fruit} $\Rightarrow$ {Potato} is not automatically the sum of the supports for the two given rules. Some transactions may contain both apple and pear.

9.1.2 Mining Generalized Association Rules

The problem of discovering generalized association rules is to find *all* possible rules $X \Rightarrow Y$ that satisfy the minimum support and confidence thresholds defined by the user. There is another user-defined threshold that indicates the minimum degree of interestingness of a rule with respect to rule redundancy, which is discussed later in the chapter.

The problem decomposition for mining generalized association rules follows a similar framework to that for Boolean association rule discovery presented in Section 8.1.3. The process is outlined as follows:

1 Find all frequent itemsets with support greater than or equal to the user-defined minimum threshold.

2 From the frequent itemsets, generate all rule expressions with confidence greater than or equal to the user-defined minimum threshold. To comply with the rule definition, no rule where items on the right-hand side are the ancestors of any items on the left-hand side is generated.

3 Evaluate the degree of interestingness of the rule expressions and prune redundant rules.

The basic Apriori algorithm presented in Chapter 8 was developed for mining Boolean association rules. The original Apriori rule generation algorithm can be used almost directly for Step 2. The only modification is to ensure that the additional constraint is enforced. The pruning of redundant rules is addressed in Section 9.3. This section therefore focuses on Step 1, the adaptation of the Apriori algorithm for finding frequent itemsets. A basic algorithm is outlined in pseudo-code as follows:

```
algorithm AprioriAdapted (DB : database; MS : support threshold) : set of
                          itemsets;
begin
   I := all items in DB;
   F₁ := {i | i ∈ I and i.count ≥ MS};
   k := 2;
   while Fₖ₋₁ ≠ ∅ do
      Cₖ := new candidate itemsets of size k generated from Fₖ₋₁;
      for each transaction t in DB do
         add all ancestors of the items in t to t and remove any duplicates;
         find all candidate itemsets contained in t and save them to Cₜ;
         for each candidate itemset c in Cₜ do
            c.count := c.count + 1;
         end for;
      end for;
      Fₖ := {c | c ∈ Cₖ and c.count ≥ MS};
      k := k + 1;
   end while;
   return (F₁ ∪ F₂ ∪ ... ∪ Fₖ)
end;
```

This adapted algorithm is almost the same as the basic algorithm for mining frequent itemsets for Boolean association rules. The only difference is how ancestors are treated. In this algorithm, the first seed set F_1 must include not only frequent items but also frequent ancestors. Any support for an item is also support for all its ancestors. The adapted algorithm can use the same apriori_gen function to generate new candidate itemsets based on frequent itemsets in a seed set. In order to count support for items and their ancestors, each transaction from the transaction database is modified to include ancestors of the items that appear in the transaction. Then the support for an ancestor is counted in the same way as that for an item. Again, efficient search structures, such as the hash tree can also be exploited to locate quickly those candidate itemsets contained in the current transaction.

For the example data set in Figure 9.1, if the minimum support threshold is set to 50%, i.e. three transactions, frequent itemsets that can be discovered include {Apple}, {Fruit}, {Bakery}, {Bakery, Fruit}, {Fruit, Loaf bread}. If the minimum confidence threshold is set to 90%, the rule {Loaf bread} $\Rightarrow$ {Fruit} has 100% confidence and is collected in the final result. It is interesting to note that a more specific rule {Loaf bread} $\Rightarrow$ {Apple} has a lower level of confidence of 67% and is, hence, excluded from the final result.

Although working correctly, the basic adapted algorithm is inefficient in counting the support. Because of ancestors, the total number of items and the average size of transactions increases substantially. Several suggestions have been made to speed up the process:

- The support for an itemset X that contains item x and its ancestor y is the same as the support for the itemset $X - \{y\}$. It is therefore unnecessary to count the support for itemsets that contain an item and its ancestors. If L_k, the set of frequent k-itemsets, does not contain any itemset involving an item and its ancestor, the collection C_{k+1} of candidate itemsets newly created using the apriori_gen operation, will not include any itemset of the same nature. It therefore makes sense to remove candidate 2-itemsets that consist of an item and its ancestor, before support is counted.

- Instead of repeatedly traversing the taxonomy to locate ancestors of an item, the ancestors of each item can be pre-computed and held in an efficient data structure, such as a hashing structure, so that quick reference can be made.

- In order to limit the size of a modified transaction, only the ancestors whose descendants are in the current collection of the new candidates are included. When the candidate itemsets only contain ancestors of items, the ancestors can replace the items in the relevant transactions rather than being added.

- In the basic algorithm, at a particular iteration, the support for all newly created candidate k-itemsets are counted by scanning the entire database once. An alternative way is to scan the database several times. The support for the candidate itemsets that contain ancestors at the top of the taxonomy are counted first. If those candidate itemsets are infrequent, any candidate itemsets containing the descendants of the ancestors must be infrequent, and hence there is no need to count their support.

- Most transaction databases in real life are huge. Searching the entire database to count the support can be expensive. A possible improvement is to use a sample of the database to estimate the support for ancestors and consequently determine whether or not to count the actual support for descendants when the entire database is later searched.

Although these improvement measures are sensible in their own right, the additional complexity and cost involved in the modified algorithm may outweigh any benefits. The scope of the problem of mining generalized association rules is, in general, much larger than that of Boolean association rules. Many rules may be discovered.

9.2 QUANTITATIVE ASSOCIATION RULES

9.2.1 Description

For Boolean and generalized association rule discovery problems, the data inputs can be considered as special tables of two columns: the record identifier and a group of values of a single attribute. Rules of those kinds represent associations among the values of the same attribute. The data input for quantitative association rule mining is a typical relational table of tuples and attributes. Each row is normally marked by a unique record identifier. The table normally has a number of attributes; some may be quantitative (i.e. numerical or ordinal) whereas others may be categorical (i.e. nominal). Because of the involvement of a number of different attributes, quantitative association rules is also known as *multidimensional* association rules.

Figure 9.2(a) shows a relational table where attributes Age and NoOfMobilesUsed are quantitative and attribute Gender is categorical. Although a relational table is different from a transaction database, it can be transformed into a transaction database in a straightforward manner as shown in Figure 9.2. The transformation is realized by creating a temporary table, Figure 9.2(b), that pairs an attribute name with

FIGURE 9.2   Transformation from a relational table to a transaction database

RecordID	Age	Gender	NoOfMobilesUsed
1	25	Male	1
2	23	Female	1
3	29	Male	0
4	33	Female	2
5	37	Female	2

(a)

RecordID	Age: 20–29	Age: 30–39	Gender: Female	Gender: Male	NoOfMobilesUsed: 0–1	NoOfMobilesUsed: 2
1	1	0	0	1	1	0
2	1	0	1	0	1	0
3	1	0	0	1	1	0
4	0	1	1	0	0	1
5	0	1	1	0	0	1

(b)

RecordID	Items
1	<Age, 20, 29>, <Gender, Male>, <NoOfMobilesUsed, 0, 1>
2	<Age, 20, 29>, <Gender, Female>, <NoOfMobilesUsed, 0, 1>
3	<Age, 20, 29>, <Gender, Male>, <NoOfMobilesUsed, 0, 1>
4	<Age, 30, 39>, <Gender, Female>, <NoOfMobilesUsed, 2>
5	<Age, 30, 39>, <Gender, Female>, <NoOfMobilesUsed, 2>

(c)

a value (or a range of values) in the original table to create a new attribute. Each row of the temporary table takes the Boolean value 1 for an attribute if the corresponding attribute in the original table has a value within the range; otherwise, 0. Then the names of the attributes in the temporary table, i.e. the pairing of the attribute and its value, are recorded as items in a transaction database, Figure 9.2(c), for those attributes of the temporary table that have the value 1.

The transformation indicates that *items* now take a rather different form. In a given relational table, for categorical attribute A with values a_1, a_2, ..., a_k, each pairing of name A and one of its values, i.e. $<A, a_i>$, is considered as an *item*. For a quantitative attribute B with a value range, the range is divided into a number of partitions, the pairing is of the attribute name with each of the partitions. In fact, a triple $<B, l, u>$ where l and u are the lower and upper bounds of the partition, is considered an item. A set of such items forms an itemset. For example, $<Gender, Male>$ and $<Age, 20, 29>$ are items, and $\{<Age, 20, 29>, <Gender, Male>\}$ is an itemset. Since there are different ways to partition a quantitative domain, for a range of quantitative values [a, b], any of the sub ranges within [a, b] can be considered as a specialization of [a, b], and [a, b] itself can be seen as a generalization of the sub ranges.

The support for an item has a different understanding in this context. A tuple of the input table supports an item $<A, a_i>$ if the attribute A is categorical and takes the exact value a_i. A tuple of the input table supports an item $<B, l_i, u_i>$ if attribute B is quantitative and has a value between the lower bound l_i and the upper bound u_i of a range. For instance, record 2 in Figure 9.2(a) supports both items $<Gender, Female>$ and $<Age, 20, 29>$ because Gender has the value Female and age 23 is between 20 and 29.

A quantitative association rule takes the form of $X \Rightarrow Y$ where X and Y are itemsets. The constraint on the quantitative association rule is that attributes of X cannot occur again in Y, i.e. attributes$(X) \cap$ attributes$(Y) = \emptyset$. The rule is said to hold in the relational table with support s and confidence c, if s fraction of tuples in the table support $X \cup Y$, and c fraction of tuples in the table that support X also support Y.

The problem of discovering quantitative association rules is to find *all* possible rules $X \Rightarrow Y$ that satisfy a minimum support threshold s and a minimum confidence threshold c, both defined by the end user. The concept of interestingness of a quantitative association rule also exists. It is discussed in Section 9.3.2.

9.2.2 Mining Quantitative Association Rules

As with generalized association rules, adapting the original Apriori algorithm to this kind of association rule is appealing. The rule generation algorithm can be easily adapted from the original. The main concern is the adaptation of the Apriori algorithm to find frequent itemsets. In principle, this is also quite straightforward. Values of quantitative attributes are discretized into partitions before the discovery. The apriori_gen operation is used to generate new candidate itemsets. The only change to make is to ensure that no candidate itemsets with items representing the same attribute are made. The relational table is then scanned record by record, and the support counters for the candidate itemsets contained in the record are incremented. There seems to be no obvious difficulty in the adaptation.

Unfortunately, there is a problem with discretization of quantitative attributes. For a quantitative attribute, if the attribute domain is divided into too many small partitions, the support for each partition remains low. Certain rules may not be found due to lack of support. For the example table in Figure 9.2, assuming the minimum support threshold is 2 transactions, item $<age, 30, 34>$ is considered not frequent.

At the same time, information may be lost when individual values are grouped into an interval. The problem worsens when an interval gets bigger. Intuitively, information loss can be understood as an increase of uncertainty and reduction of confidence level. For the table in Figure 9.2(a), the gender for the person without a mobile phone is male. Therefore, the rule $<$NoOfMobilesUsed, 0$> \Rightarrow <$Gender, Male$>$ has 100% confidence. However when the attribute values for NoOfMobilesUsed are grouped into [0, 1], this absolute certainty is lost. As a result, the confidence of the rule $<$NoOfMobilesUsed, 0, 1$> \Rightarrow <$Gender, Male$>$ is 67%.

A dilemma then exists: if intervals are too small, some rules will not be found because of lack of support. If intervals are too large, certain rules may not be found due to lack of confidence. One suggested method is to use the concept of *partial-completeness*, based on measures of confidence among rules with small intervals and their larger extended intervals, to determine the number of partitions needed, and then apply the equal-depth (i.e. equal-frequency) partitioning method mentioned in Chapter 3. The concept of partial-completeness is beyond the scope of this book. Further details can be found in the reference described in the Bibliographical Notes.

The problem of discovering frequent itemsets can now be decomposed as follows:

1 For each quantitative attribute, the number of partitions is first determined, and the equal-depth discretization method is used to partition the domain of the attribute.

2 All individual quantitative and categorical items are collected and the support for them is counted. The frequent items are then selected.

3 In order not to miss any rules on the grounds of lack of support, infrequent adjacent values or adjacent small intervals for a quantitative attribute are merged into larger intervals as long as their supports are less than a user-defined maximum.

4 Infrequent items are removed. Based on the final list of frequent items, all frequent itemsets are discovered.

Now, we use the relational table in Figure 9.2(a) as an example to illustrate the process. Suppose that the minimum and maximum user-defined support thresholds are two transactions. Suppose also that the quantitative attribute age is partitioned into four intervals and another quantitative attribute NoOfMobilesUsed is not partitioned, as in Figure 9.3(a). First, all items, i.e. individual attribute values and initial intervals together with their support are listed. The infrequent items $<$Age, 20, 24$>$, $<$Age, 30, 34$>$ and $<$Age, 35, 39$>$ are merged with their consecutive intervals, creating new items $<$Age, 20, 29$>$ and $<$Age, 30, 39$>$. The infrequent item $<$NoOfMobilesUsed, 0$>$ is merged with $<$NoOfMobilesUsed, 1$>$ to create a new item $<$NoOfMobilesUsed, 0, 1$>$. Since the newly merged items all have sufficient support, the process of merging stops. Then infrequent items are removed and the list of all frequent items is obtained as shown in Figure 9.3(b). This list is then used as the seed to generate new candidate itemsets. Figure 9.3(c) shows the other frequent itemsets discovered from the given input table.

From the frequent itemsets, quantitative association rules are generated. An example association rule for the input table is {$<$Age, 30, 39$>$, $<$Gender, female$>$} $\Rightarrow$ {$<$NoOfMobilesUsed, 2$>$}. The rule has support level of 40% (i.e. two transactions) and confidence level of 100%.

9.3 REDUNDANT ASSOCIATION RULES

Until now, we have discovered association rules according to their levels of support and confidence. A large number of association rules may be discovered but not all of them are equally useful. Among the rules, there may be associations where the two sides are statistically independent, i.e. those with a lift factor closer to 1. Since those associations only occur by chance, rules of this kind serve little purpose and should be removed from the result set. Unfortunately, the lift measure is ineffective in detecting redundant rules in the contexts of generalized and quantitative association rules.

FIGURE 9.3   Using Adapted Apriori algorithm for a data set with quantitative attributes

RecordID	Age	Gender	NoOfMobilesUsed
1	25	Male	1
2	23	Female	1
3	29	Male	0
4	33	Female	2
5	37	Female	2

Initial Partitioning	Age
1	20 .. 24
2	25 .. 29
3	30 .. 34
4	35 .. 39

(a)

All Individual Items			
Item	Support	Item	Support
<Age, 20, 24>	1	<NoOfMobilesUsed, 0>	1
<Age, 25, 29>	2	<NoOfMobilesUsed, 1>	2
<Age, 30, 34>	1	<NoOfMobilesUsed, 2>	2
<Age, 35, 39>	1	<Age, 20, 29>	3
<Gender, male>	2	<Age, 30, 39>	2

Frequent Items	Support
<Age, 25, 29>	2
<Age, 20, 29>	3
<Age, 30, 39>	2
<Gender, male>	2
<Gender, female>	3
<NoOfMobilesUsed, 0, 1>	3
<NoOfMobilesUsed, 1>	2
<NoOfMobilesUsed, 2>	2

(b)

Frequent Itemsets	Support
{<Age, 25, 29>, <Gender, male>}	2
{<Age, 25, 29>, <NoOfMobilesUsed, 0, 1>}	2
{<Age, 20, 29>, <Gender, male>}	2
{<Age, 20, 29>, <NoOfMobilesUsed, 0, 1>}	3
{<Age, 20, 29>, <NoOfMobilesUsed, 1>}	2
{<Age, 30, 39>, <Gender, female>}	2
{<Age, 30, 39>, <NoOfMobilesUsed, 2>}	2
{<Gender, male>, <NoOfMobilesUsed, 0, 1>}	2
{<Gender, female>, <NoOfMobilesUsed, 2>}	2
{<Age, 25, 29>, <Gender, male>, <NoOfMobilesUsed, 0, 1>}	2
{<Age, 20, 29>, <Gender, male>, <NoOfMobilesUsed, 0, 1>}	2
{<Age, 30, 39>, <Gender, female>, <NoOfMobilesUsed, 2>}	2

(c)

9.3.1 Interestingness of Generalized Association Rules

In the context of mining generalized association rules, a number of rules may describe the same or very similar associations at different levels of data abstraction. For instance, there may exist an association rule {Coke} ⇒ {fry} with 4% support and 80% confidence. If it is known that the Coke category consists of 50% classic Coke and 50% diet Coke, the association rule {diet Coke} ⇒ {fry} is expected to have 2% of support and 80% confidence. If the actual support and confidence for the latter rule are close to the expected 2% and 80% respectively, the rule has not provided more information than the former more general rule, and hence is considered *redundant*. The redundant rule should be removed from the final collection. In other words, there is no need to keep both rules. The domain knowledge regarding the Coke category helps to prune some redundant rules. But, in general, how is the redundancy of a rule measured, particularly in situations where no domain knowledge is available?

A method of determining redundant rules has been developed. The idea is based on the concept of estimated support and estimated confidence of a rule with respect to its close ancestor rule. Given an itemset $Y = \{y_1, y_2, \ldots, y_n\}$ and an itemset $Y' = \{y'_1, y'_2, \ldots, y'_k, y_{k+1}, \ldots, y_n\}$ where y'_i is an ancestor of y_i, the itemset Y' is called an *ancestor itemset* of Y. Given a rule $X \Rightarrow Y$, rules $X' \Rightarrow Y$, $X \Rightarrow Y'$ and $X' \Rightarrow Y'$ are also known as ancestors of $X \Rightarrow Y$. Among the ancestor rules, rule $X' \Rightarrow Y'$ is a *close* ancestor of $X \Rightarrow Y$, if no ancestor rules, where $X' \Rightarrow Y'$ is an ancestor of any of them, exist.

Based on the concepts of ancestor itemsets and rules, the expected values of support and confidence of a rule can be defined. Consider a rule $X \Rightarrow Y$. Let $Z = X \cup Y$, $Z = \{z_1, z_2, \ldots, z_n\}$ and $Z' = \{z'_1, z'_2, \ldots, z'_k, z_{k+1}, \ldots, z_n\}$ where Z' is an ancestor of Z. The expected value of support ES of Z with regard to its ancestor Z' is defined as:

$$ES_{Z'}(\sigma(Z)) = \frac{\sigma(z_1)}{\sigma(z'_1)} \times \frac{\sigma(z_2)}{\sigma(z'_2)} \times \ldots \times \frac{\sigma(z_i)}{\sigma(z'_i)} \times \sigma(Z')$$

where $\sigma(x)$ is the support of x. Similarly, let $X' \Rightarrow Y'$ be an ancestor rule of $X \Rightarrow Y$, and $Y = \{y_1, y_2, \ldots, y_n\}$ and $Y' = \{y'_1, y'_2, \ldots, y'_k, y_{k+1}, \ldots, y_n\}$. The expected value of confidence EC of $X \Rightarrow Y$ with respect to its ancestor $X' \Rightarrow Y'$ is defined as:

$$EC_{X' \Rightarrow Y'}(conf(X \Rightarrow Y)) = \frac{\sigma(y_1)}{\sigma(y'_1)} \times \frac{\sigma(y_2)}{\sigma(y'_2)} \times \ldots \times \frac{\sigma(y_i)}{\sigma(y'_i)} \times conf(X' \Rightarrow Y')$$

An association rule $X \Rightarrow Y$ is known as *R*-interesting with regard to an ancestor $X' \Rightarrow Y'$ if the actual support for $X \Rightarrow Y$ is at least R times the expected value of support or the actual level of confidence is at least R times the expected value of confidence. R can be a user-defined minimum interest threshold. An *R*-interesting rule is deemed not to be redundant and is kept in the final result together with its close ancestor. Using the R measure on both or either of the expected support and expected confidence is a matter for the data analyst to decide.

To illustrate the use of the R measure, two rules for the transaction database in Figure 9.1 are used:

(a) $\{\texttt{Fruit}\} \Rightarrow \{\texttt{Bakery}\}$ with support 50% and confidence 60%
(b) $\{\texttt{apple}\} \Rightarrow \{\texttt{loaf bread}\}$ with support 33% and confidence 67%

The expected value of support and the expected value of confidence for Rule (b) with regard to its ancestor Rule (a) are calculated as follows:

$$ES_{(a)}(\sigma(b)) = \frac{\sigma(\text{apple})}{\sigma(\text{Fruit})} \times \sigma(a) = \frac{3}{5} \times 50\% = 30\%$$

$$EC_{(a)}(conf(b)) = \frac{\sigma(\text{loaf bread})}{\sigma(\text{Bakery})} \times conf(a) = \frac{3}{4} \times 60\% = 45\%$$

The actual support for Rule (b) is 1.1 times of the expected value and the actual confidence of the rule is 1.49 times the expected value. If the minimum threshold $R = 1.5$, then Rule (b) is considered redundant with respect to Rule (a) because its actual support and actual confidence have not both reached 1.5 times the expected values. If $R = 1.3$, Rule (b) is considered not redundant with regard to Rule (a).

Given a set of generalized association rules and a minimum interest threshold, the rules are interesting if they either have no ancestors at all or they are *R*-interesting with respect to their close ancestors.

9

9.3.2 Interestingness in Quantitative Association Rules

The redundant rule problem also exists in the context of quantitative association rule discovery. Similar to the example used at the beginning of Section 9.3.1, if it is known that a third of the people in the age group between 20 and 29 have an age between 20 and 24, the rule <Age, 20, 24> $\Rightarrow$ <NoOfMobilesUsed, 1, 2> that has 3% support and 80% confidence is redundant with respect to another rule <Age, 20, 29> $\Rightarrow$ <NoOfMobilesUsed, 1, 2> that has 9% support and 80% confidence.

Similar to the situation with respect to generalized association rules, an interestingness measure based on expected support and expected confidence is developed. Consider a rule $X \Rightarrow Y$. Let $Z = X \cup Y$, $Z = \{<z_1, l_1, u_1>, <z_2, l_2, u_2>, \ldots, <z_n, l_n, u_n>\}$ and $Z' = \{<z_1, l'_1, u'_1>, <z_2, l'_2, u'_2>, \ldots, <z_n, l'_n, u'_n>\}$ where $l'_1 \leq l_i \leq u_i \leq u'_1$, and Z' is also known as an ancestor of Z. The expected value of support ES of Z with respect to its ancestor Z' is defined as:

$$ES_{Z'}(\sigma(Z)) = \frac{\sigma(<z_1, l_1, u_1>)}{\sigma(<z_1, l'_1, u'_1>)} \times \frac{\sigma(<z_2, l_2, u_2>)}{\sigma(<z_2, l'_2, u'_2>)} \times \ldots \times \frac{\sigma(<z_n, l_n, u_n>)}{\sigma(<z_n, l'_n, u'_n>)} \times \sigma(Z')$$

where $\sigma(x)$ represents the support to x. Similarly, let $X' \Rightarrow Y'$ represent an ancestor rule of $X \Rightarrow Y$, and $Y = \{<y_1, l_1, u_1>, <y_2, l_2, u_2>, \ldots, <y_n, l_n, u_n>\}$ and $Y' = \{<y_1, l'_1, u'_1>, <y_2, l'_2, u'_2>, \ldots, <y_n, l'_n, u'_n>\}$ where $l'_1 \leq l_i \leq u_i \leq u'_i$. The expected value of confidence EC of $X \Rightarrow Y$ with respect to $X' \Rightarrow Y'$ is defined as:

$$EC_{X' \Rightarrow Y'}(conf(X \Rightarrow Y)) = \frac{\sigma(<y_1, l_1, u_1>)}{\sigma(<y_1, l'_1, u'_1>)} \times \frac{\sigma(<y_2, l_2, u_2>)}{\sigma(<y_2, l'_2, u'_2>)} \times \ldots \times \frac{\sigma(<y_n, l_n, u_n>)}{\sigma(<y_n, l'_n, u'_n>)} \times conf(X' \Rightarrow Y')$$

Similar to the generalized association rule situation, a minimum threshold R is defined and used. A rule $X \Rightarrow Y$ is R-interesting and not redundant with respect to its ancestor $X' \Rightarrow Y'$ if its actual support or confidence is at least R times the expected value of support or confidence. Again, interesting rules include those without any ancestors or those that are R-interesting with respect to their close ancestors.

From the frequent itemsets in Figure 9.3, the following two rules can be derived:

(a) {<Age, 20, 29>} $\Rightarrow$ {<NoOfMobilesUsed, 0, 1>} with support 60% and confidence 100%
(b) {<Age, 25, 29>} $\Rightarrow$ {<NoOfMobilesUsed, 0, 1>} with support = 40% and confidence 100%

The expected value of support and the expected value of confidence for Rule (b) with respect to its ancestor Rule (a) are calculated as follows:

$$ES_{(a)}(\sigma(b)) = \frac{\sigma(<age, 25, 29>)}{\sigma(<age, 20, 29>)} \times \sigma(a) = \frac{2}{3} \times 60\% = 40\%$$

$$EC_{(a)}(conf(b)) = \frac{\sigma(<NoOfMobilesUsed, 0, 1>)}{\sigma(<NoOfMobilesUsed, 0, 1>)} \times conf(a) = 100\%$$

Rule (b) does not have any extra support or confidence compared to the ancestor. It is therefore considered redundant with respect to Rule (a).

This definition of interestingness is loose: because the support of an attribute within an itemset may be affected by the support of other attributes within the same itemset, a single-aspect view of interestingness is not realistic. The interestingness measure is tightened: A rule $X \Rightarrow Y$ is R-interesting with respect to an ancestor $X' \Rightarrow Y'$ if the actual support of $X \Rightarrow Y$ is at least R times the expected value of support based on $X' \Rightarrow Y'$ or the actual confidence of $X \Rightarrow Y$ is at least R times the expected value of confidence based on $X' \Rightarrow Y'$ and $X \cup Y$ is R-interesting with respect to $X' \cup Y'$. An itemset Z is R-interesting with respect to Z' if the actual support of Z is at least R times the expected support based on Z'. For any specialization $'Z$ of Z, as long as $'Z$ is also an itemset, any other specialization of Z (i.e. $Z-'Z$) is also R-interesting with respect to Z'.

9.4   DISCOVERING SEQUENTIAL PATTERNS

In certain applications, data sets may contain *sequences*. The problem of mining frequently occurring sequential patterns from a given data set can be considered as a variant of association rule mining. This section introduces the concept of sequential pattern mining and adaptation of the Apriori principles for discovering sequential patterns.

9.4.1 Sequential Data and Sequential Patterns

A sequence is a list of *elements*, ordered along the time dimension. Each element in turn is a collection of *events*. An event represents the presence of an attribute value in an abstract sense. Events within an element can occur simultaneously or in a certain order along the time dimension.

Data sets of a sequential nature exist in many applications, such as the following:

- Shopping transactions: Figure 9.4(a) shows such a database. A transaction, i.e. an element of the sequence for a specific customer, consists of a collection of purchased items that can be thought of as simultaneous events within the element. All transactions of a customer are ordered according to the shopping date and time. Figure 9.4(b) presents the transactions on a timeline, illustrating the characteristics of the sequential data.

- Visits to pages of a website: The log file on the web server records the pages that visitors have viewed. If a visit session by a visitor can be identified, the pages visited by the visitor in the session form a sequence. An example sequence may look like: <{Home page}, {Electronics page}, {Camera page}, {Digital Camera page}, {Shopping Basket page}, {Payment Confirmation page}>.

- Sequences of events: In automatic control systems, results from various sensors are recorded. The devices monitor chains of events that may lead to a serious outcome. An example sequence of events may be: <{ice on runway}, {wheels not rotating}, {brake released}, {speed not reducing}, {overshoot the runway}>.

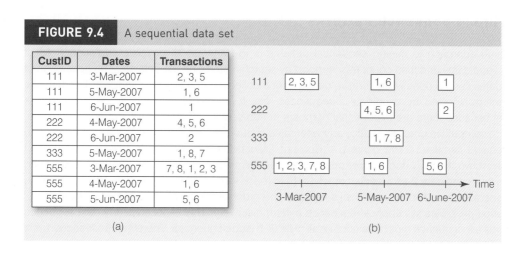

FIGURE 9.4	A sequential data set

CustID	Dates	Transactions
111	3-Mar-2007	2, 3, 5
111	5-May-2007	1, 6
111	6-Jun-2007	1
222	4-May-2007	4, 5, 6
222	6-Jun-2007	2
333	5-May-2007	1, 8, 7
555	3-Mar-2007	7, 8, 1, 2, 3
555	4-May-2007	1, 6
555	5-Jun-2007	5, 6

(a)

(b)

■ Genome sequences: DNA of different species can be recorded as sequences. Each sequence consists of an ordered list of DNA elements and each element is a permutation of the DNA bases A, T, G and C in a certain order. For instance, the sub-sequence GGTTCCGCCTTCAG may occur a number of times in a complete DNA sequence record.

There are many other example data sets of this nature, such as video frames, courses taken by students over years of study, etc. In Figure 9.4, frequent sequences may exist. For instance, sequence <{2, 3}, {1, 6}> occurs in two out of four customer records in the data set. Such a sequence may indicate the existence of an association in time between items {2, 3} and {1, 6}. Understanding such associations can be useful for profiling customer shopping behaviour over a time period.

Let $DB = \{s_1, s_2, \ldots, s_n\}$ be a set of n data sequences. Each sequence $s_i = <e_1 e_2 \ldots e_m>$, where $1 \leq i \leq n$, is an ordered list of m elements. Each element $e_j = \{i_1, i_2, \ldots, i_t\}$, where $1 \leq j \leq m$, is a collection of t events. The length of a sequence, $|s|$, refers to the number of elements within the sequence. A k-sequence refers to a sequence with k events.

Given a sequence $t = <t_1 t_2 \ldots t_m>$ and another sequence $s = <s_1 s_2 \ldots s_n>$, t is said to be *contained in* s if there exist m integers $1 \leq j_1 < j_2 < \ldots < j_m \leq n$ such that $t_1 \subseteq s_{j1}, t_2 \subseteq s_{j2}, \ldots, t_m \subseteq s_{jm}$. In this case, t is also known as a *sub-sequence* of s. The *support* for sequence s refers to the fraction of data sequences in DB that contain s.

TABLE 9.1	Data sequences
Sequence ID	**Data Sequences**
111	{2,3,5}, {1,6}, {1}
222	{4,5,6}, {2}
333	{1,7,8}
555	{1,2,3,7,8}, {1,6}, {5,6}

The transaction database in Figure 9.4 can be thought of as a set of four data sequences of different lengths, one for each customer, as shown in Table 9.1. Sub-sequence <{2, 3}, {1, 6}> is a 4-sequence with length of two. It is contained in two of the data sequences (those with IDs 111 and 555). Hence, it has the support of 50% of the data sequences. Sub-sequence <{5}, {6}> is only contained in the first data sequence and therefore only has the support of 25%.

Given a sequential data set DB and a user-defined minimum support threshold, the task of discovering *sequential patterns* is to find all sub-sequences that have support greater than or equal to the minimum support threshold. For instance, if the minimum support threshold is set to 50%, <{2, 3}, {1, 6}> is considered as a frequent sequential pattern, whereas <{5}, {6}> is not.

9.4.2 Mining Sequence Patterns

A brute-force approach to mining sequential patterns is to generate all possible sub-sequences of events as candidates and then count their support by searching through the data set. The generation of the candidates can be done in an iterative manner: for a collection of n events, candidate 1-sequences are generated, followed by candidate 2-sequences, etc. It is obvious that this simple approach is impractical because there are exponential numbers of sub-sequences contained in a data sequence, too many to compute in practice, particularly when data sequences are long. The problem is worse than finding frequent itemsets in the context of Boolean association rule mining. In Boolean association mining, given two items, i_1 and i_2, only one candidate 2-itemset, $\{i_1, i_2\}$, can be generated. However, more than one candidate 2-sequence, namely, <{i_1}, {i_1}>, <{i_1}, {i_2}>, <{i_2}, {i_1}>, and <{i_1, i_2}>, can be generated from two events. This is because the order of events matters in a sequence.

The Apriori principles still apply to sequence pattern discovery. This is because any data sequence that contains a k-sequence must also contain all of its $(k-1)$-sub-sequences. Therefore, if a k-sequence is frequent, all of its $(k-1)$-sub-sequences are also frequent. Any extensions of an infrequent k-sequence are also bound to be infrequent. The basic Apriori algorithm for finding frequent itemsets for Boolean association rule discovery can be adapted to locate frequent sequential patterns. The adapted algorithm is presented in pseudo-code:

```
algorithm AprioriAdaptedSeq(DB: database; MS: support threshold): set of
                              sequences;
begin
    F₁ := {i | i ∈ I and i.count ≥ MS};   // I is the collection of all events
    k := 2;
    while Fₖ₋₁ ≠ ∅ do
        Cₖ := apriori_gen(Fₖ₋₁);
        for each data sequence t in DB do
            Cₜ := subsequence(Cₖ, t);
            for each candidate k-sequence c in Cₜ do
                c.count := c.count + 1;
            end for;
        end for;
        Fₖ := {c | c ∈ Cₖ and c.count ≥ MS};
        k := k + 1;
    end while;
    return (F₁ ∪ F₂ ∪ ... ∪ Fₖ)
end;
```

The adapted algorithm is almost the same as the original algorithm. The apriori_gen operation needs to be modified to deal with sequences. The apriori_gen operation is meant to generate new candidate k-sequences based on frequent $(k-1)$-sequences. The merge step is modified for two specific cases: the base case when $k = 2$ and the general case when $k > 2$. In the base case, two frequent 1-sequences are merged into new candidate 2-sequences: given two frequent 1-sequences $<\{i_1\}>$ and $<\{i_2\}>$, four candidate 2-sequences, $<\{i_1\}, \{i_1\}>$, $<\{i_1\}, \{i_2\}>$, $<\{i_2\}, \{i_1\}>$ and $<\{i_1, i_2\}>$ can be made. For instance, frequent 1-sequences, $<\{1\}>$ and $<\{2\}>$ can be merged into $<\{1\}, \{1\}>$, $<\{1\}, \{2\}>$, $<\{2\}, \{1\}>$ and $<\{1, 2\}>$.

In the general case, a sequence s_1 merges with another sequence s_2 only if the sub-sequence obtained by removing the first event from s_1 is identical to the sub-sequence obtained by removing the last event from s_2. The new candidate sequence is the sequence s_1 concatenated with the last event from the sequence s_2. Whether the last event is included in the last element of s_1 or saved as a new element depends on the following situations:

- If the last two events in s_2 belong to the same element, the last event of s_2 becomes part of the last element in the newly merged sequence.

- If the last two events in s_2 belong to different elements, the last event of s_2 becomes a separate element at the end of the newly merged sequence.

For instance, frequent 3-sequences $<\{1\}, \{2\}, \{3\}>$ and $<\{2\}, \{3\}, \{4\}>$ can be merged into a new candidate 4-sequence $<\{1\}, \{2\}, \{3\}, \{4\}>$. Frequent 3-sequences $<\{1\}, \{5\}, \{3\}>$ and $<\{5\}, \{3, 4\}>$ can be merged into a new candidate 4-sequence $<\{1\}, \{5\}, \{3, 4\}>$.

As in the original apriori_gen operation, a candidate k-sequence can also be pruned in order to reduce the number of unnecessary candidates before support is counted. The idea is the same: a candidate k-sequence is pruned if at least one of its $(k-1)$-sub-sequences is not in the current seed set F_{k-1} and hence infrequent. For instance, given $<\{1\}, \{2\}, \{3\}, \{4\}>$ is a newly merged candidate sequence from <{1}, {2}, {3}> and <{2}, {3}, {4}>, if either <{1}, {2}, {4}> or <{1}, {3}, {4}> are not in F_3, then <{1}, {2}, {3}, {4}> is pruned because it is bound to be infrequent.

The process of counting support is the same as that in the original Apriori algorithm. Support for a sequence only refers to the fraction of data sequences in the data set that contain the sequence. The candidates contained in a data sequence are first located with the subsequence function. The support counters of the candidates are then incremented. By the end of the process, the infrequent candidates are discarded and the frequent ones are selected into the seed set for the next round of candidate generation. For the customer transaction data set presented in Figure 9.4, given the minimum support threshold of 50%, i.e. at least two customer transaction sequences must contain a candidate sequence, the following are some of the frequent sequential patterns:

```
<{1}, {1}>          support = 50%
<{3}, {1}>          support = 50%
<{2}, {1, 6}>       support = 50%
<{2, 3}, {1, 6}>    support = 50%
```

From a frequent sequence, a sequential rule of the form $s_1 \Rightarrow s_2$ could be derived. For instance, a rule <{2, 3}> $\Rightarrow$ <{1, 6}> holds with confidence = support(<{2, 3}, {1, 6}>)/support(<{2, 3}>) = 2/2 = 100%. This rule, in the context of a transaction database, means that customers who purchase items 2 and 3 in one transaction will definitely purchase items 1 and 6 in another transaction at a later stage.

9.4.3 Time Constraints and Counting Schemes

Counting support for a sub-sequence has so far been based on the occurrence of a sub-sequence in an entire data sequence. The time period within a data sequence is ignored. Consider Table 9.2, which contains information about students taking different courses over three years of study.

A frequent sequential pattern <{statistics}, {data mining}> is contained by all sequences in the data set. According to the current way of counting support, the pattern should have a support score of 100%. This way of counting support considers the time span as the maximum and the occurrences of the frequent sequence in all data sequences are counted. However, sometimes, time difference does matter. For instance, the time when statistics is taken may be of particular interest. In other words, there is a difference between taking statistics in the first year and taking it in the second year or the third year before the data mining course is taken in the third year.

The time gap between elements of a sequence can also be viewed from another different angle. In Table 9.2, if consecutive timestamps 1, 2, 3, etc. are assigned to elements of the data sequences, for the sequential pattern <{statistics}, {data mining}>, the time gap between {statistics} and {data mining} in the first data sequence is $3 - 1 = 2$, and the time gap in the second data sequence is $3 - 3 = 0$. If the

TABLE 9.2	Student-course data sequences
Student	**Courses**
A	<{statistics}, {database, programming}, {expert systems, data mining}>
B	<{programming}, {database}, {statistics, data mining}>
C	<{mathematics}, {statistics, database}, {data mining}>

time gap allowed is 2, the support for the pattern remains at 100%. However, if the time gap allowed is 1, then support for the sequential pattern drops from 100% to 67% because the first data sequence no longer supports the pattern. In general, maximum and minimum time gaps can be defined. Serving as a mask, the parameters determine the result of counting the support.

Events within an element of a sequence are assumed to happen at the same time; there is no temporal order among events of the same element. However, events within the same element may occur at different points in time. We can put the events within a window of a certain size where events along temporal dimension can be specified. In Table 9.2, student B takes both statistics and data mining in the third year of study. However, the student may take statistics before data mining in the same year, say in the first term.

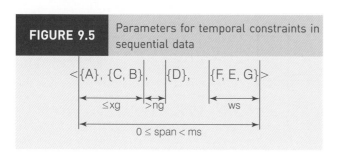

| **FIGURE 9.5** | Parameters for temporal constraints in sequential data |

For sequential pattern discovery, it is necessary to study some temporal constraint parameters and understand the corresponding mechanisms for counting support. Figure 9.5 illustrates four temporal parameters: maximum span (ms), event-set window size (ws), maximum time gap (xg) and minimum time gap (ng).

The maximum span refers to the maximum time difference allowed between the latest and earliest occurrences of events in the entire sequence. The event-set window size represents the maximum time difference allowed between the latest and earliest occurrences of events within a single element. The maximum gap is the maximum time difference allowed between the latest occurrence of an event in an element and the earliest occurrence of an event in its immediately preceding element. The minimum gap is the minimum time difference required between the earliest occurrence of an event in an element and the latest occurrence of an event in its immediately preceding event-set.

With the temporal constraint parameters, given a data sequence and a sub-sequence whose support is to be counted, a number of different counting schemes may be employed, and the results will differ. The schemes are summarized as follows:

- COBJ: This method counts the occurrence of the sub-sequence as one per data sequence (data object). This is the method that has been used so far.

- CWIN: A time window of a fixed size is defined. It slides along the timeline of an object, one unit a time. All appearances of the sub-sequence within the time window are counted as one. The method counts the number of the time windows as the support.

- CMINWIN: A minimal window of occurrence refers to the smallest time interval in which the sub-sequence occurs. The method counts the number of such minimal windows as the support.

- CDIST_O: A distinct occurrence of the sub-sequence is defined as the set of event–timestamp pairs such that there has to be at least one new event–timestamp pair that is different from a previously counted occurrence. The method counts the number of such pairs as the support.

- CDIST: This method is similar to CDIST_O, but it does not allow overlapping of event–timestamp pairs. The method counts the number of pairs as the support.

Figure 9.6 illustrates the use of the counting schemes. It assumes that ws = 0, ng = 0, mg = 1 and ms = 2 units of time. The data sequence is <{A}, {A}, {A, B}, {B}, {A, B}, {A, B}, {B}> and the candidate sequence to be counted is <{A}, {B}>.

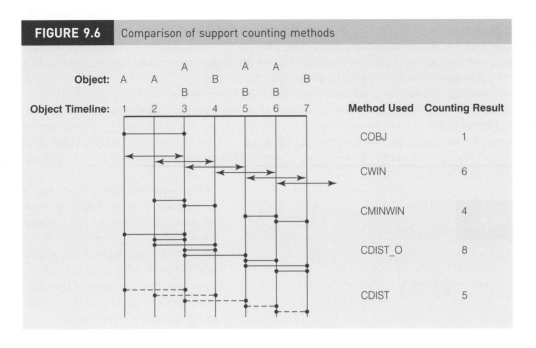

| FIGURE 9.6 | Comparison of support counting methods |

As can be seen in Figure 9.6, the COBJ method counts a candidate only once, even if it appears many times in the object. The CWIN method defines a sliding time window with maximum span of two time units. The window slides across the object by one unit of time and counts all occurrences of the sub-sequence it sees. There are six such windows and hence the support for the candidate is six. The CMINWIN method defines the minimal time interval between elements {A} and {B} as 1. The number of such minimal windows containing the sub-sequence is four. When the CDIST_O method is used, there are eight distinct occurrences of the candidate sequence at times (1, 3), (2, 3), (2, 4), (3, 4), (3, 5), (5, 6), (5, 7) and (6, 7). The CDIST method identifies five non-overlapping event–timestamp pairs: (1, 3), (2, 4), (3, 5), (5, 6) and (6, 7) for the candidate sequence.

In practice, which constraint parameters to consider and which counting scheme to use depends very much on the purpose of discovery. A good data mining software environment should allow the end user to choose the parameters and select a suitable counting scheme.

Mining sequence patterns is an expensive task. The Apriori algorithm is inefficient. This inefficiency is partly due to the size of the search space and the complexity of the problem, and partly due to the generate-and-prune strategy behind the algorithm: in sequence discovery, there are simply too many candidates to generate and the database has to be searched many times to count support.

9.4.4 Generalized Sequential Patterns

The sequential patterns so far described contain only 'items': each event within a sequence is the occurrence of an attribute value. As with generalized association rules, taxonomies over attribute values may also be available. In this case, sequential patterns state ordered appearances of not only items but also categories. For instance, if a purchase of Coke is followed by a purchase of loaf bread, and a purchase of orange juice is followed by a purchase of baguette, a sequential pattern stating purchases of soft drinks are followed by purchases of bakery products may be found.

An algorithm, known as GSP, was developed to mine such generalized sequential patterns. Based on the Apriori principles, the algorithm takes a set of data sequences and a taxonomy as inputs and discovers all sequential patterns whose support is greater than a user-defined threshold. The algorithm also considers time constraints such as maximum time gap, minimum time gap and a sliding window size all of which are specified by the user. The algorithm follows the idea of the adapted algorithm in Section 9.1.2, including the categories in the data sequences before candidate sequences are generated and their support counted.

The solution suffers the same problem as that for the generalized association rule discovery: the inclusion of categories increases the number of candidate sequences generated, prolongs the process of counting supports during the discovery process, and may result in more sequential patterns that are frequent in the end. To deal with this problem, the algorithm adopts a two-phase strategy for counting support, eliminating sequences that are not contained in the elements of a data sequence. Another follow-up algorithm, called mining frequent sequences (MFS), uses a two-stage procedure to count support: the support for frequent sequences is estimated in a sample of the database and then the database is searched to check and refine the candidate sequences. Details of the algorithms can be found in the articles referred to in the Bibliographical Notes.

9.5   ASSOCIATION RULE DISCOVERY IN WEKA

As mentioned in Chapter 8, association rule mining is a weak point of Weka. Solutions in Weka are mainly designed for mining patterns from relational tables. Because of this, the mining of Boolean association rules is indirect. This section therefore demonstrates only the mining of quantitative (or multidimensional) association rules.

9.5.1 Mining Quantitative Association Rules

The current version of Weka provides four methods: Apriori, PredictiveApriori, Tertius and a meta-learner algorithm, called FilteredAssociator, that enables the use of a filter in combination with a mining method, combining data preprocessing with association rule mining.

For the purposes of demonstration, we use the data set in `bank.arff`, which can be downloaded from the official Weka website. It contains records regarding personal details, types of bank account and whether or not to have a personal equity plan (pep) for 600 anonymous individuals. Figure 9.7(a) shows part of the data set and Figure 9.7(b) shows the summary on the Preprocess tab.

The Apriori algorithm implemented in Weka cannot adaptively deal with the merging of smaller intervals to larger intervals for quantitative attributes. This means that not only must the initial discretization of quantitative attributes be done before the mining takes place, but also the data miners have to repeat the mining process manually to find the best discretization with respect to the result rules. For this demonstration, two numeric attributes of the data set, Age and Income, are treated as follows. The attribute Age is divided into six intervals by the equal-frequency method (as recommended in Section 9.2.2). The attribute Income is divided into three intervals of roughly equal width. This decision is rather arbitrary. The discretization may have to be modified in light of the quality of any association rules.

Besides the discretization, the numeric attribute Children is converted to nominal type by using the NumericToNominal filter because there are only a few values in the domain. The rest of the attributes are all nominal and, hence, can be left without any pre-processing. Before the association rule mining, the first attribute (customer number) is removed because its unique value will prevent any association having the support of more than one transaction.

Association rule mining is performed on the Associate tab. Pressing the Choose button in the Associator block (Figure 9.8) activates the display of the method menu. For this demonstration, the Apriori method is selected from the list and the method command and its default parameters

---

FIGURE 9.7   Data set for quantitative association rule mining

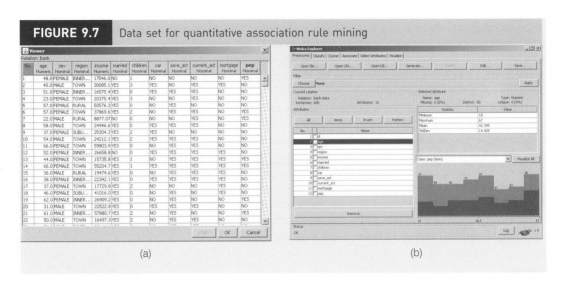

(a)   (b)

FIGURE 9.8   Mining quantitative association rules

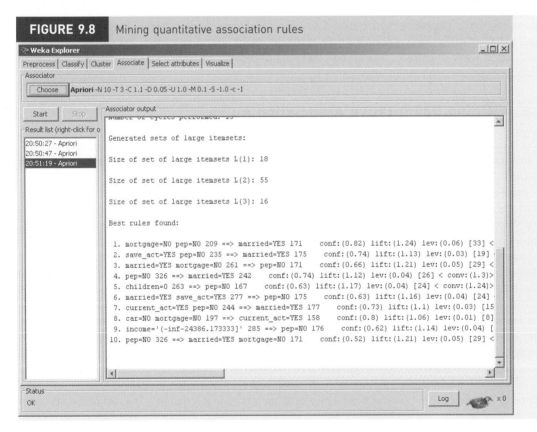

---

are displayed in the box next to the Choose button. The parameters can be modified by clicking on the command box. For this demonstration, we use the default settings except for the metricType parameter, which is set to 'Conviction' to show results of different quality evaluation parameters. The result is displayed in the Associator output window, as shown in Figure 9.8.

The top 10 rules are discovered because of the default setting of the number of rules. Rule 9 has a confidence level of 62% but a lift of 1.14, indicating many people within the income range do not have a personal equity plan. Rule 10 has confidence of 52% and lift of 1.21 states that among people without a personal equity plan, over half of them are married and do not have a mortgage. The top 10 rules will change if a different evaluation measure is used.

9.5.2 Mining Sequential Patterns

Weka version 3.6.1 offers a version of the Generalized Sequential Pattern algorithm. Unfortunately the algorithm is not available from the Explorer module, but only in the command-line module, SimpleCLI. The facility is also quite restrictive in the sense that the number of elements is fixed and none of the temporal constraints are supported.

For this demonstration, we create a data set that contains details about students taking courses over semesters is created. Figure 9.9(a) shows the contents of this file. There are three students. Each row represents the courses that a student has studied each semester. The data set shows that certain courses follow certain other courses across semesters.

FIGURE 9.9 Mining sequential patterns

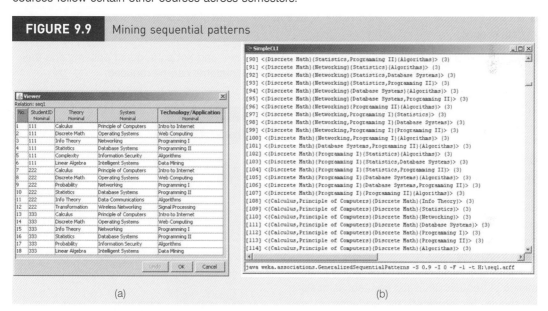

(a)   (b)

Operating the command-line module in Weka is very simple. The command is entered in the command area at the bottom of the window (see Figure 9.9(b)), referring to the data file by its full path name. The result of the data mining is displayed in the main window area. Figure 9.9(b) shows a few of the hundreds of sequential patterns that have been found.

Many sequential patterns in the list can be validated by comparing the patterns with the data set content. For example, Calculus and Principle of Computers are followed by Discrete Math, which is in turn followed by Information Theory. This sequential pattern has a support of 100%.

9.6 INCREMENTAL MINING OF ASSOCIATION RULES

Real-life databases are often dynamic in the sense that new data records are inserted and existing records are removed periodically or randomly. Such change is even more apparent in online applications. Furthermore, in certain application areas, such as share prices in stock markets and device access logs in computer network maintenance systems, data changes are frequent and constant. This type of data is known as a *data stream*.

9.6.1 The Problem

Data changes result in new association patterns and invalidation of existing patterns. If the existing knowledge about associations is not updated, inconsistency between the data content and the knowledge occurs. One simple approach is to periodically perform the association rule mining with the most updated database content. Most existing algorithms for association rule mining consider the input database as a static data set and the entire database has to be scanned many times to find the frequent patterns. Therefore, this simple approach may be feasible only when the frequency of change is low or the database is small. When the data changes frequently, the approach quickly becomes impractical: the amount of time taken to rediscover all associations does not match the speed of data change. More realistic solutions include:

■ developing new algorithms that update rather than re-discover the patterns;

■ limiting the scope of association patterns so that the update of the patterns matches the speed of data change;

■ using approximate algorithms to maintain a set of frequent and not so frequent patterns and their support so that the heavy workload of discovering new patterns can be reduced.

As with the static situation, incremental mining of association rules is mainly concerned with incremental mining of frequent itemsets. Given a database *DB*, let *L* be the set of all frequent itemsets found in *DB*. Let *db* represent a database increment and let *DB'* represent the updated database. The problem of incremental mining of frequent itemsets is to find *L'* that contains frequent itemsets which have support greater than or equal to the user-defined minimum threshold.

Figure 9.10 illustrates the route for incremental mining of frequent itemsets: frequent itemsets in *L'* should be obtained by updating *L* with reference to *DB* and *db*. Frequent itemsets in *L'* must have the support of *DB'* but they should not be directly discovered from *DB'* because of the cost involved.

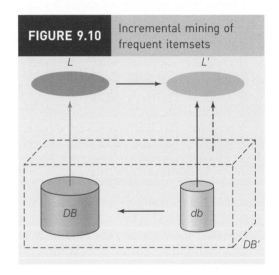

FIGURE 9.10 Incremental mining of frequent itemsets

9.6.2 Early Methods for Incremental Mining

Fast update (FUP) algorithm With *DB*, *db*, *L* and the user-defined minimum support threshold *ms* as inputs, the algorithm follows the Apriori principle of generating and pruning candidate itemsets iteratively from small itemsets to large itemsets. At iteration *k*, the algorithm performs the following steps:

1 Generate a collection C_k of candidate *k*-itemsets from the current seed set L'_{k-1}.

2 Scan through the increment *db* to count the supports for the existing frequent *k*-itemsets in L_k and for the newly created candidate *k*-itemsets in C_k.

3 Save directly into L'_k the frequent k-itemsets in L_k with support greater than or equal to $ms \times (|DB|+|db|)$.

4 Drop the remaining k-itemsets in L_k: they have become infrequent in light of increment db.

5 Prune the newly created candidate k-itemsets in C_k with support less than $ms \times |db|$ because they are bound to be infrequent.

6 Scan DB and count the supports for the remaining candidate k-itemsets in C_k, saving those with support greater than or equal to $ms \times (|DB|+|db|)$ into L'_k and dropping those with less support than that.

The algorithm terminates when no more candidates can be made.

Borders algorithm   A *border* itemset is one which is itself infrequent but all of its non-empty proper subsets are frequent. Border itemsets mark the border between frequent and infrequent itemsets in a lattice structure. For instance, in the lattice in Figure 8.2 (page 222), {A,B} and {A,E} are border itemsets. The Borders algorithm initially assumes that all border itemsets for the current collection L of all frequent itemsets are saved in set B. The algorithm then constantly maintains the support counts for frequent itemsets in L and border itemsets in B in the light of increment db. The increment is scanned and the support counters for all frequent itemsets and border itemsets are updated. The new frequent itemsets, including *promoted* border itemsets (i.e. those border itemsets that have become frequent), are saved into L. Based on the updated content of L, new border itemsets are constructed as a superset whose proper subsets with one item less are all elements of L. New border itemsets are then collected into B. The main body of the algorithm follows an iterative process similar to that of the Apriori algorithm: it generates candidate $k+1$-itemsets from previous frequent k-itemsets and promoted border k-itemsets and then searches DB and db to count the support. The newly discovered frequent candidates are added into the final collection L and the infrequent candidates are added into the collection of border itemsets. The algorithm terminates when no more frequent itemsets can be found.

The FUP algorithm is simple and several times faster than applying the original Apriori algorithm on DB' every time DB is updated. However, the algorithm is considered slow because it relies on scanning the original database at least once per iteration in order to count the support for newly created candidates. Reported experimental results show that the Borders algorithm performs well compared to the FUP algorithm. The drawback of the Borders algorithm is that both DB and db have to be searched a number of times, depending on the number of iterations required.

9.6.3 The SWF Algorithm

Some more recent algorithms have focused on how to reduce the creation of candidates and further limit the scan of DB. Among them is the sliding-window filtering (SWF) algorithm, which promises to scan the database only twice. The SWF algorithm considers a given database as a sequence of partitions collected along the time dimension. At any time, a partition Δ^- is removed from the beginning of the database and a partition Δ^+ is added at the end. The unchanged part of the database is referred to as D^-. A sliding window of n partitions reflects the current content of the database.

Figure 9.11 illustrates such a time-variant transaction database viewed through a sliding window of three partitions. The initial database $db^{1,3}$ consists of partitions p_1, p_2 and p_3, each of which comprises three transactions. Partition p_1 is then removed and partition p_4 is added. The new database, denoted as $db^{2,4}$, comes into the view of the sliding window. In the context of the changes, frequent itemsets supported by p_1 may become infrequent and be removed, frequent itemsets supported by D^- are brought forward to the new database and their support is renewed, and new frequent itemsets supported by p_4 are added into the database.

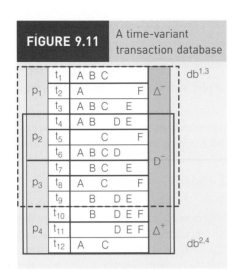

FIGURE 9.11 — A time-variant transaction database

The SWF algorithm searches for frequent itemsets of different sizes, partition by partition. The algorithm has two procedures: the pre-processing procedure and the incremental procedure. The pre-processing procedure is called at the beginning when the algorithm is used to mine frequent itemsets for the first time. The procedure returns not only a collection of all frequent itemsets in a given database, but also a collection of candidate itemsets of different sizes, known as the Cumulative Filter (CF). The incremental procedure is then used to mine frequent itemsets when Δ^- is removed and Δ^+ is added. The procedure takes the addition and deletion of partitions, the existing collection of frequent itemsets and the current cumulative filter as inputs, and returns the updated collection of all frequent itemsets and the updated cumulative filter. For each itemset in the cumulative filter, a support counter and a start partition number are maintained. The procedures are outlined and illustrated using the example database in Figure 9.11, assuming the minimum support threshold is 40%.

Pre-processing Procedure   The pre-processing procedure works as follows. Given a database db and a support threshold s, the database is first divided into n partitions p_1, p_2, ..., p_n, expressed as $db^{1,n}$. The sizes of the partitions are saved for later use. For the database in Figure 9.11, the database $db^{1,3}$ within the initial sliding window has three partitions each of which has three transactions. The filtering threshold is therefore $0.4 \times 3 = 2$ transactions.

The partitions are then searched one after another. Candidate 2-itemsets within a partition p_i are formed and the support for the candidates is counted. New candidate 2-itemsets with the support of at least $s \times |p_i|$ transactions are saved into the cumulative filter CF, and their start partition numbers are recorded as the current partition number. These numbers are used in the calculation of the cumulative support.

For the database in Figure 9.11, the pre-processing procedure scans through partitions p_1, p_2 and p_3 sequentially. In p_1, new candidate 2-itemsets AB, AC, AE, AF, BC, BE and CE are first created. Among them, only AB, AC and BC have sufficient support and are saved into the CF. If a candidate 2-itemset already exists in the cumulative filter CF (i.e. it was obtained when previous partitions were searched), its support is incremented according to the support of the transactions within the partition. Candidate 2-itemsets whose cumulative support is less than their own filtering thresholds, i.e. $s \times (|p_1|+|p_2|+\ldots+|p_k|)$, are removed from the CF. For the database in Figure 9.11, the candidate 2-itemsets for p_2 are AB, AC, AD, AE, BC, BD, BE, CD, CF and DE. Among them, AB, AC and BC are already in CF and their cumulative supports satisfy the filtering threshold of $0.4 \times (3+3) = 3$ transactions so they stay in CF. Among the rest, only AD and BD satisfy the threshold of $0.4 \times 3 = 2$ transactions and hence are saved in CF.

Finally in partition p_3, the candidate 2-itemsets are AC, AF, BC, BD, BE, CE, CF and DE. Candidates AB, AC, AD, BC and BD already exist in CF. As AB, AC and BC were created in p_1, their filtering threshold is $0.4 \times (|p_1|+|p_2|+|p_3|) = 0.4 \times (3 + 3 + 3) = 4$ transactions. All of them satisfy the threshold and are kept in CF. AD and BD have a filtering threshold of $0.4 \times (p_2|+|p_3|) = 3$ transactions. AD only has the support of two transactions and is removed from the CF; BD has the support of three transactions and stays in CF. Among the new candidates for p_3, only BE has the support of two transactions and is saved in CF.

The pre-processing procedure then uses candidate 2-itemsets to create all new candidate itemsets iteratively. The procedure assumes that all candidate 1-itemsets, i.e. individual items, are already given.

At each iteration, candidate itemsets with one extra item are merged from two candidates in the collection in the previous iteration. The support counter for a candidate itemset is initialized to zero. During the iterative process, no attempt is made to scan the database. Eventually, all candidate itemsets are saved in a collection. Then the database is scanned. The support for all candidates in the collection are counted. Candidates with support that is greater than or equal to $s \times |db^{1,n}|$ are saved into the collection of all frequent itemsets L.

For the transaction database in Figure 9.11, candidates A, B, C, D, E, F are given and CF contains {AB, AC, BC, BD, BE}. From the candidates in CF, new candidates such as ABC can be made. All candidates that have sufficient support, $0.4 \times (|db^{1,3}|) = 4$ transactions, are frequent itemsets; this includes A, B, C, E, AB, AC, BC and BE.

Incremental procedure The incremental procedure consists of three main steps:

1 Find candidate 2-itemsets in D^-, i.e. the original database after Δ^- is removed.

2 Find candidate 2-itemsets in $D^- + \Delta^+$, i.e. the new database after Δ^+ is added.

3 Scan the new database $D^- + \Delta^+$ and find all frequent itemsets.

In the first step, the candidate 2-itemsets in the cumulative filter CF obtained from the pre-processing procedure are loaded into memory. The partitions in the Δ^- portion of the database are searched one by one before the portion is removed. For each partition, each candidate 2-itemset supported by the partition is updated as follows: its support counter is reduced by the number of transactions in the partition that contain the candidate and the start partition number of the candidate is increased by 1, indicating the update to its filtering threshold. After the update, if the candidate no longer has sufficient support, it is removed from CF. For the database in Figure 9.11, the candidate 2-itemsets AB, AC, BC, BD and BE are loaded from CF. After scanning through partition p_1, AB, AC and BC are removed from CF due to lack of support.

In the second step, the partitions in Δ^+ are searched sequentially. In each partition, candidate 2-itemsets supported by the transactions within the partition are formed. The start partition number and the support counter for each candidate is set in the same way as in the pre-processing procedure. Those candidates with sufficient support according to their own filtering thresholds are added into CF if they are new. For the candidate 2-itemsets that already exist in CF, their support counters are updated with respect to the partition. For the database in Figure 9.11, the candidate 2-itemsets for p_4 are AC, BD, BE, BF, DE, DF, and EF. Among them, BD and BE are existing candidates in CF. BD has insufficient support and is removed from CF. BE has sufficient support and stays in CF. Of the new candidate 2-itemsets DE, DF and EF also have sufficient support and are added to CF.

The third step is the same as the second part of the pre-processing procedure. All candidate itemsets of different sizes are generated from the candidate 2-itemsets in CF. The procedure then scans $D^- + \Delta^+$ to count the support for each candidate in order to find the frequent itemsets. For the database in Figure 9.11, the candidates are used to generate larger candidate itemsets such as BDE and DEF. Eventually, the entire $D^- + \Delta^+$ is searched for the second time, counting the support for all candidate itemsets. As a result, the frequent itemsets A, B, C, D, E, F BD, BE and DE are found.

9.7 PARALLEL MINING OF ASSOCIATION RULES

The discovery of association rules is a combinatorial problem. Given a specific setting of parameters, such as minimum support and minimum confidence, there can be a huge number of combinations to be searched and, as a result, a large number of frequent itemsets may be discovered. In Section 8.6.1, we mentioned that the number of frequent itemsets grows exponentially as the minimum support threshold decreases linearly. Due to the fact that sufficient support for an item is also sufficient support for the categories of that item and that sufficient support for a narrow range of attribute values is also sufficient support for a wider range, the situation significantly worsens for generalized and quantitative association rule mining.

There is a limit to improving efficiency by exploiting implementation techniques and developing novel solutions based on a single processor. Ultimately, any substantial difference in speed of computation can only be made through the use of parallel or distributed processing. This section briefly introduces the principles of parallel mining of association rules and outlines a number of different approaches and algorithms.

9.7.1 Approaches

The principle behind parallel processing is 'divide and conquer', i.e. we break a big problem down into a set of smaller problems and use a number of processors to solve the smaller problems concurrently. However, how to apply the principle in finding a parallel solution depends on a number of factors.

The first influential factor is the architecture of a multi-processor machine. Each processor of the machine either has its own local distributed memory (DMM) or a shared common system memory (SMP). The DMM approach, also known as the 'shared nothing' approach, relies on local data access most of the time and hence achieves the desirable divide-and-conquer state more easily. However, in order to access data in the local memory of another processor, a processor has to synchronize with the other processor through message passing, which increases the communication cost among processors. In the SMP approach, since each processor has full access to the entire system memory, little or no communication cost is incurred. However, the bandwidth of a common bus can limit scalability and the exclusive locking mechanism can be complex. The main focus of DMM-based parallel solutions is, therefore, to minimize the amount of communication between processors. The main objective for SMP-based solutions is to minimize attempts to share the common segments of memory.

Another influential factor is the parallelism of data or tasks. Data involved in the discovery of association rules include transactions, itemsets and rules. Tasks include generating candidate itemsets, counting support and selecting frequent itemsets, and generating rule expressions. Data parallelism means that data are partitioned among the processors and located in the local memories of the processors. The partition is physical in the DMM approach and logical in the SMP approach. Each processor works on its own local memory and conducts the same discovery tasks. Task parallelism means that different processors are assigned different tasks. In order to ensure the local autonomy of each processor, data may need to be replicated.

In any parallelization of data and tasks, balanced workloads on processors ensure the best use of the divide-and-conquer strategy to share the work evenly among the processors. A good balance of workload may not always be easy to achieve. Many practical parallel algorithms utilize static load balancing by initially dividing the data or tasks evenly. However, the balance cannot be assured because some data partitions contain more patterns to be discovered than others. Some tasks may also take longer than others. Dynamic load balancing means reassigning tasks during the mining process to balance out the workload among processors. Because of the difficulties involved, not many existing algorithms take this approach.

9.7.2 Algorithms

A large number of parallel algorithms have been developed since the problem of association rule mining was first identified. Almost all the algorithms are designated for finding frequent itemsets. The

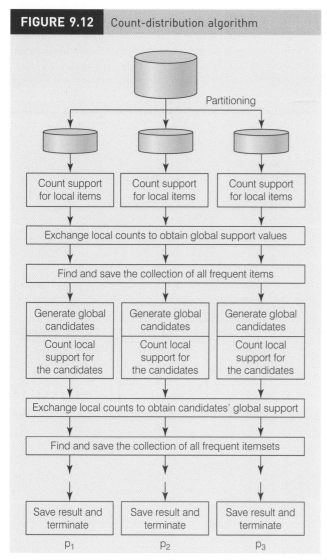

FIGURE 9.12 Count-distribution algorithm

majority of them are DMM-based, static-load-balancing methods that are further developed on the base of some known sequential algorithms. This section explains the principles of a number of methods that follow the sequential Apriori algorithm. Since many of them share the same ideas, we outline only three algorithms with three parallelization strategies.

Count-distribution algorithm The transaction database is evenly divided among the processors (Figure 9.12). In the first pass, each processor uses items from its own local partition to compile its own list of candidate items and calculates their support. Then, the processors exchange local counts to obtain a global list of candidate items with their global support and produce a global collection of all frequent items. In other iterations, each processor obtains its own collection of new candidate k-itemsets from the global collection of all frequent $(k-1)$-itemsets and searches its local memory to count the partial support for the candidates. The processors then communicate the partial counts to each other to obtain the global support for each candidate, select from their own candidates the frequent itemsets and save them into the global collection. Each processor makes its own decision whether to terminate the process or continue to the next round. Since the algorithm uses a local copy of all candidate itemsets, it limits the amount of communication between processors. The drawback is that the entire collection of new candidates is replicated, causing stress to the local memory.

Data-distribution algorithm Again, the transaction database is evenly divided among the processors (Figure 9.13). Instead of maintaining a separate copy of the entire collection of new candidates, the algorithm allocates a disjoint subset of new candidate itemsets to each processor. It is the task of each processor to count the global support for its own candidate itemsets. This means each processor must use its own data page and the data page from other processors, increasing the amount of communication between processors. Each processor then selects the frequent itemsets from its own collection of candidates and exchanges them with other processors in order to obtain a global collection of all frequent k-itemsets for the next round. Again, each processor makes its own decision whether or not to terminate the process.

Candidate-distribution algorithm Support for every newly generated candidate itemset by every transaction must be counted. This causes the count-distribution algorithm to replicate the candidate list and the data-distribution algorithm to broadcast the local partition of the database; both of them exchange partial counts in every iteration. The candidate-distribution algorithm solves the problem by reducing communication and balancing the workloads of processors at a heuristically determined iteration. Before this iteration, the algorithm behaves in the same way as either the data-distribution or count-distribution algorithm. At the iteration, the collection of frequent k-itemsets is partitioned so that each processor generates a disjoint subset of candidate $(k+1)$-itemsets, independently of the other processors. The input transaction database is also repartitioned so that each processor only needs to search its own partition to count the support for its own candidates. From this iteration onwards, each processor generates candidates, counts the support for them and selects frequent itemsets from them, independently of other processors. Once the local collection of frequent itemsets is obtained, the collection is broadcast to other processors for them to prune away unnecessary new candidate itemsets.

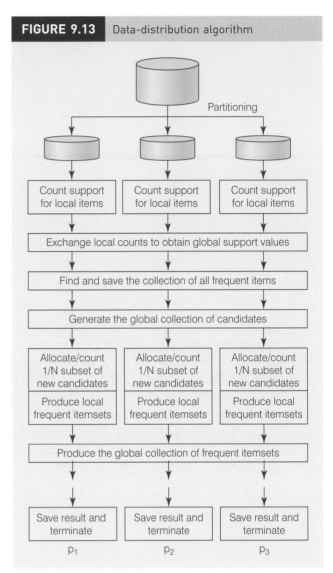

FIGURE 9.13   Data-distribution algorithm

9.7.3 Challenges

Although a lot of progress has been made in parallel mining of association rules, a number of issues are yet to be fully addressed. The following list outlines some of the difficulties that should prompt efforts towards novel solutions:

- *High dimensionality*: In association rule mining, data dimensionality refers to the number of items. In real-life applications of Boolean association rules, the number of items can be as high as tens of thousands. In the context of generalized and quantitative association rules, the number of items is even higher because of the involvement of item categories and partitioning of quantitative attributes. For many parallel algorithms, high dimensionality means large numbers of candidate itemsets to be generated, particularly the candidate 2-itemsets, where all possible combinations of pairs of items are attempted. Dealing with such a huge number of candidate itemsets even in a parallel processing environment is a big burden for algorithms. Parallel solutions that are based on new ideas of avoiding generating candidate 2-itemsets are needed.

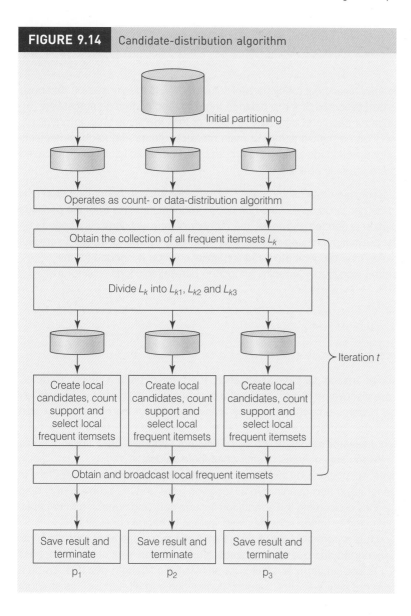

FIGURE 9.14 | Candidate-distribution algorithm

- *Large data size*: In many practical applications of association rule mining, the transaction database is often measured not in gigabytes but in terabytes. Such a large database size means that even parallel solutions have to consider reducing the number of times that the database is scanned. However, most existing solutions, showing their sequential origins, still scan the database many times. Moreover, many parallel solutions assume that the local memory is sufficient to hold a structure for candidate itemsets, but this may not be the case when the transaction database is extremely large. New solutions are needed to deal with the situation where disk access during the mining process for candidate itemsets is unavoidable.

- *Data location*: In many real-life applications, data are fragmented and distributed across a network of database servers on different physical sites. The fragmentation can be horizontal (different servers store different transactions) or vertical (different servers store different items). Most parallel solutions assume horizontal partitioning of the database, which may not be most effective for vertically fragmented distributed databases. Solutions based on vertical partitions therefore need further attention.

- *Data skewness and dynamic load balancing*: Many parallel solutions divide the transaction database evenly among the available processors in order to balance the workload so that all processors proceed at more or less the same pace and terminate at more or less the same time. In practice, however, data can be skewed: some partitions may contain more candidate and frequent itemsets than others, causing unbalanced workloads among the processors. Parallel solutions that are based on dynamic load balancing are urgently needed.

- *Rule generation*: Almost all association rule mining solutions consider the rule generation step a straightforward process and do not focus on it. If the number of frequent itemsets from the previous step is small, no parallel solution is needed. However, the number of frequent itemsets depends on factors such as the setting for the minimum support threshold. When the number of frequent itemsets is large, many association rules may be generated and a parallel solution is needed for the generation of rules, to share the workload. Currently, almost no parallel solutions exist for this process.

9.8   SUMMARY

In this chapter, the problems of mining various association rules have been studied in detail. Generalized association rules are discovered in the context of a data abstraction hierarchy. Association rules of this kind show not only patterns among data values at the leaf level of the hierarchy but also patterns between concepts of data abstraction at higher levels of the hierarchy. Quantitative rules represent associations between values or ranges of values of different attributes. Sequential patterns reflect temporal associations between sets of items or sets of attribute values.

This chapter studied possible adaptations of the basic Apriori algorithm to solve the problem of finding frequent itemsets for generalized and quantitative association rules and the problem of finding sequential patterns. Particular issues concerning the adaptation include counting support for concepts, partitioning quantitative attributes, and counting schemes with various temporal constraints.

The strength of an association rule is normally judged by the level of support and level of confidence, including the level of lift. For generalized and quantitative association rules, the level of interestingness with respect to rule redundancy is also an important factor for showing the strength of a rule. To be a strong rule, the rule should have not only sufficient support, confidence and lift, but also its strength must be significantly higher than that of its ancestor rules.

This chapter demonstrated how to use the limited facilities in Weka to mine quantitative association rules and sequential patterns.

The chapter also studied two recent developments of association rule mining, incremental mining and parallel or distributed mining of association rules. Many applications have a dynamic data source whose content changes substantially over time. Online maintenance of discovered patterns and new patterns in light of the data changes is more sensible than rediscovery of patterns from scratch. The chapter outlines two early simple algorithms and the more recent SWF algorithm for incremental mining of frequent itemsets. The chapter portrays parallel mining as the ultimate solution to the problem, and described three types of parallel solution for finding frequent itemsets that are based on adaptation of the sequential Apriori algorithm. The chapter stressed the remaining difficulties in parallel mining and the need for more novel solutions.

EXERCISES

1 Give your own examples of the following association patterns:

  (a) Boolean association rule;

  (b) generalized association rule;

  (c) quantitative association rule;

  (d) sequential pattern.

2 Use the transaction database and category hierarchy in Figure 9.1 as an example to illustrate the working of the algorithm adapted from basic Apriori for generalized association rules presented in Section 9.1.2. From the frequent itemsets found, derive at least one generalized association rule expression.

3 Apply to Exercise 2 some of the method improvements described at the end of Section 9.1.2 and observe any practical improvement for that example.

4 Use the data set in Table 9.3 to illustrate the working of the adapted basic Apriori algorithm for quantitative association rules presented in Section 9.2. From the frequent itemsets obtained, derive at least one quantitative association rule expression.

5 Use some generalized and quantitative association rules derived from the frequent itemsets obtained in Exercises 2 and 4 to demonstrate the concept of redundant association rules and the measure of interestingness in respect of rule redundancy.

TABLE 9.3	Data set for Exercises 4 and 8			
Outlook	**Temperature**	**Humidity**	**Windy**	**Class**
Sunny	85	high	FALSE	negative
Sunny	80	high	TRUE	negative
Overcast	83	high	FALSE	positive
Rain	70	high	FALSE	positive
Rain	68	normal	FALSE	positive
Rain	64	normal	TRUE	negative
Overcast	64	normal	TRUE	positive
Sunny	72	high	FALSE	negative
Sunny	69	normal	FALSE	positive
Rain	75	normal	FALSE	positive
Sunny	75	normal	TRUE	positive
Overcast	72	high	TRUE	positive
Overcast	81	normal	FALSE	positive
Rain	71	high	TRUE	negative

6 Use the transaction database presented in Figure 9.4 as an example to illustrate the following:

(a) How to create new candidate 2-sequences

(b) How to create new candidate *k*-sequences

(c) How to count the support for candidate sequences with different time constraints.

7 In Section 9.4.4, the MFS algorithm for discovering generalized sequential patterns is mentioned. Follow the reference entries provided in the Bibliographical Notes and collect more information about the algorithm. Describe how the algorithm works. What are the strengths and weaknesses?

8 Use the data set from Table 9.3 (provided as `weather.arff`) in Weka to perform the mining of quantitative association rules using the Apriori algorithm. Use a sensible filter to discretize the temperature attribute. Use different evaluation metrics to observe the top 10 to 15 rules mined from the data set.

9 The data set in Table 9.4 changes its content over time. The initial database consists of three partitions (numbered 1, 2 and 3), each of which consists of four transactions. Over a period of time, partition 1 is removed and partition 4 is added. Suppose that the minimum support threshold is 50%.

(a) Demonstrate the working of the pre-processing procedure of the SWF algorithm.

(b) Demonstrate the working of the incremental procedure of the SWF algorithm.

TABLE 9.4   Data set for Exercise 9

Partition #	TransID	Items
1	100	Apple, Bread, Coke
1	200	Apple, Flour
1	300	Apple, Bread, Coke, Egg
1	400	Apple, Dates
2	500	Apple, Bread, Dates, Egg
2	600	Coke, Flour
2	700	Apple, Bread, Coke, Date
2	800	Apple, Bread, Coke, Dates, Flour
3	900	Bread, Coke, Egg
3	1000	Apple, Coke, Flour
3	1100	Bread, Dates, Flour
3	1200	Bread, Dates, Egg, Flour
4	1300	Coke, Egg
4	1400	Apple, Coke, Dates
4	1500	Egg, Flour
4	1600	Bread

10 In medium- and large-scale network systems, accesses to switches, computers and printers are recorded by system log records. Log records are generated very fast and in large volumes. The system administrators are keen to track the log records and monitor the network traffic. Discuss the dynamic nature of the scenario, the scale of data changes, and the need for an incremental data mining solution.

11 In Section 9.7, three categories of parallel solution are described. It has been reported that the count and data distributions can be combined into a hybrid solution. Conduct an investigation in the literature into such a hybrid solution. Outline the working principles of the hybrid solution.

BIBLIOGRAPHICAL NOTES

Due to extensive interest in association rule mining, much research work has been conducted in this field, resulting in a large collection of literature on the subject. A number of survey papers have been published, for example, Ullman (2000), Hipp *et al.* (2000), Zhao and Bhowmick (2003), and Kotsiantis and Kanellopoulos (2006b). All the papers give a thorough review of the concepts of association rules of different kinds, techniques for mining those rules and the performance of the techniques. The work by Bayardo and Agrawal (1999) provides a theoretical underpinning to various measures for optimal (best and most interesting) rules that can be useful for some researchers. Besides the survey articles, this text has also used Tan *et al.* (2006) and Han and Kamber (2006) for general reference.

Three types of association (generalized, quantitative and sequential) were first introduced by the QUEST project team at IBM's Almaden research centre. The original articles by the researchers from the QUEST team (Agrawal and Srikant 1995; Srikant and Agrawal 1995, 1996) are mainly referred to for details of the adapted algorithms. The concept of partial completeness was fully explained in Srikant and Agrawal 1995. Discussions over rule redundancy are also based on the papers by Srikant and Agrawal. For sequential pattern discovery, this chapter refers to a survey article by Zhao and Bhowmick (2003) and an article by Joshi *et al.* (1999). Two more references have been used for sequential pattern mining: the GSP algorithm was first reported in (Srikant and Agrawal 1996) and the MFS algorithm was first reported by (Zhang *et al.* 2001).

The literature about incremental mining of association rules is extensive and research is continuing. Early works include Cheung *et al.* (1996) and Cheng *et al.* (1997) on the FUP algorithm and its improvement (the FUP2 algorithm), and an algorithm known as CARMA, by Hidber (1998). The Borders algorithm is reported in Aumann *et al.* (1999). A similar algorithm using the concept of negative borders, known as ICAP, is reported in Ayad *et al.* (2001). The SWF algorithm is reported in Lee *et al.* (2001).

Unlike the extensive coverage of incremental mining of association rules, the literature's coverage of parallel solutions for association rule mining appears limited. This chapter mainly draws references from two sources: the first paper to parallelize the sequential Apriori algorithm (Agrawal and Shafer 1996) and an excellent broad survey by Zaki (1999).

CHAPTER 10

Data mining in practice

LEARNING OBJECTIVES

To be aware of the industrial-standard CRISP-DM methodology for data mining projects

To study a case where data mining techniques have been successfully exploited

To provide an overview of some existing data mining software tools

To obtain an integrated view on data warehouse, OLAP and data mining

To be aware of technical and practical issues regarding data mining applications in text mining and web mining

Having explained the technical aspects of data mining in the previous chapters, this chapter focuses on the practical aspects of data mining applications. A data mining project is a complex process that requires appropriate understanding of the data involved, proper selection of suitable data mining methods and tools, sensible execution of the chosen methods with appropriate parameter settings, and objective evaluation of the result patterns. Like designing a good database, it may take years of experience to master data mining.

This chapter introduces CRISP-DM, an industrial-standard data mining methodology. Although the methodology is still in its infancy, many data mining practitioners have already started following it in their data mining practice. For a better understanding of the methodology and a taste of real-life data mining, a successful data mining project is presented as a case study.

Many data mining software tools are now available. It makes sense for this chapter to describe some of the widely used tools. The chapter gives a short introduction to the other facilities of Weka, providing a more thorough understanding of this powerful tool set.

As a summary of this text, the chapter puts data warehouse, data retrieval, OLAP and data mining into perspective in an integrated decision-support environment. To enhance understanding of data mining applications, the chapter also presents a very brief overview of web mining and text mining.

10.1 THE CRISP-DM METHODOLOGY

In the early years of data mining, many data miners used their own approaches and procedures to perform data mining projects. These approaches and procedures were heavily influenced by the nature of the input data and software tools. Quite often, trial and error was adopted in order to find the best solution after repeated attempts. Although some form of trial and error can never be completely ruled out, that approach is not only time-consuming but also open to abuse. Because of the strategic importance of data mining projects and the potential cost involved, such a project cannot be taken lightly. Any ill-conducted project may end up finding wrong patterns, which may lead to a false understanding of the data and inappropriate decision-making with dire consequences. The three-stage process for data mining outlined in Chapter 2 is sufficient to demonstrate the principle of data mining, but it lacks thorough guidance regarding the necessary activities at each stage of a data mining project.

By the mid-1990s, there was a strong desire in the data mining community for a methodology that is independent of industry, tool and application. In 1996, the Cross-Industry Standard Process for Data Mining (CRISP-DM) methodology was first proposed by three major players in the data mining field: SPSS, Daimler-Benz and NCR. A project funded by the European Commission was undertaken by a consortium including the three pioneers between 1997 and 1999. During the project, the draft standard was developed, tested and evaluated. The first version of the standard, CRISP-DM 1.0, was established in 1999. Although there was an attempt in 2006 to develop a new version of the standard, it appears that the long waited CRISP-DM 2.0 has yet been finalised. CRISP-DM 1.0 is, therefore, the only published version of the methodology.

10.1.1 Process Model

The CRISP-DM methodology describes data mining activities with a hierarchical process model (Figure 10.1). Tasks are divided at four levels of abstraction in the hierarchy: phase level, generic task level, specialized task level and process instance level:

■ The *phase* level is most general. It divides tasks into phases or stages, such as data preparation.

■ The *generic task* level describes the data mining tasks that are applicable to all data mining situations. A generic task for the data preparation phase, for example, is about cleaning the data.

■ The *specialized task* level specifies how the generic tasks are implemented for a specific data mining situation, such as removal of outliers.

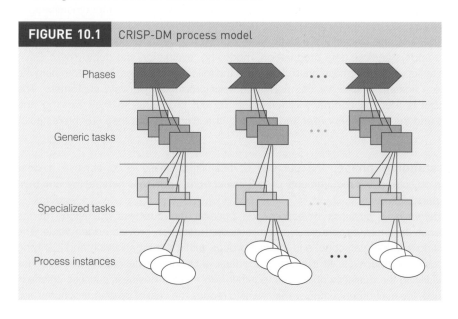

FIGURE 10.1 CRISP-DM process model

Phases

Generic tasks

Specialized tasks

Process instances

■ The *process instance* level records actions, decisions and results of a specific data mining activity. It describes what actually happened in a particular activity. For instance, an outlier identification method is used to locate outlier objects for a given data set.

Two points are worth mentioning. First, the hierarchical view does not provide a clear understanding of the order among the tasks at different levels although there is an indication of order at the phase level. Quite often in data mining, the process must backtrack to a previous stage and certain tasks need to be repeated under different settings. There are simply too many possibilities. In order to avoid being too complex, the methodology does not give full guidance on this point except what is specified in its reference model (see Section 10.1.2).

Second, meaningful mapping from higher-level generalized tasks to lower-level specialized tasks and actions must be and can only be achieved in a given data mining context. In CRISP-DM, four data mining contexts are summarized:

■ The *application domain* outlines the area for which the data mining project is undertaken. The context helps to clarify the 'business problem' to be resolved through the project. For instance, an application domain may be about customer profiling and segmentation.

■ The *problem type* refers to the type of data mining problems that the project involves. For instance, customer profiling and segmentation may involve clustering.

■ The *technical aspects* refer to specific technical concerns that the project may face. For instance, missing values may be a factor of technical concern that needs to be addressed.

■ The *tools and techniques* specify which data mining tools and solutions are used for the project. For instance, the K-means method in Weka may be exploited for clustering.

10.1.2 Reference Model

CRISP-DM 1.0 presents the methodology through the CRISP-DM Reference Model, which provides a hierarchical overview of the process and tasks, and the CRISP-DM User Guide, which specifies actions taken under each task and offers hints and tips for conducting each task. This section outlines the CRISP-DM Reference Model. You can find the User Guide in the CRISP-DM 1.0 document mentioned in the Bibliographical Notes.

According to CRISP-DM, the lifecycle of a data mining project consists of six phases: business understanding, data understanding, data preparation, modelling, evaluation and deployment. Each phase and the main tasks within the phase are explained in the following sections. In order to help the explanation, we use a fictional mail-order company that sells products to private customers. The basic business model is that the company regularly sends out brochures to their existing and potential customers and the customers order and purchase the products that they are interested in via post.

Business understanding phase The purpose of this initial phase is to achieve a clear understanding of the objectives and requirements of the project from a business perspective and then from a data mining perspective.

In the task of *determining business objectives*, we observe the business operations of the organization and identify business opportunities where collected data can provide added value. The task involves interacting with key personnel and interest groups within the organization and clarifying the organization's business objectives. At the end of the task, a document describing the business background and specifying the business objectives together with a set of business success criteria is produced. For instance, the mail-order company may want to reduce the cost of posting brochures and increase the customer order rate. The success criteria include the amount of cost reduction and increased customer orders within a period of time.

In the task of *assessing the business situation*, we identify factors affecting the business objectives and the successful completion of the project. The main factors include available resources (e.g. data, data domain experts and computer resources), business and data assumptions and constraints (e.g. existing domain knowledge), and risk factors affecting the completion of the project and contingency plans (e.g. staff turn over, limitations of computing resources). The purpose is to gain a balanced understanding of the costs and benefits of the project to the business. The task produces an assessment document that identifies these factors. The document reports the readiness of the organization in undertaking the project. For the mail-order company, resources include existing mail order data and a relevant software tool. The company may assume that mail order is still popular with private customers. A likely constraint is that the company is more interested in sales of summer items. The direct benefits of the project are to cut down postal costs by targeting customers who are more likely to respond. Risk factors may include whether household demographic data that are essential for the investigation can be obtained on time.

In the task of *determining data mining objectives,* we often discover that business objectives for data mining are not exactly the same as data mining objectives. This task involves translating business objectives into data mining objectives. The output of the task is a list of clearly stated data mining goals together with the success evaluation criteria. For instance, cutting down the postal costs is a business objective for the mail-order company. The data mining goals are to build a good quality predictive or classification model to determine if a customer is likely to respond and hence to decide whether to post the customer the brochures. The success criterion is the accuracy of the prediction.

The final task of this phase is *project planning*, which is not described here in detail because it is a generic task for every project. This does not in any way underestimate the importance of the task itself.

Data understanding phase   The purpose of this phase is to gain a general understanding of the data to be used. Such an understanding is essential to ensure the relevance, suitability and quality of the data for the project.

In the task of *collecting and integrating data,* the data source identified should be investigated. The relevance of the data features in relation to the project objectives needs to be assessed. Sometimes, data may come from different sources and must be integrated into a single data collection. The data collection report produced at the end of the task provides the criteria for feature and instance selection at a later stage. For the mail-order company, data may be collected from their existing customer and sales databases. Data regarding household demographics may be collected from third-party sources, such as local government authorities or agencies.

In the task of *describing data*, we compile feature descriptions in terms of attribute types, values and distributions, and instance descriptions in terms of overall instance quantity and instance quantity for different feature–value combinations. These details are recorded in the data description report. For the mail-order company, this task may reveal that there is a mixture of different types of feature in the data set collected. Some of the features, such as age and income, are ratio types whereas others, such as postcode, are nominal types. For some features, such as return rate, there is a great imbalance between 'active' (i.e. returned an order) and 'dormant' (i.e. no response).

In the task of *exploring data*, we gain initial understanding of the data collected. Any data exploration method (e.g. descriptive statistics, data visualization, OLAP) may be used (see Chapter 3). At the end of the task, a data exploration report is produced. This level of understanding is more in-depth than simple data description. For the mail-order company, not only can the distribution of the values for the feature Age be understood through descriptive statistics and visualization tools, but a strong correlation between age and return rate may also be established.

10

In the task of *assessing data quality*, we examine all aspects of data quality as described in Chapter 3, with regard to its relevance to the purpose of data mining. The most important question is whether the quality of the data collected is sufficient for the mining project. At the end of the task, a quality assessment report is produced. For the mail-order company, it may be realized that missing values is a major quality concern.

Data understanding may require more understanding of the business side. It may be necessary to go back to the business understanding phase and repeat some of the tasks designated for that phase. For instance, some data understanding may lead to modifications to the project objectives.

Data preparation phase The data preparation phase includes all tasks that are necessary for producing a final input data set. This phase can be time-consuming and tasks may have to be repeated before the final data set is ready. The main tasks for the phase include the data pre-processing tasks described in Chapter 3.

The *data selection* task selects attributes and records that satisfy conditions relevant to the goals of the data mining project. Supporting arguments for the selection decisions must be documented at the end of the task. For the mail-order company, attributes describing an address detail may be excluded except for the postcode. Random sampling without replacement may be used to select training, validation and testing examples for developing a predictive model.

The *data cleaning* task aims to improve the data quality. The task may include activities such as repairing missing values, resolving any data inconsistency, using more suitable default values, and correcting errors, if possible. Any cleaning actions together with a justification for them must be recorded in the data cleaning report. For the mail-order company, data cleaning may include using zero as a suitable default value for a derived attribute representing the number of orders made in the past and removing extreme outlier instances from the data set.

The *data construction* task refers to the activities that involve deriving new attribute values from existing ones. The new attribute values may be the results of data aggregation, data transformation or data discretization. For the mail-order company, the total quantity and value of items purchased by each customer may be derived from the existing records of the quantity and unit prices of items. The Age values may be discretized into a number of age groups. Again, all the actions and their justifications must be recorded in a written document.

The *integrating data* task refers specifically to actions taken to combine separate partial data records into a single complete data record in the output data set. The integrated data should provide an understanding of a data record in its entirety. Again, the rationale behind the integration must be explained in a document. The mail-order company may realize the importance of household demographics and decide to integrate such data from a third-party source with the company's own data to form a fuller data record on customers.

The *formatting data* task is the final preparation of the data set into the format required by the chosen software tool. The formatting should normally change only the syntactic appearance of data rather than their semantic meaning. The output of the task is the reformatted data set. In the mail-order company data set, if Weka is to be used, all NULL values in the original data set must be replaced by '?' and the ARFF file format must be adhered to.

Modelling phase Modelling is the actual mining phase. A variety of data mining techniques may be employed and their parameter values are calibrated to optimal values. Several techniques are often available in a software tool for solving one data mining problem. In this case, some or even all of the alternatives are often tried in order to consolidate the findings.

Technique selection involves selecting mining techniques that are suitable for the input data set. The data understanding phase provides the opportunity to get to know the data characteristics and the business objectives can also influence the choice of mining technique. At the end of the task, the chosen mining techniques and the justifications for selecting them should be recorded. The mail-order company may realize that very few of the data attribute values follow a normal distribution. Some techniques, such as the GMM method, assume normal distribution and, therefore, are not suitable. The company may also be interested in the explanation of classification decisions made by the predictive model. This requirement further narrows down the possible techniques to decision tree induction and rule-based methods.

Test design is an optional task that may be needed for certain types of data mining problems, such as classification. To validate the classification model, the available data records may be divided into training, test and validation sets and the selection method for the different purposes must be recorded. For the mail-order company, it may be decided that the test method using 10-fold cross-validation is to be used.

Building and assessing models are two closely related tasks. The selected data mining techniques with particular parameter settings are applied and the resulting models are obtained. The data miners must then measure the performance of the models against predetermined evaluation criteria. During the tasks, different parameter settings and evaluation results may be recorded. The result of model evaluation may suggest another round of model building and assessment. Eventually, the best-performing model or models are obtained. The mail-order company may select the C4.5 method with default parameter settings. The result tree may have only around 60% accuracy. Settings, such as a pruned tree with at least 50 examples in the leaf node may be added, and another round of modelling may produce a result tree with 80% accuracy. After attempting a number of other mining techniques and obtaining similar levels of accuracy, it is concluded that the decision tree with the accuracy rate of 80% is the best model to be obtained from the input data set.

It is often necessary, particularly when the modelling results are not satisfactory, to return to the data preparation phase, modify and repeat some of the data preparation tasks, and re-attempt the modelling. For instance, building a decision tree directly over numeric attributes may produce less than satisfactory accuracy. It is quite common for the data analysts to return to the data preparation phase and discretize some or all numeric attributes before attempting decision tree modelling again.

Evaluation phase By this phase, we have obtained good models (from the data analysis perspective). The evaluation phase further examines the validity of model development and model performance, and assesses the result models from a business perspective, i.e. how well the models meet the business objectives, by checking whether all important business issues have been considered.

Evaluating data mining results is a task that checks how well the results apply in the business context. Ideally, a small-scale pilot application in a real-life surrounding should be attempted and the effect evaluated. Indirect results from the data understanding and modelling phases should be looked into for a fuller understanding of the data mining results and explanations for the truthfulness of the results. By the end of the task, the assessment of the results against the business success criteria are summarized and the best-performing model becomes the approved model to be used in the practice. The mail-order company may select a few hundred households for a pilot study on the predictive model obtained from the modelling stage. The business success criteria are used to test the success of the model's predictions.

Reviewing the data mining process is a task that takes place before the result model is released. This review should check objectively every stage of the data mining process to ensure that important factors have not been overlooked and that little or no soft decisions based on groundless assumptions and personal opinions are made. If any doubts exist, concerns should be raised and tasks of the relevant phases must be repeated. The mail-order company locates some extra data for testing purposes. It decides to perform a new round of modelling using the extra data set as the test set. The results must be compared to the results produced by using the cross-validation test option. The evaluation may show that there is no difference between the two rounds.

Determining the next step is carried out after evaluation. The data mining process can either proceed to the next deployment phase, indicating successful completion of the project, or return to the business understanding phase to go through another round of data mining or to start a completely new project with different business objectives. The final decision with its supporting arguments should be documented as the output of the task. For example, the mail-order company may decide to deploy the model in practice, signalling the end of the current data mining project.

Deployment phase This phase is the final phase of a complete data mining life cycle. During this phase, the results of data mining are applied to the business practice. Actions that apply the models and are meant to bring positive results to business should be specified. The schedule of the actions should be carefully planned. The defined actions must have parameters with which the effects of the actions can be measured. The measurements must be objective and on a sound footing. The measurement of business actions may result in modifications to the specification of the original business problem, which may trigger another data mining project.

Although most of the deployment tasks require the involvement of the intended clients, data miners should also be consulted to ensure good and sound use as well as continuing monitoring the use of the data mining results. As far as the data miners are concerned, this phase also serves as the conclusion stage for the data mining project. Data miners should produce a final report on the project and present an objective view of the data mining results and their use in practice.

The mail-order company may realize the positive result of a pilot study and decide to deploy the predictive model in practice on a larger scale. It works out a schedule for rolling out the model. The company must also make changes to its way of running business to accommodate the use of the predictive model, that is, to send out a brochure only when the predictive model indicates a strong likelihood of return.

10.1.3 Summary

The CRISP-DM methodology is the first attempt to promote data mining as an engineering process that standardizes tasks in different phases of the data mining process. However, compared to database design methodologies, the issue of standardization is far from being settled: it is yet to be accepted by the majority of the data mining community. The standard is not without its limitations. For instance, it hardly addresses the roles that data miners or data analysts should play in a data mining project, nor does it describe the roles of domain experts whose involvement in the project is essential for its success. This issue may need to be accommodated in future editions of the standard.

The vendor-specific SEMMA (abbreviation for Sample, Explore, Modify, Model, Assess) approach to data mining has also been called a methodology. However, SEMMA has not investigated thoroughly all levels of activities as CRISP-DM has done. Even the vendor, SAS, claims that SEMMA should not be taken as a full data mining methodology. It is therefore safe to suggest that the CRISP-DM is the only data mining methodology in existence.

10.2 CASE STUDY

This section presents a data mining project as a case study. Finding successful data mining projects with sufficient detail is not easy. The shroud of secrecy surrounding data mining in commercial companies often prevents details being revealed to their potential competitors. Many successful cases give very little detail on what was really done.

The data mining project presented here is one of the rare success cases that have been fully reported. The project was conducted by Gary Saarenvirta and his team for Loyalty Group Canada in

1998. The approach taken by the project is consistent with the CRISP-DM methodology though the project itself was not the direct result of following the methodology. This section presents the case study from the perspective of the methodology.

10.2.1 Business Understanding, Objectives and Readiness

Customer profiling is an important business strategy for database marketing and customer relationship management. One main approach to customer profiling is to segment customers according to 'shareholder values' variables, such as customer profitability and customer retention probability, that can be derived from customer shopping transactions. By dividing customers into high-profit and low-profit groups according to their shopping behaviours, more detailed studies regarding customers' demographic properties can reveal potential opportunities for cross-selling (selling additional products that complement existing purchases) and up-selling (selling more expensive products).

The Loyalty Group Canada is a coalition of more than 125 Canadian companies from different sectors of industry and commerce such as finance, banking, retailing, grocery, petrol supply, telecommunications, etc. The coalition runs a programme known as the Air Miles Reward Programme (AMRP) that aims at promoting more frequent shopping by customers in the companies that sponsor the programme. The idea of the programme is that customers shop at the sponsor companies, collect and accumulate air miles as reward, and redeem the air miles against flight tickets, hotel accommodation and theatre tickets. The programme is popular, with nearly 60% of Canadian households taking part.

In the past, the coalition has used recency, frequency and monetary value (RFM) analysis, OLAP and linear statistical methods to evaluate the success of marketing initiatives undertaken by the coalition and its sponsor companies and to seek new marketing opportunities. The coalition wants to investigate the potential of data mining in customer segmentation and to identify further data mining initiatives. For comparison, there is an existing segmentation created using the RFM analysis. The business problem in this case directly corresponds to the problem of clustering in data mining. The general idea is to group customers according to their shopping behaviours and to understand the characteristics of the groups.

The coalition possesses its own data warehouse that stores data about customer shopping transactions provided by the sponsor companies. The data warehouse contains 6.3 million household records and more than 1 billion customer transaction records. The project team has access to the data warehouse and the data mining software IBM Intelligent Miner for Data. The software runs with the DB2 Universal Database Enterprise-Extended Edition on a five-node RS/6000 SP massively parallel hardware platform. IBM Intelligent Miner for Data is capable of the intended purpose and the parallel platform ensures speedy discovery of patterns from large data sets. In other words, the organization is ready to undertake this project.

10.2.2 Data Collection

This investigation involves six tables: promotion history, customers, transactions, sponsor companies, census and tax data. Among them, census and tax data are from third-party sources and describe demographic properties of customers. Figure 10.2 shows the tables and their relationships.

From the tables, 50,000 customer records and associated shopping transactions over a period of 12 months are extracted. 'Shareholder value' variables for the project include revenue, period of customer tenure, number of sponsor companies shopped at over the customer tenure, number of sponsor companies shopped at over the last 12 months and the customer shopping *recency* represented by the number of months since the last transaction. Some business-specific variables are also included. Values for these variables are aggregated from the transactions table by using a cross-tabulation query over the first two quarters of 1997. The sponsor companies are divided into

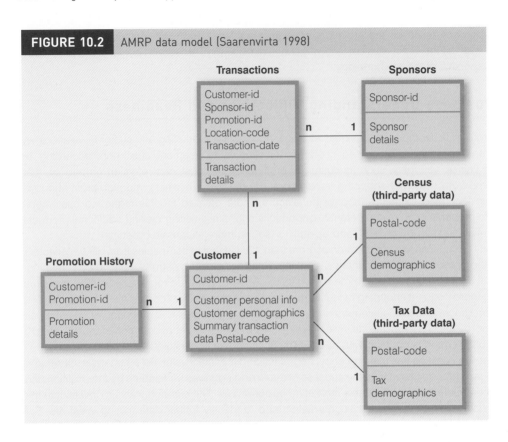

FIGURE 10.2 AMRP data model (Saarenvirta 1998)

14 categories and three transaction variables (revenue, travel miles collected and number of transactions) are used for each category over two quarters. There are, therefore, 84 variables summarizing the customer shopping behaviours.

10.2.3 Data Understanding and Preparation

The main data preparation work is focused on handling missing values and data transformation.

The data set contains missing values for different types of variable. After further investigation into the meaning of the variables and the meaning of missing values, it is decided that the missing values for categorical variables representing customer demographic features should be replaced with a special missing value code (such as U). This is because unknown values themselves may reveal some patterns. A binary field is also created to mark out the coded records for each categorical attribute with missing values. Different ways of handling missing values for numeric variables are considered. For transaction variables, such as revenue, travel miles collected and the number of transactions of a customer, it is decided that a natural and cautious solution is to fill missing values with zero. In other words, if the value is not known, it is assumed to be zero.

The general reasons for data transformation include eliminating the effect of outliers, making the values of variables more comparable and making the data more interpretable. The first concern over the transaction variables is that the values for these variables may not be directly comparable. Suppose that there are two customers making profit contributions to a business by purchasing different items over a period of time. Customer 1 makes a total profit contribution of 100 units: 50 on item A, 20 on item B and 30 on item C. Customer 1 has been with the business for 10 months. Customer 2 makes a total profit contribution of 10 units: 5 on item A, 2 on item B and 3 on item C. Customer 2 has been with the business for only 1 month. If the contribution amounts are used directly, the first customer is clearly more profitable than the second. However, there is a good reason to believe that the two are similar. For this reason, ratios instead of actual amounts should be calculated. For this project, all transaction variables are normalized with such ratios. For instance, the total number of miles collected for Category 1 companies in the second quarter is now calculated as a ratio of the total number of miles collected by the customer for all categories of company over all quarters.

From data understanding and exploration, it is realized that values for transaction variables are very skewed with most customers having lower values for the variables. For some of the variables, discretization with percentiles is applied. For instance, the values of the variable representing the number of travel miles are discretized at percentile break points 10%, 25%, 50%, 75% and 90%. Eventually, seven bands are obtained: 0, 1, [2, 39], [40, 514], [515, 1151], [1152, 1824] and [1825, ∞) and are assigned integers 0, 1, ..., 6. Logarithmic transformation is also applied to some transaction variables to curb the extremely skewed distributions of the original values. After transformation, the skewed values are more stretched out.

Throughout the data preparation stage, the descriptive statistics facility of IBM Intelligent Miner for Data has been used to gain understanding about the values of the interested variables. The software is equipped with a visualization facility to illustrate the distributions of data values in bar charts (for numeric attributes) or pie charts (for categorical attributes). Figure 10.3 shows the visualizations of the distributions of original data, distributions of discretized data and distributions of log-transformed data for various variables. A pie chart represents the value distribution for a categorical variable, and a bar chart represents the value distribution (histogram) for a numeric variable.

An additional data preparation task for this project is to introduce some time-derivative variables for capturing the change of data over time periods. For instance, a variable is introduced to represent the difference in the numbers of miles for a certain category of companies between two quarters, capturing the data change over the period of two quarters.

10.2.4 Data Mining (Modelling)

IBM Intelligent Miner for Data provides two clustering solutions: demographic clustering and neural network clustering. The project uses both solutions over the same set of data, aiming to find common clusters and hence consolidate the finding.

Demographic clustering in IBM Intelligent Miner for Data produces good and more interpretable results for variables with discrete values. Therefore, all continuous variables are discretized before the demographic clustering is conducted. Data analysts select the attributes, known as active fields, upon which clusters are defined and also choose some attributes as supplementary fields that are not used in defining the clusters but are used to gain understanding about them. The active fields include: total number of products purchased, number of products purchased in the last 12 months, customer's total revenue contribution, customer tenure in months, ratio of revenue to tenure, ratio of number of products to tenure, recency and region. These variables are all important 'shareholder value' variables. All other variables including other 'shareholder value' variables are used as the supplementary fields.

The demographic clustering algorithm in IBM Intelligent Miner for Data requires data analysts to set several parameters including the maximum number of clusters, the maximum number of data passes, the accuracy threshold and the similarity threshold. Unlike the K-means method, which produces exactly K clusters, the demographic clustering algorithm may produce fewer clusters than the maximum. The maximum number of data passes indicates the maximum number of times that the algorithm scans through the data set. If the accuracy criterion is not satisfied, this parameter eventually stops the clustering process. The accuracy threshold is the normal stopping point for the algorithm. The

FIGURE 10.3   Effects of pre-processing on data (Saarenvirta 1998)

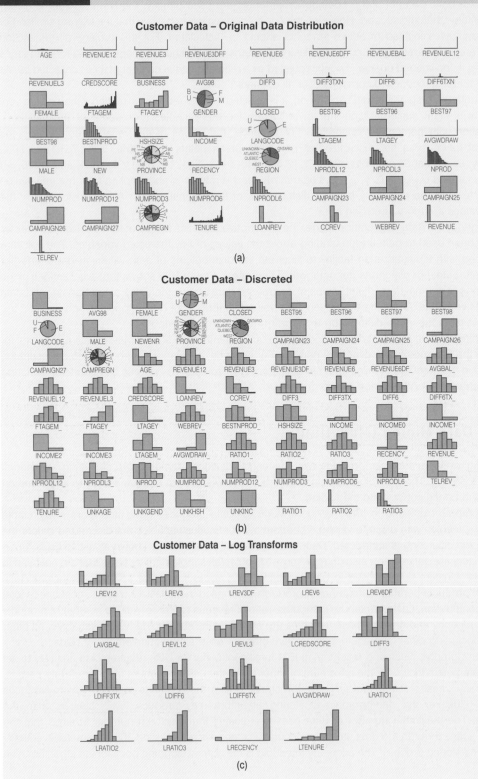

threshold refers to the amount of change of measures between data passes. The Condorcet criterion is a measure of cluster quality with a value between 0 and 1 where 1 indicates perfect clustering, i.e. all clusters are homogeneous and entirely different from each other. The accuracy threshold is measured as a percentage. The lower the threshold, the better the quality of the clusters. The combined setting of a low accuracy threshold and a high maximum number of data passes should produce better quality clusters. The similarity threshold defines the value difference at which two distance measures are considered equal. For instance, if the threshold is set to 0.5, any two distances with a difference between them less than or equal to 0.5 are considered equal.

In the first demographic clustering run, the data analysts set parameters for a maximum of nine clusters and five data passes, an accuracy threshold of 0.1. They used the default setting for the similarity threshold of 0.5. The cluster identifiers assigned to data records are added as an output variable. Including this variable allows the data analyst to cross-tabulate the results of demographic clustering against those of neural clustering so that commonality and difference between the different solutions can be seen.

Figure 10.4 shows the visualization of the clustering results. A stripe represents a cluster with the rightmost integer as the cluster identifier and the leftmost number as the proportional size of the cluster as a percentage. For instance, 24% of customers belong to Cluster 6. The clusters are listed in descending order of size. The variables listed from left to right along a stripe indicate the significance of the variable to the cluster membership based on a chi-square test between the variable and the cluster identifier field. For each variable, its value distribution within the cluster is outlined either in the form of a bar chart (for numeric attributes) or a pie chart (for a categorical field). In order to give a comparative understanding, the value distribution for the

---

FIGURE 10.4 Visualization of demographic clustering results (Saarenvirta 1998)

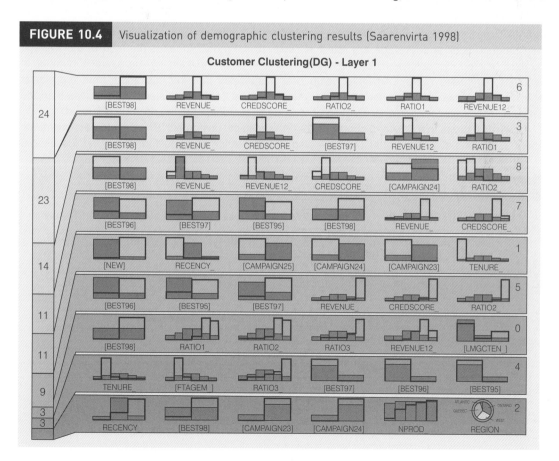

variable in the whole data set is also present as a shaded bar in the background for a bar chart or a ring around the outside of a pie chart. Interesting clusters are those where the distributions of attribute values within a cluster is very different from the distributions of the same attribute values for the whole data set.

After the clustering, the data analysts start to characterize the resulting clusters qualitatively. In general, they find that the clustering results confirm the findings about *gold* customers identified by an earlier RFM analysis. Most of the clusters have either almost all gold customers or no gold customers at all. For instance, Cluster 6 contains almost all gold customers, whose values for important 'shareholder value' variables are all in the 50th and 75th percentiles. Cluster 3 contains no gold customers and its customers have much lower values for the same 'shareholder value' variables. Validating a known pattern increases the level of confidence in using data mining tools. The clustering results also further identify clusters within the gold customer category, indicating additional knowledge. For instance, the data analysts find that Cluster 5 contains not only gold customers validated this year (1998), but also gold customers in the previous years (1995, 1996 and 1997), indicating a year-on-year increase of this kind of customer. The cluster itself is also interesting because the values for most 'shareholder value' variables are in the 75th and even the 90th percentiles.

After demographic clustering, a further round of clustering using the neural network algorithm in IBM Intelligent Miner for Data is conducted. This round uses the log-transformed variables. All the discretized variables are treated as the supplementary attributes. This round of clustering is done for comparison purposes. Common clusters can be used with confidence.

10.2.5 Result Interpretation and Deployment of Business Actions

In order to assist in interpretation, the value distributions of some 'shareholder value' variables together with product index and leverage are listed in Table 10.1. Product index is the ratio of the average number of products purchased by the customers in a cluster divided by the average number of products purchased overall. An index value over 1 indicates that the customers from the cluster purchase more than the average; otherwise, the customers from the cluster purchase less than the average. The leverage represents the ratio of revenue to customer, i.e. the revenue per head.

Table 10.1 shows that Cluster 5 contains the most profitable customers: 9% of customers contribute about 35% of the overall revenue. The table also shows that the good customers are in Clusters 2, 5

TABLE 10.1	Cluster profiling (Saarenvirta 1998)				
Clusterid	**Revenue**	**Customers**	**Product Index**	**Leverage**	**Tenure**
5	34.74%	8.82%	1.77	3.94	60.92
6	26.13%	23.47%	1.41	1.11	57.87
7	21.25%	10.71%	1.64	1.98	63.52
3	6.62%	23.32%	.73	.28	47.23
0	4.78%	3.43%	1.45	1.40	31.34
2	4.40%	2.51%	1.46	1.75	61.38
4	1.41%	2.96%	.99	.48	20.10
8	.45%	14.14%	.36	.03	30.01
1	.22%	10.64%	.00	.02	4.66

and 7. These customers have higher revenue per person than the customers of other clusters, as indicated by the leverage. The table confirms that as profitability increases, so does the average number of products purchased and that customer profitability increases as tenure increases.

From this study, the following business strategies are recommended to the client:

- Clusters 2, 5 and 7 contain the best customers. The client should therefore develop a retention strategy to keep the customers.

- The product indices of the customers in Clusters 2, 6 and 0 are very close to those for the customers in Clusters 5 and 7. Therefore, the client should develop cross-selling strategies by comparing their purchased products and promoting the products across the two sides, hoping to convert customers currently in Clusters 2, 6 and 0 to Clusters 5 and 7. Since the product indices of the two sides are so close, it is believed that this objective should be achievable.

- In Cluster 1, the patterns are not yet mature due to the percentage of customers in the group and the very short customer tenure, so the client should apply a 'wait-and-see' policy.

- Customers in Cluster 8 are poor-quality customers. They count for more than 14% of all customers but contribute less than 0.5% revenue. The client should avoid spending too much on customers in this cluster.

This project was a success, not only because the recommendations list was derived, but also the Loyalty Group was convinced that data mining is a promising technology for them. As a result, they planned a further clustering project with more behaviour variables, a new classification project for building predictive models for direct mail targeting and an association rule project for identifying new marketing opportunities with the results of the customer segmentation project.

10.3 DATA WAREHOUSING, OLAP AND DATA MINING IN PERSPECTIVE

In Chapter 3, data warehouses were presented as a source for data mining. This section describes data warehouses as part of an integrated environment for data retrieval, data reporting and data mining, helping to put data warehousing, OLAP and data mining into perspective, known sometimes as *business intelligence*. As explained in Section 3.3.1, a data warehouse is an organization-wide database designated for the purpose of data analysis and decision support. A typical data warehouse system has a multi-tier architecture similar to that shown in Figure 10.5.

The data warehouse consists of a central data repository and a collection of data marts. The repository is the central data store that holds all types of data in their entirety. Data marts are smaller-scale data warehouses for a specific department of the organization. Data from the operational database systems within the organization and data from external data sources are pulled into the central repository by the *data loading manager* of the warehouse DBMS. The raw data collected from different operational systems are integrated into the central repository by the *warehouse manager*. The warehouse manager is also responsible for collecting metadata and maintaining mapping between the central repository and the data marts.

Data in the warehouse (or in individual data marts) are viewed as a collection of connected tables by data retrieval tools, a multidimensional hypercube by OLAP tools and a large flat table that holds data in their entirety by most, if not all, data mining tools. The *query manager* of the warehouse DBMS is responsible for creating and maintaining such views. The data retrieval tools search the raw data and compile them into useful reports. OLAP tools summarize data in various ways along chosen dimensions and produce data summary results. Data mining tools comb through the data table many times and induce hidden patterns. All the processed information, i.e. the reports, summaries and patterns, are

FIGURE 10.5   A Multi-tier data warehouse architecture

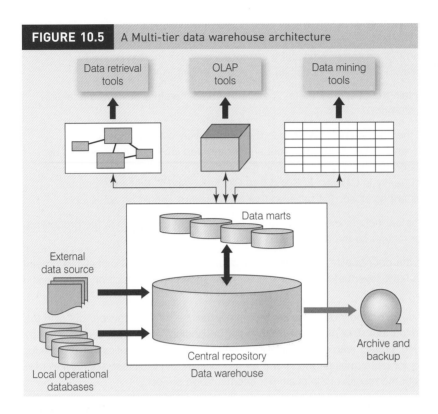

collected into a knowledge base to support decision-making for the organization. This information-based, decision-making route from raw data in operational systems to knowledge in a knowledge base is becoming increasingly important and vital for organizations of various kinds. The route also echoes the pyramid structure shown in Figure 1.1.

10.3.1 Data Representations in a Data Warehouse

Data in different parts of the data warehouse environment may take different forms. The representations of data from the operational systems can be either homogenous or heterogeneous. They can be tables of a single relational DBMS or from different relational DBMSs, such as Microsoft SQL server 2000, MySQL, DB2 and Oracle, or even representations in different data models, such as relational tables, networks and objects. In real-life cases, it is more likely that data in the operational systems are heterogeneous.

For convenience and uniformity, data stored in the central repository and data marts are represented in a single data model. Because most retrieval and analysis tools assume that data are represented as two-dimensional, flat tables, the relational model therefore becomes a natural choice. Thus, the central repository should normally consist of a set of conceptually related tables, organized in a suitable structure such as star schema (see Chapter 3). A data mart can be a real partition of the central repository if the warehouse is distributed, or merely an external schema if the warehouse is centralized. As with any other database, a date warehouse also has backup facilities for the purpose of system recovery.

The central data repository contains not only raw data values pulled from the operational systems but also pre-computed data summaries and derived attribute values in order to save time for the data analysis. For instance, the warehouse may contain not only transaction records for individual customers but also the total number of transactions over a period of time.

Besides data values, data about data, known as *metadata*, are also an important part of the data warehouse. In a typical data warehouse, there exists different types of metadata that include the following:

- metadata associated with data loading and transformation, which includes descriptions of source data, description of destination data and mappings from the source to the destination;

- metadata associated with data management, which includes schematic metadata, such as attributes, domains, tables and relationships; system level metadata, such as indices, views, security and integrity constraints; and description metadata for any data aggregations and their associated queries;

- metadata associated with knowledge, which includes domain knowledge about data, heuristics about data and validated information patterns discovered from the databases.

In most application databases, metadata are hidden from the end user. For data understanding and analysis, metadata are very valuable. For instance, when an attribute about seasons of the year is used in clustering, knowledge regarding the attribute's circular domain helps to derive a correct way of measuring the difference between seasons. Clearly, treating the domain as a nominal type is not sensible because there is a sense of order and a sense of difference among the seasons. One possible way is to take the difference between two adjacent seasons to be twice as small as the difference between two non-adjacent seasons. For example, the difference between autumn and winter is 0.5 while the difference between autumn and spring is 1.

10.3.2 Data Warehousing Functions

All functions regarding the effective maintenance and operation of a data warehouse can be called data warehousing functions. This section briefly introduces three major functions: data loading, data integration and metadata management. All these functions are direct or indirectly related to the effect of data mining.

Data loading This important function loads data from the operational systems into the central repository. The function must solve a number of problems. First, many operational systems are developed as 'sealed units'. In such a system, data can only be accessed via a purpose-built user interface. However, data loading requires accessing the entire database, including data stored in the system catalogue. Such access cannot be conducted simply via the existing user interface. Specially designed software routines may have to be used to break this access barrier. Second, a large amount of data may be frequently transported from different operational systems. Such a transfer should not affect the working of the operational systems. Sometimes, data transfer is needed to keep the content of the central repository updated when the contents of the operational systems have changed. The changes need to be synchronized, either constantly or regularly with a time gap between the updates.

Data integration This function combines data records about the same entity loaded from different operational systems into a single data record in the central repository. A number of problems may be encountered. First, there may exist conflicts and inconsistencies between data values over similar features from different sources. For instance, two operational systems may both have a variable representing customer performance. The variable in one system marks the performance out of three values (excellent, good and poor) whereas the variable in the other system marks the performance with a number between 1 and 10. When the customer records are integrated, this inconsistency must be resolved through some form of data transformation. Worse still, if the variable in one system indicates poor performance whereas the other system shows a performance score of 9 out of 10, a clear conflict exists and it has to be resolved before the data records can be combined. The second problem is that data integration may cause incomplete records even when the data records are complete before integration. For instance, if one operational system S1 has complete records over attributes A and B and another operational system S2 has complete records on attribute A only, then joining the two data sources creates null values on B for those records that exist only in S2. Handling missing values is very important in a data warehouses and has a knock-on effect on data mining.

Metadata management In a data warehouse environment, this includes metadata exchanges between different software tools that create, access and update metadata. Exchanges of metadata information across all the tools are needed to keep the metadata consistent across software tools. In order to enable the exchange, metadata must be standardized. Recently, there is a move to use XML as the standard notation for describing metadata. XML has been used by a number of business information system software tools, such as SAP. Besides the issue of a standard notation, metadata standardization still faces a number of difficult problems, such as how to resolve conflicts on various aspects of data definitions and business rules created by different operational systems. The history of metadata evolution may also reveal important information about the data. One suggestion in keeping the history is to use metadata versioning: all previous versions of metadata are backed up in the system.

10.4 DATA MINING SOFTWARE TOOLS

Since the establishment of data mining, many commercial and non-commercial data mining software tools have been developed and widely used. Throughout this book so far, Weka has been used to demonstrate how to apply data mining algorithms and solutions to data sets. It is useful to be aware of other tools that are available besides Weka. This section hence briefly introduces a few of them. However, this section should not be taken as a complete survey of all existing software tools.

10.4.1 Survey of Tools

Existing software tools can be categorized according to the data mining solutions they provide. Some products are single-purpose tools, such as See5 for decision tree induction only. Others are suites of solutions, offering algorithms of different kinds for different data mining tasks. Some data mining utilities are extended from existing data analysis capabilities while others are built from scratch. A number of frequently used software tools are listed as follows:

■ *SAS Enterprise Miner* is a commercial product, part of SAS suite for data analysis. The software provides a range of solutions for different data mining tasks, such as classification, clustering and association rule discovery. The solutions for classification include neural networks, decision trees and regression analysis. The software is also equipped with facilities for data exploration and preparation, and evaluation and visualization of mining results. With an easy-to-operate GUI, the user can interactively conduct data mining tasks.

■ *Clementine* is a data mining extension of the commercial statistical software SPSS. Since the product complies with the CRISP-DM methodology, it provides various solutions for different phases of a data project. The modelling solutions include classification solutions, such as neural networks and decision tree induction; clustering solutions, such as the K-means method; association rule solutions, such as Apriori and sequence detection; and regression analysis solutions, such as linear and logistic regressions. Through a GUI, the user can build a stream of data mining tasks similar to a Knowledge Flow in Weka (see Section 10.4.3).

■ *RapidMiner*, previously known as YALE, is a free software tool under a GNU licence. Built on the collection of various data mining solutions in Weka, RapidMiner provides a more effective GUI and visualization tools for enhancing the understanding of data as well as patterns. According to a latest survey, the software is becoming popular.

■ *Microsoft SQL Server* has been extended with data mining and OLAP capabilities since Microsoft SQL Server 2000. At the beginning, the data mining functions were limited and OLAP and warehousing were the main interest. However, Microsoft SQL Server 2008 has been equipped with data mining plug-ins which can be accessed from an Excel spreadsheet, allowing mining tasks to be performed on an Excel worksheet. The available data mining solutions include those for clustering, classification, estimation and association discovery.

■ *Oracle Data Mining*. From Oracle 9*i*, Oracle has provided data mining facilities as an extended option of its own database server (a similar extension for OLAP also exists). Adapting the CRISP-DM methodology of data mining, Oracle's data mining option is equipped with data preparation, modelling and evaluation tools. The data mining solutions include naïve Bayes, decision trees, support vector machines, generalized linear models, K-means and orthogonal partitioning clustering, and association rules for the purposes of classification, regression analysis, feature extraction, anomaly detection, association rule mining, etc. The system is also equipped with a GUI for assisting data exploration and visualization.

There are many other software packages available on the market. New ones are still being developed, and some old ones are fading away. None of the products are yet in a position to completely dominate the data mining market. The general trend behind the tools is towards an effective and easy-to-use visual system not only for the visualization of data and patterns but also for the specification of mining tasks. Some software tools, such as Clementine, Oracle Data Mining and SAS Enterprise Miner, promote a data mining methodology whereas others do not. The popularity of the tools may be indicated by the surveys that are frequently conducted by the kdnuggets.com website.

10.4.2 IBM Intelligent Miner for Data

As an alternative to Weka, this section briefly shows the use of another data mining tool known as IBM Intelligent Miner for Data. It is one of the earliest software tools in data mining as a result of the QUEST research project. The software has a client–server architecture with IBM's DB2 Universal Database as the supporting backend DBMS. It operates in both Unix and Microsoft Windows environments. The software has been successfully used many times for real-life data mining projects.

The IBM Intelligent Miner for Data provides the following facilities:

■ *Data definition*. This facility enables the user to specify input and output data sets. The input data can be represented in IBM DB2 tables or flat ASCII files on disks. Through this facility, derived attributes representing computed results based on existing attributes can be defined. Once a data set is defined, its content can be browsed as HTML pages.

■ *Data preparation*. The software is also equipped with various data pre-processing facilities including data aggregation, data filtering, data sampling, data grouping, data discretization, data transformation and treating missing data. These facilities work on the defined data sets using the data definition facilities.

■ *Data mining tools*. The software provides a range of data mining techniques. For cluster detection, the software offers a demographic solution and a neural network solution. Boolean and generalized association rules can be discovered with the Apriori algorithm. The software provides both neural network and decision tree induction solutions for classification. The software also offers facilities for mining sequential patterns and building prediction models. Statistical methods such as linear regression, principle component analysis, bivariate statistics, etc. are provided for data understanding and mining.

■ *Result viewing*. The software is equipped with good facilities for visualizing data and patterns as well as for setting up data mining tasks. Association rules are presented both as textual rules and as a directed graph. Decision trees are presented in a visual tree structure. The result of clustering is also visualized in boxes associated with bar charts and pie charts.

Figure 10.6 illustrates the graphical user interface of the software. A data mining project is known as a *mining base* that can be created, saved and edited. The detailed tasks within the scope of the project are defined and created as project components under different categories and listed in a tree view panel on the left. Details of the highlighted component are displayed in the top right panel. Relevant components of a specific mining project can be dragged and dropped in the Workarea panel for better organization and ease of use.

With a new mining base, relevant project components need to be defined by setting a number of options via a sequence of dialogue boxes. The final summary of the definition is saved and can be viewed at request. The data analysts then choose a component task and press the Play button to perform the task. The data analyst must be fully aware of the correct order of the tasks.

Normally, the first task for a project is to define the input data set in the Data category. During the data definition process, details such as the data source, the treatment of attribute domains, any new derived attributes, etc. are specified. Next, a mining task of a specific type is defined. During the definition, the input data set and attributes, the mining algorithm, and the associated parameters are specified.

As an example, we define an input data set in the Data category. The demographic clustering algorithm is selected. The parameters for the algorithm, e.g. the maximum number of clusters, the maximum number of passes and the accuracy threshold, must then be specified. The active attributes upon which clustering is conducted are named, as are supplementary attributes for cluster understanding. When the Play button is pressed, the result of clustering is saved in the Results category and can be selected and viewed. Figure 10.7 shows the result displays for (a) a demographic clustering, (b) a decision tree classification, and (c) Boolean association rule mining.

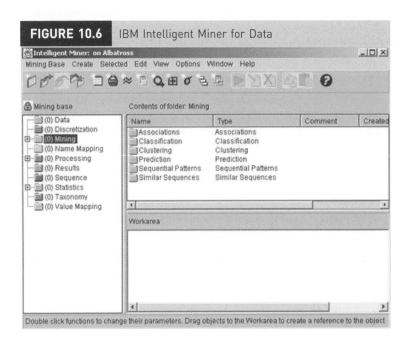

FIGURE 10.6   IBM Intelligent Miner for Data

FIGURE 10.7   Mining results in IBM Intelligent Miner for Data

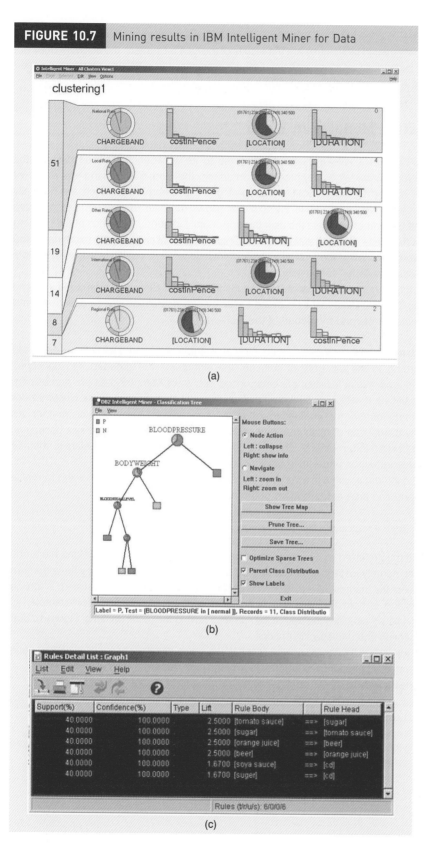

(a)

(b)

(c)

10

In general, the software is a solid and reliable tool. The graphical user interface is reasonably easy to use. Since most of the data mining techniques are the results of the QUEST project, the software does not offer as wide a range of techniques as those in Weka. Using a normal desktop PC, the processing speed can be slow. Recently, the software has been absorbed into the new DB2 Data Warehouse Edition.

10.4.3 Other System Modules in Weka

As explained briefly in Chapter 1, Weka offers other routes to its workbench facilities besides the Explorer. While the Explorer provides a graphical user interface, the simple command-line route (or module) offers a direct access to Weka facilities via short one-line commands, which are normally appreciated only by experienced users. While the Explorer allows the user to conduct a single data mining task at a time, the Experimenter offers the user the opportunity to conduct a series of data mining tasks with different techniques, different parameter settings and different remote machines, and compare the results statistically. While the Explorer gives interactive access, the Knowledge Flow route provides a batch-processing style for data mining.

This section introduces briefly and broadly the workings of the Simple Command-Line and Knowledge Flow routes. The statistical test side of the Experimenter has already been described and access to remote machines is beyond the scope of this book.

Simple Command-line route In Weka, data mining algorithms and other facilities are designed as Java classes. According to the category of solution, the algorithms are grouped into *packages* in a hierarchy. At the top level, Weka facilities are categorized into *weka.filters* for data pre-processing, *weka.classifiers* for classification, *weka.associators* for association pattern mining, *weka.clusterers* for clustering, *weka.attributeSelection* for evaluating attribute importance, and *weka.estimators* for estimating the probability distribution of attribute values. Each category is further divided into packages, each of which is in turn divided into methods. For instance, *weka.classifiers.trees.J48* refers to the J48 algorithm for decision tree induction under the classifier category.

Weka's command-line interface works in a very simple fashion. A command in the following format is entered into the command line area at the bottom of the main panel window:

```
java weka.⟨category⟩.⟨package⟩.⟨algorithm class⟩ [options] ⟨data set⟩
```

A data mining algorithm is referred to by using the usual dot notation from top level of the hierarchy down to the bottom level, namely, category name followed by package name followed by the algorithm name. To assist the user, the names of all solutions, packages and categories are listed in online documentation. A command is normally used with a set of generic or tool-specific. For example, '-t' specifies the training set and '-d' specifies the output file name for saving the result patterns. Figure 10.8(a) shows some example generic and J48-specific options.

The pathname of the input data file can be *relative* to the Weka home directory or *absolute* with all parts of the pathname enumerated. For instance in Figure 10.8(b), the pathname is `data/weather.arff`. In Section 9.5.2, the pathname was `H:\seq1.arff`. The full command in Figure 10.8(b) is:

```
java weka.classifiers.trees.J48 -t data/weather.arff
```

The command is activated by pressing the Enter key. The data mining result is, by default, displayed in the main area of the panel window, as in Figure 10.8(b).

FIGURE 10.8	Weka command-line interface

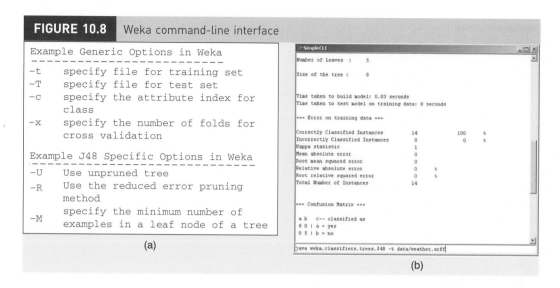

Example Generic Options in Weka

-t   specify file for training set
-T   specify file for test set
-c   specify the attribute index for
      class
-x   specify the number of folds for
      cross validation

Example J48 Specific Options in Weka

-U   Use unpruned tree
-R   Use the reduced error pruning
      method
-M   specify the minimum number of
      examples in a leaf node of a tree

(a)

(b)

Knowledge flow route

The Knowledge Flow module of Weka offers an effective alternative to the Explorer. The module can cope with large data sets. It specifies an entire data mining task from the data source to the final inspection of result by creating a knowledge flow layout. This way of setting out data mining tasks has the following advantages. First, an overview of the entire data mining process is always available. Second, the flow layout can be saved and changed so that a whole history of data mining processes can be tracked.

The module is activated by selecting the Knowledge Flow option in the Weka root window. Figure 10.9 shows the Knowledge Flow window in Weka version 3.6.1. The window consists of tabbed toolbars at the top, a canvas window named Knowledge Flow Layout in the middle and a feedback window at the bottom. The tabbed toolbar contains command buttons for various Weka facilities, divided into categories. For instance, the DataSources toolbar contains command buttons for Arff Loader, etc. The Knowledge Flow window also includes buttons for saving and loading a knowledge flow.

A knowledge flow is a directed graph composed by creating components and links between them in the canvas window. A component is created by pressing a command button in a tabbed toolbar for the component type and clicking at an appropriate location in the canvas. An icon image is then displayed at the location. Each component's properties can then be configured by selecting the Configure option from the component's pop-up menu. The component can be connected to another component by selecting a suitable option from the pop-up menu for the first component, and then dragging and dropping the 'rubber-band' that appears over the icon image for the other component.

Configuring a knowledge flow

We now demonstrate how to construct a knowledge flow with an example. The purpose of the knowledge flow is to perform classification using the J48 and Simple Naïve Bayes methods on a given data set and observe their performances.

An Arff Loader component is created by pressing Arff Loader on the Data Sources toolbar. The component is configured to represent the data set in the `weather.arff` file by selecting the Configure option from the pop-up menu and opening the file. The component is a representation of the data set in the flow chart. A Class Assigner component from the Evaluation category is needed to specify which attribute of the data set serves as the class attribute. The component is connected to the

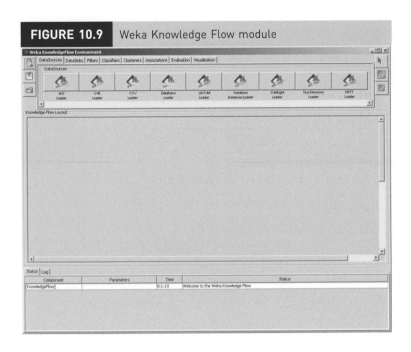

FIGURE 10.9 Weka Knowledge Flow module

Arff Loader component by selecting the Data set option from the pop-up menu of the Arff Loader and dragging and dropping the 'rubber-band' onto the Class Assigner component. Figure 10.10 shows the class attribute being selected.

For the purpose of data exploration, a Data Visualizer of the Visualization category is added below the Class Assigner. To test the working of the flow so far, we can select the Start Loading option from the Arff Loader menu and then select the Show plot option from the Data Visualizer menu. A 2D scatter plot for a pair of attributes is shown on the screen. The user can then choose any pair of attributes for data visualization.

The test option for using J48 is the training–testing split and the test option for using the Simple Naïve Bayes is cross-validation. For this purpose, a CrossValidation FoldMaker and a TrainTest SplitMaker are created, from the Evaluation toolbar. A connection is made between the Class Assigner and each of the makers. Now, J48 and Simple Naïve Bayes methods are created as classifier components from the Classifiers category. A connection link is drawn from each test option to the correct classifier. The link must be drawn twice: one to select the TrainingSet option and once to select the Testset option because both test options use the same data set for training and testing. A TextViewer component of the Visualization category is created and connected to the Simple Naïve Bayes classifier by selecting the Text option from the pop-up menu of the classifier. Through this text window, each naïve Bayes classifier for each fold of the cross-validation can be observed. Figure 10.11 shows the interface after creating these components.

Two Classifier Performance Evaluator components, from the Evaluation toolbar, are created to measure the performance of the classification methods over the data set. The results of the evaluations are connected to another TextViewer component. The connections from the classifiers to the performance evaluators are set by selecting the batchClassifier option from the pop-up menus of the classifiers. The connections from the performance evaluators to the text viewer component are created by selecting the Text option from the pop-up menu of the evaluators. Figure 10.11 shows the whole knowledge flow.

Once the knowledge flow has been formed, the data mining process can be started by selecting the Start Loading option from the pop-up menu of the Arff Loader, the start of the flow. The results can

FIGURE 10.10   After creating the Class Assigner component

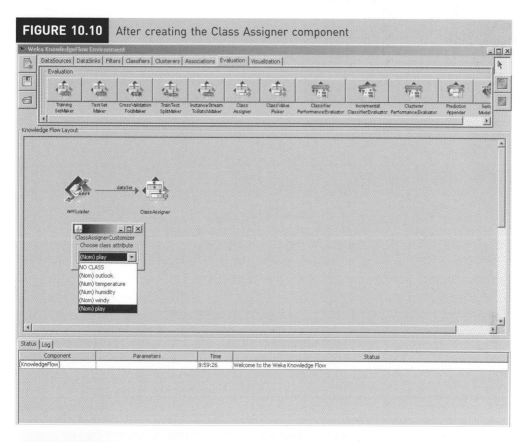

FIGURE 10.11   After creating Classifier components

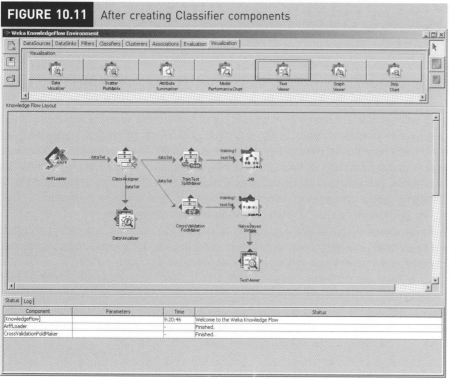

10

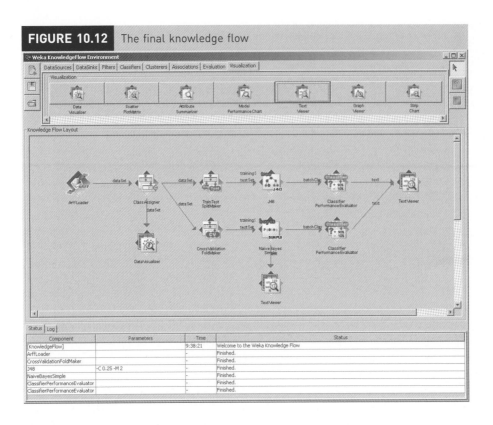

FIGURE 10.12 The final knowledge flow

be read in the text viewer window by selecting Show results from the pop-up menu of the TextViewer at the end of the flow. Figure 10.12 shows progress messages for the process at the bottom of the window. Selecting Show results from the menu of the TextViewer below the Naïve Bayes Simple classifier also reveals the naïve Bayes coefficients.

10.5 DATA MINING APPLICATIONS: TEXT MINING AND WEB MINING

Although structured data records are stored in databases, what exists more in reality are unstructured documents. In a typical organization, there exists electronic documents of various kinds, such as memoranda, emails, faxes, handbooks, manuals, papers, web pages, etc. The mountains of documents can be even bigger than the mountains of data. The mountains form another potential 'gold mine' for useful information patterns. *Text mining* is about discovering information patterns from unstructured texts whereas *web mining* is about discovering information patterns from web page structures and components. The two fields have attracted a great deal of attention in recent years.

Because of the unstructured nature of text documents and web page contents, text mining and web mining face a new set of problems and challenges. In fact, what patterns to discover, how to discover them and how to measure the usefulness of the patterns all require a thorough rethink.

On the other hand, there are similarities among data mining, text mining and web mining. Text mining and web mining can be considered, to a certain extent, as an application and extension of data mining. Therefore, this section briefly describes the application of data mining techniques to solving some of the problems in text mining and web mining. To address all of the problems in the fields of text mining and web mining and discuss their solutions, a separate book is needed.

10.5.1 Text and Text Pre-processing

In text mining, a collection of text documents of a particular content domain, known as a *corpus*, is processed. Each document within the collection is a unstructured text, but may have a set of attributes such as author, date of publication, number of pages, etc. that can be transformed into alphanumeric codes, known as *tags*. Most unstructured texts are written in natural-language sentences that can be decomposed into words. Words therefore become the basic components of text. Collectively, these words reflect the meaning of a document and embed the message that the document tries to deliver. That meaning or message is what information extraction is about.

In preparation for text mining, words are extracted from a text. A single text document may contain millions of words. Not all words are useful. Words with extremely high frequencies of occurrence, such as articles (e.g. 'the', 'a' and 'an'), prepositions (e.g. 'in', 'on', 'about') and pronouns (e.g. 'these', 'that', 'they') are not useful in reflecting the meaning of the documents and hence are normally removed as *stop words*. Words with extremely low frequency of occurrence are not likely to relate to the main meaning of the document and hence can also be removed. Many words may have a common stem. For instance, 'program', 'programs', and 'programming' all have the same stem 'program'. It is normally desirable to keep the stem of words and remove the different suffixes. Synonyms are different words that have the same or very similar meanings; sometimes, it may be desirable to unify synonyms into the same word.

All the actions of filtering stop words, stemming words and unifying synonyms help to reduce the number of words to be kept as keywords. Methods also exist for further selecting keywords from a document in the context of a corpus. For instance, the entropy keyword selection method uses the amount of entropy to determine whether a word is a useful keyword. If words are considered as dimensions of a document, reducing the number of keywords is a reduction of dimensionality.

Also in preparation for text mining, texts may be pre-processed to impose some structure on them. For instance, based on the words extracted from documents, a document–word matrix can be constructed. In such a matrix, a row represents a document identified by a document tag. A column represents a word. The content of a cell at a specific row and a specific column represents the frequency of the word occurring in the document. Such a matrix normally forms the basis for further text mining.

10.5.2 Text Mining

Association analysis After text pre-processing, such as parsing and filtering stop words, keywords are extracted from a document. The document identifier and the list of keywords contained in the document can be viewed as a transaction where the document identifier is taken as the transaction identifier and the list of keywords is taken as the list of items. For example, a document 12202 containing the keywords Computer, Database, Programming can be seen as the following transaction:

```
(12202, {Computer, Database, Programming})
```

A collection of documents, then, forms a transaction database. In this case, Boolean association rule mining solutions such as the Apriori algorithm can be used to mine the association between keywords. Given a collection of computing books, there may be an association rule:

```
{Database, Programming} ⇒ {Web page, connectivity, scripting}
```

with support and confidence above a given minimum threshold, indicating a strong association between programming database applications and website development.

10

A potential problem with this kind of keyword-level association discovery is that many association patterns may be discovered. Among them, many chance associations may exist between random words. This level of association can be shallow in meaning, indicating only the co-occurrences of keywords.

Some frequently occurring keywords may form meaningful *terms* or *phrases*. For instance, the keywords 'computer', 'human' and 'interaction' may occur frequently together, indicating the existence of a term 'human–computer interaction'. The term should be taken as a single unit in further association rule discovery. The discovery of association patterns at the term level tends to be more interesting. Useless associations of random words can be reduced, making the discovery process faster.

Related to association rule discovery is the use of categories of words that are similar in some sense for generalized association rule mining. Words of similar meaning or words that often describe the same concepts are categorized. Associations between categories can be of interest. For instance, 'human–computer interaction' and 'human–machine interaction' may be considered to be the same and used as the same term in association mining.

Association analysis at keyword and term levels assists information extraction from documents. As described earlier, frequently occurring keywords may already serve the purpose of term or phrase extractions. The existence of certain collections of keywords and terms may indicate the existence of entities or objects with properties.

Document classification   Document classification, also called *text categorization*, is concerned with classifying a given document into one of several predefined classes. Taking a collection of documents with their own sets of keywords as training examples, a classification model may be constructed and evaluated. Such a classification model is then used for classifying an unseen document according to the set of keywords extracted from the document. So far, this sounds straightforward.

However, unlike a structured relational table, documents may contain different sets of keywords. Classification models that rely on attribute–value pairs to discriminate between classes may not work very well. This is because there are no well-structured attributes available for text. If each keyword is taken as an attribute, this creates the following problems for classification models:

- Many attributes exist and it is extremely inefficient for decision tree induction methods to calculate information gain across all attributes for the selection of the root of a tree.

- Even if it is feasible for an algorithm to complete the tree induction, the tree is likely to be large, complex and suffer the problem of overfitting, causing poor performance.

- Because different documents may have different sets of keywords, many null values are introduced into the training set and the performance of a classification model further deteriorates.

According to research conducted in this area, some classification approaches can solve the problem of text categorization. The *k*-nearest neighbours model, mixture models, Bayesian classifiers and association-based classification have been used successfully. Take the *k*-nearest neighbours approach as an example. A collection of training documents is prepared. For each document, a set of keywords describing the document is extracted and organized into a vector. A class tag is assigned to each document. When an unseen document needs to be categorized, a set of keywords is extracted from the unseen document into a vector. The distance between the unseen document and each of the training documents is calculated. The nearest *k* training documents are located. The class of the unseen document is taken as the class of the majority of the *k*-nearest neighbour training documents. The key here is a sensible way of measuring similarity between documents based on keyword vectors.

Document classification can enable automatic categorization of documents according to their contents and has many areas of application. IT system administrators can use such a classification model to determine whether incoming emails are junk emails. Software agents can search web page contents and automatically categorize URLs for effective indexing of the links. Even a personal organizer on a desktop PC can use the classification model to help organize files on the local disk.

Document clustering Sometimes it is necessary to group documents containing similar words. In a typical organization, emails about a specific subject matter are written and exchanged. Minutes of meetings regarding a certain long-term issue may contain repeated discussions about the issue over a period of time. It may be useful to track all or some emails or meeting minutes of this kind.

Document clustering is about partitioning documents into groups according to similar keywords contained in the documents. Like many other text mining methods, the clustering is conducted over keywords extracted from the documents. The clustering algorithms of data mining are faced with the problem of the high dimensionality of text documents. In high-dimensional space, data objects are diverse and distances between them become uniform. It is then difficult to separate documents into groups because similarity within groups is more or less the same as similarity between groups. Inevitably, dimension reduction is an essential step for real-life documents. Dimension reduction techniques such as principal component analysis (PCA) and wavelet transformation (DWT) can be used. Some dimension reduction methods are specifically developed for reducing the dimensions for text documents, including latent semantic indexing (LSI), probabilistic latent semantic indexing (PLSI) and locality preserving indexing (LPI).

With reduced dimensions, document clustering can be conducted using the clustering algorithms described in Chapters 4 and 5. For measuring similarity between two given documents, a popular measure is the ratio of common keywords, i.e. the number of common keywords divided by the total number of words in the two documents. This measure is a version of the Jaccard's coefficient. Alternatively, the cosine distance function described in Chapter 4 is also a suitable similarity measure between text documents.

10.5.3 Web Mining

The web offers a platform for a huge amount of online documents. Compared to off-line text documents, documents on the web tend to be semantically rich, multimedia, semi-structured, and dynamic. Semantic richness refers to the content of a web page. It is not uncommon for a web page to contain not only text on a specific subject, but also advertisements, flash animations and images. This makes information extraction more difficult than in a text mining context. Web pages can be considered as semi-structured documents where the mark-up tags indicate certain structures but text within a paragraph remains unstructured. Web pages often contain hypermedia links to text documents, audio files, image files and video files. These multimedia documents may also contain valuable information. Web pages are dynamic in the sense that new pages are added constantly and old pages are removed constantly. Even the content of a web page can be dynamic, if a database is used underneath the page. All of these features of web documents make web mining more challenging but at the same time more promising.

Web mining has its own set of problems to solve. Our focus here is on the application of data mining techniques for the purposes of web mining. Keyword- or term-level association analysis, document classification and document clustering are relevant for web documents. However, the semantic richness of web pages means a greater presence of *noise*, i.e. irrelevant materials in the same pages. Because of this, all three types of mining task are more difficult and challenging. At the same time, labels and hyperlinks embedded in a web page may also provide strong hints and indications about the meaning of text on the page. These hints and indications may assist in the discovery of strong associations, induction of more accurate classification models and even more sensible measures of similarities.

10

One important area in which data mining techniques should be able to assist is web usage mining. A web server normally maintains a log file of web page visits as part of system administration. In such a *web log file*, each log entry contains the visitor's IP address, the timestamp of the visit, the URL of the web page visited, the browser and communication protocol used, the number of bytes of data transferred, etc. These log record details collectively provide a rich source of data.

Web log records should be cleaned, transformed and even re-structured before mining takes place. For instance, since the HTTP communication protocol is a stateless protocol, each access to a page is considered as a separate visit. There is no concept of a 'session'. Some preparatory operations may be needed to introduce the concept of sessions based on a heuristic time period measurement.

Boolean associations among page visits can be discovered by using methods such as Apriori (see Chapter 8). Sequential patterns among page visits can also be discovered. Web log records may be grouped according to similar page visits. These patterns may help e-commerce website owners to monitor customer online shopping behaviour and website designers to discover design flaws and improve website structure.

10.5.4 Text Mining Problems

As indicated at the beginning of this section, text mining and web mining have fundamental problems that arise from their own domains. Although this is not the focal point of this section, it is useful to gain some awareness of these problems. Interested readers can find more information about various solutions to the problems from the references given in the Bibliographical Notes.

Since text documents consist of words, understanding what role a word serves in a sentence is essential for understanding the meaning of the sentence. In the sentence 'Tim emails the busy Head of Department', for example, 'Tim', 'Head' and 'Department' are nouns and 'busy' is an adjective, but 'emails' serves here as a verb. Normally, without any context, the word 'emails' would be considered as the plural form of a noun. One important task of text mining in relation to natural-language processing is to identify the correct *part of speech* (POS) of a word and tag the word. The task is known as *POS tagging*. The problem can be seen as a form of classification where the classes are parts of speech (noun, verb, adjective, adverb, preposition, conjunction, pronoun and determiner), and the sentence structure and position of the word, etc. are descriptive features. The objective is to find the highest scored tag among the classes to assign to a word. The literature reports effective use of hidden Markov models (HMM) in solving this problem.

A written text uses words and symbols to convey a message or to describe the meaning of something. Even if a message is quite short and the meaning quite straightforward, the meaning is buried among the words of the text. For instance, the paragraph above tries to describe the meaning of 'POS tagging'. That is the information embedded in a paragraph of 175 words (or word occurrences). Information extraction is about extracting information from a body of text. It can be put into perspective as follows. The most trivial level of extraction is keyword extraction. Based on the keywords, terms and phrases that are more meaningful are extracted. Based on keywords, terms and phrases, compound entities corresponding to objects of certain kind are extracted. Again, the literature reports some success in exploiting the HMM method.

Related to information extraction but different is the problem of text summarization, which tries to summarize a large document into a concise version that still captures the most important statements. In a way the process is very much like compression. The difference is that the compressed version must be easily comprehensible without the need to 'decompress'. The objective of the process is to select key sentences. The literature reports some success in the use of Bayesian classifiers in extracting such sentences.

10.5.5 Web Mining Problems

Information retrieval (IR) has been a field of research for several decades. Information retrieval engines search unstructured text documents and, ideally, pull out those that meet the user's query condition. In the context of the web, information retrieval has a close link with search engines whose main function is to find and return the most relevant links to web pages. For both, the success of the search result is judged by the precision and recall rate (see Chapter 7). In the context of document retrieval, precision is the ratio of the number of relevant documents retrieved to the total number of documents retrieved; recall rate is the ratio of the number of relevant documents retrieved to the total number of relevant documents. The two measures can be combined into a single F-score that is the ratio of the product of the two measures against the average of the two measures.

Finding a few truly relevant documents from a sea of documents is not an easy task. A straight keyword-based search requires the user to know exactly the right keywords in describing the documents. If not, the results of retrieval are very poor. Given the existence of synonyms (different words with the same or very similar meaning) and homonyms (the same word with different meanings), the job of finding the right documents can be much harder. Google's text indexing and PageRank algorithms have achieved a reasonable degree of success in returning a ranked list of relevant documents, which is the main reason for its popularity. However, the road to the summit of total success still seems very long.

Web pages are semi-structured documents that contain mark-up tags and hyperlinks to other documents. These features result in tasks such as mining web page structure and mining web page links. Mining page structure aims to discover a semantic structure among the components of a page rather than the presentation structure of HTML mark-up tags. The structure divides and groups web page components according to relevant topics and purposes. Such a semantic structure does not contain components irrelevant to the topic, such as navigation buttons. Finding such a structure from a web page and across web pages helps the organization of semantic content within an page and in gaining a semantically homogeneous view of web site content across pages. This type of mining task may require its own solutions. A reported algorithm, known as 'vision-based page segmentation', works on the HTML mark-up structure and divides page components according to positions of the components as perceived by human vision.

Web link analysis is a task of analyzing hyperlinks in web pages. Depending on the purpose, different analyses can be performed using different methods. One of the purposes is to automatically determine the authoritative pages on a certain topic, known as *authority*. Embedding a hyperlink in a page normally indicates the author's approval and endorsement of the page to which the link refers. There even exist pages, known as 'hubs', particularly designed to refer to useful external links. Normally, the quality of the authority can be judged by the number of links that refer to it. The quality of a hub can be measured by the number of high-quality authorities to which it refers. An algorithm known as HITS has been developed for determining authorities and hubs and has proved successful.

Web link mining goes beyond determining authoritative pages. Because a web page normally contains more than one semantic component, analysis between semantic blocks within or across pages can be of interest. In addition, hyperlinks form a directed graph. The study of such a graph helps the understanding of the content.

10.6 SUMMARY

In this final chapter, some important issues regarding application aspects of data mining have been summarized and discussed. The cross-industry standard methodology for data mining (CRISP-DM) was introduced. In order to enhance understanding of the methodology, a case study about customer segmentation was presented. The case study demonstrates the activities carried out by the project team and decisions taken by the data analysts during the project lifecycle. Practical data mining is a science as well as an art. Not only must it be done properly in a way that is statistically sound, but it also requires years of experience. Data mining can be done badly and many data mining projects do fail. This is why a methodology specifying how to do things properly is very useful.

This chapter presented data mining as a data analysis tool within the context of a greater integrated decision-making system that involves related technologies such as data warehouse and OLAP. The chapter described data warehousing issues that relate to the use of data mining. The positioning of data mining in this way clarifies the role that data mining plays within an information-based decision-making environment, particularly in large size organizations.

We also provided a brief overview of a number of data mining software tools that are currently available. The working principles of IBM Intelligent Miner for Data were shown. For practical data mining, Weka facilities besides the Explorer and Experimenter, i.e. the Knowledge Flow and Simple Command-Line modules, were introduced. These modules offer effective alternatives to the Explorer. The Simple Command-Line enables fast execution of an individual data mining or preparation operation. The Knowledge Flow module enables streaming a complex discovery project from the start of data preparation to the final evaluation of patterns in terms of a connected graph of individual tasks. This facility promotes careful setting up of data mining activities and is endorsed by a number of data mining tools.

Finally, the chapter provided a brief introduction to the subjects of text mining and web mining as applications to and extensions of data mining. The chapter describes how existing data mining techniques can be used to solve some discovery problems in text documents and web pages. Text mining and web mining have immense potential for practical use and hence should be studied as a separate subject.

EXERCISES

1 In the previous chapters, various data mining techniques to solve three types of data mining problem (classification, clustering and association) have been described. Using some of the techniques as an example, describe how to use them for other data mining problems.

2 Discovering anomalies, known as 'outlier mining', is about finding abnormal and outlier patterns that may exist in a data set. Such a kind of discovery can be useful for fraud detection and product fault diagnosis. It is an area of data mining that this text has not covered. Discuss possible uses of existing clustering techniques for the detection of such patterns.

3 Describe the main phases and major tasks in each phase of a data mining project lifecycle according to the CRISP-DM methodology. Conduct some research on the Internet to find an interesting data mining project, and study it from the perspective of the CRISP-DM methodology.

4 Conduct some research into the SAS SEMMA data mining approach. Compare SEMMA to CRISP-DM and describe the major similarities and differences of the two schemes.

5 Exercise 10 in Chapter 6 presented an application scenario about an estate agency selling houses. Use this application scenario as an example to illustrate some major tasks for each phase of the data mining lifecycle.

6 Figure 10.5 outlines a multi-tier architecture of a data warehouse environment for a typical organization. Use your organization as an example to show the working of the data warehouse environment. In particular, attempt to address the following key points during your work:

(a) data representations in the operational systems, the central repository and the data marts;

(b) any metadata to be kept in the central repository;

(c) specific problems that may be encountered during data loading and integration, and the consequences of these problems to the later data analysis and mining stage;

(d) example data analysis tools that should be available in the environment.

7 CBA and See5 are two single-purpose data mining tools. CBA is an association rule mining tool that can discover Boolean and quantitative association rules. See5 is a decision tree induction tool that uses the C4.5 algorithm (the successor of ID3) to induce decision trees. Both tools are free to download. Obtain a copy of the software and practise some mining operations with the data sets provided with the software. Because of its reliability and quality of product, the See5 software is still used for real-life data mining.

8 Practise using the Simple Command-Line module of Weka with some data sets provided. (Note that the location for a data set is `data/<data set>.arff`.)

9 Practise using the Knowledge Flow module of Weka by setting a data mining task layout specified as follows:

(a) a knowledge flow connection to the data set `iris.arff`;

(b) a knowledge flow specification of the class as different types of iris flowers;

(c) the 10-fold cross-validation test option;

(d) any three classification techniques provided by Weka with their own classification evaluations;

(e) a knowledge flow viewer to view the classification results of all three classifiers.

Perform the mining operation specified by the flow layout and observe the results.

10 Describe the similarity and differences between text mining and web mining. Summarize and highlight the main categories of mining task for each. Give an example for each task.

11 Use the bank data set downloaded from Weka website as an example to conduct a data mining project. Create your own business objectives according to your understanding of the data set, and apply the CRISP-DM methodology. In the mining/modeling stage of the project, try to use the Knowledge Flow route to specify any data mining tasks.

BIBLIOGRAPHICAL NOTES

References for this chapter are from various sources. Chapman *et al.* (2000) is the main reference for the coverage of the CRISP-DM methodology. The document covers both the reference model and the user guide of the methodology. Larose (2005) and Connolly and Begg (2005) give a shorter and more concise coverage of the methodology. The vendor-specific data mining approach SAS SEMMA is explained briefly by short articles on the Internet and by Randall (2007). The customer segmentation case study is cited (with permission from the author) from an article in the online *DB2 Magazine* (Saarenvirta 1998).

Early references on data warehousing include Kelly (1997) and Anahory and Murray (1997). Database texts such as Connolly and Begg (2005) include a single chapter on the subject. It is not easy to find recent comprehensive texts on the subject. Ponniah (2001) is one of the few available. References to data mining software tools are mainly from short articles on the Internet and www.kdnuggets.com. The Kdnugget newsletter runs surveys of the software tools used. It is intriguing to see the rapid change in popular tools from year to year. Early surveys of data mining tools include a tutorial by Elder and Abbott (1998) and a survey by Goebel and Gruenwald (1999). Section 10.4.2 mainly refers to the author's teaching notes in early years before IBM Intelligent Miner for Data was replaced by Weka due to the withdrawal of technical support by IBM. Witten and Frank (2005) provide comprehensive coverage of other Weka modules, including using data mining solutions through application program interfaces.

A number of references are used for Section 10.5. Han and Kamber (2006) provide a concise but systematic coverage of the two subjects. Konchady (2006) gives a comprehensive coverage of text mining although the same text also addresses most web mining issues. A short survey of web mining is given by Kosala and Blockeel (2000). Berry (2003) and Berry and Castellanos (2008) present more thorough reviews of the field of text mining.

10

BIBLIOGRAPHY

Aggarwal, C.C. (2003) Towards Systematic Design of Distance Functions for Data Mining Applications, *In Proceedings of the 9th ACM SIGKDD International Conference on Knowledge Discovery and Data Mining*, Washington, D.C. USA, August, pp. 9–18.

Agrawal, R. and Shafer, J.C. (1996) Parallel Mining of Association Rules, *IEEE Transactions on Knowledge and Data Engineering*, Vol. 8, No. 6, pp. 962–969.

Agrawal, R. and Srikant, R. (1994) Fast Algorithms for Mining Association Rules in Large Databases, *In Proceedings of the 20th International Conference on Very Large Data Bases*, Santiago, Chile, September, pp. 487–499.

Agrawal, R. and Srikant, R. (1995) Mining Sequential Patterns, *In Proceedings of the 11th International Conference on Data Engineering*, Taipei, Taiwan, March, pp. 3–14.

Agrawal, R., Gehrke, J., Gunopulos, D. and Raghavan, P. (1998) Automatic Subspace Clustering of High Dimensional Data for Data Mining Applications, *In Proceedings of 1998 ACM SIGMOD International Conference on Management of Data*, Seattle, Washington, USA, June, ACM Press, pp. 94–105.

Agrawal, R., Gupta, A. and Sarawagi, S. (1995) Modeling Multi-dimensional Databases, *IBM Research Report*, IBM Almaden Research Center, California, USA.

Agrawal, R., Imielinski, T. and Swami, A. (1993) Mining Association Rules between Sets of Items in Large Databases, *In Proceedings of 1993 ACM SIGMOD International Conference on Management of Data*, Washington, D.C. USA, May, pp. 207–216.

Agrawal, R., Mannila, H., Srikant, R., Toivonen, H. and Verkamo, A. (1996) Fast Discovery of Association Rules in Fayyad, Piatetsky-Shapiro, Smyth and Uthurusamy (eds), *Advances in Knowledge Discovery and Data Mining*, Chapter 12, AAAI/MIT Press.

Aleksander, I. and Morton, H. (1995) *An Introduction to Neural Computing*, 2nd Revised Edition, International Thomson Publishing.

Anahory, S. and Murray, D. (1997) *Data Warehousing in the Real World: A Practical Guide for Building Decision Support Systems*, Addision-Wesley.

Aumann, Y., Feldman, R. and Lipshtat, O. (1999) Borders: An Efficient Algorithm for Association Generation in Dynamic Databases, *Journal of Intelligent Information Systems*, Vol. 12, No.1, pp. 61–73.

Ayad, A., El-Makky, N. and Taha, Y. (2001) Incremental Mining of Constrained Association Rules, *In Proceedings of the 1st International SIAM Conference on Data Mining*, Chicago, USA, April.

Bayardo Jr., R. and Agrawal, R. (1999) Mining the Most Interesting Rules, *In Proceedings of the 5th ACM SIGKDD International Conference on Knowledge Discovery and Data Mining*, San Diego, CA, USA, August, pp. 145–154.

Berkhin, P. (2002) Survey of Clustering Data Mining Techniques, http://citeseer.ist.psu.edu/berkhin02survey.html, accessed 19 March 2008.

Berry, M. (ed.) (2003) *Survey of Text Mining: Clustering, Classification, and Retrieval No.1*, Springer.

Berry, M. and Castellanos, M., (eds) (2008) *Survey of Text Mining: Clustering, Classification, and Retrieval No. 2*, 2nd Edition, Springer.

Berry, M.J.A. and Linoff, G. (1997) *Data Mining Techniques for Marketing, Sales and Customer Support*, John Wiley & Sons, Chapters 1–3, pp. 1–62.

Berry, M.J.A. and Linoff, G. (2004) *Data Mining Techniques for Marketing, Sales and Customer Relationship Management*, 2nd Edition, John Wiley & Sons, Chapters 1–3, pp. 1–42.

Borg, L. and Groenen, P. (1997) *Modern Multidimensional Scaling: Theory and Applications*, Springer-Verlag.

Bouman, C.A. (2005) CLUSTER: An Unsupervised Algorithm for Modeling Gaussian Mixtures, https://engineering.purdue.edu/_bouman/software/cluster/, accessed 29 March 2009.

Breiman, L., Friedman, J., Olshen, R. and Stone, C. (1984) *Classification and Regression Trees*, Belmont, CA: Wadsworth International Group.

Buntine, W. (1991) Learning Classification Trees, in Hand, D. (ed.), *Artificial Intelligence Frontiers in Statistics*, London: Chapman & Hall, pp. 182–201.

CACM (1996) *Communications of the ACM*, Vol. 39, No. 11.

CACM (1998) Examining Data Quality, *Communications of the ACM*, Vol. 41, No. 2.

Cai, Y., Cercone, N. and Han, J. (1990) An Attribute-Oriented Approach for Learning Classification Rules from Relational Databases, *In Proceedings of the 6th International Conference on Data Engineering*, IEEE Computer Society, Los Angeles, California, USA, February, pp. 281–288.

Centrowska, J. (1987) PRISM: An Algorithm for Inducing Modular Rules, *International Journal for Man–Machine Studies*, Vol. 27, No. 4, pp. 349–370.

Chapman, P., Clinton, J., Kerber, R., Khabaza, T., Reinartz, T., Shearer, C. and Wirth, R. (2000) *CRISP-DM 1.0: Step-by-Step Data Mining Guide*, www.crisp-dm.org, accessed 27 August 2009.

Chen, M-S., Han, J. and Yu, P.S. (1996) Data Mining: An Overview from a Database Perspective, *IEEE Transactions on Knowledge and Data Engineering*, Vol. 8, No. 6, pp. 866–883.

Cheng, C-H., Fu, A.W. and Zhang, Y. (1999) Entropy-based Subspace Clustering for Mining Numerical Data, *In Proceedings of the 5th ACM SIGMOD International Conference on Knowledge Discovery and Data Mining*, San Diego, California, USA, August, pp. 84–93.

Cheung, D.W., Han, J., Ng, V. and Wong, C.Y. (1996) Maintenance of Discovered Association Rules in Large Databases: An Incremental Updating Technique, *In Proceedings of the 12th International Conference on Data Engineering*, IEEE Computer Society, Washington, D.C. USA, February-March, pp. 106–114.

Cheung, D.W., Lee, S.D., and Kao, B. (1997) A General Incremental Technique for Maintaining Discovered Association Rules, *In Proceedings of the 5th International Conference on Database Systems and Advanced Applications*, Melbourne, Australia, April, World Scientific Press, pp. 185–194.

Clark, P. and Boswell, R. (1991) Rule Induction with CN2: Recent Improvements in *Machine Learning: Proceedings of the 6th European Working Session on Learning (EWSL-91)*, Portugal: Springer-Verlag, pp. 151–163.

Cohen, W.W. (1995) Fast Effective Rule Induction, *In Proceedings of the 12th International Conference on Machine Learning*, Lake Tahoe, California, USA, July, Morgan Kaufmann, pp. 115–123.

Collobert, R., Bengio, S. and Mariêthoz, J. (2002) Torch: A Modular Machine Learning Software Library, Technical Report IDIAP-RR 02–46, http://www.torch.ch/introduction.php, accessed 30 March 2009.

Connolly, T. and Begg, C. (2005) *Database Systems: A Practical Approach to Design, Implementation and Management*, 4th Edition, Addison Wesley, Chapters 31–32.

Cost, S. and Salzberg, S. (1993) A Weighted Nearest Neighbour Algorithm for Learning with Symbolic Features, *Machine Learning*, Vol. 10, No. 1, pp. 57–78.

Du, H., Jassim, S. and Obatusin, M.F. (2000) Effects of Attribute Selection Measures and Sampling Policies on Functional Structures of Decision Trees, in Ebecken, N. and Brebbia, C.A. (eds) *Data Mining II: Second International Conference on Data Mining*, Cambridge, UK, July, WIT Press, pp. 391–400.

Dunham, M., Xiao, Y., Le Gruenwald, L. and Hossain, Z. (2000) A Survey of Association Rules, http://www2.cs.uh.edu/%7Eceick/6340/grue-assoc.pdf, accessed 28 January 2010

Economist (1995) How to turn junk mail into a goldmine – or perhaps not, *The Economist*, April 1st.

Elder, J. and Abbott, D.W. (1998) A Comparison of Leading Data Mining Tools, In Proceedings of the 4th International Conference on Knowledge Discovery and Data Mining, https://www.aaai.org/Papers/KDD/1998/Tutorials/Abbott.pdf, accessed on 27 August, 2009.

Elmasri, R. and Navathe, S.B. (2007) *Fundamentals of Database Systems*, 5th Edition. Addison Wesley.

Ertöz, L., Steinback, M. and Kumar, V. (2003) Finding Clusters of Different Sizes, Shapes and Density in Noisy High Dimensional Data, *In Proceedings of the 3rd SIAM International Conference on Data Mining*, San Francisco, California, USA, May.

Ester, M., Kriegel, H-P., Sander, J., Wimmer, M. and Xu, X. (1998) Incremental Clustering for Mining in a Data Warehousing Environment, *In Proceedings of the 24th International Conference on Very Large Data Bases*, New York City, USA, August, Morgan Kaufmann, pp. 323–333.

Ester, M., Kriegel, H-P., Sander, J. and Xu, X. (1996) A Density-based Algorithm for Discovering Clusters in Large Spatial Databases with Noise, *In Proceedings of the 2nd International Conference on Knowledge Discovery and Data Mining*, Portland, Oregon, USA, August, AAAI Press, pp. 226–231.

Fasulo, D. (1999) An Analysis of Recent Work on Clustering Algorithms, http://citeseer.ist.psu.edu/fasulo99analysi.html, accessed 19 March 2008.

Fayyad, U.M., Piatetsky-Shapiro, G. and Smyth, P. (1996) *Advances in Knowledge Discovery and Data Mining*, AAAI Press, pp. 1–34.

Frawley, W.J., Piatetsky-Shapiro, G. and Maltheus, C.J. (1991) *Knowledge Discovery in Databases: An Overview*, AAAI/MIT Press.

Geng, L. and Hamilton, H.J. (2006) Interestingness Measures for Data Mining: A Survey, *ACM Computing Surveys*, Vol. 38, No. 3.

Goebel, M. and Gruenwald, L., (1999) A Survey of Data Mining and Knowledge Discovery Software Tools, *ACM SIGKDD Explorations Newsletter*, Vol. 1, No. 1, pp. 20–33.

Gunopoulos, D., Khardon, R., Mannila, H. and Toivonen, T. (1997) Data Mining, Hypergraph Transversals and Machine Learning, *In Proceedings of the 6th Symposium on Principles of Database Systems*, Tucson, Arizona, USA, May, pp. 209–216.

Han, J. and Kamber, M. (2001) *Data Mining: Concepts and Techniques*, San Francisco: Morgan Kaufmann Publishers.

Han, J. and Kamber, M. (2006) *Data Mining: Concepts and Techniques*, 2nd Edition, Morgan Kaufmann Publishers.

Han, J., Pei, H. and Yin, Y. (2000) Mining Frequent Patterns without Candidate Generation, *In Proceedings of 2000 ACM SIGMOD Conference on Management of Data*, ACM Press. Dallas, Texas, USA, May, pp. 1–12.

Hand, D., Mannila, H. and Smyth, P. (2001) *Principles of Data Mining*, MIT Press.

Hart, A. (1984) Experience in the Use of an Inductive System in Knowledge Engineering, in Bramer, M. (ed.), Research and Developments in Expert Systems, Cambridge: Cambridge University Press.

Hartigan, J.A. (1975) *Clustering Algorithms*, New York: John Wiley & Sons.

Haykin, S. (2008) *Neural Networks and Learning Machines*, 3rd Edition, Prentice-Hall.

Hidber, C. (1998) Online Association Rule Mining, Technical Report #UCB//CSD-98–1004, Department of Electrical Engineering and Computer Science, University of California at Berkeley.

Hipp, J., Guntzer, U. and Nakaeizadeh, G. (2000) Algorithms for Association Rule Mining: A General Survey and Comparison, *ACM SIGKDD Explorations Newsletter*, Vol. 2, No. 1, June, pp. 58–64.

Holte, R.C. (1993) Very Simple Classification Rules Perform Well on Most Commonly Used Datasets, *Machine Learning*, Vol. 11, No. 1, pp. 63–90.

Jain, A.K. and Dubes, R.C. (1988) *Algorithms for Clustering Data*, Englewood Cliffs, NJ: Prentice Hall.

Jain, A.K., Murty M.N. and Flynn P.J. (1999) Data Clustering: A Review, ACM Computing Surveys, Vol. 31, No. 3, pp. 264–323.

Jarvis, R.A. and Patrick, E.A. (1973) Clustering Using a Similarity Measure Based on Shared Nearest Neighbours, IEEE Transactions on Computers, Vol. 22, No. 11, pp. 1025–1034

Jones, D.S. (1979) Elementary Information Theory, Oxford: Oxford University Press.

Joshi, M., Karypis, G. and Kumar, V. (1999) A Universal Formulation of Sequential Patterns, Technical Report #99–21, University of Minnesota, Minneapolis.

Karypis, G. (2006) CLUTO – Family of Data Clustering Software Tools, http://glaros.dtc.umn.edu/gkhome/views/cluto/, accessed 30 March 2009.

Karypis, G., Han, E-H. and Kumar, V (1999) CHAMELEON: A Hierarchical Clustering Algorithm Using Dynamic Modelling, IEEE Transactions on Computers, Vol. 32, No. 8, pp. 68–75.

Kaufman, L. and Rousseeuw, P.J. (1990) Finding Groups in Data: An Introduction to Cluster Analysis, New York: John Wiley & Sons.

Kelly, S. (1997) Data Warehouse in Action, John Wiley & Sons.

Keogh, E. and Pazzani, M. (2001) Derivative Dynamic Time Warping, In Proceedings of the 1st SIAM International Conference on Data Mining, Chicago, IL, USA, April.

Konchady, M. (2006) Text Mining Application Programming, Charles River Media.

Kosala, R. and Blockeel, H. (2000) Web Mining Research: A Survey, ACM SIGKDD Explorations Newsletter, Vol. 2, No. 1, pp. 1–15.

Kotsiantis, S. and Kanellopoulos, D. (2006a) Discretisation Techniques: A Recent Survey, GESTS International Transactions on Computer Science and Engineering, Vol. 32, No. 1, pp. 47–58.

Kotsiantis, S. and Kanellopoulos, D. (2006b) Association Rule Mining: A Recent Overview, GESTS International Transactions on Computer Science and Engineering, Vol. 32, No. 1, pp. 71–82.

Langley, P., Iba, W. and Thompson, K. (1992) An Analysis of Bayesian Classifiers, In Proceedings of the 10th National Conference on Artificial Intelligence, San Jose, California, USA, July, pp. 223–228.

Larose, D.T. (2005) Discovering Knowledge in Data, New Jersey: John Wiley & Sons.

Lee, C.H., Lin, C.R. and Chen, M.S. (2001) Sliding-Window Filtering: An Efficient Algorithm for Incremental Mining, In Proceedings of the 10th International Conference on Information and Knowledge Management, Atlanta, Georgia, USA, November, pp. 263–270.

Lewis, D.D. (1998) Naïve Bayes at Forty: The Independence Assumption in Information Retrieval, In Proceedings of the 10th European Conference on Machine Learning (ECML1998), Chemnitz, Germany, April, pp. 4–15.

Little, R.J.A. and Rubin, D.B. (2002) Statistical Analysis with Missing Data, 2nd Edition, New York: John Wiley & Sons.

Liu, H. and Motoda, H. (eds) (1998) Feature Extraction, Construction and Selection: A Data Mining Perspective, Kluwer Academic Publishing.

Liu, W.Z. and White, A.P. (1994) The Importance of Attribute Selection Measures in Decision Tree Induction, Machine Learning, Vol. 15, No. 1, pp. 25–41.

Loftus, R. and Loftus E.F. (1988) Essence of Statistics, 2nd Edition, Alfred A. Knoff Inc.

Luan, J. and Zhao, C-M. (eds) (2006) Data Mining in Action: Case studies of Enrolment Management, New Directions for Institutional Research, No. 131, Jossey-Bass.

Ma, J. and Drury, C.G. (2003) The Human Factors Issues in Data Mining, In Proceedings of the Human Factors and Ergonomics Society 47th Annual Meeting, Communications, Vol. 47, pp. 716–720.

MacQueen, J.B. (1967) Some Methods for classification and Analysis of Multivariate Observations, In Proceedings of the 5th Berkeley Symposium on Mathematical Statistics and Probability, Berkeley: University of California Press.

Magnani, M. (2004) Techniques for Dealing with Missing Data in Knowledge Discovery Tasks, http://magnanim.web.cs.unibo.it/data/pdf/missingdata.pdf, accessed on 15 May 2008.

Mendenhall, W. and Sincich, T.L. (2003) A Second Course in Statistics: Regression Analysis, 6th Edition, Prentice-Hall.

Michalski, R.S., Mozetic, I., Hong, J. and Lavrac, N. (1986) The Multi-Purpose Incremental Learning System AQ15 and Its Testing Application to Three Medical Domains, In Proceedings of the 5th National Conference on Artificial Intelligence, Philadelphia, Pennsylvania, USA, August

Michie, D., Spiegelhalter, D.J. and Taylor, C.C. (1994) Machine Learning, Neural and Statistical Classification, Prentice-Hall.

Mingers, J. (1989) An Empirical Comparison of Selection Measures for Decision-Tree Induction, Machine Learning, Vol. 3, pp. 319–342.

Molina, L.C., Belanche, L. and Nebot, A. (2002) Feature Selection Algorithms: A Survey and Experimental Evaluation, In Proceedings of the 2002 IEEE International Conference on Data Mining (ICDM'02), Maebashi City, Japan, December, pp. 306–313.

Murthy, S.K. (1998) Automatic Construction of Decision Trees From Data: A Multi-disciplinary Survey, Journal of Data Mining and Knowledge Discovery, Vol. 2, No. 4, pp. 345–389.

Nagesh, H.S. (1999) High Performance Subspace Clustering for Massive Data Sets, Master's Thesis, North-western University.

Nagesh, H.S., Goil, S. and Choudhary, A. (2000) A Scalable Parallel Subspace Clustering Algorithm for Massive Data Sets, In Proceedings of International Conference on Parallel Processing, Toronto, Canada, August, pp. 477–484.

Parsons, L., Haque, E. and Liu, H. (2004) Subspace Clustering for High Dimensional Data: A Review, ACM SIGKDD Explorations Newsletter, Vol. 6, No. 1, pp. 90–105.

Pasquier, N., Bastide, Y., Taouil, R. and Lakhal, L. (1999) Discovering Frequent Closed Itemsets for Association Rules, In Proceedings of the 7th International Conference on Database Theory, Jerusalem, Israel, January, pages 398–416.

Piatetsky-Shapiro, G. (2007) www.kdnuggets.com, accessed 29 October 2007.

Ponniah, P. (2001) Data Warehousing Fundamentals: A Comprehensive Guide for IT Professionals, John Wiley & Sons.

Quinlan, J.R. (1986) Induction of Decision Trees, Machine Learning, Vol. 1, pp. 81–106.

Quinlan, J.R. (1987) Simplifying Decision Trees, *International Journal for Man–Machine Studies*, Vol. 27, pp. 221–234.

Rabiner, L.R. (1989) A Tutorial on Hidden Markov Models and Selected Applications in Speech Recognition, *In Proceedings of IEEE*, Vol. 77, No. 2, pp. 257–286.

Randall, M. (2007) *Data Mining Using SAS Enterprise Miner*, John Wiley & Sons.

Rees, D.G. (2001) *Essential Statistics*, 4th Edition, Oxford: Chapman & Hall/CRC Press.

Saarenvirta, G., (1998) Mining Customer Data: A Step-by-Step Look at a Powerful Clustering and Segmentation Methodology, http://www.dbmag.intelligententerprise.com/db_area/archives/1998/q3/98fsaar.shtml, accessed on 27 August 2009.

Salvador, S. and Chan, P. (2007) FastDTW: Toward Accurate Dynamic Time Warping in Linear Time and Space, *Journal of Intelligent Data Analysis*, Vol. 11, No. 5, pp. 561–580.

Sander, J., Ester, M., Kriegel, H-P. and Xu, X. (1998) Density-Based Clustering in Spatial Databases: the Algorithm GDBSCAN and its Applications, *Journal of Data Mining and Knowledge Discovery*, Vol. 2, No. 2, pp. 169–194.

Silberschatz, A., Korth, H.F. and Sudarshan, S. (2002) *Database Systems Concepts*, 4th Edition, McGraw-Hill.

Smith, L. (2002) A Tutorial on Principal Components Analysis, http://users.ecs.soton.ac.uk/hbr03r/pa037042.pdf, accessed 14 September 2009.

Soukup, T. and Davidson, I. (2002) *Visual Data Mining: Techniques and Tools for Data Visualization and Mining*, John Wiley & Sons.

Srikant, R. and Agrawal, R. (1995) Mining Generalised Association Rules, In Proceedings of the 21st International Conference on Very Large Data Bases, Zurich, Switzerland, September, pp. 407–419.

Srikant, R. and Agrawal, R. (1996) Mining Quantitative Association Rules in Large Relational Tables, In Proceedings of the 1996 ACM SIGMOD International Conference on Management of Data, Montreal, Quebec, Canada, June, pp. 1–12.

Tan, P-N., Steinbach, M. and Kumar, V. (2006) Introduction to Data Mining, Addison-Wesley.

Taylor, J, K. and Cihon, C. (2004) *Statistical Techniques for Data Analysis*, 2nd Edition, Oxford: Chapman & Hall/CRC Press.

Thomsen, E. (2002) *OLAP Solutions: Building Multidimensional Information Systems*, 2nd Edition, John Wiley & Sons.

Tsai, P.S.M., Lee, C.C. and Chen, A.L.P. (1999) An Efficient Approach for Incremental Association Rule Mining, in Methodologies for Knowledge Discovery and Data Mining, *Lecture Notes for Computer Science*, SpringerLink, pp. 74–83.

Ullman, J. (2000) A Survey of Association-Rule Mining, Proceedings of the 3rd International Conference on Discovery Science, *Lecture Notes in Computer Science*, Springer-Verlag, pp. 1–14.

Vapnik, V. (1998) *The Nature of Statistical Learning Theory*, New York: John Wiley & Sons.

Verbeek, J-J., Vlassis, N. and Kröse, B. (2003) Efficient Greedy Learning of Gaussian Mixture Models, *Journal of Neural Computation*, Vol. 15, No. 2, MIT Press, pp. 469–485.

Vlachos, M., Hadjieleftheriou, M., Gunopulos, D. and Keogh, E. (2003) Indexing Multi-dimensional Time-series with Support for Multiple Distance Measures, *In Proceedings of the 9th ACM SIGKDD International Conference on Knowledge Discovery and Data Mining*, Washington, D.C, USA, August, pp. 216–225.

Weka (2008) http://www.cs.waikato.ac.nz/ml/weka/, accessed 14 January 2008.

Wilson, D.R. and Martinez, T.R. (1997) Improved Heterogeneous Distance Functions, *Journal of Artificial Intelligence Research*, Vol. 6, pp. 1–34.

Witten, I.H. and Frank, E. (2005) *Data Mining: Practical Machine Learning Tools and Techniques*, 2nd Edition, Morgan Kaufmann Publishers.

Wu, Y. and Chang, E.Y. (2004) Distance-Function Design and Fusion for Sequence Data, *In Proceedings of the 13th ACM International Conference on Information and Knowledge Management*, Washington, D.C, USA, November, pp. 324–333.

Zaki, M. (1999) Parallel and Distributed Association Rule Mining: A Survey, *IEEE Concurrency*, Vol. 7, October–December, pp. 14–25.

Zaki, M. and Orihara, M. (1998) Theoretical Foundations of Association Rules, In Proceedings of the 3rd ACM SIG-MOD Workshop on Research Issues in Data Mining and Knowledge Discovery, Seattle, Washington, USA, June.

Zhang, M., Kao, B., Yip, C. and Cheung, D. (2001) A GSP-based Efficient Algorithm for Mining Frequent Sequences, In Proceedings of the 2001 International Conference on Artificial Intelligence (**IC-AI'2001**): Las Vegas, Nevada, USA; June, pp. 497–503.

Zhao, Q. and Bhowmick, S.S. (2003) Association Rule Mining: A Survey, Technical Report No. 2003116, Singapore Nanyang Technological University.

INDEX